CLASSIC GUIDEBOOKS TO THE

Egyptian Architecture as Cultural Expression

by

EARL BALDWIN SMITH

with an introduction
by
ALAN GOWANS

AMERICAN LIFE FOUNDATION
1968

Distributed by Century House, Watkins Glen, N.Y.

Library of Congress Card No. 68-31027

CONTENTS

EARL BALDWIN SMITH AS AN ART HISTORIAN

In his lifetime (1888-1956) E. Baldwin Smith was well respected in the academic world as a sound scholar, an effective teacher, and a competent administrator, the kind of man people call a "pillar" of whatever organization he belongs to. He was not, however, the kind generally labelled "brilliant" or "exciting." For all their talk of free-ranging inquiry, academics in fact habitually think in terms of little slots, fit their colleagues into them, and leave them there; so by his contemporaries Baldwin Smith was set down essentially as a follower of archaeologist Howard Crosby Butler (whose chair at Princeton he eventually came to occupy), and of Charles Rufus Morey, whom he succeeded as chairman of Princeton's Department of Art and Archaeology — someone, in short, who consolidated achievements rather than broke new paths. But time, shifting perspectives and sifting reputations as always, has made Baldwin Smith's contribution to scholarship seem increasingly more significant. In particular it has vitiated his contemporaries' criticism of his not "specializing" as "true scholars" should. What seemed to them dilettantish wanderings off into other fields from his first "slot" — *Early Christian Iconography and a School of Ivory Carvers in Provence* (Princeton University Press, 1918) — in retrospect has proved his great strength.

From the point of view that equates "scholarly depth" with concentration on some narrow area of learning, Baldwin Smith's two most heinous sins were *Egyptian Architecture as Cultural Expression*, and the course he insisted on giving for many years in Modern Painting. Since Provence ivories could be considered as related both to the Late Antique and early medieval "fields," there was some excuse for Smith's books on *Early Churches in Syria* (1929), *The Dome* (1950) (emphasizing as it did Late Antique and early medieval Syria) and *Architectural Symbolism in Imperial Rome and the Middle Ages* (1956). But when he wrote on Egypt he invaded territory which, with the single exception of Ancient Greece, is probably the most rigorously guarded preserve in all scholarship. For the Establishment that dominates Egyptology, like its Hellenic counterpart, the most essential qualification is philological — if you can't read hieroglyphics or demotic or archaic Greek script like the daily newspaper, you have no business presuming to talk about anything Greek or Egyptian, much less publish. As for teaching Modern

Painting, that was even worse; only Painters should talk about Painting in any case, and certainly not an "Ancient and Medieval man."

And Baldwin Smith was neither a hieroglyphics expert nor a Painter — for Egyptological expertise, he relied on his former pupil William C. Hayes of the Metropolitan Museum, and while he had studied at Pratt Institute and was a very competent draughtsman (as the illustrations he drew for his own books, including *Egyptian Architecture*, show very well), he was in no sense a professional artist. His "problem" (as the Establishment mentality would see it) was that he had a genuine and probing interest in art as cultural expression. He did not see statues and paintings and buildings from the past as "Art Objects" to be "appreciated" in a historical void. Neither did he share the fashionable iconologists' view of historic art as a collection of puzzles to be solved; he did not imagine that Pausanias described the Agora or Van Eyck painted madonnas with the idea of providing occasions for twentieth-century archaeologists and iconologists to demonstrate their cleverness. He believed that painters and sculptors and builders in the past worked to satisfy specific given needs in their societies, and that the proper business of art historians, like historians in general, was not to pass judgement on the past but to explain why things had happened as they did — why Egyptians built Egyptian temples and not Greek ones, why Picasso painted differently from Perugino (to say "because their taste was different" is no answer; *why* was it different?). Such an approach was not entirely new, but it was far enough from scholarly fashion in Smith's time to ensure his never being labelled "brilliant."

For that matter, Baldwin Smith's basic approach still is out of fashion. Romantic "appreciation" and iconology have in their turn been superseded by technological rationalization; the "in" thing to maintain now is that all architecture was composed, and can be explained, on the same rationale as Walter Gropius's Fagus Shoe Factory: once somebody discovered how to build pointed rib-vaults, Gothic cathedrals inevitably replaced Romanesque ones; once somebody discovered how to put a dome on squiches, Justianian naturally insisted on his palace-church of Holy Wisdom being constructed with them; once steel became cheap enough to use structurally, there could be no possible reason why bridges and courthouses, derricks and palaces should not all be built exactly the same way. It follows that if only steel and concrete had been known in the Ancient world, Perikles' Parthenon and Rameses' Temple of Karnak would have looked exactly like the Seagram Building on Park Avenue.

To all such nonsense Baldwin Smith's works, and especially *Egyptian Architecture as Cultural Expression*, are standing rebukes. It is not so much that he refuted the technological rationalists by facts, though of course Egyptian Architecture implicitly does so: if (as it points out for one instance) Egyptians knew how to build true arches two or three millenia before the Romans, clearly you cannot distinguish Roman architecture from Greek merely by its use of arches, but must explain why Roman builders suddenly adopted and made such extensive use of a technique known so long before them. It is that he more decisively than anyone before him and most after showed that the art of architecture is to be distinguished from mere building not by "aesthetics" but by "meaning." Norris Kelly Smith put the matter succinctly in his *Frank Lloyd Wright: A Study in Architectural Content* (New York, 1966):

> According to Nikolaus Pevsner, "A bicycle shed is a building, Lincoln Cathedral is a piece of architecture . . . The term architecture applies only to buildings designed with a view to aesthetic appeal." [Bruno] Zevi disputes this [in his essay on architecture in *Encyclopaedia of World Art*] contending, rightly enough, that a bicycle shed may be so designed as to be aesthetically appealing. But would this make it a work of architectural art? I think not, because it would still be unrelated to any area of institutional meaning. Palace, house, tomb, capital, court, temple, church — these, mainly, are the buildings which stand for the institutionalized patterns of human relatedness that make possible the endurance of the city, or of society, or of the state; and these have provided almost all the occasions for meaningful architectural art for the past five thousand years. They bear upon realms of experience which have given rise to great quantities of painting and poetry; but one would be hard put to find either a painter or a poet who could make much out of the occasion or the experience of bicycle-parking. Nor can the architect endow it with significance.

"Buildings which stand for institutionalized patterns of human relatedness" — Baldwin Smith does not use this phrase, but he would have approved of it; indeed, it could hardly have been written without his precedent. For that is what *Egyptian Architecture as Cultural Expression* is about; essentially, Baldwin Smith here said, that is what all Architecture is about. And he proved it.

Baldwin Smith's views have not been refuted, any more than Norris Kelly Smith's will be. They have been, and will be, largely ignored, or at best dismissed with a supercilious "I cannot agree." For of course such a concept of architecture is even more offensive to current orthodoxy than it was to past dogmatism. Where it had something at least in common with romantic appreciation, and more than a little with iconology, it is the very antithesis of technological rationalism. In particular it is fatal to the basic premise on which that system depends — that to understand architecture you have to think like an architect.

Now it may be true that to understand the New Brutalism you have to think like a New Brutalist, to understand Bauhaus building you have to think like Gropius (though even this is open to question); but the idea of having to think like such men in order to understand the history of architecture is valid only if you assume that architects today think like architects in the past. And precisely because he not only knew architectural history thoroughly, but understood its practise as well (being twice acting director of Princeton's School of Architecture and teaching a course in it for many years) Baldwin Smith better than anyone in his time was able to realize what a highly dubious proposition this is.

In *The Restless Art* (New York, 1966) I demonstrated (at least to my own satisfaction, and without being refuted), that what we call Painting today not merely looks different from what was called Painting in, say, 1750; it *is* different — a different kind of activity, dedicated to different ends and pursued by different means. It follows that to think like a Painter today is worse than useless if you want to understand what painters were doing two or three or four hundred years ago; it will positively mislead you. And I think the same observation holds true for architecture. If you imagine that I. M. Pei or Kahn or Rudolph or Mies are performing basically the same function in our society as Imhotep or Pheidias or Pierre de Montereau or even Pugin performed in theirs you are sadly mistaken. Like modern painters, they may be going through the same motions, but their ends are basically different. All these earlier architects were concerned with meaning, with compelling images of the social and political and cultural institutions in and with which they lived. Fashionable architects today are concerned with solving building problems. Not that historic architects were uninterested in problem-solving, of course; the difference was that for them solving problems was not an end in itself, it was only a beginning. Problems were solved in order to do something else — to set forth in tangible form beliefs and aspirations and ideals; they began where our so-called avant-garde architects leave off. Of this process it so happens that Ancient Egypt is a conspicuous example, and that is perhaps why Baldwin Smith chose it to demonstrate his ideas. He did so with clarity and brilliance — and irrefutably. Time may have made some of his data obsolete, but it has left his central thesis unchallenged — indeed, made it more apposite than ever. Sometime the scholarly world in general will wake up to its importance; perhaps even those architects who wonder whether egg-crate-construction and sociological problem-solving really satisfies the soul of man will realize its relevance.

ALAN GOWANS
Victoria, April 1968

Earl Baldwin Smith (1888–1956)

PREFACE

ANCIENT buildings, in spite of their appeal to the imagination and at times their real beauty, are little more than a series of unexplained phenomena until they have been brought into a comprehensible relationship and given environmental significance as the embodiment of social needs, conventions, and aspirations. As a tangible record of human endeavour they are a form of history. History has been defined as "an imposition of form upon the otherwise meaningless images of the past." In this book a form, or a unifying pattern of interpretation, has undoubtedly been imposed upon the disconnected ruins of Egyptian architecture. It is to be hoped that the author has been successful in presenting a clear verbal distinction between possibility, probability, and actuality. Exactly how objective and historically justified his interpretations may be, it remains for the illustrations and inscriptions to prove and for the reader to judge.

No one book can be all things to all men. Certain specific aspects of Egyptian architecture have been more or less excluded, partly because they represent a highly specialized interest in the subject, but primarily because they have been adequately presented in a few recently published and accessible volumes. Details of Egyptian masonry are thoroughly treated in Clarke and Engelbach's *Ancient Egyptian Masonry,* 1930; the origin and development of various architectural elements are competently handled in G. Jéquier's *Manuel d'archéologie Égyptienne,* 1924; and excellent large size illustrations of the buildings are available in the three folios of G. Jéquier, *L'architecture et la décoration dans l'ancienne Égypte,* 1920-1924.

My indebtedness to Egyptologists for materials and ideas I hope is fully indicated by the bibliography in the notes. References, however, cannot express my obligation to H. E. Winlock and his colleagues in the Egyptian Department of the Metropolitan Museum of Art, who have been so generous with their advice and assistance. It was W. C. Hayes who, without regard for time, season, or the annoyance of our respective wives, took me and my manuscript in hand and in more ways than I can enumerate contributed to whatever value the book may prove to have. In the process he tactfully reversed an earlier relationship of student and teacher, transforming a community of interests into a permanent friendship.

In Egypt my studies were not only greatly aided but made most pleasant by the kindness of Mr. and Mrs. Davies and Mr. and Mrs. Burton. Also I wish to thank Dr. Nelson for extending to me the privileges of the Library of the Institute of Oriental Studies at Luxor. Both in Egypt and in Princeton Donald Wilber has been a valuable friend and helpful critic, even assisting me with the lettering of plates when he felt dissatisfied with my results. In more ways than I can express in words I am deeply indebted to my colleagues, Professors Friend, Stillwell, Forsyth, and Egbert. It is not merely that they read my manuscript and criticized my drawings. After years of association with them I know that it was their interest, friendship, and the stimulation of their ideas which made the book what it is, if that is not asking them to assume too great a responsibility. There is nothing like the final drive to finish a book, and the resultant neglect of departmental duties, to test out friendships.

E. B. S.

Brick Making, Tomb of Rekhmara, Thebes

P. E. Newberry, *The Life of Reḵhmara* (1900, Pl. xxi.

1. *ENVIRONMENT*

PRIMITIVE and unreflective architecture is never "frozen music." In Egypt, however, architecture is the frozen record of habits and customs which went back to a formative period long before the beginning of Dynastic history and the adoption of stone as a building material. The student of Egyptian architecture, to adapt a statement of an Egyptologist, "is like a man who has come late to the play and beholds before him the great spectacle of the second act, but does not know what has gone before, except in so far as the bald and brief statements upon his program can serve to enlighten him." Before there were any buildings which to-day can be seen and admired, in fact, before there was any recorded Egyptian writing or any known kings ruling over the whole land, Egyptian culture was not only formed in a definite pattern, but it was far from being crude and experimental. The realization that a study of Egyptian architecture must begin, as far as existing monuments are concerned, at a time when the fundamental traditions of the culture were already fixed not only helps to explain many characteristics of the buildings which still exist, but also throws a different light upon the part that environment played in their origin and development.

The presence in Egypt, three thousand years before the Christian Era, of the earliest stone architecture in the history of the world seems in itself some proof of precocious originality; but any valuation of Egyptian architecture which accepts its buildings at their face value, which judges them by the æsthetic standards of our Western civilization, and assumes that the whole history of Egyptian architecture is preserved in the stone structures, must be revised when it is realized to what extent the stone monuments were sculptural reproductions of venerated and traditional types which originated in wood and brick.

Actually architecture never took shape in stone. Without the primitive prototypes to furnish the customary form and usage, there were no structural and utilitarian reasons to compel the Egyptians to cut their first stone buildings in the elaborate decorative fashion which they so tenaciously preserved for thousands of years. As far as any architectural necessity was involved, the early columns and architraves might as well have been rough hewn and crude, provided the uprights were strong enough to support their horizontal load. It merely begs the question and introduces a false criterion into our study of this architecture if we suppose that the stone forms arose from the instinctive æsthetic desires of the Egyptian race. The problem of the extent to which the Egyptians had an æsthetic attitude towards architecture can be more profitably discussed in the last chapter. At this point it is perhaps enough for those who see so much abstract beauty and creativeness in Egyptian architecture to explain why the Egyptians wanted a stone architecture, and why they went to such endless trouble in their use of stone. Some significance must be attached to the fact that the earliest methods of building were not in stone, and that stone, throughout the whole history of Egypt, was only used for religious and sepulchral monuments. The immutable mold of conservatism in which Egyptian civilization was set at such an early period is proof in itself that stone architecture came into existence in order to preserve something venerated and unchangeable.

Environment supplies the materials and the conditions of life, but in the end is not the only factor in shaping the materials to a style of architecture. Physical environment is frequently overemphasized as the formative element in the genesis of a civilization. Man, not nature, makes a style of architecture. A culture is the soil adapted to the will of man. Some writers have insisted that Egypt had no culture, but only an acquired civilization, the product of intruders who found life easy in such an artificial hothouse. Herodotus wrote, "Egypt is acquired land and the gift of the Nile," and ever since his statement has been quoted in nearly every book on Egypt as if it entirely explained all the peculiarities of the land and its forms of expression. Egypt to-day has very little wood of any architectural value, and therefore the environmentalists insist that wood could not have played an important part in the origin of the stone forms of Egyptian building. Because the bordering hills are flat, some romantic moderns see a reflection of this environmental motif in the flat low masses of the temples, ignoring the fact that for a thousand years or more the dwellings of Egypt did not have flat roofs.

The misinterpretation both of the origin of the culture and the significance of the architecture as a reflection of the physical conditions arises because by the time Egyptian forms were recorded in stone, and hence available for study, the culture was already set into a rigid and somewhat artificial repetition of venerated and hence significant forms. By 3000 B.C. environment in its broadest sense was a beneficent tyrant which had already imposed a monotonous mimesis upon the necessary routine of life.

The human element in the drama assumes greater importance and the Predynastic age takes on greater significance when an Egyptologist like Newberry writes, "The agricultural Egypt of modern times is as much the gift of man as it is of the Nile." "We are accustomed," he writes, "to regard Egypt as a paradise, as the most fertile country in the world, where, if we but scratch the soil and scatter seed, we have only to wait and gather the harvest. The Greeks spoke of Egypt as the most fit place for the first generations of men, for there, they said, food was always ready at hand, and it took no labour to secure an abundant supply. But there can be no doubt that the Egypt today is a very different place from the Egypt of pre-agricultural times. There has been a great, but gradual, change in the physical condition of the whole country." [1]

[1] P. E. Newberry, "Egypt as a Field of Anthropological Research,' *Proceedings of the British Association for the Advancement of Science,* Liverpool (1923).

The change was a desiccation of North Africa. Its effect upon the nomadic hunters who formerly wandered the grass-lands, which are now a desert, is set forth by Toynbee.[2] He explains very clearly how the challenge of nature forced the forefathers of the Egyptians either to follow their receding habitat into the Sudan, where they could continue to live an easy but uneventful existence, or plunge into the marshes of the Delta and evolve an agricultural culture by changing their habits, cutting ditches, rescuing land from the waters of the Nile, and in so doing make a new social environment. Once the initial change was made from a nomadic existence on the steppes to an agricultural life along the river, the fundamental habits of Egyptian civilization were rooted. Then the physical environment, as it was given usefulness by the routine of human effort, asserted itself. In the end the river and all it meant in the life of man made a stultifying hothouse where every product continued for thousands of years to be reproduced true to type.

THE NILE. The Nile, bringing its yearly offering of rich, life-giving mud, flows north to the Mediterranean through a narrow valley cut off by the cliffs from the dry, barren waste of the desert on either side. The total area of Egypt does not exceed 40,000 square miles, and of this only 13,000 square miles are habitable and a mere 10,000 are capable of cultivation. Yet this bit of land, little larger than the kingdom of Belgium, supported about 7,000,000 people and still teems with a startling variety of life.

Living was comparatively easy in the valley once agriculture and a protecting social system were developed. Every year the Nile rose with cosmic precision to flood its banks and deposit the fertile, black earth brought down from Africa. With relatively little effort on the part of man this mud under the intense heat of the sun yielded several crops a year. It is no wonder that the Egyptians worshiped the river and wrote hymns in adoration of it: "Praise to thee, O Nile, that issueth from the earth, and cometh to nourish Egypt. Of hidden nature, a darkness in the day. Thou that vomitest forth, giving the fields to drink and making strong the people." [3] The yearly cycle of barren dryness and magical growth played a compelling part in the perpetuation of Egyptian habits. It gave a monotonous regularity to the order of life which was reflected in the ritualistic conservatism of all Egyptian forms of expression, and the Nile, its creator, carved as permanent a channel in the religious thought of Egypt as it did in the rocks of its river-bed. "They tremble that behold the Nile in full flood. The fields laugh and the river banks are overflowed. The gods' offerings descend, the visage of man is bright, and the heart of the gods rejoiceth." [4] Although the "Black Land" acted like an incubator to create life and traditions at an incredibly early date, there was an inclination for its oasis culture to become formalized; such easy regularity and dependence upon the soil in the end tended to discourage initiative and imposed a ritual upon the society and its art. The "Red Land" of the desert at the same time served as a barrier to protect the social institutions and was therefore conducive to an inbreeding of ideas. The isolation of the valley, however, was more mental than physical; Egypt from primi-

[2] A. J. Toynbee, *A Study of History*, 2d ed. (1935), I, p. 305; E. Meyer, *Geschichte des Altertums* (1928), I, 2.

[3] "Hymn in Adoration of the Nile," A. Erman, *The Literature of the Ancient Egyptians* (1927), p. 146; A. Moret, *The Nile and Egyptian Civilization* (1927).

[4] "Pyramid Text," A. Erman, *op. cit.*, p. 10.

tive times had extended contacts with other regions by trade and war; it suffered many invasions; but in the end its environment always assimilated the invader and perpetuated its own time-honored traditions.

THE CLIMATE. The most obvious of the many environmental factors is climate. The brilliant sunlight, intense heat, scarcity of rain, which amounted to arid dryness in Upper Egypt, and the absence of any severe changes of temperature, undoubtedly affected the development of architecture. Windows, in a land where light had such searing intensity, were developed largely for ventilation. The earliest types of houses had curved roofs made of bent reeds or branches; but certainly by Dynastic times there was no climatic necessity for sloping roofs to shed rain. Therefore, as soon as there were tools capable of cutting large, rigid timbers, the roofs began to be flat. At an early time the flat roof was used as a terrace where much of the work and relaxation of the home became bearable in the cool of the evening.

It was the absence, however, of any indoor hearth [5] which most definitely influenced the evolution of the house types. Cooking for the most part took place in the open courtyard or on the roof, and such heat as was desirable within the house during the winter months was supplied by braziers, that is, for those few who could afford such comfort. Without the necessity of the hearth, where the family could gather about the glowing fire and the smoke would escape from under the high roof, Egyptian houses, as they grew in size and comfort, had no reason to retain the original single-roomed structure. Instead, the interiors could be divided by light partitions of wood, brick, or hangings, into airy and ventilated arrangements of rooms opening off the central hall. Also as a result of the climate the open courtyard in front of the house became an essential element of the dwelling where much of the activity of the home took place out-of-doors. In fact the unroofed enclosure, at first round and later rectangular, which must have been the prototype of the courtyard, was probably one of the earliest and most rudimentary forms of shelter in Egypt.[6]

THE MATERIALS. Available materials were a second environmental factor which exerted an obvious influence upon the methods of building. These materials, considered in the order in which they were adopted for construction, were varied and accessible.

1. *Pliable materials,*[7] such as *reeds, rushes, palm fronds, papyrus stalks* and small *branches*—all growing along the banks of the Nile—were used to make the primitive shelters because they did not require tools, and could be gathered, bound together, and interwoven by hand.

2. *Mud* from the river was the next material to be adopted by the early builders, and ever since has remained the cheapest, easiest, and most common building material of the country. At first it was probably plastered onto reed latticework and woven mats, and later was used to make solid mud walls. Like the earlier wattle construction the pliable mud required no tools.

[5] The central hearth occurs in the Neolithic period (see pp. 20, 21), but disappears in the later primitive houses.
[6] See p. 23.
[7] A. Lucas, *Ancient Egyptian Materials and Industries,* 2d ed. (1936), p. 42.

3. *Wood,* although scarce in the valley since historic times, nevertheless played a more important part in the origin of many Egyptian architectural forms than is generally realized. There are indications that vegetation was more luxuriant in primitive times than during Dynastic history. The local woods, which supplied timbers of small dimensions to be used for the construction of boats and houses, consisted of *palm, sycamore,* and *acacia.* For some purposes *thorn* and *tamarisk* were used. *Ebony,* by the I Dynasty, was brought down from the Sudan, and *fir, pine, cedar,* and *cypress*[8] were imported, principally in the Delta, from a very early period. The whole history of Egyptian craftsmanship gives evidence of a highly developed technique of wood-working. The extremely early use of the hard, red acacia, which was cut scale-shape and carefully fitted together, shows the Egyptian habit of working in the available small pieces of wood. This habit and necessity had an evident bearing upon the subsequent stone architecture.

4. *Brick,*[9] in its turn, was either developed naturally from plastered mud, which seems the more likely, or was introduced from Mesopotamia, the other old fluvial civilization, long before the end of the Predynastic period. The mud of the Nile made excellent brick when dried in the fierce rays of the sun. By the end of the III Dynasty the Egyptians were masters of such essentials of brick architecture as the arch and the vault. Kiln-baked brick was almost never used, and the few examples of glazed tile, appearing in a highly developed technique in both the I and III Dynasties, prove that it was not technical ignorance, even at an early date, which kept the Egyptians from developing the possibilities of this method of wall decoration and protection.[10] The present method of making sun-dried brick in Egypt is the same as is pictured on the wall of a Middle Kingdom tomb and is evidence of the extreme conservatism of the land.

Although Egypt had an old and fully developed tradition of brick architecture, she never evolved, as did Mesopotamia, a monumental style in this material. While brick continued to be the most common building material throughout Egyptian history, it was used more for practical construction than for important monuments. This utilitarian attitude towards brick and the relatively sudden shift to stone for religious and sepulchral architecture cannot be explained by the mere accessibility of stone throughout the length of the valley. Stone was always accessible, and the ultimate Egyptian method of quarrying it by slow, pulverizing blows of a stone hammer could have originated at almost any early date. Therefore its comparatively sudden adoption for monumental architecture is an astonishing event, presupposing a highly organized and directed central government. If tradition was as dominating as it seems to have been, there must have been a great necessity, or compelling desire, which altered the habitual routine, impelled the builders to undertake the difficult task of quarrying and cutting stone for their temples and tombs, and brought about the first lithic architecture in the history of the world.

5. *Stone,* although it was both plentiful and accessible, was not used in any real architectural sense until the III Dynasty.[11] *Limestone* and *sandstone* were both common and easily cut from the cliffs

[8] A. Lucas, *Ancient Egyptian Materials and Industries,* p. 379.
[9] A. Lucas, *op. cit.,* p. 43, gives bibliography.
[10] Petrie, *Abydos,* II, pp. 25, 48.
[11] Lucas, *op. cit.,* p. 45.

which flanked the valley. *Granite,* while occurring in various localities, was most accessible in the great ledges crossing the valley to form the cataracts of the Nile. The pink and gray granite of Aswân was most favored. In addition to these principal building stones, various uses were also made of *basalt, schist,* hard *quartzite,* and soft *alabaster.*

THE SOCIAL CONDITIONS. Social customs and beliefs were a more important part of the general environmental matrix out of which the architecture was formed than were climate or even available materials. With this aspect of the human environment it is no longer a question of simple and logical sequence in which certain religious beliefs and social institutions gave rise to specific forms of architecture. The necessity for architecture grew with the need for more elaborate institutions, and in many cases architecture had as much influence in formulating ideas as customs had in developing architecture. There is an unfortunate rigidity in human thinking which unconsciously works to force any unified process of creation into a rational, although unreal, sequence which the mind can follow step by step. This mental limitation, which is reflected in our language, makes it difficult both to see and describe a natural evolution. The very necessity of beginning and ending a verbal description of intricate change involves choice and the inherent artificiality of an imposed sequence.

Egyptian ideas seem distant and unreal without art to give them appreciable form, and their art seems strange and even incomprehensible without ideas to give it meaning. Therefore the least artificial approach to the unity of the Egyptian outlook, as reflected in the architecture, is to omit the human equation from its logical place in the general environment, and instead develop the basic ideas of the social institutions along with the architecture which embodied them. One institution, however, and its ramifications, so completely dominated all others that it requires special emphasis. Practically all extant Egyptian art, whether sculptural, graphic, or architectonic, was in some sense mortuary. This does not mean, however, that the Egyptian was always weighed down with his thoughts of death. Actually he had a cheerful and childlike enjoyment of life, and for practical purposes developed a civic architecture in brick of which we know very little. Nevertheless, the ritual and beliefs concerning death most definitely shaped architecture. The Middle Kingdom poet in his poem, "A Dispute with his Soul of One who is Tired of Life," voiced what was never far from the Egyptian's mind when he wrote, "Death is before me today." [12] The Egyptian's obsession with death and his unending effort to obtain immortality was a quest for certainty which, it will be seen, goes far to explain the tenacity of his traditions, the despotism of his priesthood, and the unyielding conservatism of architectural conventions. But before the effects of these ideas can be developed in an architectural sequence, an historical framework is necessary.

THE CHRONOLOGY. The long and intricate history of Egypt can be compressed into significant periods. Predynastic history is in the process of being discovered,[13] and, important as this period

[12] A. Erman, *The Literature of the Ancient Egyptians,* p. 91.

[13] A. Scharff, *Die Altertümer der Vor- und Frühzeit Aegyptens* (*Mitt. aus d. Aeg. Sammlung,* Berlin, 1931, Vol. IV), Einleitung; Petrie, *Prehistoric Egypt* (1920).

was as the formative age when the basic ideas of the culture and the architecture were evolved, it will always remain obscure. Thousands of years of development went by before the curtain rose on what we know as Dynastic history. This long evolution, which went back to a time when the Nile valley was humid and tropical and the bordering deserts were grassy steppes, has no known dates. Its records and relative chronology are now ingeniously arranged by means of *sequence dates*. These sequence dates divide all possible Egyptian history into one hundred parts and assume that the unification of Egypt and the beginning of Dynastic history took place in Sequence Date 78. When Sir Flinders Petrie first established this theoretical order, the beginning of the primitive age was set at S.D. 30, thereby leaving time for earlier stages, which have now been uncovered at Merimda, Helwan, El-Tasa, Badari, and in the Fayum. Thus we have a period of vague duration which extends back to 6000 B.C. or even to 10,000 B.C. as Petrie claims.

The transformation of nomadic life into an agricultural culture must have first taken place in the Delta. Consequently civilization in Lower Egypt was more advanced in the late Predynastic period than it was in Upper Egypt, where the social units were for a longer time isolated and warlike. Long before what we know as Egyptian history began, the communities in the Delta were unified under the chief of the city-state of On, which later became Heliopolis. Two apparently contemporaneous events introduced Dynastic history: one, the appearance of a written language, and the other, the forceful unification of Egypt by Menes, a ruler of the Hawk clan from Upper Egypt, who finished the conquest of the Delta begun by his immediate predecessors. After the unification Menes built the city of Memphis, near modern Cairo, and probably transferred the seat of government from Thinis, which was at or near Abydos, to the new city where he could better control his long kingdom. It was at Saqqara, the necropolis of Memphis, and not at Abydos, that he was finally buried, as recent discoveries have shown. Very little is known about the ancient sites and early life in the Delta because its marshy soil has made excavations almost impossible. Undoubtedly the Southern conquerors borrowed many of the "Northland's" customs, such perhaps as the use of a calendar, when they unified the land.

Unfortunately there is still a serious doubt as to when the unification took place. Petrie set the date as early as 5546 B.C., Borchardt established it as 4186 B.C., Breasted reduced it to 3400 B.C., Meyer first brought it down to 3315 and later to 3197 B.C., while Scharff has reduced it to 3000 B.C. It is easy to believe that the truth lies somewhere within these limits. Fortunately it is not so much the specific dates as the sequence of periods which are important for the study of architecture. Therefore it is convenient for our present purpose to follow the short and more generally accepted chronology of Meyer.[14] His subdivision of the Old Kingdom into Thinite and Memphite periods is followed because the first two Dynasties are architecturally closer to the Predynastic period than to the innovations of the III Dynasty. The reader who desires a fuller historical background is referred to the following books: J. H. Breasted, *History of Egypt;* H. R. Hall, in the *Cambridge Ancient History* I, and E. Meyer, *Geschichte der Altertum*.

[14] E. Meyer, *Geschichte der Altertum*, I², 1909, p. 17; *Chronologie Égyptienne*, trans. by A. Moret, 1912; *Die Altere Chronologie Babyloniens, Assyriens und Aegyptens*, 1931.

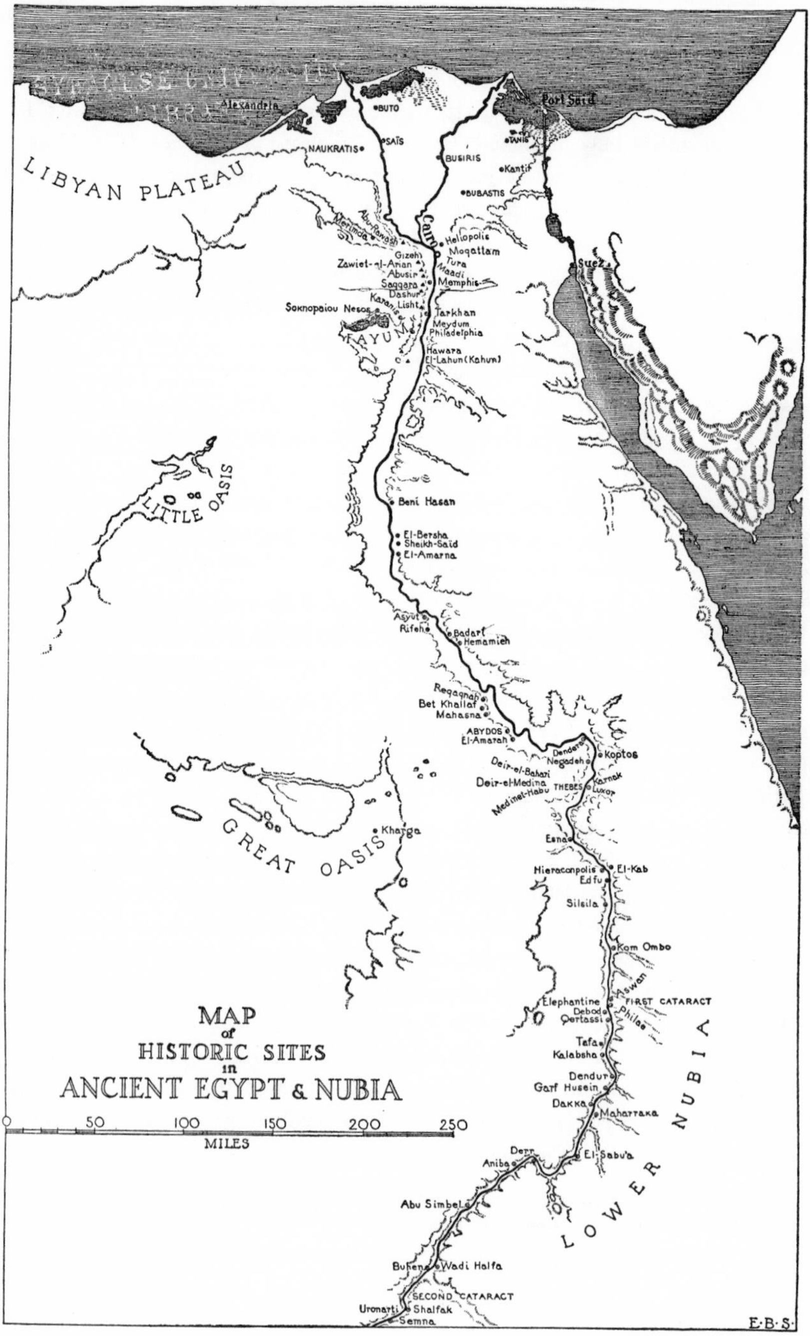

Alexandria
BUTO
SAÏS
NAUKRATIS
BUSIRIS
Port Said
TANIS
Kantir
BUBASTIS
LIBYAN PLATEAU
Abu Roash
Merimda
Cairo
Heliopolis
Moqattam
Gizeh
Tura
Zawiet-el-Arian
Maadi
Abusir
Saqqara
Memphis
Dashur
Karanis
Lisht
Soknopaiou Nesos
Tarkhan
Meydum
Philadelphia
FAYUM
Hawara
El-Lahun (Kahun)
Suez
LITTLE OASIS
Beni Hasan
El-Bersha
Sheikh-Saïd
El-Amarna
Asyut
Rifeh
Badari
Hemamieh
Reqaqnah
Bet Khallaf
Mahasna
ABYDOS
El-Amarah
Dendera
Koptos
Negadeh
Deir-el-Bahari
Deir-el-Medina
THEBES
Karnak
Medinet-Habu
Luxor
Kharga
GREAT OASIS
Esna
Hieraconpolis
El-Kab
Edfu
Silsila
Kom Ombo
Elephantine
Aswan
FIRST CATARACT
Debod
Qertassi
Philae
Tafa
Kalabsha
Dendur
Garf Husein
Dakka
Maharraka
LOWER NUBIA
MAP of HISTORIC SITES in ANCIENT EGYPT & NUBIA
0 50 100 150 200 250
MILES
Derr
Aniba
El-Sabu'a
Abu Simbel
Buhen
Wadi Halfa
SECOND CATARACT
Uronarti
Shalfak
Semna
E·B·S·

2. *THE FORMATION OF IDEAS*

MANY PEOPLE feel that architecture, as an art, is limited in some mysterious way to monumental and elaborate buildings, while all else is mere utilitarian construction, unworthy of the artistic label. Inasmuch as Egyptian architecture was always tectonic and, from the Egyptian viewpoint, highly utilitarian, it is essential to ignore all questions of artistic valuation until all the evidence is presented and the question of the Egyptian's æsthetic enjoyment of architecture can be reviewed. Historically and critically it is more comprehensible and objective to discard æsthetic valuations and assume that architecture began when the first shelters were erected. Architecture was on the way to becoming something more than mere construction when simple huts acquired in the imagination of men the significance of a type, an ideal, a concept, to which was associated meaning and importance. Once men began to value their structures, no matter how simple, and so formed the habit of thinking of them as something more than physical protection, the mere construction was elevated into art, even if there was no conscious enjoyment of the results as an æsthetic experience such as a modern man may experience in the presence of a work of art. After that, the kind and amount of significance which was present in each building became a matter of degree relative to the viewpoint and prejudices of subsequent critics.

The only way to acquire even a slight insight into the past, so that we may begin to see its creative efforts with a sympathy approaching understanding, is to examine the beginnings of ideas and follow their evolution as an expression of cultural experience. Otherwise Egyptian architecture must seem inexplicably strange or beautifully exotic.

Egypt is the oldest country with a comparatively continuous development from a primitive stage of social thinking to an elaborate and highly organized state of civilization which is reflected in the architecture. Ideas change slowly, and much of the fascination of Egyptian art, quite apart from its force and early productivity, is its *magnificent perpetuation and embodiment of primitive beliefs.*

Man, in the slow and difficult process of evolving tools and ideas, for the two were mutually dependent, had to work from the known to the unknown. Even in periods of creative incentive his greatest inventions and most exalted ideas have been built upon past experience, have taken shape gradually, and at no stage in their development have they been more than an inspired re-application of known forms and concepts. Egyptian architecture is a graphic record of this instinctive conservatism.

Life for man has always been a struggle, more desperate under primitive conditions than it is today. Primitive man, such as the early nomadic hunters in the Nile valley, in a life and death battle with the forces of nature, working with limited understanding and imperfect instruments, was forced to think only of protection. Protection meant shelter, food, and the propitiation of those phenomena of nature which threatened him and over which he had no control. *Protection, both in the beginning and throughout the history of Egypt, was the compelling incentive which brought about all the essentials of architecture.* In the early stages of this "Quest for Certainty" the house, in its simplest and crudest beginnings, was man's first architectural effort. *The concept of the house must, therefore, underlie all subsequent architectural needs.*

In time man came to enjoy and suffer an imaginative experience of life. He dreamt about his departed ancestors, thought wonderingly of his own life in the hereafter, dreaded the possible action of disembodied and unhappy spirits who troubled his mind, and so evolved a conception of life after death. Inevitably this conception was constructed out of his experiences in a material world. So the dead required dwellings, weapons, food, and all that would make an everlasting existence comprehensible. *The idea of the tomb as an eternal home for the dead had to originate in man's mind as a replica of the dwelling of the living.* When the standard of physical comfort and social distinction required more and more elaborate physical protection, the accommodations for the dead kept pace with those for the living.

The need of the temple arose last. *The first temples were only shelters for the divinity, and, as such, they were houses of the living transformed gradually to a religious use, thereby acquiring a new significance.* Any generalization, however necessary it is when dealing with a social complex of ideas and instincts, can only approximate the truth. In general, the awakening of a religious instinct in primitive man began with fetishism, in which specific rocks, trees, aëroliths, and features of the landscape were given magical significance. Much of this first phase of religious thinking was preserved in Egypt. After fetishism came zoömorphism, finally to be followed by anthropomorphism. The evidence suggests that during the first stages of society in the Nile valley, when animals were the source of food, danger, and social power among the hunters, and later, when the engendering powers of the Nile and the sun were the mysterious sources of sustenance for the agriculturists, the Egyptians visualized the supernatural in animal and in plant shapes. As villages and clans became communal organizations, each group took unto itself a totem which became the protective and invigorating spirit of the whole group. For ages there was no conception of the supernatural in human form as a being who shared man's need of food and shelter. Such ideas came only when an individual—chieftain, priest, or ancestor—was remembered and thought of as the personification, and finally as the incarnation of the totem.

At such times as the priest and chieftain, who was usually the same powerful man, and whose duty it was to guard and propitiate the totem, was imagined as the incarnation of the supernatural, then his temporal dwelling, which was already the important place where offerings and tribute were made, where justice was rendered, and where the assurance of protection was maintained by mysterious rites, became a sanctuary. The slowness with which these ideas evolved is indicated by the persistent survival of primitive beliefs throughout Egyptian history. Egyptian divinities kept their animal forms, and the great stone temples of the New Kingdom were places, not of communal worship, but of divine abode. There the Pharaoh, the great chieftain and high priest, either served the divinity or was himself enshrined as the personification of the gods (Plate II–7).

Egyptian religion never acquired a permanent system. Instead it preserved a loose flexibility in which the primitive regional gods appear and disappear, combine and then recombine, sometimes being associated in celestial families, and at other times taking on characteristics of new divinities.[1] The divinities were from the outset communal guardians leading their clans in battle, and their importance was always a reflection of the fluctuations in the political fortunes of their followers. At first there were only local gods, who were in time superseded in importance by the cosmic divinities of which Osiris and Re, the sun-god, became the most powerful. Apparently both were once local gods of the Delta, perhaps with accretions from the outside; Atum of On became Re-atum of Heliopolis; Osiris, whose earliest form was a bundle of reeds, the *dedu,* was later, after he became the great god of resurrection, remembered as a legendary Delta king. Outside religious elements, when they appeared, were either grafted onto existing Egyptian divinities or completely assimilated by the environment. What is essential to the architecture is the evidence that the *house of the powerful one eventually grew into the temple.*

THE HOUSE

The house, then, was the architectural embryo, not only because it was the first structural requirement, but also because it naturally came to assume a vital and constant importance in the primitive imagination. It is well to realize that the size and decoration of the house have ever since tended to manifest social distinctions and stand as symbols of power.

In spite of its importance the specific history of the house in Egypt is obscure because so little remains of the actual dwellings. Except for a few models, some schematic and ideographic pictures, and the imprint of houses among the ruins, the story of domestic architecture has to be reconstructed from the evidence of the tombs and the persistence of primitive forms in the monumental, religious, and mortuary architecture. Even from this evidence, suggestive and important as it is, the probable evolution of the basic house types can not be followed with any smoothly developing continuity.[2]

At first Egypt, throughout its length, was occupied by isolated groups in relatively different stages of cultural development. This is indicated by the persistence of various primitive house-types, in spite of the fact that Egypt is generally recognized to have had a curiously uniform and widespread racial and cultural background from remote times. While the Egyptian state and society, as we know them, give little indication of having developed from an organization by tribes and families, but rather seem to have been based upon divisions which were merely a matter of locality, there still must have been tribal units at some early stage of social development which gave way to regional communities. There must also have been periodic infiltrations and invasions which brought new and different social customs—each with some rudimentary kind of architectural embodiment. Every new racial factor meant either cultural recession or stimulation, depending upon the background and adaptability of the newcomers. Moreover, the conservatism and per-

[1] A. W. Shorter, *An Introduction to Egyptian Religion* (1931); J. H. Breasted, *Development of Religion and Thought in Ancient Egypt* (1912); G. Steindorff, *The Religion of the Ancient Egyptians* (1905); A Moret, *Du Caractère Religieux de la Royauté Pharaonique* (1902); *Mystères Égyptiens,* 3d ed. (1922).

[2] The standard study of early house forms is F. Oelmann, *Haus und Hof im Altertum,* I (1927).

PLATE I: HOUSE FORMS AND HUT-SHRINES

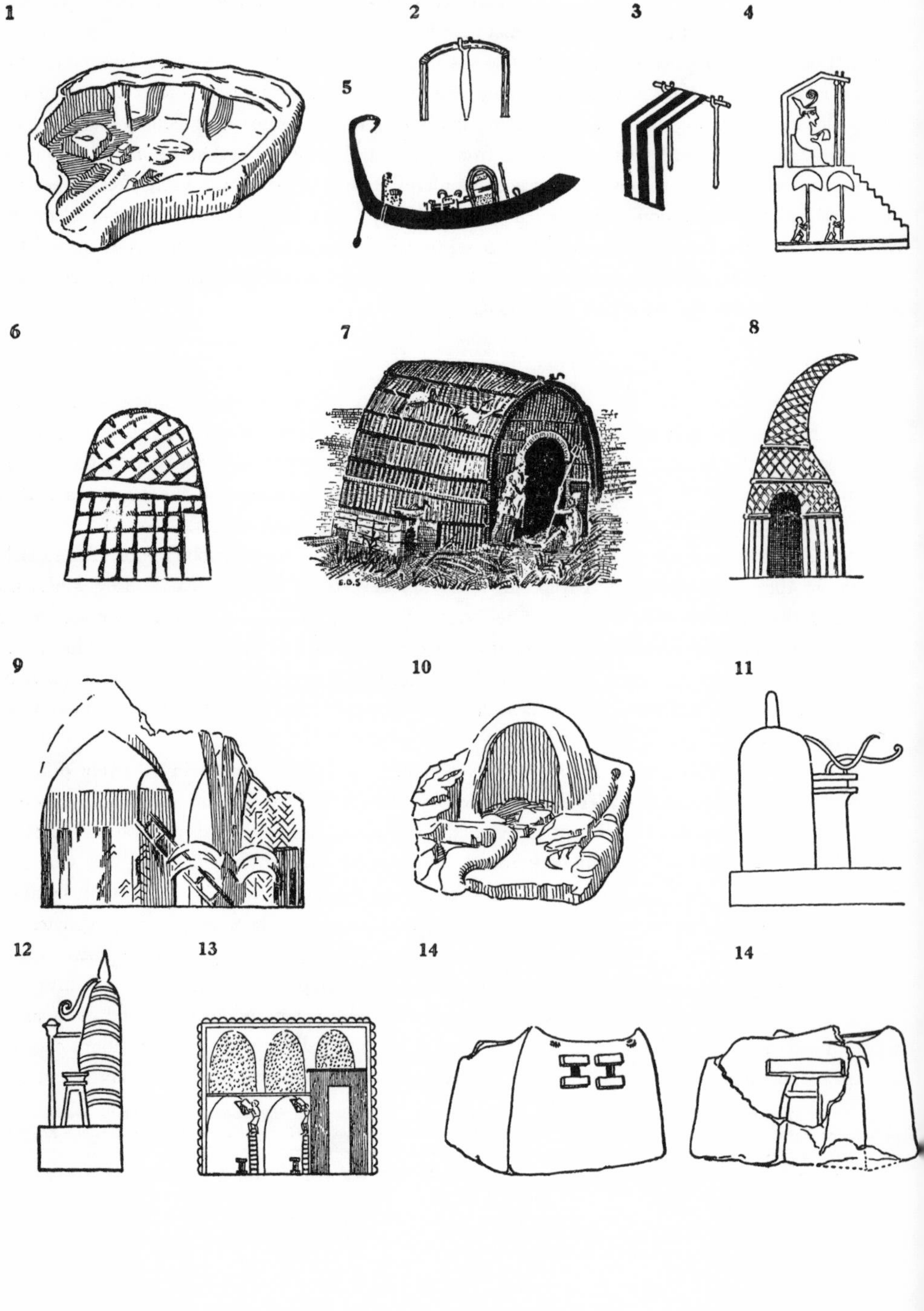

sistence of architectural traditions must have been even more rigid in such a period of regional isolation than later when there was a natural mingling of ideas. Some communities were living in tents at a time when others were settling down to agriculture and the beginnings of urban architecture. In fact this mingling of new and old is still apparent in Egypt to-day.

As new social conditions arose and the primitive customs mingled through tribal or regional conquests, compulsory exogamy and the inevitable transmission of ideas, the *rudimentary forms of architecture persisted unchanged long after more elaborate and permanent types were evolved.* For purposes of actual dwelling the primitive house-types sank lower and lower in the social order and were continued by those classes of society whose habits and resources were nearest to the level at which such architctural forms originated. To-day the natives working in the fields build temporary straw and reed shelters which are exactly like primitive huts.

THE POLE AND COVERING. When the valley was first occupied in the Quaternary age by nomad hunters forced out of the tablelands of North Africa by the increasing desiccation, there was no architecture. The hunters lived in pits and caves. The first shelters were of two different types which may have occurred simultaneously in different parts of the long valley. The simplest was the tent, a universal primitive shelter, consisting of one or more poles, hung at first with skins, then matting, and finally with patterned fabrics. One of the earliest known Nile cultures, which existed in a time when the valley was damp and tropical with a rich vegetation, was the Badarian.[3] Even then the Badarians were advanced beyond an elementary stage of living: they were agriculturists in villages, growing barley, making a kind of linen, and practising a fairly developed art of pottery and a crude figure sculpture. Taking their graves as imitations of their dwellings, we

[3] G. Brunton and G. Caton-Thompson, *The Badarian Civilization* (1928). The beginnings of culture are being steadily pushed back for already the Badarian culture has been superseded by a still earlier Tasian culture which as yet has not contributed anything to the origin of architecture.

PLATE I

1. Tent-shelter, soul-house 106 from Rifeh (Petrie, *Gizeh and Rifeh,* 1907, Pl. xv).
2. Hieroglyph for "tent" (F. L. Griffith, *Hieroglyphs,* 1898, Pl. VII/103).
3. Tent-shelter on model of a boat from Deir-el-Bircheh, XII Dyn. (*Annales du Service,* I, 1900, p. 31).
4. King in tent-shelter, Predynastic mace of Narmer (J. E. Quibell, *Hierakonpolis,* I, 1900, *Pl.* XXVI-B).
5. Reed cabin on Predynastic boat (Quibell, *op. cit.,* II, 1902, Pl. LXXV).
6. Reed hut, I Dyn. ivory from Abydos (Petrie, *The Royal Tombs,* II, 1901, Pl. IV).
7. Reed hut, Palestrina mosaic in Palazzo Baronale, Rome (*Alinari,* 27287).
8. Libyan hut, mosaic of El-Alia, Tunis (Daremberg et Saglio, *Dictionnaire des Antiquités,* Fig. 4828).
9. Round house of matting, Temple of Hatshepsut (E. Naville, *Temple of Deir-el-Bahari* III, 1898, Pl. LXXI).
10. Model of mud hut, British Museum, no. 32612.
11. Round hut-shrine of Min (G. Jéquier, "Les temples primitifs," *Bull. de l'Inst. française d'arch. orientale du Caire,* VI, 1908, p. 36).
12. Round hut-shrine of Min (*op cit.*).
13. Granaries, tomb painting at Thebes (J. G. Wilkinson, *The Manners and Customs of the Ancient Egyptians,* I, 1878, p. 371, Fig. 142).
14. Predynastic house model, El-Amrah (D. Randall-Maciver and A. C. Mace, *El Amrah and Abydos,* 1902, Pl. x).

PLATE II: HOUSE FORMS AND HUT-SHRINES

1

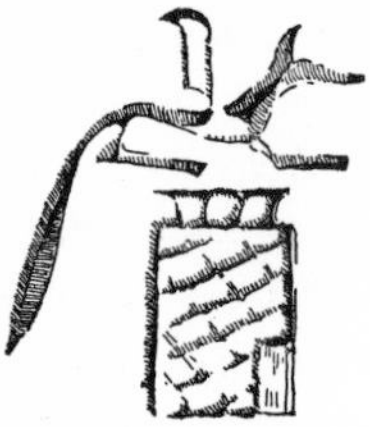

2

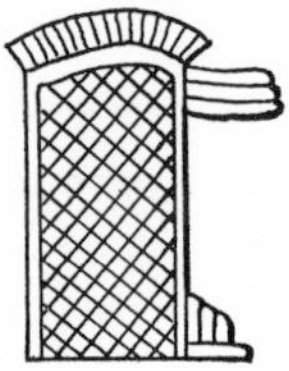

3

4

5

6

7

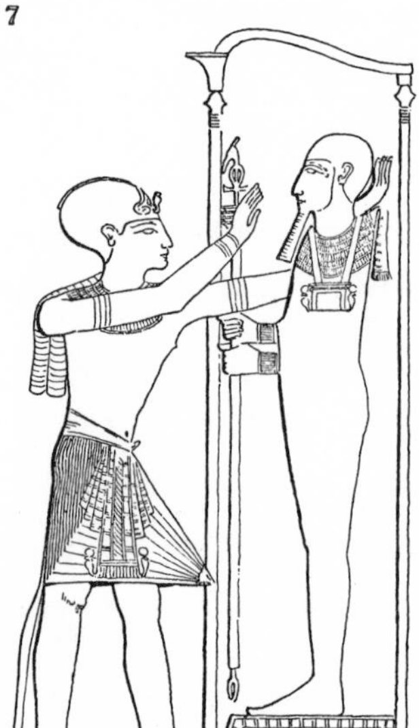

8

may believe that they lived in shelters made of poles covered with skins and matting. A survival of such a primitive tent shelter is reproduced in the clay model of a soul-house, found at Rifeh and dating perhaps from the VI Dynasty (Plate I–1).

The tent, as might be expected, continued to be a common form of light protection, just as it is still the dwelling of wandering nomads in the valley. Because of the importance of the tent among the early tribesmen, its form retained a social and religious distinction which was perpetuated for certain traditional purposes. The hieroglyphic sign for "tent," "shelter," "canopy," or "booth" (Plate I–2) shows a light structure, open in front and made of a framework of bundled reeds; the roof, slightly curved, is supported by a central forked pole, prototype of the saddle capital. The same sign, compounded with a determinant, meant "festival," indicating that this form was at an early time associated with ritualistic gatherings. The first appearance of this shelter in Egyptian art occurs on the mace of Narmer, who was the conquering predecessor of King Menes. The warrior king sits in royal, if not divine, state on a raised platform under a tent-shelter (Plate I–4). The same form, because of its primitive associations, persisted as a shrine, naos, or holy of holies (Plate II–7, 8). Also it continued to be used throughout Egyptian history as a kiosk, or movable pavilion, which served as a portable protection from the sun, easily moved when the land was inundated.[4] A tomb painting (Plate II–6) depicts the priest Urarna surveying the gathering of his crops from a portable kiosk, hung with patterned mattings. A still simpler form is represented as a cabin in a boat model of the XII Dynasty (Plate I–3). Later it will be seen how other features of the tent-shelter, such as its curved roof of matting[5] and its tenoned posts[6] survived in stone architecture.

It is conceivable that this rudimentary tent-shelter, with vertical supports and open in front, evolved into the columnar portico (Plate III–7) which was apparently used as an open shelter, without rooms behind it, as late, at least, as the Middle Kingdom, and was an ideograph representing "house" and "palace." Therefore it is presumable that the form, idea, and connotation of a columnar portico were derived in the first place from a primitive type of shelter associated in men's minds with a chieftain, and that therefore the colonnade continued in Dynastic architec-

[4] J. Capart, *Egyptian Art (Eng. trans.)* (1923), p. 76.
[5] Pages 22, 118, 169.
[6] Page 165

PLATE II

1. Hut-shrine of Anubis, seal of King Qa from Abydos (Petrie, *The Royal Tombs,* I, Pl. XXIX/86).
2. Hut-shrine of Set, III Dyn. stele of Ha'b'w-Sokar (M. A. Murray, Saqqara Mastabas, I, 1905, Pl. XXXIX/43).
3. Hut-shrine, seal of King Zer (Petrie, *op. cit.,* II, Pl. XVI).
4. House-shrine, clay cylinder from Negadeh (G. Jéquier in de Morgan's *Recherches sur les origines de l'Égypte,* p. 170, Fig. 561).
5. Hut-shrine, ivory from Abydos (Petrie, *op. cit.,* II, Pl. VII/8).
6. Kiosk, depicted in Tomb of Urarna (N. de G. Davies, *The Rock Tombs of Sheikh Saïd,* 1901, Pl. XV).
7. Naos of Ptah with Seti I in attendance, relief from Abydos (J. Capart, *Le Temple de Seti I,* I, 1912, Pl. XXIV).
8. Naos of Osiris, Book of the Dead, British Museum (*The Papyrus of Ani,* 1894, Pl. 20).

PLATE III:HOUSE FORMS AND HUT-SHRINES

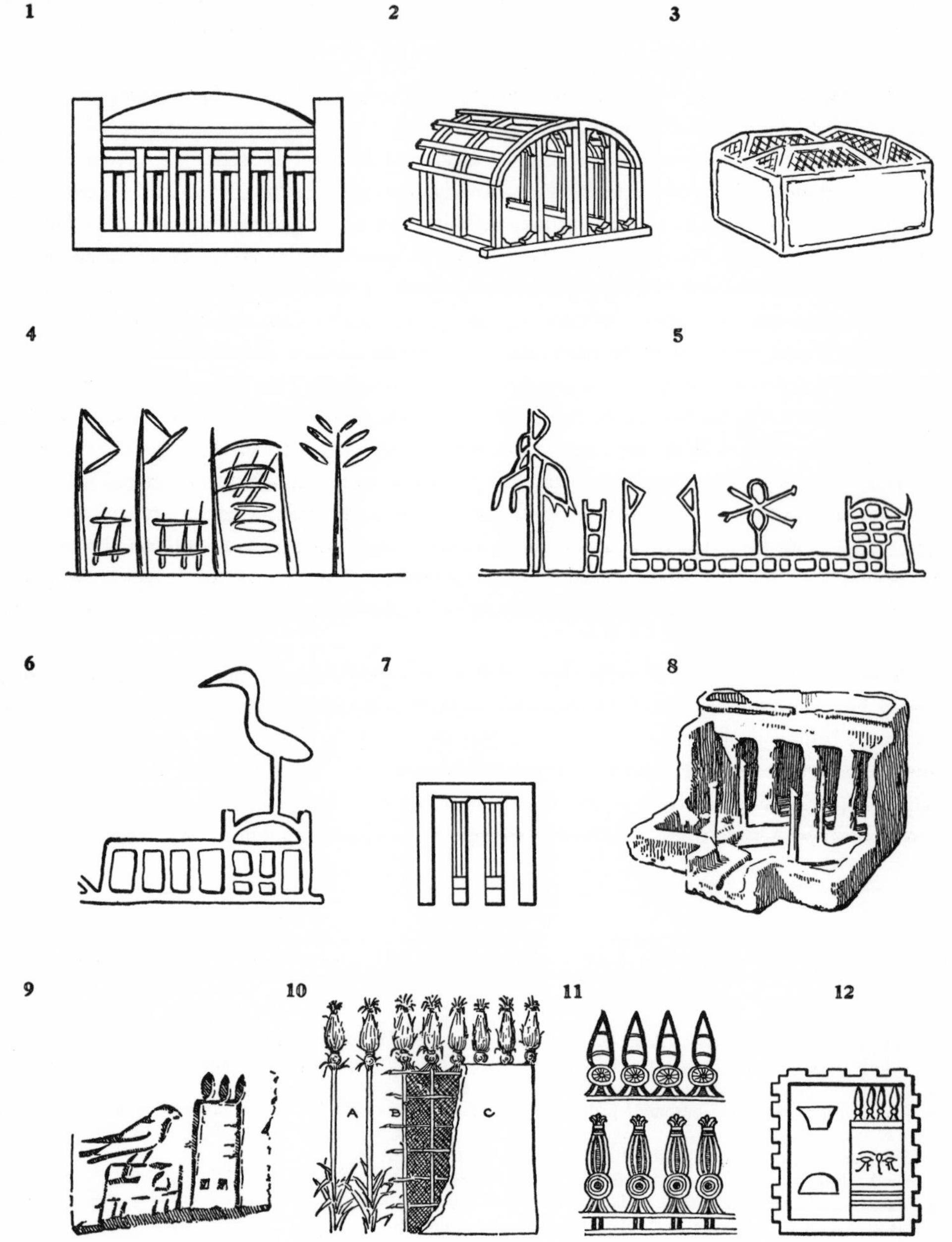

ture to be a mark of royal distinction. The inscription of Kheti reads, "Behold, thy name shall be forever in the temple of Upwawet, thy memory shall be beautiful in the colonnade." [7]

THE WATTLE AND THATCH HUTCH. The other elementary dwelling was the wattle and thatch hutch, consisting at first of a semicircle of bundled reeds bound together into a point at the top or bent over to form a conical or hoop roof. Something similar to this crude structure survives in the shepherd huts illustrated in late Nilotic landscapes. Closely related to the thatch hutch was the circular hut made of interwoven reeds, branches, or other pliable materials.[8] The evidence is conclusive that this was a very early form of house. Little cabins which appear in the pictures of Predynastic boats (Plate I–5) were obviously made of bendable materials and had curved roofs. The same form of woven construction, with an archlike roof, is seen at the opening of Dynastic history in a small house-sanctuary, cut on an ebony table of King Menes (Plate I–6), and at the end of Dynastic history on Roman pavements representing Nilotic scenes (Plate I–7).

Undoubtedly the earliest Egyptian wattle houses were circular, or at least curved, in plan. The curvilinear plan of a house is universally an instinctive and primitive shape, because it requires no preconception, and is the natural result, best illustrated by the nests of birds, of starting at one point, with pliable materials which do not require tools, and returning to the same place after a space has been enclosed. Its existence in Egypt is supported by the widespread persistence of the circular and thatched house throughout Africa (Plate LXIV–1), especially among the pagan tribes of the Nilotic Sudan,[9] whose modes of life approximate the tribal conditions in Prehistoric Egypt. Furthermore, remains of hut circles have been uncovered at Hemamieh [10] which varied in diameter from three to seven feet. They had low, mud walls, about a sunken floor, which show the imprint of an outer layer of vertically set bundles of reeds, and were only a skirting, or sup-

[7] Breasted, *Ancient Records of Egypt,* I, No. 403.

[8] Diodorus (I, 43) wrote in the first century A.D., "and their dwellings they built of reeds. And traces of these customs still remain among the herdsmen of Egypt, all of whom, they say, have no other dwelling up to this time than one of reeds."

[9] C. G. and Brenda Z. Seligman, *Pagan Tribes of the Nilotic Sudan* (1932).

[10] G. Brunton and G. Caton-Thompson, *The Badarian Civilization,* p. 82.

PLATE III

1. Hieroglyph for "sarcophagus" (M. A. Murray, *Saqqara Mastabas,* Pl. XXXVIII/39).
2. Wooden cabin on a boat, Cairo Museum.
3. House, ivory model in Cairo Museum.
4. Hut-shrine on cylinder, Berlin (A. Scharff, *Die Altertümer der Vor-und-Frühzeit Ægyptens,* II, 1929, Pl. 25/136).
5. Hut-shrine of goddess Neith, ebony tablet of King Menes (Petrie, *The Royal Tombs,* II, Pl. X/2).
6. Hut-shrine (*op. cit.*).
7. Hieroglyph for "palace" (Murray, *op. cit.,* Pl. XXXVIII/37).
8. Soul-house from Rifeh (Petrie, *Gizeh and Rifeh,* Pl. XV/100).
9. House, ivory of King Menes (Petrie, *The Royal Tombs,* II, Pl. III/4).
10. *Khekher* cornice: A (Petrie, *Egyptian Decorative Art,* 1895, Fig. 184), B & C by Author.
11. *Khekher* borders from Theban Tombs.
12. Hieroglyph for "house" or "tomb" (Murray, *op. cit.*).

porting base for a superstructure and roof of thatch. A tamarisk pole was driven into the ground on each side of the hut, almost touching the walls. Also at Merimda Beni-Salaam,[11] in the West Delta, Junker discovered remains of oval houses with sunken floors, a rim of plastered mud, and a superstructure of reeds, or wattle. At Maadi[12] were found houses of circular and oval plan, made of posts stuck in the ground and with the space between these posts filled with daub and wattle.[13] Each house had a central hearth; their size, however, makes it seem doubtful if they could have had roofs.

Round houses, made of plaited basketwork and with curved roofs, of the type still common in Negro Africa to-day, are depicted in the XVIII Dynasty on the reliefs of the mortuary temple of Queen Hatshepsut at Deir el-Bahari (Plate I–9). They were meant to represent typical dwellings of the inhabitants of the land of Punt which corresponds to modern Somaliland on the Gulf of Aden, and was the region where the Egyptians believed their race originated. Late classic representations of houses in Libya and North Africa show circular cabins and rectangular huts made of rushes and thatchwork (Plate I-8). Herodotus (IV, 190) describes the Libyan houses as mobile huts made of rushes interlaced with leaves of asphodel. Sallust describes the rural Numidian house as a *mapalia,*[14] with a conical incurving roof somewhat resembling the prow of a ship (Plate I-8).

THE MUD HOUSE. The mud house started with sticky, Nile mud plastered on the thatched and plaited walls of the more primitive structures, thereby producing a kind of daub and wattle. At first it continued the tradition of the semicircular or round form of dwelling, illustrated by a model of an Egyptian semicircular, mud house, dating from the Old Kingdom, in the British Museum (Plate I–10). In Libya, which was closely related to Lower Egypt in Predynastic times, the round house and its related form, the round tomb, survived as a traditional mode of building.[15] In Egypt, however, by the Dynastic period the round house,[16] with its curved roof, made of either mud or pliable materials, had become either a venerated shrine type or a utilitarian structure used for granaries, storerooms, bakeries, and the like (Plate I–13). Its persistence and religious significance through Dynastic times indicates its early importance in the culture. The shrine of the God

[11] H. Junker, *Anzeiger d. Ak. d. Wissenschaften d. Wien,* 1932; A. Scharff, *Die Altertümer d. Vor- und Frühzeit Aegyptens,* I, (*Mitt. aus d. Aeg. Santmlung,* Berlin, 1931, IV), p. 9 *seq.*

[12] Oswald Menghin and Mustafa Amer, *The Excavations of the Egyptian University in the Neolithic Site at Maadi* (1932).

[13] At Maadi the excavators have also discovered rectangular houses made by wooden posts stuck into the ground, the door off center on the long side, and a *circular* hearth inside. O. Menghin, "Die Grabung der Universität Kairo bei Maadi," *Mitteilungen der Deutschen Instituts für Aegyptsche Altertumskunde in Kairo,* V (1931), p. 111.

The Predynastic site at Mahasna revealed the remains of "wood piles" arranged in some system; between the piles were abundant traces of small twigs intertwined and indications of powdered mud. There is some doubt as to whether these remains were covered dwellings or only open wind-break shelters (J. Garstang, *Mahasna and Bet Khallaf,* 1902).

[14] "Mapalia" in Daremberg et Saglio, *Dictionnaire des Antiquités.*

[15] Oric Bates, *The Eastern Libyans* (1914); Sir Arthur Evans, *The Palace of Minos,* II, p. 39; there is also the evidence of the circular tombs in Nubia (W. E. Emory, "Archæological Survey of Nubia," *Annales du Service,* XXX (1930), p. 127).

[16] In the Old Kingdom hut-circles, for the use of workmen, made of rough stone and laid without mortar, have been found in the Fayum (G. Caton-Thompson and E. W. Gardiner, *The Desert Fayum,* 1934, pp. 120-121) and at Helwan (Petrie and E. Mackay, *Heliopolis, KafrAmmar and Shurafa,* 1915, p. 39). Also circular silo-pits, in some cases lined with coiled matting of corn straw, were found in the Fayum from the Neolithic period (*The Desert Fayum*).

Min, for example, is the replica of the round house of a tribal chieftain (Plate I–12), conical in shape, with painted bands of color, and having a totem mast before the entrance.

THE RECTANGULAR HOUSE. Simple as the rectangular form may seem, it has never been a natural shape in which men instinctively built their first houses. The idea of a structure with straight walls at right angles did not arise until builders began to work with rigid materials which required tools. The change from the curved to the rectangular plan began to take place in Egypt about S.D. 40. The early type is remarkably preserved by a clay model from a Predynastic tomb at El-Amrah (Plate I–14). The model reproduces what, at the time, was probably an upper-class house, even though it conforms to what later became the common type of Egyptian dwelling. The walls of the El-Amrah house were presumably of mud and wattle, although mud brick appears in Egypt by the middle of the Predynastic period. The doors and windows were framed in wood, and the door placed off center in the long side remained a persistent feature of Egyptian domestic architecture.

The transition from curved to rectangular houses either took place in the wattle and plaited mode of construction, or was introduced into the valley by invaders. Rectangular shelters of latticework, with a cresting of stalks projecting above the flat roof to form a parapet, or what eventually became the cavetto cornice in the stone architecture, were depicted in the Old Kingdom as the traditional shrine of Anubis (Plate II–1), suggesting that this type of house had once been associated with the jackal clan. There were some early minglings of the rectangular house with its projecting parapet and the wattle house with its curved roof, as indicated by another pictograph of the Old Kingdom, a house shrine of the God Set with a curved roof surmounted by a reed cresting (Plate II–2).

The natural evolution of the Egyptian house from the circular hut, through the oval form, to the rectangular dwelling is actually illustrated, sometime between about 2250 and 1650 B.C. at Aniba [17] in Nubia, where cultural development was more retarded than in Egypt. Here at Aniba in the First Period are the plans of circular tent-like huts, with a central post, which must have had conical roofs.[18] During the Second Period there are twelve circular huts with stone orthostates, an inner ring of posts, and a hearth at the center. Also from this period there are houses of oval and horseshoe plans. Finally in the Third Period rectangular houses of brick occur.

THE KHEKHER HOUSE. A distinctive form of the early house, probably indigenous to some special district and clan, is the rectangular dwelling made of light construction, with a peculiar cornice or parapet. This type is first represented as a pictograph on a I Dynasty ivory of King Menes from Abydos (Plate III–9). Here it is a sign depicting in ideographic form what may have been a two-storied house. In hieroglyphic writing the sign continued to signify "palace," "hall,"

[17] A. Langsdorff, "Eine Siedlung der C-Gruppe Leute in Aniba," *Annales du Service* (1932), p. 24 *seq.* abb. 1.

[18] The author compares these houses to the type illustrated by F. Oelmann, *Haus und Hof im Altertum*, I (1927), p. 24, abb. 4-b.

or "tomb"; at Saqqara it occurs as a house, or tomb, within a protective enclosure (Plate III–12). The striking feature of this sign, in addition to the fact that it usually denotes a two-storied palace, is its cresting of what the Egyptians called *ḳheḳhers*.

According to Sir Flinders Petrie,[19] this form of decorative parapet originated on the light cabins for boats, made of papyrus stalks with the ends tied together at the top (Plate III–10a), but it is more probable that it developed on one type of dwelling shelter and was transferred as an emblem of power to boat shelters. Whether the original structures had vertical stalks, or latticed-worked walls (Plate III-10b), the bundled tops were stylized into *ḳheḳhers*. When such primitive shelters were plastered with mud, the bound tops projected above the roof and made a memorable and valued decoration. Hence in hieroglyphic writing the *ḳheḳhers* came to signify "ornament," and when used on a house they meant a palace. Therefore at an early date the *ḳheḳher* house must have been the dwelling of a great chieftain, while later the *ḳheḳher* frieze (Plate III–11) came to be always associated with tomb decoration, for reasons which will become evident.

THE PANELED FRAME HOUSE. During the late Predynastic period, perhaps in the Delta, a new type of domestic construction appeared. Lower Egypt at the opening of the historic period had had for a long time a more advanced culture than existed in Upper Egypt. It was the first settled part of the valley; its longer history, early unification, and contacts with the East developed the methods of living in the Delta beyond the isolated and warlike life of the Southern tribes. The more advanced mode of construction, which was in wood, was undoubtedly limited to the ruling class. It is possible that it evolved naturally out of the inevitable mingling of the two elementary traditions of building. Whether it was a fusion of wattled wall construction and the tent, with its poles and hangings, or merely an importation, certainly a type of light timbered construction appeared before the I Dynasty. It consisted of a paneled framework made of small pieces of wood skilfully squared and joined together.

This type is twice pictured as a venerated house-shrine on sealings of King Zer of the I Dynasty (Plate II–3). The drawings show the vertical poles, the cross-bars, a door off center on the long side, and the evident sag of a tent-like hanging stretched over the bent hoops of the roof. A larger house, long and rectangular, with two doors and built of the same paneled timbering, is represented on a clay cylinder of the I Dynasty from Negadeh (Plate III–4). It is impossible to tell from the representations whether the openings of the frame walls were filled with wattle and mud, or covered with hangings. If this mode of construction was the prototype of the somewhat similar small-wood, recessed construction which we will see depicted on the Old Kingdom stelæ and imitated in the tombs of the Old and Middle Kingdoms, then the walls were hung with fabrics serving to keep out the heat and wind, and yet capable of being opened for ventilation.

THE CURVED ROOF. It is necessary to emphasize the early prevalence of curved roofs in order that later the presence of curved ceilings in stone will not necessarily connote vaulting. The bent

19 Sir Flinders Petrie, *Egyptian Decorative Art* (1895), p. 101; E. Mackay, "Khekher frieze," *Ancient Egypt* (1920), p. 111.

hoop-roof, covered with woven matting, which went back in origin to tent and reed forms, continued to be used long after the customary roof of the Egyptian house had become flat (Plate I–7).

The tent, it has been seen, developed before Dynastic times into a portable structure with a curved roof, covered with matting. Because of its primitive importance as the seat of the tribal chieftain and guardian of the clan's totem, it continued to be used throughout Egyptian history as the most common symbol of the sacred shrine. It first occurs on a sealing of the I Dynasty (Plate II–5). In the New Kingdom it is still represented as the naos, or shrine, of Osiris (Plate II–8) in a later transcript of the *Book of the Dead,* where it preserves the characteristics of the primitive structure and shows a stylized representation of uprights of small-wood and a bent-wood roof.

What is significant at this stage is not the influence of the tent kiosk upon Dynastic architecture, but the overwhelming evidence of an early tradition of curved roofs. The curved roof was carefully imitated in the early wooden sarcophagi (Plate V–2), which were themselves thought of as houses, and it therefore also figured as the hieroglyph for a sarcophagus (Plate III–1). The light framework of this prevalent type of bent roof is seen in a cabin of a XII Dynasty boat from the tomb of Masakt at Asyut (Plate III–2). As late as Roman times typical Nilotic scenes, such as occurs on the mosaic pavement from Palestrina, depict long huts with hoop roofs (Plate I–7). These examples indicate that the appearance of a semicircular roof does not necessarily imply vaulting.

THE GABLED ROOF. Obviously there was no climatic reason such as snow and rain for the curved roof to develop into a pointed gable as it did in Asia Minor and probably in Greece. By the Old Kingdom the flat roof was common, if not already customary. Therefore it is difficult to explain the small ivory model of a house, dating from early in the Old Kingdom, which was found at Abu Rawâsh (Plate III–3). The type of house represented in this model is unique, for neither its gabled roof nor its U-shaped plan seem to be Egyptian. At present the most satisfactory explanation is that it depicts a form of dwelling seen by its creator outside of Egypt.

THE FORECOURT. The enclosed forecourt was an early and important feature of the Egyptian house and therefore remained a prominent characteristic of all Egyptian architecture. Perhaps the court came before the house and should have been included among the earliest types of shelter. Not only do open, court-like shelters survive in modern field-camps, but it is also possible to assume that primitive men made open enclosures, defensive stockades, and wind-break shelters by sticking bundled reeds into the ground before they thought of bending the walls together as a roof. Prehistoric remains from Maadi and Mahasna [20] indicate the existence of such open shelters, and the simplest hieroglyph for house [21] is generally assumed to be a court, rather than a covered dwelling. With the growth of a more complex society, the mere one-roomed structure did not provide defensive security and privacy for the family and its possessions; moreover, in a country where there was little rainfall and so much of the domestic life took place out-of-doors, the space in front of the house was as much a part of it

[20] Page 20.
[21] F. L. Griffith, *Hieroglyphs,* p. 35, Fig. 193.

as the interior. The early forecourt, in combination with the simple hut, appears in the first representations of sacred dwellings, such as the hut-shrine on a sealing at Abydos (Plate II–5), a sanctuary of wattled construction on a cylinder (Plate III–4), a shrine of the goddess Neith on an ivory tablet of King Menes (Plate III–5), and another shrine on the same tablet (Plate III–6). The religious import of all these representations may be disregarded for the moment and the buildings considered as early house forms. They all show either a plaited wattle or a small-wood construction.

THE PORTICO. It is impossible to say whether the columnar porch which figures so prominently in Egyptian architecture developed as an addition to the house, or had a separate origin in the early tent-shelters (Plate I–1) and was later enlarged by the addition of rooms. Although it is conceivable that both processes of evolution took place at different times and in separate localities, there is evidence to suggest that the open shelter was the prototype. The portico became a prominent and symbolic feature of early mortuary temples, as at Abusir (Plate XXXIV), and as a hieroglyph it signified "palace" (Plate III–7); furthermore, there are small, clay models of soul-houses (Plate III–8), consisting of a forecourt and a columnar portico, but without rooms behind the porch.

THE VESTIBULE. Associated in use, if not in origin, with the columnar portico, was the enclosed vestibule which was common in domestic architecture and occurs in house plans used for tombs. Sometimes the vestibule is a small, entrance anteroom (Plate LXVI–7), and at other times it is a projecting porch, as is best illustrated by the I Dynasty tombs at Tarkhan (Plate X–10). Apparently both the vestibule and the portico began to assume architectural importance after the opening of Dynastic history.

THE SEREKH HOUSE. On the banners and stelæ of the kings of the Hawk clan, whose chieftains unified Egypt at the beginning of the I Dynasty, appears an heraldic emblem, a building which signifies both "palace" and "tomb." Such a banner of King Menes' is depicted on an ivory from his tomb (Plate III–9), and the finest example of this "palace façade" is carved on the grave stele of King Zet (Plate IV–1). The *serekh* building was undoubtedly a royal house, made of small pieces of wood carefully fitted together, which must have antedated the Dynastic age, and was, perhaps, the distinctive dwelling of the nobility of Lower Egypt. Inasmuch as this type of house, or palace, represented an advanced stage of wooden architecture and exerted a great influence on Egyptian architecture at the beginning of the Dynastic period, it will be treated separately in the next chapter.

THE TOMB

Although prehistoric tombs can hardly be called architecture, they supply important evidence regarding the beginnings of architecture, inasmuch as they were imitated from the customary dwellings of the living. The first graves in Egypt were shallow, round pits in which the bodies were wrapped or covered with either skins or crude matting, and laid on the left side in the embryonic position.

Even in such early graves as those at Badari, dating before S.D. 30, the utensils and pots buried with the dead show the existence of a developed ritual of death and a cult of careful preparation for the hereafter.

The round graves, shaped after the circular huts, persisted with varying tenacity in different parts of the valley (Plate X–1), but in time they gave place to oval graves where the body was still laid on its side in a contracted posture and covered with matting, as in sleep. Before the end of the first half of the Predynastic period, the rectangular trench, like the rectangular house, appeared; and before S.D. 52 brick had begun to be used for the walls of the tombs. At El-Amrah the trenches were at first lined with wood and later with sun-dried brick—a sequence which indicates the order in which the building materials were adopted. About contemporary with the appearance of brick in the graves, the roof of the tomb was made stronger by laying poles across the top. These poles were covered with matting and buried under a mound of earth.

While the lower classes continued to be buried in shallow trenches, the more prosperous and powerful members of the communities sought greater protection for their final resting place. The rulers initiated new modes of tomb construction, and it will be seen what a passion their desire for everlasting security became. Though the tomb grew more elaborate, the dead were still laid, as in sleep, on a mat of plaited reeds; but towards the end of the Predynastic period the body was at times wrapped in woven fabrics. At all times the dead were supplied with food, drink, weapons, palettes to prepare the pigments for painting the face, and models of boats for the final journey "to the West." At Hierakonpolis a Predynastic tomb was unearthed in which the mud walls were washed over with yellow ochre and then painted with the first extant Egyptian mural, showing the journey of the soul by boat.

Naïve as these sepulchral beginnings may seem, they formulated ideas which came to dominate Egyptian culture. The careful preparation for immortality arose from a natural ideology and an instinctive conviction so universal and persistent that we still perpetuate it with our expensive mortuary parlors and acres of elaborate grave monuments. At the moment when men began to reflect, there was the realization of some significant relation between the body and the spirit: the body, they saw, decomposed when the spirit left it; and the spirit—or the vital force, which the Egyptians called the *Ka*—remained, they realized, a vague and incomprehensible nothingness unless it had some material aspect. Experience demonstrated that there could be no shadow, or reflected image, without a tangible body to make it. The vivid images of the departed which men saw in their dreams were convincing proof of the continued existence of the dead. Thinking, then, as they had to, from the known to the unknown, the Egyptians pictured the everlasting life in terms of the material present. Therefore when the dead went "West," to where the Sun-god sank into his grave every night and where the reincarnated Osiris ruled, "the Westerners" needed food, raiment, and all things to make death comprehensible.

In addition to the *Ka,* the Egyptians believed also in a *Ba,* or soul, which was visualized most often as a bird flying in the trees, but could appear as a flower or an animal. The *Ka,* or what is often called *the double,* could not wander about as an unhappy and disembodied spirit without working evil. In fact, it seems as if there were more fear than love in the Egyptians' concern for the comforts of their departed and in their special kind of ancestor worship. Because of this primitive animism, which they never outgrew, every statue was a possible embodiment for the *Ka* in its after life. While such a belief gave a powerful significance to all figurative art, it also brought all representational sculpture and painting under a strict priestly and ritualistic control.

Two persistent elements in the effort to thwart death directly influenced the history of the architecture. They were *the idea of worship at the grave* and *the desire that the occupant of the grave should be physically protected.* The desire for security did not become an obsession until the Old Kingdom, when the kings of unified Egypt considered themselves divine mortals. Worship at the grave, which in time became a tremendous ritual and supplied the incentive and forms from which the great mortuary temples of the New Kingdom evolved, went back to a natural instinct. Breasted writes of "the offering to the dead, originally only a small loaf in a bowl, placed by a son, or wife, or brother on a reed mat at the grave." Even in the early graves a ledge was added where such offerings could be left. By the end of the Predynastic period the rectangular chamber of the dead had a small recess, or vestibule, which in time *developed into the mortuary chapel.*

It seems unlikely that the mortuary chapel developed directly and solely from the vestibule of the tomb. Some intimation of another tradition may be derived from the early Dynastic tombs where the rooms for the service of the dead are always *above the actual burial chamber.* In Mesopotamia it was customary to bury the dead in the floor of the house, using either the whole house, or a room of it, as a chapel. Such must have been the case during the Predynastic period in certain parts of Egypt, presumably in the Delta where deep burials underground would have been impossible because of the marshy ground.[22] In fact, the close relation between the house and the tomb in Egypt suggests this possibility, while the prevalence of burials either under the house or in front of the door among the pagan tribes of the Sudan, whose crude culture shows so many primitive Nilotic survivals, furnishes strong evidence for the assumption.[23] At the opening of Dynastic history, the royal graves, although built in imitation of houses, were underground and covered for protection with mounds of earth on which stood grave stelæ. In spite of Sir Flinders Petrie's belief that there were no superstructures on the royal mounds at Abydos, it now seems probable that shelters of reed, wattle, and wood were built above these graves to serve as chapels, and were perhaps the survival of the house with the grave beneath it.

Unfortunately no chapels of this kind remain because they were built of perishable materials, but some evidence for such a genesis of the tomb superstructure is supplied by the evolution of the Dynastic tomb.[24] It is imaginable, however, that the reed house, plastered with mud and crowned with *ḳheḳher* cornice (Plate III–9, 12), was one type of royal chapel, perhaps the kind erected above the I

[22] House burials were found in the West Delta at Merimda Beni-Salaam (A. Scharff, *Die Altertümer der Vor- und-Frühzeit Aegyptens,* I, (1931), p. 9).

[23] C. G. and Brenda Z. Seligman, *Pagan Tribes of the Nilotic Sudan* (1932), pp. 112, 133, 290, 302, 470, 534; C. G. Seligman, "Egyptian Influences in Negro Africa," *Studies presented on his Anniversary to F. H. Griffith* (1932); N. W. Thomas, "Some Ibo Burial Customs," *Journal Royal Anthropological Institute,* XLVII (1912), p. 170, "For a rich man his grave is dug by four young men in his house or garden."

[24] Page 48.

Dynasty tombs at Abydos. Not only did this type of house keep the double meaning of "palace" and "tomb" in hieroglyphic writing, but the *khekher* cornice survived in Egyptian art solely as a frieze painted along the top of the interior walls of tomb chambers. In the next chapter it will be seen how another type of royal palace, through the same process, became in time entirely limited to sepulchral usage. Speculative as these suggestions must at first seem, it is necessary to realize how closely related were all Egyptian ideas. The fact that all house signs in Egyptian writing may be used as determinatives of and for either "house" or "tomb" is evidence of such a fusion of ideas and customs.

THE TEMPLE

Religion antedates temples. Temples were fixed concepts which could only take shape when religious ideas were firmly established in a relatively stable culture, when supernatural spirits and powers were visualized as sufficiently human to require a permanent abode and the service of an organized household. Therefore they reflect a comparatively late stage in the growth of religious institutions.

The first necessity of the religious instinct, after it emerged as a vague consciousness of impotence, was to turn the inexplicable and aimless chance of primitive life into something ordered and in part controlled. It was ages before men could distinguish between the various beliefs, customs, and ceremonies which this necessity evolved. To understand the thinking which made Egyptian architecture, it must be understood that the primitive mind *experienced life as a whole,* and so could not isolate its activities into separate and specialized faculties. To the primitive ritualist, religion was not the care of the soul, medicine the care of the body, agriculture the care of the crops, and government the care of the people. Religion, because it dealt with the whole apparent reality of existence, was everything. It supplied all explanations: its feasts established the calendar; its usages formed the basis of education; and its needs created both science and art. *Art therefore was not for the delectation of the senses.* In Egypt art was a great necessity and had tremendous usefulness. To the primitive imagination, its forms were related to reality itself, and its representational images were of magical significance. It is the simple and indivisible oneness of such naïve thinking, so inherent in Egyptian civilization, whether early or late, which furnishes us with an interpretation of the forms of architecture.

At the time when men in Egypt were settled in communal organizations, dependent as agriculturists upon the bounty of the Nile, the two life-giving elements which required explanation and control were the River and the Sun. Furthermore, men saw all forms of nature animated by good or evil spirits. Osiris, for example, was worshiped as a pillar, or bundle of reeds, long before he was thought of in human form. Each community set up one particular spirit whose power it most dreaded or whose qualities it most wished to possess, and the spirit became the protector and totem of the locality. The physical attributes of the fetish were by necessity material, and usually animal. The hawk, the bee, the cow, the eagle, the cat, the lion, and the elephant were a few of the protecting totems which in the end gave their names to the clans and later to the nomes, or provinces, of Egypt. In time, of course, many of these divinities merged with one another or otherwise lost their original significance.

What was it, then, which turned animal and pillar spirits into gods with human needs, thus giving rise to the necessity of religious abodes for them? In tribal society the sorcerer became the priest and chief, the powerful one, and eventually the king. His magic propitiated the spirits and his house was their residence. Gradually in men's memory he stood forth as the representative of the unknown, then as the possessor of its attributes, and finally as its incarnation. His justice was the will of the spirit, and his house was related in men's minds to the divinity. At this stage the incipient idea of the temple began to take shape. Chief, priest, divinity, house, and ritual were all intermingled as one essential whole. Therefore it might be said that there were no temples in Predynastic times; instead there were all the elements from which the need and the conception of the temple could evolve. Towards the end of this formative period when more than one god was worshiped in a community, there were the great house of the chief and shelters for the other communal divinities, while the common people propitiated many vague powers and spirits of good or evil either in the home or in the open.

It is necessary, within the compass of this book, to skip boldly and rapidly over these complex and uncertain religious origins in order to lay the foundations for the Egyptian's outlook on life which justified his rigid architectural conventions. For example, the lotus and papyrus flowers, so faithfully reproduced as columns in all periods of Egyptian architecture, derived from primitive religious usage. The "Bee" chief of Lower Egypt, who ruled from his "Red House" at Buto, wore the red cap with the ureus, or cobra, as a sign of life and death power, and his "speaking arms" were the WAZ, or papyrus, which was a common river plant of the Delta. In Upper Egypt a Southern chief, called NSWT, which was the lotus sign, ruled from his "White House." With the unification of the North and South, the kings of the Dynastic period absorbed the attributes of the conquered localities with the result that the lotus and the papyrus became symbolic of the union of the two regions.

The value of the lotus and papyrus, however, and their eventual perpetuation in architectural forms, went back in Egyptian minds to something more fundamental than political symbolism. In some way their significance in Egyptian eyes was related to the primitive dependence upon the life-giving vegetation arising out of the waters of the Nile. The chief was the one whose magic helped to regulate and assure the order and abundance of the life-sustaining growth. His house, in the season, was undoubtedly hung with either lotus or papyrus, and the flowers were tied to the supporting posts so that his dwelling was a festal bower. At such times his house was the abode of the godhead and imaged in small and comprehensible terms the reproductive idea of growing life on which man was so dependent. Thus within this microcosm the columns were the life-producing flowers themselves, pushing up from the ritualistically fertilized earth, and the painted ceiling was the heavenly but present abode of the gods. The architecture dramatized the life process of flowering growth so that columns were not seen as functional supports, but as symbols of growth. With the formality of Egyptian culture it was natural for the house and temple to preserve a distinct memory of the forms of this early magic.

It is more confusing than helpful to consider the innumerable and none too clearly defined gods who were honored in the Egyptian temples. Besides the local totems who became divinities, or merged with similar divinities, the two gods who rose above all others were Re, the Sun-god, and Osiris, the god of vegetation and the dead. In the Old Kingdom the anthropomorphic conception of divinity became a fixed habit, and on the Palermo stone both Re and Osiris are listed as prehistoric kings of Egypt. It was then, as Breasted wrote, "that the Sun-god shifted to the world of men where he became an Ancient King who, like a Pharaoh, had once ruled Egypt." His primitive, reed boat, by which in his daily journey he traversed the heavens, turned into a royal barge, and the reigning Pharaoh became the incarnation of the giver of ight. In the same way Osiris, who personified the life cycle of death and resurrection, the periodic rise and fall of the food-giving waters of the Nile, an ancestral spirit, and the great judge of the underworld, came also to be incarnate in the person of the Pharaoh.

Actually the "daily divine cult" which was pictured in all the temples of Egypt down to the coming of Christianity, was a royal domestic ritual,[25] "consisting of a series of acts of service such as the servants of a king, or man of high rank, would perform for their master each day." "His dwelling was cleansed and perfumed, a fire kindled, his soiled garments were taken from him and removed, and when he had been washed, anointed, scented, and re-dressed in suitable apparel, and his jewelry and other ornaments placed on him, and the symbols of his authority put in his hands," [26] he was given food and drink.

Since the forms and ritual of anthropomorphic worship were derived from the home life of the mighty one of the clan, all the earliest shrines depict house types which in different localities were the dwelling of the ancestor of the mighty one, who in men's minds was either a god himself or the descendant of the gods.[27] This combination of ideas kept the primitive type of the clan house as a traditional abode of the god long after the actual dwellings of the rulers had become more elaborate structures.[28]

All the hut-shrines which were venerated at the opening of Dynastic history have already been illustrated as houses. The best of these to consider as an embryonic temple is the shrine of Neith, a goddess of the Delta, which is represented on a I Dynasty ivory of King Menes from Abydos (Plate III–5). Here are depicted all the simple elements of a temple, elements which continued to persist even after Egyptian temples had become gigantic structures of stone in the New Kingdom. The naos, or shrine proper, is a single-roomed hut with a curved roof of matting. In front of it is a courtyard in which stands the totem pole carrying the emblem of the goddess; and at the entrance to the court are

[25] A. Moret, *Le Rituel du Culte Divin Journalier en Égypte* (1902); A. M. Blackman, "The Sequence of the Episodes in the Egyptian Daily Temple Liturgy," *Journ. of the Manchester Egyptian and Oriental Soc.* (1918-1919), p. 27.

[26] E. A. W. Budge, *Osiris,* I (1911), p. 252.

[27] Rémy Cottevieille-Giraudet writes, "Ainsi il apparaît que dans l'Égypte primitive le dieu loge dans une habitation identique à cette du chef de ville ou du roi: palais et temple sont tout un; le seigneur est un maître, le dieu en est un autre qui a les mêmes besoins" ("Note sur le Kiosque de Fête Sed," *Fouilles de l'Institut français d'Archéologie orientale du Caire,* IX, 1933, p. 40).

[28] Among the Pagan tribes of the Nilotic Sudan the shrine of the god, such as the sanctuary of Nyakang, among the Shilluk, consists of a group of circular, thatched houses arranged like a homestead within an enclosing fence (C. G. Seligman, *op. cit.,* p. 78).

poles from which banners fly. The relation of this representation to actual temples will appear later. At the present stage it is more important for the reader to see why there were as yet no specialized temple types; house, tomb, and shrine were as yet only different aspects and uses of the same customary and natural forms.

3. *THE BEGINNINGS OF DYNASTIC ARCHITECTURE*

Copy thy fathers which have gone before thee.
INSTRUCTION OF THE KING OF UPPER AND LOWER EGYPT TO HIS SON MERY-KE-RE.

THE EGYPTIANS themselves looked back with awe and reverence to the Thinite Kings, at the opening of the historic period, whose power unified the land and whose will brought about the social and artistic development which created the wonders of the Old Kingdom. Those divine Lords of Thinis whose tombs have been discovered at Abydos are no longer the legendary figures which they were to the later Egyptians and the early Egyptologists. While they were undoubtedly warrior kings, their administrative control of the country was sufficiently developed so that from the time of Menes they took a census every two years for the purpose of taxation. Their unification of the country influenced architecture, although at first the new rulers from Upper Egypt either followed their own building traditions or adopted those of the more prosperous and civilized Delta. In fact, the first two Dynasties of the Old Kingdom were a transition between a vague Prehistoric age and the splendor of the III and IV Dynasties.

The architecture of the first two Dynasties was entirely in mud brick, wood, and light pliable materials. The tombs, reliefs, paintings and scanty remains of actual buildings furnish but slight evidence of what their architecture was like. The picture becomes clearer when it is understood how much of this wood and brick construction was literally copied in the new stone architecture of the III Dynasty.

THE SEREKH BUILDING

At the beginning of the Old Kingdom there was a distinctive, although presumably local, style of wooden architecture which had a curiously persistent influence on subsequent buildings, even though its particular wooden construction went out of use at an early date.[1] This wooden tradition either developed or was introduced somewhere in Egypt as a *type of ruling house,* and, as such, became a venerated *symbol of power.*

Its schematic appearance is first reproduced on the banners of the Thinite Kings of the I Dynasty where the name-panel is the "palace-façade," or the so-called *serekh* building, which represents a royal palace. Ever since Perrot wrote his history of Egyptian art it has been generally, although not univer-

[1] While the *serekh* name was continued in use to designate the seat of the high administrative offices of the government, there is no reason to think that the VI Dynasty letter from Saqqara, which speaks of workmen being "clothed in his (the Vizier's) presence at the very beautiful *serekh* building," refers to a structure of small-wood such as is depicted on the early banners (A. H. Gardiner, "An Administrative Letter of Protest," *Journal of Egyptian Archaeology,* XIII, 1927, p. 75).

PLATE IV: HOUSE AND TOMB

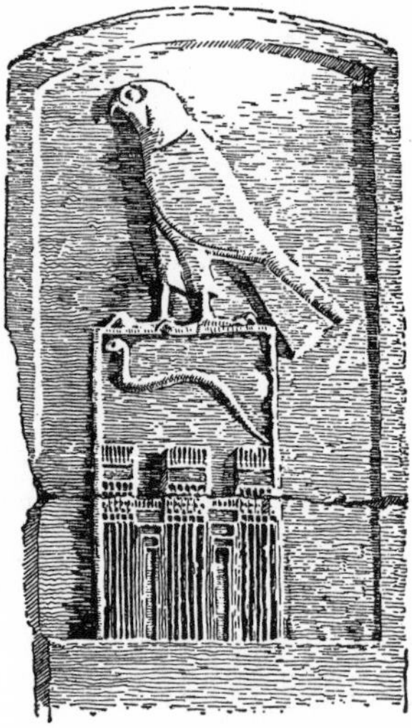

2

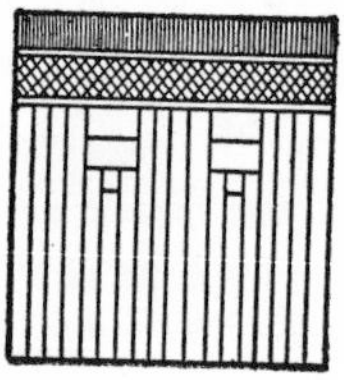

3

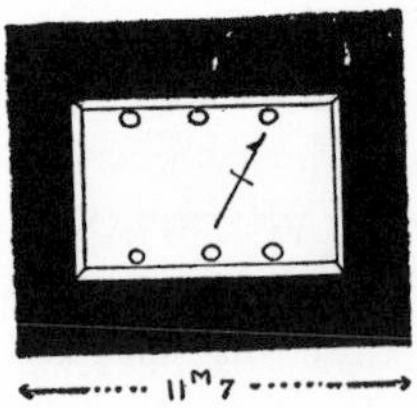

4

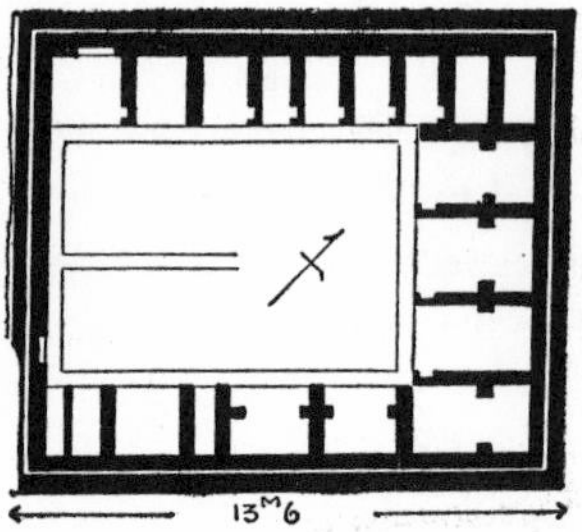

5

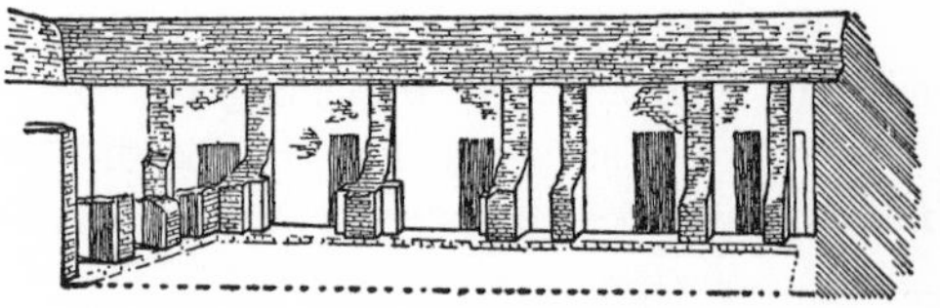

6

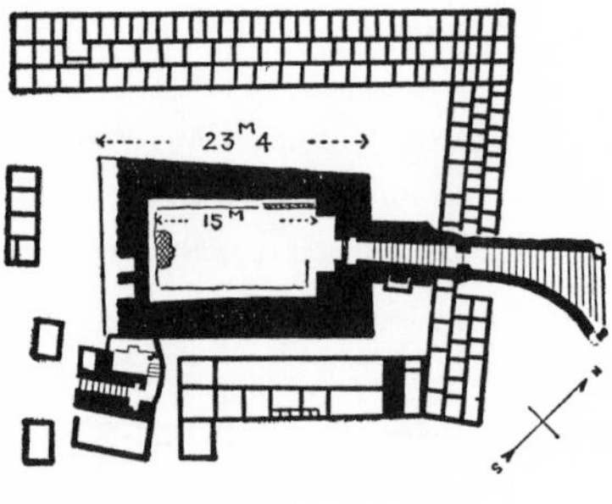

7

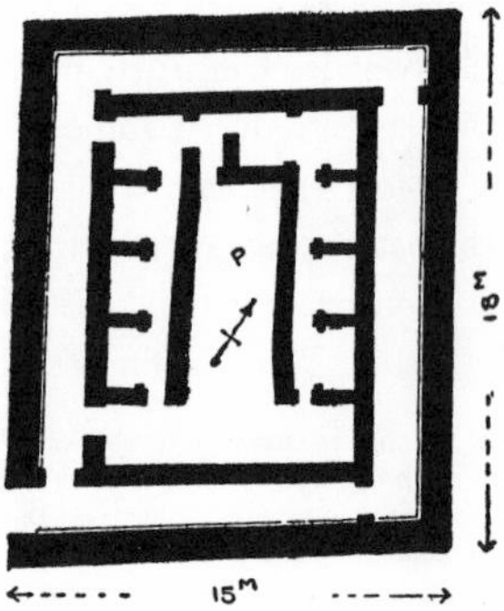

sally, recognized that the palace style of the *serekh* building was constructed of small pieces of carefully joined planks and squared timbers, so fitted together as to form a light and open framework. Its exterior appearance is clearly preserved, the finest reproduction being the towered façade upon the gravestone of King Zet (Plate IV–1), who was probably the second ruler after Menes.

The relief shows a system of slender, wooden uprights, strengthened by overlapping timbers, rigidified by crosspieces, and so built that the whole façade appears to be composed of vertical, recessed niches. The building is a defensive stronghold with two narrow doorways between three towers that project on the front and rise above the flat roof. Along the top of both the roof and the towers is a parapet, probably made of papyrus stalks. The relief, it must be realized, is no fanciful representation, for Egyptian art was always strictly literal within its ideographic conventions. The "palace-façade," surmounted by the snake emblem of the King and the Horus of his clan, was the heraldic emblem of the first Pharaohs of Egypt. The many other representations of this façade show how in time the towers disappeared and the roof became flat, with a continuous cornice, but the vertical niche pattern of small-wood construction still continued schematically to be preserved (Plate IV–2).

What the interior of the *serekh* palace was like is more problematic. There is good evidence, which does not amount to proof, that it consisted of recesses or small alcoves, made by wooden partitions and hangings, around a large central hall. Sir Flinders Petrie describes what he considers to have been the established type of wooden building of this period. "We must remember," he writes, "that a great chief's house was used by night as well as by day. By day it was needful to be able to open the house widely, or to close it altogether, so as to let in an abundance of cooling breezes, or to keep out the dust storms and extreme heat. It was thus requisite to have the system of a great number of small doorways easily closed; usually with a single board, and therefore narrow. Sometimes these openings were wider and were then barred across to prevent men and animals entering, as is shown in a house model in a wooden coffin (Plate V–2).... In all parts of the world—be it in Polynesia, Africa, or in the life of the Norse sagas—the chief sleeps with his household of retainers, ready for the fight if he be attacked. When no fire-hearth is the focus, they would naturally sleep round the sides of the great hall. Each space between the openings of the doors would be a sleeping place," screened and protected from draughts.[2]

This description by the distinguished Egyptologist is very specific, but it raises many questions upon which there is as yet no agreement. A few archæologists still believe that the recessed niche con-

[2] Sir Flinders Petrie, *Tarkhan,* II, p. 8.

PLATE IV

1. Grave stele of King Zet, Louvre.
2. "Palace-façade" of King Den (Petrie, *The Royal Tombs,* II, Pl. VII/12).
3. Plan of tomb of King Menes, Abydos (Petrie, *op. cit.,* II, Pl. LIX).
4. Plan of Tomb of King Zet, Abydos (Petrie, *op. cit.,* I, Pl. LXI).
5. Interior of tomb of King Zet, south wall (Petrie, *op. cit.,* I, Pl. LXIII).
6. Plan of tomb of King Den (Wedymuw), Abydos (Petrie, *op. cit.,* II, Pl. LXII).
7. Plan of tomb of King Perabsen, Abydos (Petrie, *op. cit.,* II, Pl. LXI).

struction, indicated in the reliefs and imitated in the tombs, was derived directly from brick construction. There are also differences of opinion as to whether the small-wood construction of the *serekh* building originated elsewhere or was a local tradition in Egypt. Some scholars believe that it developed in the traditional strongholds of the conquering chiefs of the Falcon clan from Upper Egypt; others insist that it was an indigenous method of building in the Delta, and a few hold to the idea that it was a method of construction introduced into Egypt by invaders from the East.

In order to escape some of the confusion arising from archæological controversies, and yet to test the evidence for the wooden palace style, it is clearest to follow the most reasonable explanation, while admitting the possibility of other theories. That the Falcon kings, when they conquered the Delta, took the *serekh* house as an heraldic emblem does not prove that its method of construction came from Upper Egypt. Presumably its small-wood, paneled construction was the old and royal method of building in Lower Egypt, which had developed there before the I Dynasty during the period of the "First Union." [3]

THE ROYAL TOMBS AT ABYDOS. So that the reader may consider for himself the evidence regarding the character and origin of the *serekh*-façade type of building, and at the same time follow the development of early Dynastic architecture in nearly chronological sequence, it is essential to begin with the royal tombs at Abydos. They give a reality to the warrior rulers who began Dynastic history; they introduce for the first time that desire for sepulchral permanency which became an insatiable passion of later Egyptian kings; and because they fail to imitate the sunken paneling of the *serekh* façade these tombs not only furnish some indication of what the royal abode in Upper Egypt was like, but they at once suggest that the *serekh* façade was a symbol of power borrowed presumably from Northern Egypt, rather than a traditional mode of construction in Southern Egypt.

The tombs at Abydos of the kings of the I Dynasty, and four of their immediate predecessors, are made of sun-dried brick. The five earliest ones, of which three have been identified as the tombs of Ka, Narmer, and Menes, consist of a single rectangular chamber with *plain* walls which are progressively thicker in the later examples. Each of these brick dwellings of the royal dead was buried in the sand and covered by a mound, in some cases held by a retaining wall. The mound, it is to be imagined, was surmounted by a small mortuary chapel of perishable materials, as well as the two stone grave stelæ and the offering table. The tomb of Menes (Plate IV–3), like the tombs of the four earlier kings, had an interior peristyle of wooden posts, driven into the ground, to carry the woden beams which formed the flat roof.[4] If these tombs imitated the houses of the

[3] H. Balcz, "Die altägyptische Wandgleiderung," *Mitteilungen d. Deutsche Inst. für Aegyptische Altertumskunde in Kairo* (1930), pp. 38-92; "The palaces of the early kings of the Delta were built of coniferous wood hung with tapestry-woven mats," P. E. Newberry, "Egypt as a Field for Anthropological Research," *Annual Report of the Smithsonian Institution* (1924), p. 454.

[4] The tomb is about 26 ft. long and 17 ft. wide according to Petrie, or 11.7 m. by 9.4 m. according to Reisner. There is now serious doubt regarding the attribution of this tomb to Menes, especially since the recent discovery of a tomb at North Saqqara (p. 39) which probably belonged to him. However it is reasonable to suppose that Menes, after the conquest of the Delta, initiated the custom of building two royal tombs, one as King of Upper Egypt in the land of his Fathers, and the second as King of Lower Egypt near his capital at Memphis.

living, then the royal abode of the Falcon clan was a single-roomed, primitive house, enlarged into a fair-sized hall by means of interior supports.

The tombs of Kings Zer and Zet (Plate IV–4) and Queen Merneit, which follow in chronological order, suggest the influence of a different tradition, coming perhaps from the palace architecture of Lower Egypt. With these tombs the exterior walls are still thick and *plain,* but the interiors are divided by brick cross-walls into a perimeter of small alcoves about a central chamber in which the body was buried. The central chamber in the tomb of King Zet had a plank floor and was *timber-lined throughout.*[5] Its inner walls are plastered and whitewashed (Plate IV–5), and have red panels painted on both the projecting and surrounding partitions. These red panels represented *wooden doors* through which the soul could pass. Red was the symbol of wood during the Old Kingdom, and it is possible that the projecting walls of the interior of the tomb of Zet imitated in brick the wooden partitions of a perimeter of alcoves about a central hall. The outer wall of this tomb was carried up above the roof, like a parapet, to form the retaining wall for a mound of sand piled upon the roof.[6]

The tomb of King Den (Plate IV–6) shows a return to the earlier, undivided, single chamber, and at the same time represents an advance in tomb construction. It has what was probably the first flight of stairs leading down on the north side to the burial chamber. While the interior chamber was originally still lined with wood, its floor was made of red granite,[7] which is the *earliest extant use of stone* in Egyptian architecture. The tomb of King Azab resembles that of Den and the tomb of "Qa," the last ruler of the I Dynasty, shows a still more developed continuation of the same tradition, save that it has separate chambers for offerings on either side of the entrance vestibule.

At the beginning of the II Dynasty, the tomb of King Perabsen (Plate IV–7) presents another innovation.[8] Although still built of brick, it has an enclosing wall, like a house set within a protecting court. The interior has short walls at right angles, which again form alcoves as in the tombs of Zer, Zet, and Merneit.[9] An advance in tomb construction is indicated by the carefully finished pilasters at the ends of the projecting walls and by the use of brick, instead of wood, for the greater protection of the inner burial chamber.

Finally, the tomb of King Khasekhemui (Plate V–1) has a much larger and more elaborate treatment of the recessed type of "palace interior." Khasekhemui is a clear-cut, historical person-

[5] This central chamber was about 20 ft. wide, 30 ft. long, and 6 ft. high according to Petrie, 9.3 m. wide, 11.9 m. long, and 2.6 m. high according to Reisner.

[6] G. A. Reisner (*The Development of the Egyptian Tomb down to the Accession of Cheops,* 1936) believes on rather slight evidence, in part refuted by Petrie after excavating the tombs, that there were rectangular mastabas of brick above the graves of Narmer and Menes, and that the superstructure of the tomb of Zer "was in fact a stepped pyramid with two layers of brick work outside the kernel structure, making a two-stage or three-stage, stepped pyramid," the first of its kind. For a reconstruction of this entirely theoretical prototype of the pyramid see p. 324, Fig. 172.

[7] Reisner, *op. cit.,* p. 58.

[8] Reisner, *op. cit.,* p. 125, believes that a small number of sacrificial burials were made in the alcoves around the central chamber and that the roof was of corbelled brick construction instead of being made of logs of wood. He thinks it also had a stepped mastaba made by sloping "accretion faces" (p. 355).

[9] On the tomb of Merneit "at the edge of chamber 2 is the cast of plaited palm-leaf matting on the mud mortar above this level," Petrie, *Royal Tombs,* I, p. 11.

PLATE V: TOMBS

1

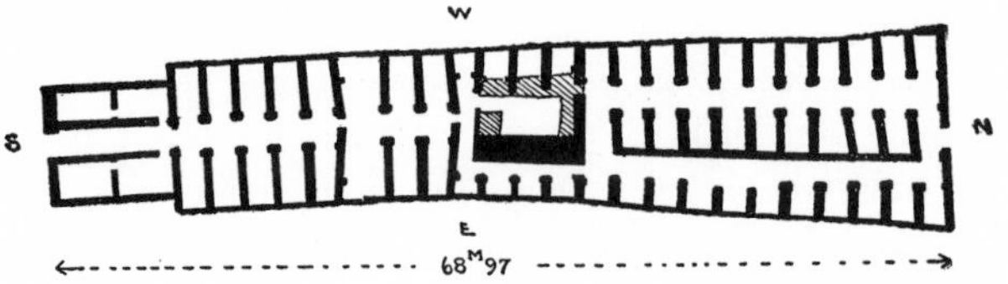

2

3

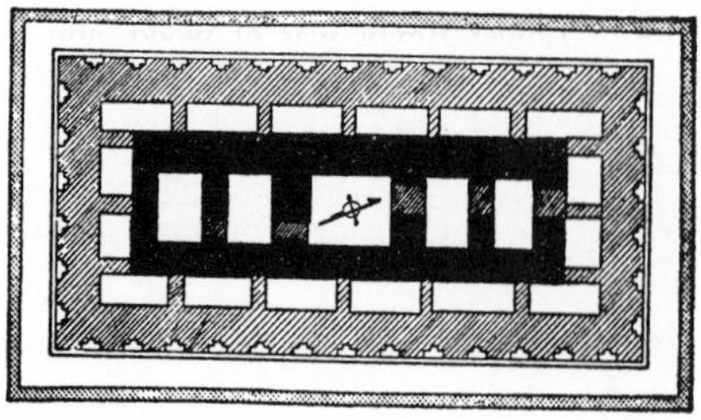

4

ality who may be perhaps identified with Khasekhem whose statue was found at Hierakonpolis. His reign closed the II Dynasty, his family established the III Dynasty, and during his reign there was marked progress in all the crafts. It is fitting that this southerner, who again had to conquer the Delta, should have the largest and most remarkable of any of the tombs at Abydos. Its total length is 68.97 m. and at its broadest part it measures 17.6 m. In front of the entrance are vestibule rooms for offerings on either side of what may have been a towered façade. Down the long interior are rows of recesses; the short brick walls, terminating in pilaster ends, probably imitate, as at Saqqara,[10] bundled reed or wood uprights and the light partitions which connected them to outer walls. The inner burial chamber, 5.4 m. long, 3.25 m. wide, and 1.75 m. high, is of stone—the first stone chamber in Egypt.[11]

These tombs at Abydos suggest the fusion of two distinct house traditions. If the palace architecture of Lower Egypt was of wood, and red was the color which designated wood, then the fact that the exteriors of these Upper Egyptian tombs were whitewashed makes it tempting to believe that the royal titles of the "White House" of Upper Egypt and the "Red House" of Lower Egypt were as much associated with the traditional exterior aspects of the seat of authority as with the color of the crowns, from which the titles are now believed to be derived.

TOMBS WITH IMITATION OF NICHE PANELING. As yet there has been no evidence that the "palace-façade" was connected with Lower Egypt. Since no early tombs have been uncovered in the Delta because of its marshy soil and the accumulations of mud deposits, it is significant that the most specific and important sepulchral imitations of the *serekh* façade are seen on a large group of tombs, all, with one exception, found on the border of Lower Egypt. All the tombs of this type, except one, have an interior arrangement of alcoves, or chambers, such as were seen in the tombs of Zer, Zet, Meneit, and Perabsen. In addition, they all have an exterior treatment of the walls on which the bricks are laboriously set to imitate the recessed niches of the small-wood, paneled construction, such as was seen on the palace-façade of the gravestones of King Zet. The most southern example of the type, and hence the most distant from the Delta, is at Negadeh (Plate v–3, 4), which dates from the time of Menes and was formerly thought to have been his second tomb.

The earliest example yet found of the "palace-façade" type of tomb, and the one which most definitely links the type with Lower Egypt, is the recently discovered brick tomb at North Saq-

[10] Page 67.
[11] Reisner, *op. cit.*, p. 357, believes that there must have been a stone mastaba as a superstructure above the tomb of Khasekhemui.

PLATE V

1. Plan of tomb of King Khasekhemui, Abydos (Petrie, *op. cit.*, II, Pl. LXIII).
2. Wooden sarcophagus of III Dyn. (Petrie, *Tarkhan and Memphis,* 1913, Pl. XXVIII).
3. Plan of I Dyn. tomb, Negadeh (G. A. Reisner, *The Development of the Egyptian Tomb,* 1936, Fig. 21).
4. Exterior of I Dyn. tomb, Negadeh (Capart, *L'art Egyptien,* I, Pl. 3).

PLATE VI: TOMBS AND SEREKH FACADE

1

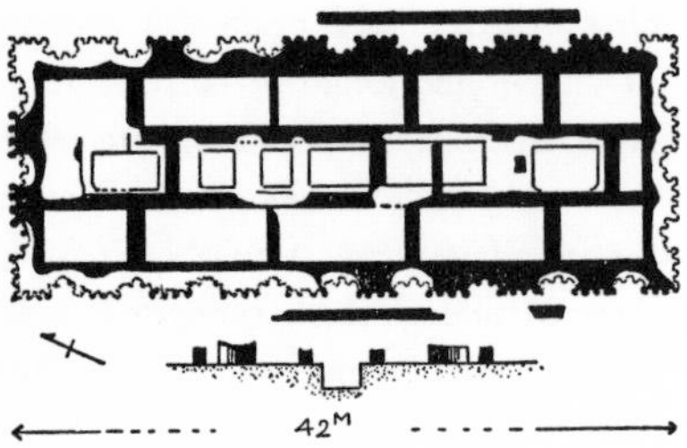

2

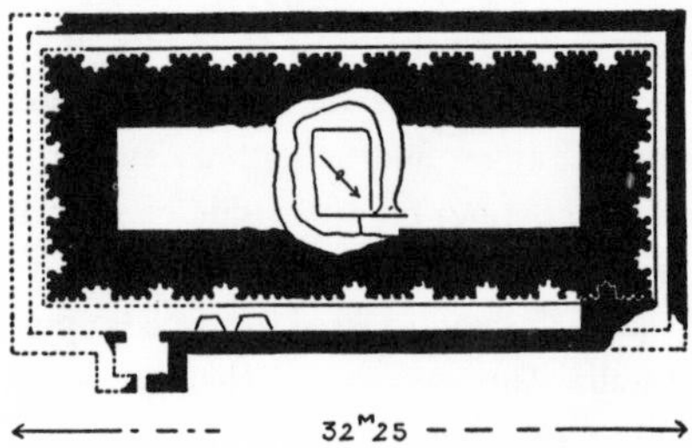

3

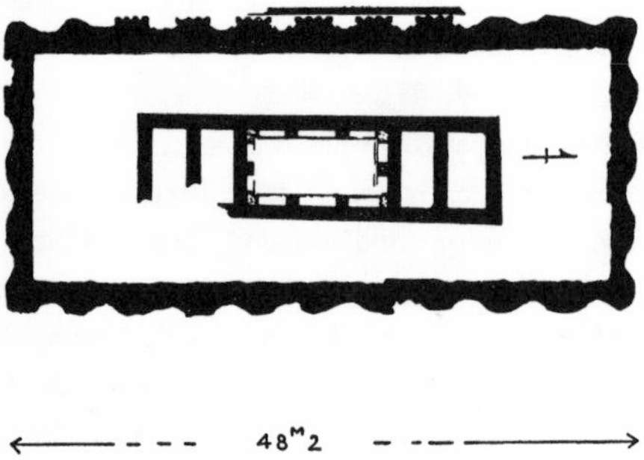

4

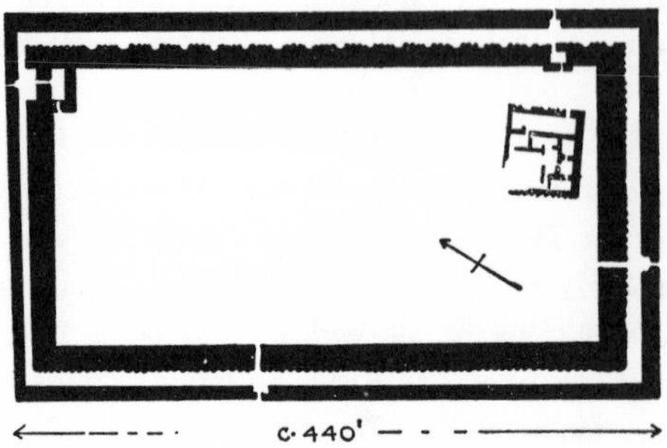

5

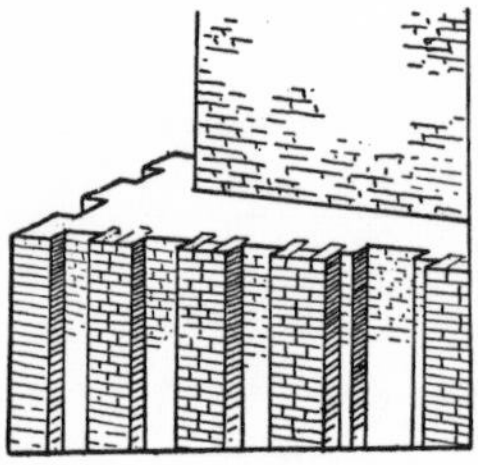

6

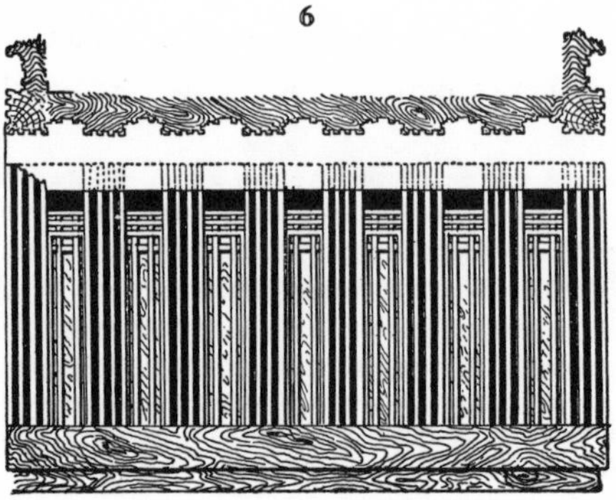

7

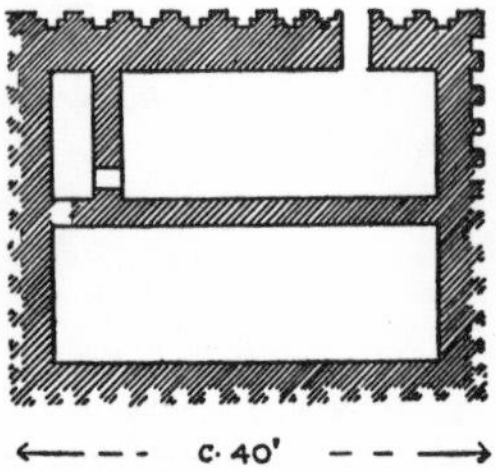

qara, quite certainly attributed to King Menes.[12] Menes presumably built his first tomb in Upper Egypt at Abydos, but when he shifted his capital to Memphis in order to control the Delta, he constructed another tomb, this time in imitation of the traditional *serekh* palace of the earlier Delta kings. His Saqqara tomb, 42.0 m. by 15.50 m., is almost exactly like the tomb at Negadeh, which is now assigned to his wife, Neith-Hetep, who may have been a Delta princess. The interior is divided by cross-walls into twenty-seven compartments, or magazines, all above the ground level, and it also has five underground chambers. In the middle subterranean chamber were found the scattered bones of two adults and the remains of a wooden bed. The magazines have false doors, and the interior brick walls are faced with mud to which were attached colored reed-mats, indicating clearly that patterned mattings were part of the original *serekh* palaces.

The next example is a large tomb of the time of Zer at Saqqara (Plate VI–1). Not far from Saqqara at Tarkhan, Petrie discovered three more brick tombs of the same type, two of which had interior chambers, while the third, dating from the reign of Zet (Plate VI–2), had an undivided interior hall. Still further north at Gizeh (Plate VI–3) is another example, also dating from about the time of Zet. Here at Gizeh the type persisted through the III Dynasty, and at Meydum it was still used in the IV Dynasty for the great brick mastabas of Prince Ranofer and Prince Rahotep.[13] In the course of the Old Kingdom the recessed paneling on the brick tombs went out of use except for small provincial mastabas.

These tombs with recessed sinkings on their exterior walls are architecturally important because they supply an explanation of much which went on in Egyptian construction both before and after the I Dynasty. When first discovered, the sinkings, from an analogy with Mesopotamian brick architecture where somewhat similar niches and buttress strips occur, were believed to have originated in brick. Before it was discovered that even in Mesopotamia the recessed sinkings in brick began in early Sumerian times as an imitation of a more primitive method of building in bundled reeds[14] and perhaps in small and overlapping pieces of wood, it was generally admitted that in Egypt the panel decoration of tombs was a copy in brick of an old and revered system of building in wood.

12 Walter B. Emery, "The Tomb of the First Pharaoh," *The Illustrated London News,* Vol. 193 (Feb. 12, (1938), p. 247.
13 A Rowe, "New Light on Egypt about 3000 B.C.," *The Illustrated London News,* Vol. 179 (1931), p. 741.
14 W. Andrae, *Das Gotteshaus und die Urformen des Bauens im Alten Orient* (1930), p. 73 *seq.*

PLATE VI

1. Plan of tomb 2185, Saqqara (J. E. Quibell, *Archaic Mastabas,* 1923, Pl. v.).
2. Plan of tomb 2038, Tarkhan (Petrie, *Tarkhan,* II, 1914, Pl. XVIII).
3. Plan of tomb 5, Gizeh (Petrie, *Gizeh and Rifeh,* 1907, Pl. VI).
4. Plan of "Schunet ez Zebib" (E. R. Ayrton, *Abydos,* III, 1904, Pl. III, VI).
5. Wall construction of palace of "Schunet ez Zebib."
6. Wooden sarcophagus of Princess Nefert, Meydum (A. Rowe, "New Light on Egypt about 3000 B.C.," *The Illustrated London News,* Vol. 179, 1931, p. 741).
7. Plan of "Middle Fort," Abydos (Ayrton, *op. cit.,* Pl. VIII).

The *serekh* façade on the gravestone of King Zet (Plate IV–1), it can be seen, has paneled niches which are identical with the sinkings on the end of the mastaba tomb at Saqqara (Plate VI-1). The dependence of both the tombs and the palace-façade banners upon an old system of small-wood construction becomes conclusively clear as more architectural evidence is reviewed. One Egyptologist [15] has recently pointed out how all the tombs of this paneled type belong to grandees of Lower Egypt and how they reproduce, as faithfully as the different structural material permitted, the wooden palace architecture of the Delta, which the Southern conquerors took over as an emblem, just as they appropriated the red crown, ureus, and other emblems and titles of the North.

PALACES AT ABYDOS. At Abydos, and dating from the II Dynasty, are the ruins of two defensive, brick palaces, which have been called forts, in spite of the facts that they are unlike any known Egyptian forts and that any ruling house in the early period of pacification must have been defensively fort-like. The so-called "Middle Fort" (Plate VI–7) has recessed sinkings on the outer surface of the brick walls, and around the base of its brick walls is a strip of symbolic red, four inches broad at a height of twenty-two inches. The other palace, known as Shûnet-ez-Zebib (Plate VI–4), has an outer and inner wall, with defensive gateways and vestibules in the inner wall. Its outer wall has a slight batter, is 201 inches thick, and even in its ruined state rises to a height of thirty-six feet.[16] Inside its great enclosure is the ruin of what was undoubtedly the actual palace. While not clear in the small scale drawing, both the inner defensive walls and the actual palace walls have recessed sinkings somewhat simplified (Plate VI–5). There is another large palace of the same early period, built by Khasekhemui, also with panelled recesses, farther up the Nile at Hierakonpolis.[17]

When the mastabas of Saqqara, Tarkhan, and Gizeh are compared with the palace of Shûnet-ez-Zebib (Plate VI) simply as plans, without regard to scale or purpose, the similarity suggests a common origin. They all have a plain outer wall and the sinkings on the interior wall, while the mastaba at Tarkhan, like the palace at Abydos, has an entrance vestibule. The presumption that the ruins at Abydos were defensive palaces, "strongholds" imitating in brick the older wooden tradition of the *serekh* palace, is further strengthened by the use in the III Dynasty of the same recessed panel treatment on the stone walls surrounding King Zoser's royal layout of sepulchral buildings at Saqqara, which copied his official residence at Memphis.[18] Moreover, the manner in which the bricks are laid and bonded in projecting strips to form the recesses on the palace walls at Abydos proves that these strips could not have originated in brick construction; for only every third course of these strips is bonded (Plate VI–5), indicating that the strips were merely imitative.

[15] H. Balcz, *op. cit.;* C. M. Firth (*Annales du Service,* XXXI (1931), p. 47) discovered two more large brick mastabas of the I Dynasty at Saqqara, on the border of Lower Egypt, which were burial places of noblemen and were decorated with the paneled, recessed brickwork.

[16] E. R. Ayrton, C. T. Currelly, and A. E. P. Weigall, *Abydos,* III (1904), p. 3.

[17] J. E. Quibell, *Hierakonpolis,* II (1902), pp. 19-20, Pl. LXXIV.

[18] Page 63.

SEPULCHRAL SURVIVALS OF SMALL-WOOD CONSTRUCTION. More conclusive evidence of the wooden origin of the paneled sinkings in brick is preserved in the later sepulchral monuments. Therefore it is necessary to follow the paneled decoration through the Old Kingdom when it became an ideographic emblem, entirely associated with the monuments of the dead. The tenacity of the idea and its purely symbolic application furnishes an excellent introduction to Egyptian architectural habits.

At Tarkhan in a tomb of the III Dynasty Petrie uncovered a wooden sarcophagus (Plate v–2) which is a small replica of a house. The coffin is interesting—both because it illustrates the literal Egyptian conception of a burial place as a house, and because it reproduces a simple, and hence ordinary, method of wood construction. The coffin, like a house, is made of upright posts, let into the floor and ceiling beams, and the open spaces between the posts are closed by boards held in place by round rungs. Its construction reminds one of the I Dynasty drawing (Plate II–4) and the sign for a sarcophagus (Plate III–1); but it is not very close to the recessed paneling of the palace-façade architecture. Another wooden coffin, however, exactly reproduces the system of small-wood joinery represented on the gravestone of King Zet and imitated by the brick tombs (Plate VI–6). This elaborate sarcophagus was discovered in a IV Dynasty mastaba at Meydum and was the property of the Princess Nefert. Although nothing now remains of her wooden dwelling, its imprint was so accurately preserved, even to the veining of the wood, in the wet mud poured about it after the sarcophagus was placed inside its mastaba, that a cast and working drawings have been made from the mold.

Another reproduction of the same type of royal house is the sarcophagus of Menkaura, one of the great Pharaohs of the IV Dynasty (Plate VII–1). Although the depth of the recessed niches is reduced in the stone copy, the four faces of the sarcophagus faithfully reproduce all the external details of what was the palace style of building in wood. Above the doorways are the grilled transoms, and even though the actual elevation of the towers seems forgotten or abandoned, the vertical paneling still indicates the tower construction. Along the edge of the flat roof is a typical Egyptian cornice, an obvious translation into stone of the old defensive parapet of stalks of the papyrus.

Innumerable sarcophagi of stone and painted wood preserve the stylized features of the old *serekh* building. One example is the sarcophagus of Fefi (Plate VII–2), discovered at Gizeh and probably dating from the IV Dynasty. Here the niche pattern has become standardized and, what is more important, its decorations prove that in combination with the small-wood framework went *curtains of stretched fabric.*

"FALSE DOORS." Before the details of the *serekh* building can be explained it is necessary to realize why its memory was so accurately preserved in sepulchral architecture. Above the tombs of the first Thinite Kings were probably two grave stelæ, decorated with the palace-façade as an emblem and name panel. Such prayers and offerings as were accorded to the royal dead were made before the gravestones. By the III Dynasty, when the tombs had massive superstructures, and

PLATE VII: SARCOPHAGI AND SEREKH FACADE

1

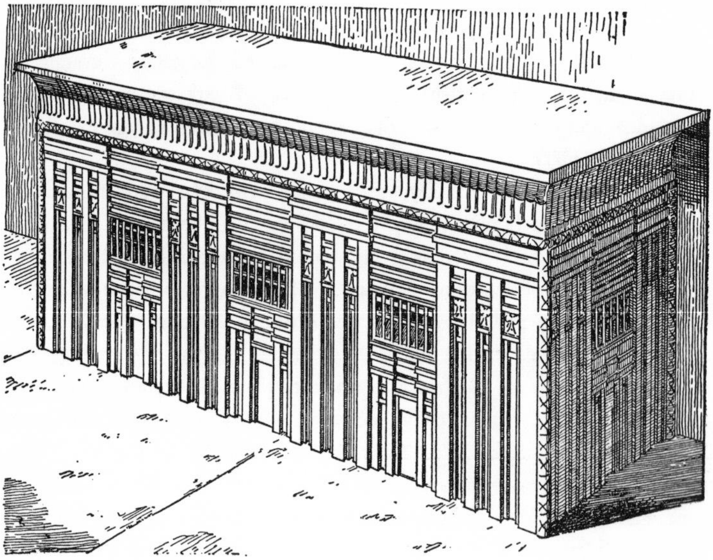

2

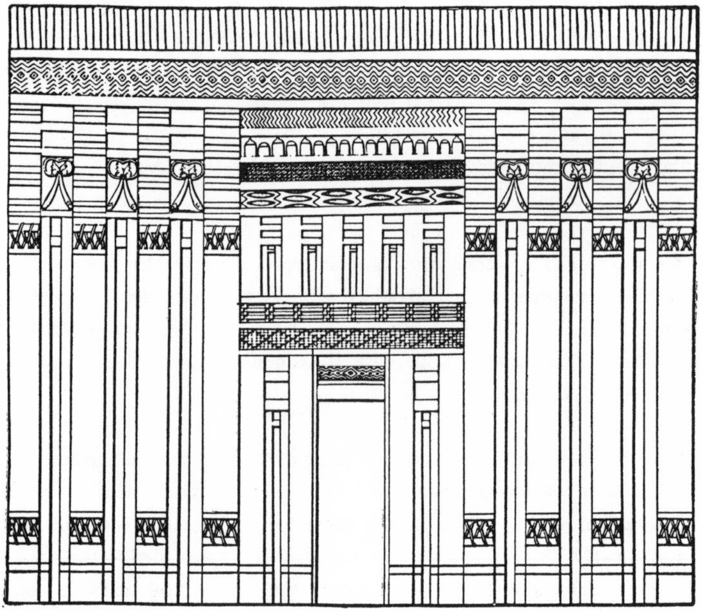

the actual burial chamber was sunk into the sand or rock beneath it, the stelæ were set up in front of the mastaba. Later they were incorporated into the face of the mastaba. At this time the palace-façade, which had been thought of as a magical dwelling associated with the divine and legendary Kings of the Delta, was simplified into an ideographic symbol, and only one of its doors, flanked by paneled and theoretical towers, was represented in stone. Even in schematized form it was still the sign of the house before which offerings and prayers to the dead were made. Where the palace-façade had been a royal emblem, signifying "palace," by the IV Dynasty it had become a formal symbol, associated entirely with the ritual of the grave. In its abbreviated and ideographic form it gives the appearance of a "false door," although it still represented a house.[19] In the Egyptian's mind it was thought of as a ritualistic door through which the dweller of the "Eternal House" might pass. The spirit, in returning from the realm of the dead in the West in order to revisit his former haunts, had to go East. Therefore all doors, either false or real, were usually on the eastern side of the tomb, and the "false door," or abbreviated *serekh* façade, became the ceremonial exit through which the dead could come, as from his house, in order to receive at his threshold the offerings of his estate. In this way the palace-façade became the "false-door" stele of all upper-class mastabas.

At Saqqara in the famous brick tomb of Hesy the whole palace-façade treatment of niches was moved back on to the east wall of an inner corridor, or small courtyard (Plate VIII–1, 2, 3, 4). Within each niche was an actual wooden door on which was carved the figure of Hesy himself. One door, beautifully executed, was emphasized by the seated figure of Hesy receiving food on an offering table (Plate VIII–3). In later tombs it is not uncommon to find the sculptured double of the dead standing in formal frontality within the niche of the "false door." With the development of an actual chamber within the tomb to be used as a chapel for the dead, the stele, or "false-door" symbol of the house, was moved inside. Hence in the vestibule of the tomb of Ptahotep at Saqqara, dating from the V Dynasty, there are two doors on the wall of the chamber, one the simplified survival of the palace-façade, and the other an imitation in stone of a more ordinary door of wooden construction (Plate XXII–3).

CONSTRUCTION OF THE SEREKH BUILDING. On the Fefi sarcophagus are carved the thongs which appear to stretch woven mats upon the framework of the niche construction. At Saqqara the niches of the Hesy tomb are actually painted in rich colors of white, yellow, blue-green, red, and black (Plate VIII–4), to imitate the yellow veining of the wood, the variegated

[19] "The stele has not only the value of a façade, or a door,—but a complete building of which only the façade is represented" (J. Capart, *Egyptian Art*, Eng. trans., 1923, p. 84).

PLATE VII

1. Stone sarcophagus of King Menkaura (Perrot et Chipiez, *Histoire de l'art*, 1, 1882, Fig. 289.
2. Stone sarcophagus of Fefi (S. Hassan, *Excavation at Giza*, 1932, Pl. LXV).

PLATE VIII: TOMBS AND SEREKH FACADE

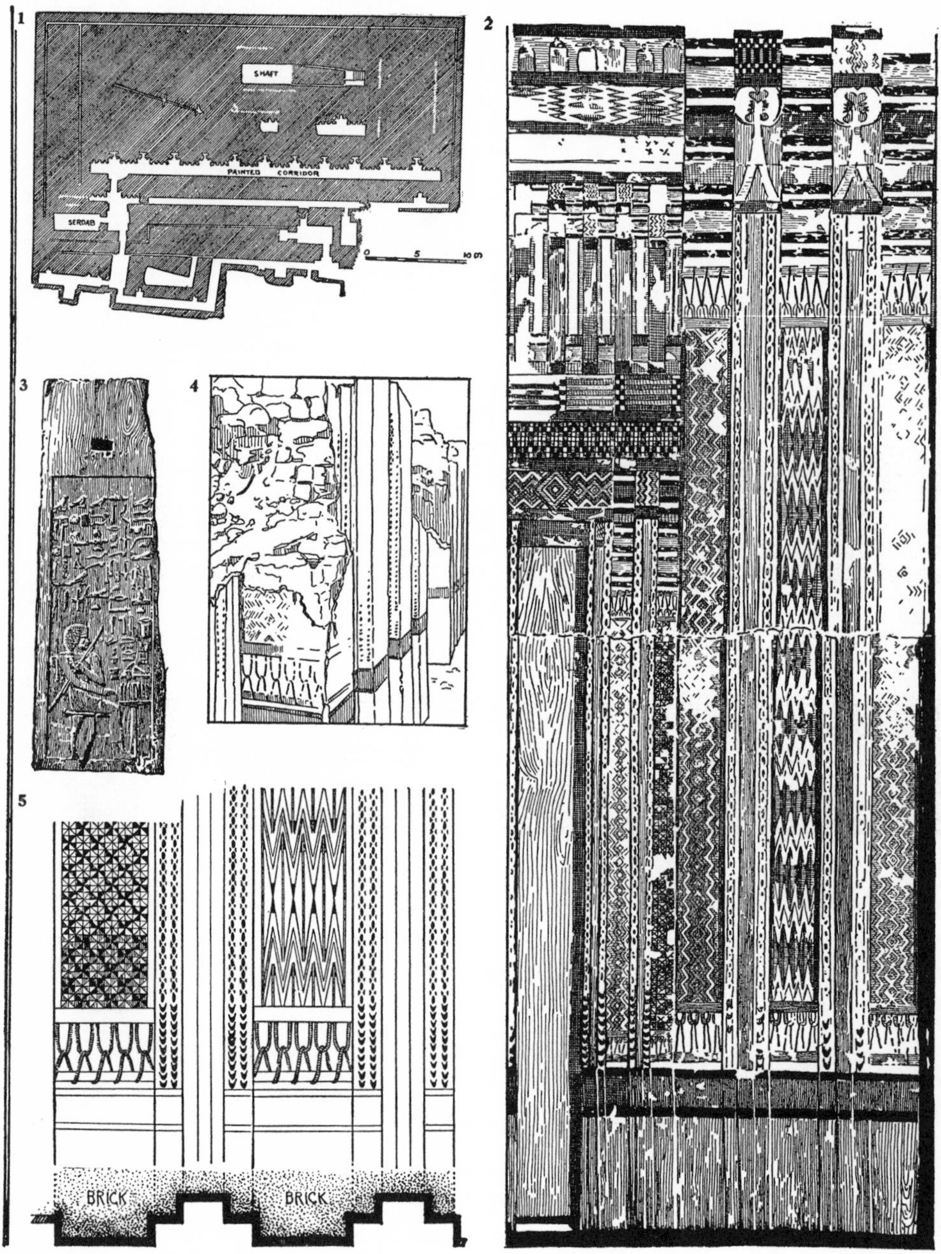

patterns of the woven textiles, and the thongs which stretched the mats from the top and bottom bars. The Hesy tomb and the other painted examples of niche paneling, such as the false-door of the Vizier of Neuserre of the V Dynasty (Plate VIII–2), and the burial chamber of the Chief Priest of Ptah, Senwosret-ankh, of the XII Dynasty at Lisht,[20] prove how the palace-façade treatment was derived from a light wooden construction combined with partitions of matting. At the same time there still remains the troublesome question of explaining structurally exactly how the prototypes of these painted versions could have been built.

When the painted patterns of the panels on the tomb of Hesy (Plate VIII–5) are compared with the plan of the niches, it is seen that the stretched mats are reproduced upon the broad faces of the projecting pilasters, while the narrow, sunken surfaces are depicted as upright, wooden posts. Thus there is represented a combination of plan and elevation which was impossible in real construction. The apparent discrepancy can be explained in one of two ways, either of which would have been natural to the Egyptian habits of thought.

There is first the possibility that the painted versions represent the interior of a "palace-façade" house imposed upon the exterior. Textile wall coverings were undoubtedly used on the interiors, and the inner face of the wall would have been the same as the exterior, only with the order of the niches reversed, as can be seen in the next illustration. Hence within the sunken niches on the interior, corresponding to the projecting pilasters on the exterior, the mats may have been stretched from upper and lower horizontal bars mortised into the side boards, in order to make a flat and attractive interior. Then with the Egyptian's ideographic habit of combining different significant and memorable aspects of the same object, the hanging decoration of the interior niches was transferred to the corresponding pilasters on the exterior.

Equally possible is the assumption that the plastic and painted versions of the revered, but no longer practised, method of construction were handed on by unquestioning craftsmen as two separate technical traditions, which were regularly combined without any regard to structural logic. Egyptian memory-images were always literal and stereotyped, but they were never organically logical, because they were ideographically descriptive.

The problem of reconstruction may not seem settled, but some actual idea of the small-wood joinery of this kind of building can be derived from Petrie's finds at Tarkhan. In one tomb Petrie

[20] W. C. Hayes, "The Texts in the Burial Chamber of Se'n-Wosret-'ankh," *Bulletin of the Metropolitan Museum of Art,* XXVIII (Nov. 1933), p. 33, Fig. 40.

PLATE VIII

1. Plan of mastaba of Hesy, Saqqara (J. E. Quibell, *Excavations at Saqqara,* 1913, Pl. 1).
2. Painted "false door," mastaba of Djedj-em-'onch, Abusir (L. Borchardt, *Das Grabdenkmal des Königs Ne-user-re,* 1907, Pl. 24).
3. Wooden door, mastaba of Hesy (Quibell, *op. cit.,* Pl. 31).
4. Painted corridor, mastaba of Hesy (Quibell, *op. cit.,* Pl. IV).
5. Painted niches, mastaba of Hesy (Quibell, *op. cit.,* Pl. VIII).

PLATE IX: SEREKH FACADE

1

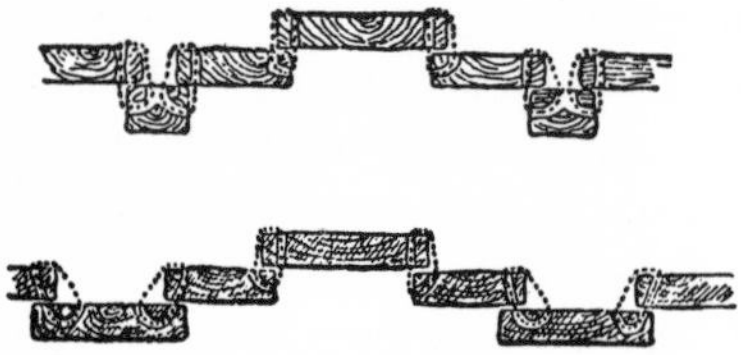

2

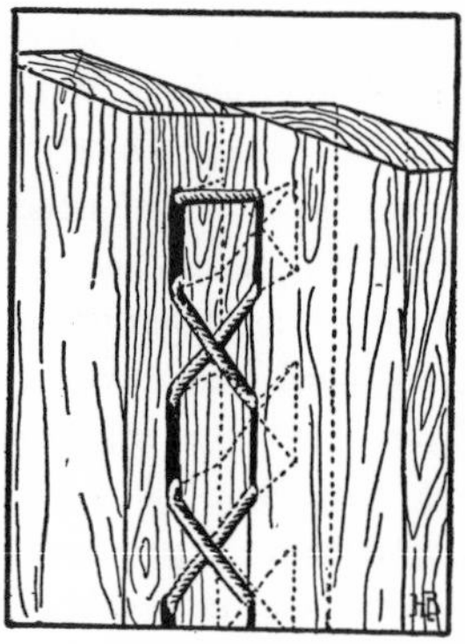

3

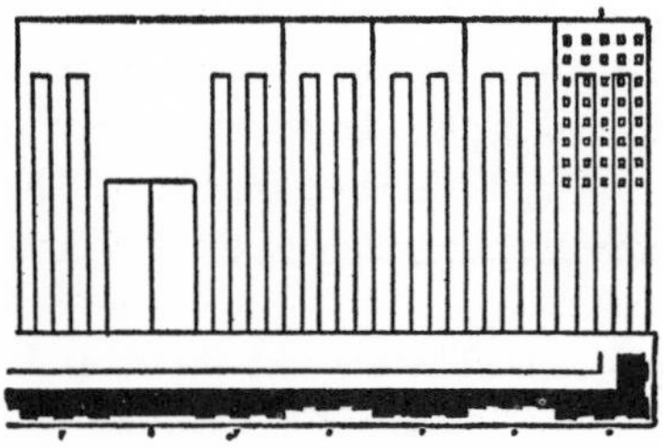

4

5

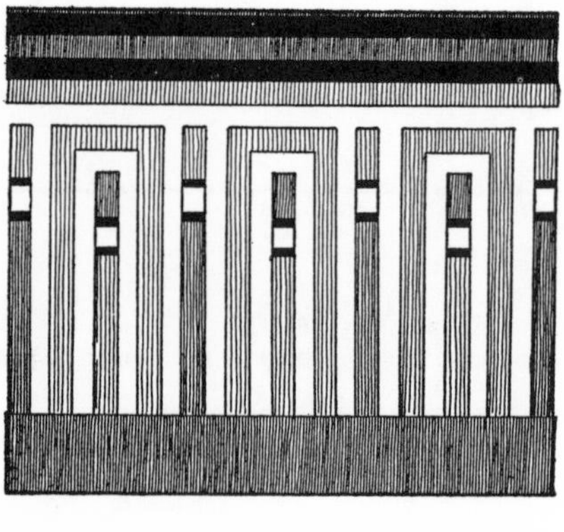

discovered a number of boards with regularly arranged borings on the edges. By fitting the holes together he proved how these boards overlapped in a form of niche construction and were bound together by thongs (Plate IX–1). However strange it may seem to us, who are accustomed to nails and screws, the wooden sarcophagi show how skilful the Egyptians were in using this primitive carpenter's method of fastening. Firmly tied lacings, moreover, were far stronger than joinery by wooden nails. It is Petrie's idea that the lacings were visible on the sides of the niches in exactly the place where the chains of ellipses appear on all the painted versions of this construction.

After the IV Dynasty the sepulchral tradition of the "palace-façade" tended to become a provincial mode. In the Middle Kingdom its use was revived, as can be seen in the painted burial chamber of Senwosret-ankh at Lisht and on the painted, wooden sarcophagus of King Mentuhotep (Plate IX–4). After the XII Dynasty a few graves, such as that of Pedi-Amen-em-Opet in the XXVI Dynasty, and a number of wooden sarcophagi, preserve the form, but in general it sank to a decorative, but still symbolic, usage upon the painted and carved dados of mortuary temples (Plate IX–5).

THE TOMB

During the first three Dynasties the grave grew from its simple Predynastic beginnings into a monumental structure of architectural significance, and at the same time retained in the Egyptian mind its association with the house. The earliest burials, while reproducing the shape of contemporary dwellings, were only shallow pits, at first round, then oval, and eventually rectangular (Plate X–1, 5). The pits were covered with branches and mounds of sand, and in the course of time were lined with matting, wood, and finally brick. It was not until the grave developed a permanent superstructure that the tomb took on architectural importance.

From the onset the death ritual and the growth of the Osiris cult stirred Egyptian thought with a great hope and laid what became a crushing burden upon the energies and resources of the living. Nowhere else in the history of mankind have natural and primitive instincts of self-preservation perpetuated themselves so tenaciously and in the end acquired such colossal proportions. Architecturally it was the dual function of the tomb which brought about its development and caused the elephantiasis. Above everything else the grave provided everlasting protection. As the abode of the dead it was also the place where offerings and prayers were made to the departed. Thus the desire for greater, and still greater, *protection,* combined with the growth of an elaborate

---

PLATE IX

1. Small-wood construction, coffin from Tarkhan (Petrie, *Tarkhan,* I, Pl. IX).
2. Wood lashings (Balez, "Die altægyptische Wangleiderung," *Mitteilungen des Deutschen Instituts für Ægyptische Altertumskunde in Kairo,* I, 1930, Fig. 19).
3. Stone sarcophagus, Lahun (Petrie, *Lahun,* II, 1923, Pl. XXIII).
4. Painted wooden sarcophagus of King Mentuhotep (G. Steindorff, *Das Grab des Mentuhotep,* 1896, Pl. II).
5. Dado decoration, tomb of Queen Tyi of XVIII Dyn. (Prisse d'Avennes, *Histoire de l'art Égyptien,* 1879).

ritual of *offerings* were the motivating factors which produced the sepulchral architecture and influenced the evolution of the temple.

At least two distinct traditions of burial influenced one another at an early time, and by the I Dynasty produced the conception of a sepulchral superstructure. One tradition began with burials in the floor of the house, or in front of the entrance, with the result that the superstructure was from the outset the essential part of the tomb, and only the need for greater protection forced the burials deeper and deeper underground. The other tradition, much better preserved in its early beginnings, started with an underground dwelling for the dead and only gradually evolved a permanent superstructure as a place of offering.

At the opening of Dynastic history the tomb in Upper Egypt was still a simple, rectangular chamber cut underground in the sand and for the most part was without interior divisions. The royal tombs at Abydos, which must have represented the most elaborate provisions of the region, were at first brick structures of one large chamber, built underground and covered with beams of wood on which a mound of sand was piled. Petrie, it is true, insists that there were no superstructures, not even an appreciable tumulus, above these tombs; the vertical gravestones of the attendants buried about the royal grave made, he says, an enclosure within which stood the two kingly stelæ above the east face of the buried tomb. The cult-house of the tomb, according to Petrie, therefore, started with the two stelæ and the offering table in front of them. Reisner, however, insists that "every substructure implies a superstructure of some sort" and so believes that the rectangular graves had rectangular mounds with retaining walls at first built of wattling or wood.[21]

ABYDOS TOMBS. Before this question of the origin of the architectural superstructure can be connected with the development of the typical mastaba tomb, certain features of the Abydos tombs must be emphasized because of their subsequent influence. Around the burial chambers of these first kings are systematic rows of large numbers of small tombs.[22] These dependent graves contained the bodies of the royal household, most of whom were ceremoniously slaughtered at the death of the king, just as the early kings of Ur in Mesopotamia killed their attendants and wives, in order to assure the royal master of fitting service in his eternal dwelling. The custom of *Sati,* or *sacrificial burials,* existed in Egypt and survived until modern times in the Sudan.[23] Whether

[21] Reisner, *op. cit.,* pp. 237, 238. He also suggests that the early paneled wood coffins were actually a representation of the old wattle grave-mound of the Predynastic period, but at the same time he denies any relation between the Egyptian tomb and house.

[22] Petrie's examination of the graves of the courtiers at Abydos leaves no doubt that the royal attendants were sacrificed by binding and burying them alive, for their positions show an effort to move after they were covered with sand. Around the tomb of Zer, arranged in two tiers, were 595 graves, around Zet's 328, around Merneit's and Den's 121, Azab's 63, and Q's only 26, all indicating a not unnatural decrease in the popularity of the custom. (Petrie, *Tombs of the Courtiers,* 1925, p. 8).

[23] Among the Anuak "when a King dies two members of his mother's family are killed and buried with him" (C. G. and Brenda Z. Seligman, *Pagan Tribes of the Nilotic Sudan,* p. 111); among the Azande "formerly several of his favorite wives were placed in the grave with their limbs broken, the chief's body supported by their outstretched legs" (*op. cit.,* p. 539); among the Bari "in the old days two *dupi* (assistants) were buried with the rain-maker, one with his stool and the other with his pipe" (*op. cit.,* p. 294n); and among the Lotuko a living man was buried with the rain-maker (*op. cit.,* p. 339).

such a practice, or only its form, still persisted through the I and II Dynasties is a disputed question,[24] *but its previous existence undoubtedly established the custom of having the family, courtiers, and servants buried about the royal dead, thereby making the sepulchral plan a replica of a royal palace, village, or stronghold, where the spirit of the dead still ruled over its domain.*

The tombs at Abydos illustrate the rising level of domestic comfort and structural improvements. By the middle of the I Dynasty, the tombs of Zer and Zet (Plate IV–4) have an interior arrangement of rooms, or alcoves, about a central burial hall. In the II Dynasty an enclosing wall, like the protecting wall of a defensive palace, is built around the tomb of King Perabsen (Plate IV–7), and at the end of the Dynasty, Khasekhemui (Plate V–1) has an ambitious imitation in brick of a long hall, divided into aisles and alcoves by supports of bundled reeds, or wood, which in the brick construction and as a means of carrying the load of the roof were built as cross-walls, ending in pilasters. Here for the first time stone was used for the actual burial chamber.

The tomb of King Den (Plate IV–6) introduces an important innovation. In addition to its very thick walls and its earliest use of stone paving, it has an open stairway, 23.6 m. long, leading down on the north side to a vestibule at the entrance. Although Garstang[25] considers descending stairs to have been developed gradually in the late Predynastic burials of El-Kab and Reqaqnah, it seems more likely that this mode became popular because of its introduction by King Den.

EARLY MIDDLE-CLASS GRAVES. While royal graves always set the subsequent style, the middle-class burials of the early Dynastic period show a natural conservatism which only gradually tends to elaborate the rectangular underground chamber. Like the houses of the living, which such tombs continued to imitate, the rectangular grave chambers in the cemeteries of El-Amrah and Negadeh, begin at this time to be divided into interior compartments (Plate X–1, 2, 3, 4, 5). By the II Dynasty the use of descending stairways is a common feature (Plate X–6, 7, 8), and at first the stairs, following the practice in the tomb of King Den, are outside the tomb and its superstructure. Also by this time all such tombs have a rectangular superstructure above ground.

MASTABA TOMB. Although no structures of any kind appear above the graves at Abydos, other burials in the same region, especially those at Negadeh, have rectangular and solid superstructures faced with brick. Nothing in Egypt was made out of whole cloth, and we come back to the question of how these rectangular superstructures originated. The usual explanation, which seems a little too logical and practical to be entirely true, is that they developed from the use of brick as retaining walls to hold the mound of sand protecting the grave beneath it. A more natural explanation, for which there is some evidence, and widespread as well as persistent parallels in the Sudan and other parts of Africa, is the primitive custom of burial in the house, or in front of it, and the subsequent use of the house as a place to propitiate the dead.

[24] Reisner, *op. cit.*, pp. 117-121.
[25] Garstang, *The Third Egyptian Dynasty* (1904), p. 35.

PLATE X: TOMBS

1

2

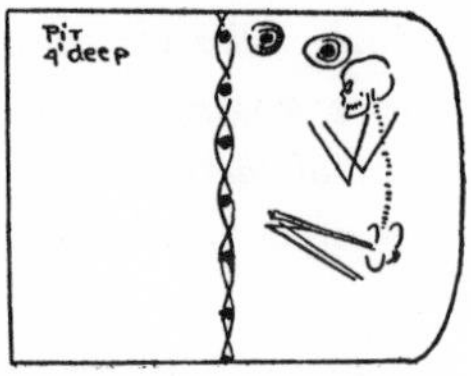

3

4

5

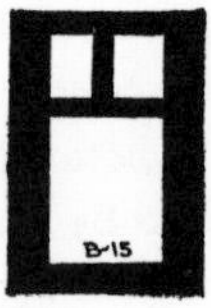

6

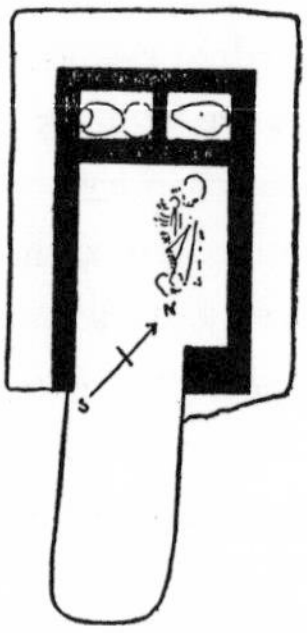

7

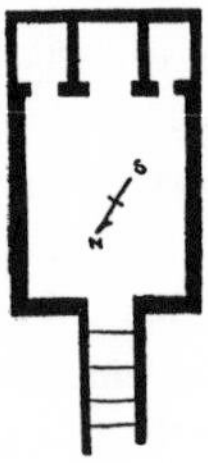

9

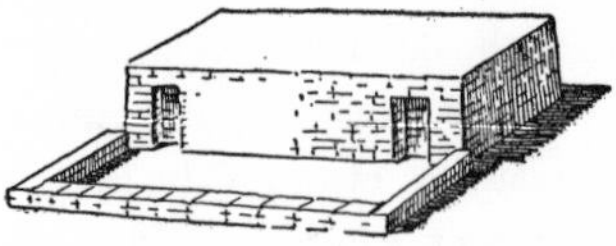

10

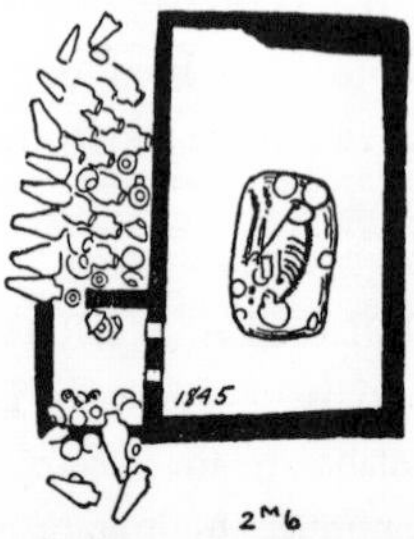

8

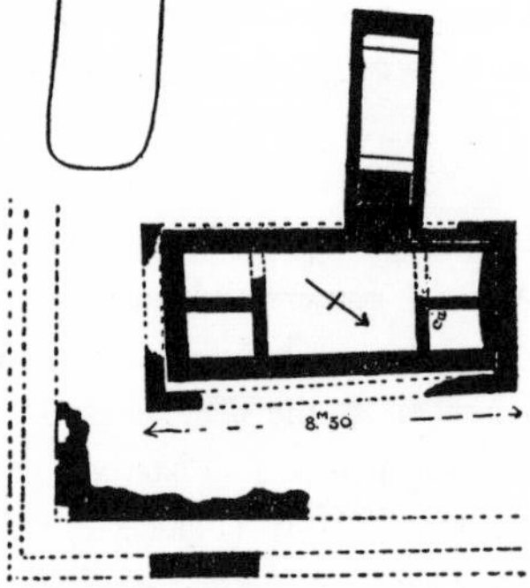

12

11

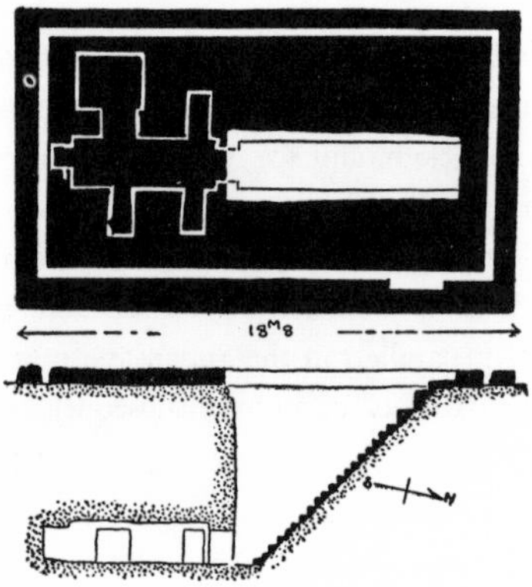

Petrie himself says, "Probably at first a chief was buried in a pit in the midst of his house, much as various burials in the floors of houses have been found in Egypt and are usual in other lands."[26] In the marshy Delta deep underground burials were impossible, and some of the lack of evidence as to the prevalence of this custom in Egypt is because the excavators cannot obtain as much information regarding early burials in Lower Egypt as they have unearthed from the dry sand of Upper Egypt.

The actual house was the primary prototype of the grave superstructure.[27] Were there no other evidence than the prevalence of burials in houses throughout Africa, the conclusion would be strongly sustained. "On the Upper Nile there dwell to-day people allied to the oldest Egyptians in appearance, stature, cranial proportions, language, and dress. They are ruled by rain-maker magicians or by divine kings who were until recently ritually slain, and the tribes are organized in totemic clans.... It really looks as if among these tribes on the Upper Nile social development had been arrested at a stage that the Egyptians had traversed before their history began. There we have a living museum whose exhibits supplement and vivify the prehistoric cases in our collection."[28] Even if the reader is not prepared to go as far as Toynbee,[29] who writes, "The fathers of the Egyptiac civilization (perhaps accompanied by the forefathers of the Dinka and Shilluk before the parting of the ways) were squat-

[26] Petrie, *Tarkhan,* II, p. 9.

[27] Reisner, an authority on the details of early Dynastic burials, denies all relation between the tomb and the house. "The external part of the known tombs," he writes, "fails even to hint at such a reproduction.... Naturally the forms of the doors were reproduced from actual doorways used in houses, but it is quite beyond the effect of this evidence to conclude that therefore the whole form of the mastaba was a reproduction of the house type of the time in question" (p. 244). Some of Dr. Reisner's explanations for the origin of the tombs are only tenable when the symbolic importance of doors and other features are connected with house forms. His theory as to the origin of the palace-façade mastabas only becomes natural and comprehensible when the relation between the tomb and the house is admitted. Regarding the royal tombs, he writes, "I feel constrained to add to the tombs of Menes and Narmer some sort of valley shrine or temple. I imagine this shrine to have arisen from the temporary mat pavilion erected immediately after the death of the king on the edge of the desert, to contain the funerary equipment during the few days required for the construction of the burial place. This funerary pavilion was built of mats and poles lashed together with cords.... In the time of one of the first three kings of Dynasty I this temporary pavilion was replaced by a c. b. (brick) structure, the so-called Valley Shrine, which took the form of a filled c. b. mastaba with nearly vertical faces, with palace-façade panelling on all four sides, painted to imitate the mat structure of the temporary *sh* pavilion" (p. 349). Even in his own theory there is a definitely implied relation between tomb form and primitive house structure, and no explanation why the palace-façade paneling did not survive in the existing "Valley Shrines."

[28] V. G. Childe, *The Most Ancient East* (1928), pp. 10-11.

[29] A. J. Toynbee, *A Study of History,* I (1935), p. 313.

PLATE X

1. Predynastic round grave, El-Amrah (D. Randall-Maciver and A. C. Mace, *El-Amrah and Abydos,* Pl. iv).
2. Grave with recess, B-135 El-Amrah (*op. cit.,* Pl. iv/4).
3. Brick grave, B-57 El-Amrah (*op. cit.,* Pl. iv/5).
4. Brick grave, B-14 El-Amrah (*op. cit.,* Pl. iv/6).
5. Brick grave, B-15 El-Amrah (*op. cit.,* Pl. iv/7).
6. Brick tomb, 3014 Negadeh (G. A. Reisner, *The Early Dynastic Cemeteries of Naga-ed-Der,* i, p. 79, Fig. 149).
7. Brick tomb, Mahasna (Garstang, *Mahasna and Bet Khallaf,* 1902, Pl. xxxiii).
8. Brick tomb, 1581 Negadeh (G. A. Reisner, *The Development of the Egyptian Tomb,* p. 69).
9. Mastaba, Negadeh (A. C. Mace, *The Early Dynastic Cemeteries of Naga-ed-Der,* ii, 1909, p. 13, Fig. 20).
10. Mastaba, 1845 Tarkhan (Petrie, *Tarkhan,* ii, Pl. xiv).
11. Mastaba, K-4 Bet Khallaf (Garstang, *op. cit.,* Pl. xxv).
12. Mastaba, R-40 Reqaqnah (Garstang, *The Third Egyptian Dynasty,* 1904, Pl. iv/B).

ting on the edge of the jungle-swamp which at that time occupied the Lower Nile valley and the Delta," the evident persistence of Nilotic traditions among the present natives throws very definite light on the original customs in the Nile valley. Among the Acholi,[30] for example, "much of the ritual of the cult of the dead—so far as it applies to male ancestors—is performed at certain (circular hut) shrines called *Kac,* and in considering this shrine it should be remembered that the dead are buried at the side of the entrance to the huts." The actual *Kac* is a crude imitation, made of rocks, of the Egyptian offering table, which is built opposite to the door of the hut.

In the I Dynasty the rectangular brick superstructures at Negadeh were undoubtedly thought of as houses. Although they had a solid core of sand and stone, their brick exteriors reproduced a house form (plate IX–9) with a forecourt and two doors. As such, they became the standard type of tomb during the Old and Middle Kingdoms and are called *mastabas.*

While it is customary to attribute the origin of the mastaba tomb to an enclosed tumulus of sand above the grave, the house-burial theory accounts better for some of the evidence. At Tarkhan, which is near to the borders of Lower Egypt, Petrie discovered a large I Dynasty cemetery in which the tombs were like mud-brick houses with the dead buried in shallow holes dug in the floor (Plate X–10) and the house filled with sand to make a mastaba tomb. Each tomb has a little courtyard, like an entrance vestibule, or chapel, before which the offerings were made as if at the door of a house. In these tombs, some of which go back a generation before Menes, we have the essential elements of subsequent stone mastabas, namely: an entrance vestibule, or chapel; a chamber, here filled with sand, but later to become the *serdab;* and an actual interment beneath the floor. Furthermore, as has been seen, *all* the brick mastabas of the I Dynasty, which imitated the niche decoration of what was probably the wooden palace construction of the Delta, were above ground, had very shallow burials in the center (Plate VI–2, 3), and were located on the outskirts of Lower Egypt.

In tomb 1060 at Tarkhan (Plate VI–2), where all the exterior faces of the mastaba imitate the small-wood paneling of the royal house, the central niche on the *eastern face* is painted red in imitation of a wooden door, and in front of this presumably "false door" is a wooden floor, the remains, undoubtedly, of a wooden, offering chapel.

By the II Dynasty sepulchral traditions began to mingle, and in the province of Girza, which includes Abydos, there remain tombs illustrating all essential stages in the evolution of the typical mastaba. Before the beginning of the III Dynasty the *solid mastaba had enclosed the descending stairway* (Plate X–11). The stairs still continued to descend from north to south, going down an open passage as in the earlier tomb of King Den. By this time the search for protection led the builders to dig the underground burial chamber so deep that it is subterranean and has a series of storerooms cut out around it.

Somewhat later in the III Dynasty the descending stair passage in the mastabas of the same province is lined with brick and strengthened by cross-walls so as to withstand the pressure of the gravel (Plate X–12). These cross-walls are penetrated with arched openings through which the stairs can pass, and the entrance to the underground chambers is closed by a large rock, lowered into place

[30] Seligman, *op. cit.,* p. 133.

down what has become a *vertical shaft.* With the inevitable thickening of the cross-walls the descending stairway becomes a covered and vaulted passage with vertical shafts opening into it (Plate XI-1).

These modifications eventuated in the *shaft mastaba* and the *portcullis* system of protection, ideas best illustrated by the great mastaba of King Zoser at Bet Khallaf (Plate XI–2). The mastaba, which was the abode of the king's *Ka,* while his actual remains were far more magnificently preserved at Saqqara, is 280 feet long, 153 feet wide, and 33 feet high. The stairway descends 91 feet below the top of the mastaba and is protected by a tunnel vault of true arch construction. Still greater safety for the burial is obtained by using the six vertical shafts as openings, down which large stones were dropped so as to block the passage. The stones were actually larger than the shafts and grooves were cut in the sides of the shafts to allow the portcullis blocks to slide down into place.[31] There is some question as to where the stelæ and place of offering were, now that the passage to the burial chamber is closed. Presumably there was a small cult building attached to the side of the mastaba, for on mastaba K-2 at Bet Khallaf, which was also a royal tomb, there are indications of a small chapel built onto the south end.

ORIENTATION. Matters of orientation were of the greatest concern to the Egyptians in their burial customs, but during the first three Dynasties there were apparently different beliefs about the significance of the four cardinal points. From prehistoric times, however, the rectangular tomb was oriented north and south, or at least laid out roughly parallel to the edge of the desert, which followed the northerly course of the river. "In the majority of cases in the Predynastic period the body lies on the left side with the face to the west, on both banks of the river, but the rule is not absolute.... I believe that it is necessary to assume that the offering-place in each case corresponded to the direction in which the body faced." [32] The entrance to the tomb of King Den and the royal tombs at Bet Khallaf were on the north side. During the III Dynasty, under the influence of the solar cult of Heliopolis, the offering chapel with its stele was shifted to the east side [33] because the "Westerners" had to come East in order to revisit, with the sun, their earthly haunts. In the case of the royal pyramids, however, the traditional entrance to the tomb remained on the north side and was only shifted during the Middle Kingdom as a means of baffling the tomb robbers.

The contracted position of the body prevailed without exception from earliest times to the end of the II Dynasty. Then the half-extended position was gradually adopted by the royal family and nobles, but for the poorer classes the embryonic posture persisted into the Middle Kingdom.

VAULTING. The development of the tomb passages in the III Dynasty royal mastabas at Bet Khallaf suggests that the arch and vault originated in Egypt as a protection for the roof of the descending stairway, but its use, from the very first, was not limited to the passageways. During the II Dynasty many tombs at Negadeh had vaults over the burial chamber (Plates XI–4 and X–6). In origin

[31] The I Dynasty tomb of King Den had grooves within which a portcullis slab was lowered in order to close the entrance.

[32] G. A. Reisner, *The Development of the Egyptian Tomb* (1936), p. 12.

[33] Page 81.

PLATE XI: TOMBS AND ARCHES

1

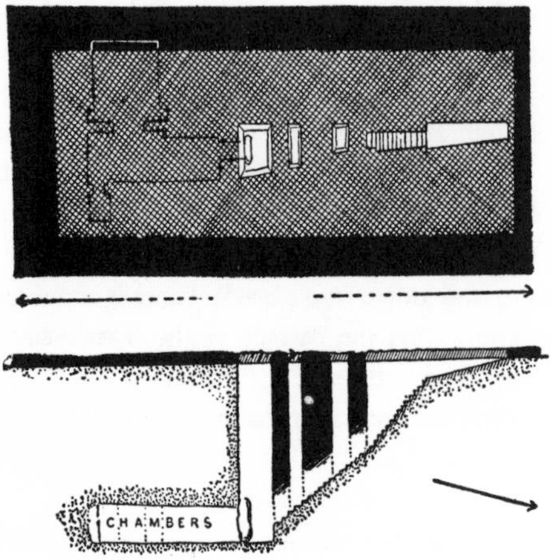

2

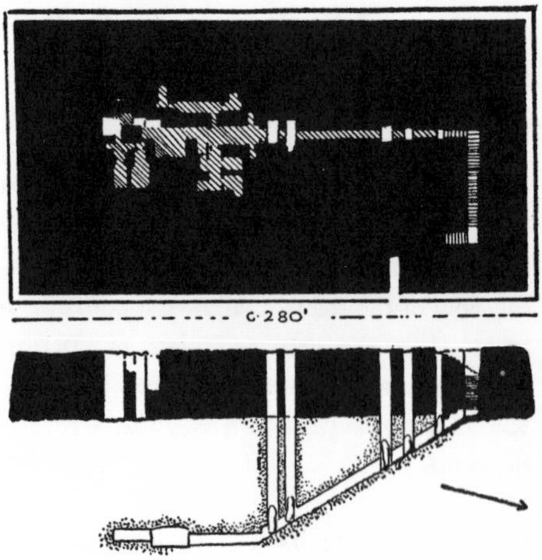

4

3

5

the vaults were of simple corbeled construction in which the bricks were laid horizontally, overlapping one another. Apparently it was not until the III Dynasty that this early corbeling turned into true arch construction with actual voussoirs, either trimmed into wedge-shaped pieces of mud (Plate XI–5) or given the necessary voussoir shape by attaching pieces of mud to their upper edges. In spite of having the elements of an arcuated style of building at this early date, the Egyptians considered the vault a purely utilitarian feature because it was not an old form consecrated by long usage.[34] So they persisted in treating it as a practical expedient, and having neither great spans, nor need of much interior space to cover, they made very little use of it in their monumental architecture.

MODIFICATIONS IN THE MASTABA. Before the end of the III Dynasty further modifications were made in the already established mastaba type of tomb. Where the I Dynasty mastabas of Lower Egypt had imitated the paneling of the wooden house on all four sides (Plate VI), the III Dynasty tomb of Hesy at Saqqara (Plate VIII), as we saw, limited this niche treatment to the *east façade* where the painted imitation of the house with its actual wooden doors was protected by an outer wall, forming a corridor, or narrow courtyard, in front of the ritualistic entrance.

Somewhat later in the same Dynasty a still greater simplification was made in the niche treatment on a mastaba at Reqaqnah (Plate XII–3). Here an actual *vestibule* in front of the door leads into the court, or corridor, and at the south end of the corridor is a single-paneled niche, or "false door," serving at the offering stele. Next to this niche an actual door opens into a chamber which may have been the *serdab* in which stood the statue of the dead. The same tomb also shows a combination of the mastaba type of lower Egypt with the stairway type of Upper Egypt, for within the solid core of the tomb a flight of stairs leads down to the burial pit. At the end of the III or the beginning of the IV Dynasty, another mastaba at Reqaqnah (Plate XII–2) has only one, small "false-door" niche on the east wall, while all that is left of the interior stairway tradition is a single *vertical shaft* descending to the burial chamber. Finally, in another small mastaba at the same place, there is a chapel on the east face of the tomb *into which* the "false door" is set (Plate XII–1). The next important change in the mastaba came at the end of the III and the beginning of the IV Dynasty when stone, because of its durability, was substituted for brick.

[34] The origin of the Egyptian vault, like that of the Mesopotamian vault, was apparently utilitarian and imitative. In discussing the early tunnel-vaulted graves of Ur and Nippur, Andrae says that the grave vault is the *subterranean hut* which had to be made of stronger material since it was underground, and also had to serve as the dwelling for the dead during an unlimited period, but its vault form is only an imitation of the curved roof (Andrae, *Das Gotteshaus und die Urformen des Bauens im Alten Orient*, 1930, p. 63).

PLATE XI

1. Mastaba, R-1 Reqaqnah (Garstang, *The Third Egyptian Dynasty*, Pl. IV/A).
2. Mastaba of Neter-Khet, Bet Khallaf (Garstang, *Mahasna and Bet Khallaf*, Pl. VII).
3. Arched passage, tomb R-1 Reqaqnah (Garstang, *The Third Egyptian Dynasty*).
4. Brick vault, tomb 3014 Negadeh (Reisner, *The Early Dynastic Cemeteries of Naga-ed-Der*, I, Pl. 65).
5. Brick arch, tomb R-110 Reqaqnah (Garstang, *op. cit.*, Pl. XIV).

PLATE XII: TOMBS AND TEMPLES

1

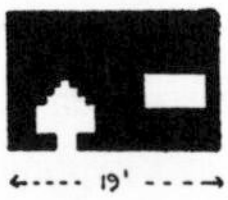

2

3

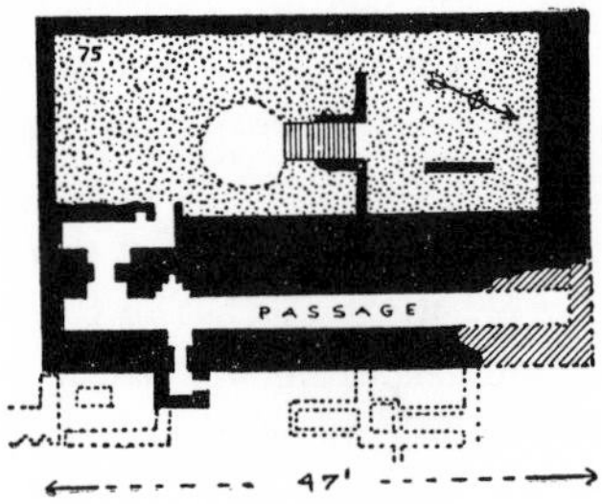

4

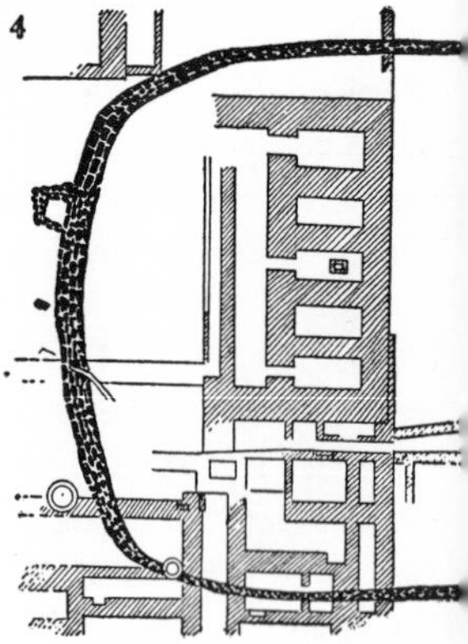

5

6

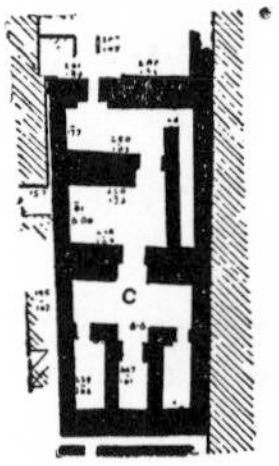

7

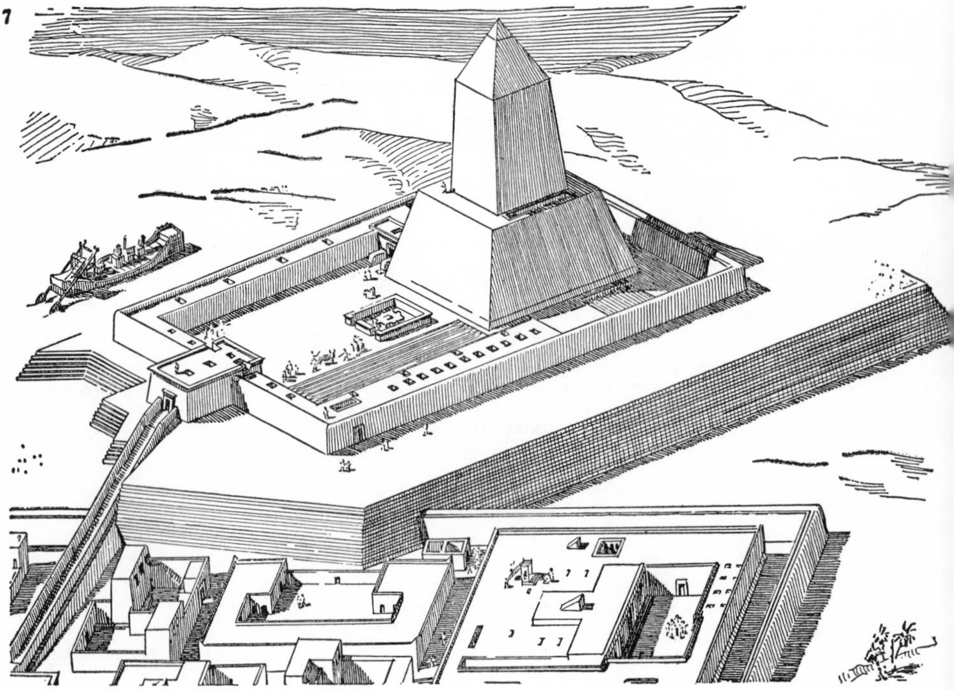

THE TEMPLE

The temple concept took shape along with the formation of a belief in the anthropomorphic divinities at about the opening of the historic period. The primitive fetishism, which worshiped rather vague powers in certain trees, stones, and mysterious places, visualized its divinities as objects and animals, and so did not conceive of an architectural abode for superhuman beings who as yet did not have mortal shape and physical needs of food, shelter, and service. Even after the birth of anthropomorphic gods the Egyptians never forgot the early fetish and animistic beliefs: the bundle reed *dedu* of Osiris might take on arms and legs but it was still the inorganic sign of the fertility spirit; the post continued to be worshiped at Busiris; the great stone *ben-ben* was elaborately honored at Heliopolis; and the sacred sycamore of Hathor and the lotus flower of Nefertem were never forgotten.

The temple, however, did not evolve out of the worship of the post, the stone, and the primeval hill. An actual dwelling for the divinity was not required until chieftain and sorcerer were imagined as the personification and eventually as the embodiment of the mysterious powers of nature. At the opening of Dynastic history, worship was still naïve and primitive, and the temples were no more than hut shrines and shelters. Even as late as the IV Dynasty, when the temple acquired more imposing proportions, there was no elaborate priestly caste such as later strangled all initiative and actually dominated the country, for the care of the gods was still a responsibility of the chief man. The religious service, in fact, was a survival from a not too distant past when the care of the totem was a tribal, communal, and family affair. During the early Dynasties religious ritual was at about the same level as exists in many parts of Africa to-day.

The representations of Protodynastic shrines are very similar to the round and long houses in which the African negroes still perform their magical rites. The shrine of Min (Plate I–12), for example, was a circular hut of reeds and mud, painted with horizontal bands of color, like the house of an African chieftain. In front it had streamers flying, the totem erected on a pole, and the phallic emblem of the god at the top of the conical roof. At first, each important tribal divinity had a time-honored and local type of house-shrine; the hut of Anubis had walls of woven reed matting (Plate II–1); the sanctuary of an unknown divinity at Abydos was a tent-like kiosk which became the common Egyptian symbol of a sacred naos (Plate II–5); and the shrine of some lion divinity was a long house set in a grove of trees (Plate II–4).

PLATE XII

1. Mastaba, R-62 Reqaqnah (Garstang, *op. cit.*, Pl. XXI).
2. Mastaba, R-54 Reqaqnah (*op. cit.*).
3. Mastaba, R-75 Reqaqnah (*op. cit.*).
4. Early temple area, Hierakonpolis (J. E. Quibell, *Hierakonpolis*, II, 1902, Pl. LXXIII).
5. Temple of Osiris (?), II Dyn. Abydos (E. R. Ayrton, *Abydos*, III, 1904, Pl. VIII).
6. Protodynastic temple, Abydos (Petrie, *Abydos*, I, Pl. L).
7. Sun temple of Ne-user-Re, Abusir (F. W. v Bissing, *Das Re-heiligtum des Königs Ne-Woser-re*, 1905, I, Pl. I).

How long such venerated shrines of perishable materials lasted and how frequently they were rebuilt no one will ever know. By the I Dynasty some temples were constructed of brick,[35] and at Hierakonpolis the temple had a granite gateway.[36] At Abydos, Petrie found the imprint of a simple rectangular temple of the I Dynasty, 21 feet by 42 feet, with walls 8 feet thick, which, like the tomb of King Menes, must have had its presumably flat roof supported by bundled reed or wooden supports. Near to this early temple of the local divinity, Wep-wawet at Abydos, and at a little higher level, Petrie uncovered the plan of a brick temple of the II or III Dynasty (Plate XII–6). It has a triple arrangement of small sanctuaries at one end which resemble an early tomb at Mahasna (Plate X–7) and a much later type of house and temple plan (Plate LXV–4). Also at Abydos was found the problematic II Dynasty plan of a brick temple, perhaps of Osiris, which must have been only the traditional rectangular building with the entrance on the long side (Plate XII–5).

Not far from Abydos, at the very ancient site of Hierakonpolis, Quibell unearthed an early temple area consisting of a nearly circular mound or platform of sand, its sides retained by rough stones, on which must have stood one or more primitive shrines (Plate XII–4). During the II Dynasty this sacred high place was encroached upon and more or less leveled in order to build crude brick temples.[37] Inasmuch as sun-dried bricks do not make permanent walls, the temple plans which can now be traced within the primitive circular enclosure probably date from the New Kingdom.

One of the oldest, and for centuries the most important, religious center in ancient Egypt was Heliopolis, near Cairo, which was formerly the city of On and the Predynastic capital of Lower Egypt. Here the Sun was worshiped as Re-atum, whose college of priests became renowned as the most learned of all the priestly groups in Egypt. Nothing remains of Re's early temple,[38] but it was a high place, the primeval mound, on which stood the great stone, known as the *ben-ben*. This venerated stone fetish, whose pyramidal top reflected the rays of the sun, eventually developed into the obelisk, and supplied the ideographic shape which turned the step-tomb of the III Dynasty into the pyramids of the IV Dynasty.

Some idea of this holy place of Re can be obtained from the later sun-temple which King Neuserre built in the V Dynasty near his pyramid at Abusir. Although built of stone on a larger scale, Neuserre's temple was undoubtedly modeled after the famous shrine of the god at Heliopolis. The temple at Abusir was built on the high ground at the edge of the desert and consisted of a great open court, 330 feet long and 250 feet broad (Plate XII–7). The entrance was at the east end, above which the sun rose, and at the opposite end of the court stood the *ben-ben*. This symbol and embodiment of the sun was a huge, ungainly, embryonic obelisk, consisting, according to Borchardt, of a pedestal measuring about 130 feet square and 100 feet high; on it stood the squat obelisk with its gleaming pyramidal top rising 56 meters above the pavement of the court. In front of the *ben-ben*

[35] G. Jéquier, *Manuel d'Archéologie Égyptienne* (1924), p. 151, describes a very early and unpublished circular, brick temple discovered at Heliopolis, which had concentric walls pierced with numerous doorways.

[36] J. E. Quibell, *Hierakonpolis,* I, (1900), pl. II.

[37] The temple remains at Badari, which go back to the Old Kingdom and perhaps earlier, are too confused to be very significant (G. Brunton, *Qua and Badari,* I, 1927, p. 18 *seq.*).

[38] A building inscription refers to Senwosret I's enlargement of the temple in Middle Kingdom (Breasted, *Ancient Records,* I, 498-504).

was the large sacrificial altar and a large rectangular slaughter area with long, parallel troughs cut in its stone pavement to catch the blood, while around the sides of the court were priestly storerooms and a royal chapel. The entrance was approached by a long, covered corridor leading up from the reception pavilion on the plain below. Most curious of all the features of this exceptional temple was the great brick model of the barque in which the sun made his daily voyage across the sky.

A clearer and more intelligible picture of the religious and mortuary architecture of this early transitional period can be pieced together from the great complex of buildings around King Zoser's step-pyramid at Saqqara.

View of the Stepped Pyramid at Saqqara from Heb-Sed Court

4. *THE STEPPED PYRAMID AT SAQQARA*

THE REMARKABLE FINDS made by the government excavators in the acres of mortuary buildings around the step-pyramid at Saqqara have added a new chapter to the history of Egyptian architecture. The gigantic complex was built early in the third millennium by Zoser, who was the first or second king of the III Dynasty. The work represents what was probably the beginning of monumental architecture in stone. Some popular writers have felt that the ruined results of Zoser's efforts exist as an inexplicable phenomenon. Unable to explain the forms, building methods, and what they call "the classic beauty" of the buildings, such writers have taken refuge in assuming a long period of transition to stone which may have taken place outside of Egypt. It has even been suggested that Zoser and his architecture represent an intrusion from the West, an offshoot of that mythical mother culture of Atlantis. How else, we are asked, are Saqqara and Mayan architectures to be explained?

Leaving Central American art to its own side of the Atlantic, we find at Saqqara many unanswered problems, but nothing which is inexplicable. The Egyptians in the Memphite region had begun to experiment with the technique of cutting stone as early as the I Dynasty.[1] Even though the magnitude, ingenuity, and complexity of the work may seem astounding, the architectural forms themselves are petrified evidence of mental habits and building traditions which have been inferred in the previous chapters. If it is admitted that the Egyptian environment intensified the natural conservatism

[1] The recent discovery at Saqqara of the rock-cut tomb of Hemaka, a Vizier of the I Dynasty, proves that stone cutting was already advanced beyond an experimental stage. The Tomb of Hemaka is cut 25 feet below the surface, and the burial chamber is surrounded by 42 magazines, each one devoted to a particular article of food (*The Illustrated London News*, vol. 188, April 25, 1936, p. 722).

of the human race, that the earliest architecture was in mud brick, wood, and pliable materials, and that stone at first could only have been used as a more permanent method of sculpturally reproducing traditional forms, then we have only to recognize the existence of some bold thinker who at Saqqara undertook, for the first time, to translate the architectural conventions of his day into what he thought was indestructible stone.

IMHOTEP. Zoser, "The Holy," was one of Egypt's greatest Pharaohs. Tradition kept alive his fame as a man of knowledge, a mighty builder, and a patron of the arts. But much of his prestige and accomplishments were due to his vizier, Imhotep, the first great architect in the history of the world.[2] Imhotep, formerly thought to have been a purely legendary figure, was actually born near Memphis about 2900 B.C.; he was perhaps the son of a distinguished architect, Kanofer, who was "architect of southern and northern Egypt" and was, presumably, the architect of King Khasekhemui who made the stone burial chamber at Abydos. Under Zoser, Imhotep became Vizier, High Priest, "First after the King of Upper Egypt," and "Chief of all the works of the King of Upper and Lower Egypt." Because of his great wisdom he was revered all through Egyptian history as a scribe, sage, astronomer, magician, the father of medicine, and the first user of stone; finally, centuries after his death, he was deified, temples were dedicated to him,[3] and when the priests of Edfu were describing the origin of their temple they said, "The master craftsman was Imhotep, the son of Ptah, the great god of Memphis; father and son united their powers and produced the first temple of Edfu in one of the earliest periods of Egyptian history."

THE SITE AND THE PLAN. What Imhotep undertook at Saqqara was to make permanent an everlasting establishment for the king, by reproducing about his tomb the buildings of wood, wattle, and brick which made up the royal residence at Memphis. The site was the necropolis of Memphis from the I Dynasty, but until recently it has been thought that there were no royal burials there before Zoser, because all his predecessors were buried in Upper Egypt. Zoser himself followed the old custom and erected for his *Ka* a gigantic brick mastaba at Bet Khallaf,[4] but when he shifted his permanent residence to Memphis he began his great tomb at Saqqara, changing the plans several times in order to adjust his sepulchral arrangements to the influence of the Heliopolitan sun worship and the fusion of Upper and Lower Egyptian funereal traditions.

THE PLAN AND WALLS. Imhotep's mortuary plan for his master was certainly altered as the work progressed. The plan, as it has been carefully uncovered by Firth[5] and Lauer,[6] is a great walled enclosure 544.90 m. by 277.60 m. (Plate XIII). Since it is almost exactly 1000 Egyptian cubits

[2] J. B. Hurry, *Imhotep* (1928); K. Sethe, "Imhotep, der Asklepios der Aegypter," *Untersuchungen zur Geschichte und Altertumskunde Aegyptens*, II (1902).

[3] Pages 193, 195.

[4] Page 53.

[5] C. M. Firth and J. E. Quibell, *The Step Pyramid* (1936).

[6] J. Phillippe Lauer, *La Pyramide à Degrés* (1936).

PLATE XIII: STEPPED PYRAMID AT SAQQARA

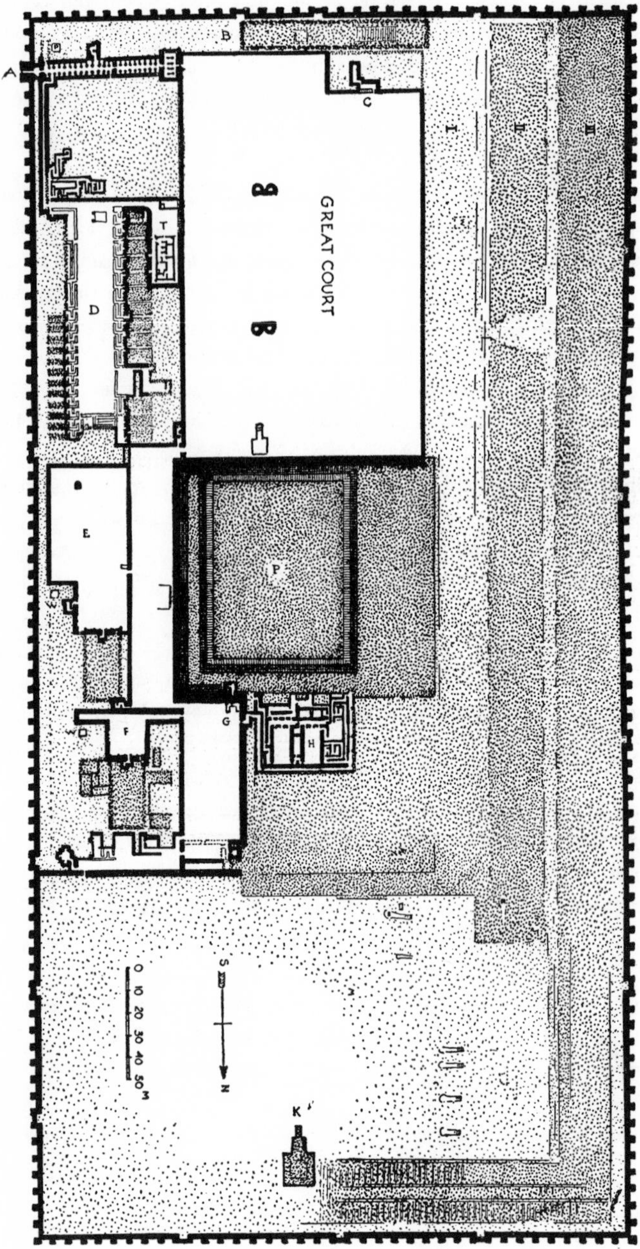

from the inner face of the southern wall to the north end, the implication is that the work began with the long mastaba which is now incorporated in the south wall. The space surrounded by the walls is not so much an enclosure as it is a great artificial terrace with open courts in it. The walls, which are really only a facing of the terrace, and even on the south side, where they have an exterior and interior surface, are 14.80 m. thick, have an interior core of cloisonettes filled with chips, bricks and rubbish, and are faced with cut limestone.

The decoration of these walls, which are 9.60 m. high, consists of recessed niches, each grooved pilaster of which is 2.35 m. deep; at irregular intervals are fourteen bastions, three at the ends and four on the sides, which imitate towered gateways with closed, doubled doors carved on them. These paneled walls, with their sinkings and closed doors, it has been suggested, copied the walls of brick which Menes built around Memphis. Probably the brick defenses of "the City of the White Walls" had this niche treatment, but we have to go further back to get the ideographic meaning of this decoration. Along the top of the walls were eight rows of slightly sunken rectangles which had no relation to the stone coursing, but were arranged vertically in the center of each sunken panel and projecting pilaster (Plate XIV–1). The effort to interpret these non-structural, rectangular sinkings has resulted in several fanciful theories. Some scholars have called them beam ends, while others have tried to make them out as windows. The explanation is simple, if they are included as part of the whole decorative, or better, symbolic, treatment of the walls, and then considered with the *serekh* palace-façade tradition.

The house was always a mark of power, and in all primitive societies the actual dwelling of the ruling family possessed special social and religious distinction. The various titles of the "Red House" and "White House" and Pharaoh, meaning "Great House," indicate how important this association of ideas was in the Egyptian mind. Therefore the niche pattern of the old *serekh* façade—the wooden palace of the legendary rulers of the Delta—acquired, as we have seen, a tremendous significance. When the southern kings of the warlike Hawk clan conquered the more civilized North, they took over the sign of this house to show their rights to the power of those demi-gods who had once reigned in the Delta. In much the same way the Dorian Greeks took over the Megaron palace of the Achæan kings, who in their minds had become heroes and semi-divinities, and made it into a cult-house. The niche pattern, which was reproduced in brick on the palace walls at Abydos, and was probably on the walls around Memphis as indicated by the sign of the Memphite nome, was by the III Dynasty largely related in men's minds with the house of the dead.

When translated into brick, either on palace or mastaba walls, it was impossible to imitate accurately the reticulated pattern at the top of the wooden framework. Because no brick walls and

---

PLATE XIII

1. Plan of mortuary precinct: *A* entrance to Hall of Colonnade, *B* Great Tomb, *C* Chapel, *D* Heb-Sed Court, *E* Court of the Southern Palace, *F* Court of the Northern Palace, *G* Serdab, *H* Mortuary Temple, *K* Great Altar, *P* Pyramid, *T* "Temple of Osiris," *W* Wells, I, II and III terraces with chambers (after Lauer in C. M. Firth and J. E. Quibell, *The Step Pyramid,* 1936, Pl. 1).

PLATE XIV: STEPPED PYRAMID AT SAQQARA

1

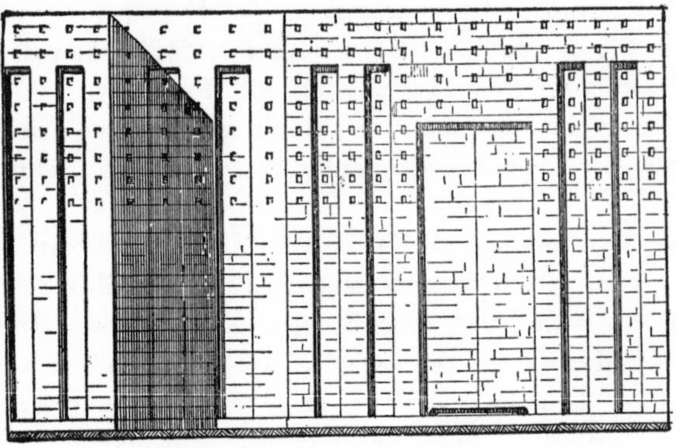

2

3

4

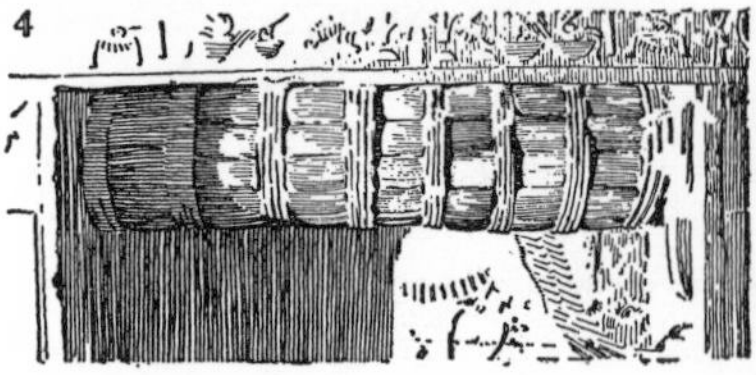

5

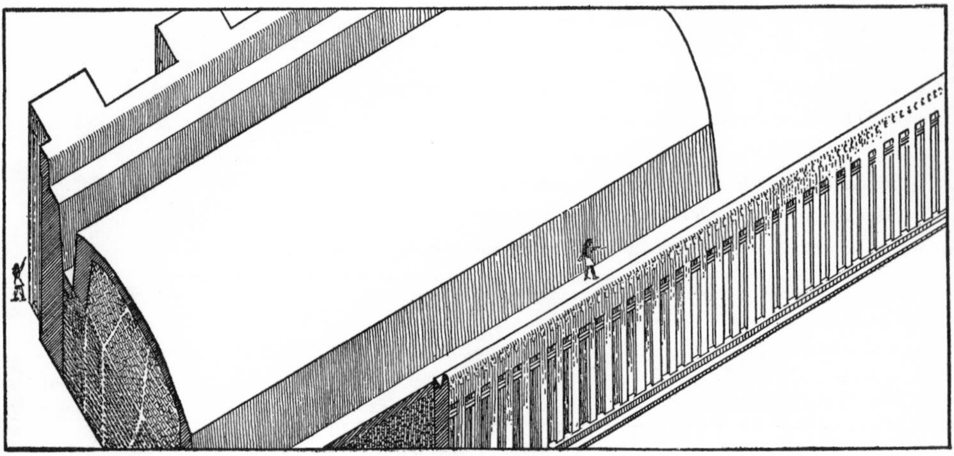

mastabas are preserved to the height where such square paneling would have occurred is no proof that the Egyptians did not schematize the effect as best they could by making shallow, rectangular sinkings in the bricks. If a section of the wall at Saqqara (Plate XIV–1) is compared with a piece of the painted sarcophagus of King Mentuhetep (Plate IX–4), it will be seen that the two-leaved doors, swung high on pivots, are the same, while both examples have three projecting pilasters and two sunken niches on either side of the closed doors. Furthermore, on the painted version of the "palace-façade," the paneled cross-timbering at the top is reduced to an arrangement of vertical squares. There are several examples, including a stone sarcophagus found at Dashur (Plate IX–3), where the symbolic small-wood pattern was simplified to exactly the diagrammatic treatment seen on the walls at Saqqara.[7]

THE GREAT TOMB. Incorporated into the south wall of the temenos, and rising above it, is the great tomb whose purpose is still unexplained. Its superstructure, on top of the wall, is 85 m. long by 13 m. wide, and its stone facing was originally built with a curved top (Plate XIV–5). Stairs, starting at the west end, descend for 30 m. down an open passage cut in the top of the tomb; then they become subterranean and continue for 24 m. when they open on a well which goes down to the burial chamber. At the bottom of the well is a small sarcophagus chamber of granite, and above it another chamber in which to handle the granite stopper giving access to the sarcophagus room. The shaft was dug first, and then the inclined trench was cut, open to the sky, primarily as a means of removing the débris, and later as a ceremonial passage for the interment of the king. After the burial the trench was entirely filled, just as the shaft had been. Subterranean corridors give access to the chambers with the famous blue-green tiles. These chambers are lined with magnificent glazed tiles [8] in imitation of walls hung with green reed-matting (Plate XIV–3); the tiles are let into grooves cut in between narrow bands of limestone carved to represent the cords by which the reed mats were bound together, and were held in place by a rush or flax stalk, threaded through the holes cut in the limestone bands. In one of these rooms is a door surmounted by the carved representation of a grilled transom, the uprights consisting of symbolic *dedu* pillars of Osiris (Plate XIV–3). The carving shows how

[7] Other examples of the *same* stylization of "palace-façade" pattern are: a sarcophagus (Petrie and Brunton, *Lahun,* II, Pl. XXIII); an alabaster offering table from Mit Rahine in the Cairo Mesum (*Le Musée Égyptien,* I, p. 9, Pl. IV); Borchardt, Ae. Z., XLI, p. 85, 86; Laure, *La Pyramide à Degrés,* Fig. 69; a similar method of generalizing the "palace-façade" by reducing it to rectangular sinkings occurs in the I dynasty on a faience bracelet from the tomb of Zet (V. Gordon Childe, *The Most Ancient East,* 1928, Pl. XII–a); and a somewhat similar simplification occurs on the tomb of Ptahshepses I of the VI Dynasty (M. A. Murray, *Saqqara Mastabas,* I, Pl. XXVI); other early examples are a fragment from Heliopolis (Lauer, *op. cit.,* Fig. 70) and a sarcophagus of wood in the Cairo Museum, No. 28029 (P. Lacau, *Sarcophages Antérieurs au Nouvel Empire,* Pl. XV).

[8] A. Lucas, *Ancient Egyptian Materials and Industries* (1934), p. 101 *seq.*

PLATE XIV

1. Exterior walls of precinct restored (J. P. Lauer, *La Pyramide à Degrés,* 1936, Pl. XXVIII).
2. Exterior walls from south.
3. Blue-tiled chamber in Great Tomb.
4. Curtain rôle of tile in stele doorway of Great Tomb (Lauer, *op. cit.,* Pl. XXXVI).
5. Great tomb on south wall restored.

the originals of these Osiris pillars were made of sheaves of bundle reeds, bound together and stuck into the spreading ends of one another. A second tiled room has three "false doors" with reliefs of Neterkhet (Zoser). At the top of one door, within the frame, is a horizontal drum which later occurs frequently in sepulchral doorways, and has caused much speculation (Plate XIV–4). Some writers have interpreted this door drum as a wooden strut originally intended to wedge the door jambs apart. Others have called it a curtain roll. The cord and matting pattern carved on the Saqqara example and on the sarcophagus of Fefi (Plate VII–2) shows that these cylinders reproduced mat curtains which could be rolled up or down.

The Great Tomb raises many unanswerable questions. Was it originally a free standing mastaba, the first tomb which Zoser undertook before abandoning it for the stepped pyramid idea? As a free standing mastaba its orientation, running east and west and with the entrance at the west end, is curiously exceptional. Zoser, we saw, had a large but traditional tomb in the region of his ancestors at Bet Khallaf. Was this Saqqara tomb, then, only a temporary resting place, pending the completion of the great pyramid? The objection to this suggestion, quite apart from the work involved and the probability of Zoser's not making a temporary resting place while he was still alive to plan a new type of tomb, is the fact that the great pyramid started modestly as a mastaba, not much larger than this tomb. Furthermore it is difficult to explain why the tile work in the temporary tomb was finished while the tile work, by the same hand, in the great pyramid was left unfinished.

It is no more satisfactory to assume that after the tomb was finished the stone was found faulty. Perhaps it was a symbolic tomb intended to commemorate the ritual of the king's sacrifice at the time of the Heb-Sed festival.[9] The burial chamber in this tomb was only large enough for a contracted burial, such as is found in all graves before the III Dynasty, while the sarcophagus room in the great pyramid allowed an extended burial. Therefore the Great Tomb was presumably abandoned because of a change in royal funereal custom. Another possibility, however, is its use as the ceremonial tomb of Zoser, as the King of Lower Egypt, where his Delta subjects might worship him. This idea is strengthened somewhat by the little chapel (Plate XIII–c) beneath the tomb and the use of the *uræus* decorations on the inner face of the temenos wall, for the cobra was the royal insignia of the Delta kings at Buto.[10]

THE ENTRANCE CORRIDOR. The only entrance to the walled city of the dead was in the bastion at the southeast corner, which was probably a towered gateway. Within the gateway are the stone copies of two open doors; then another open door gives access to the long corridor. Inside the doorway, a passage at the left leads into the solid terrace and may have had a staircase ascending to the top of the walls; at the right another passage goes to the Heb-Sed court, passing a complex of small chapels and chambers. The long entrance corridor is divided into two parts by a cross-wall (Plate XV–1). In the first part are two rows of twelve columns. The columns,

[9] Firth, *Annales du Service,* XXVIII, pp. 85-87.

[10] Lauer, *La Pyramide à Degrés,* I, pp. 110-112; inasmuch as an actual funerary ceremony took place in this tomb, and all access to the chamber was closed, Lauer suggests that the Great Tomb was built to preserve the "placenta" which would have been buried before the royal mummy was interred.

which are *cir.* 6 m. high, and tapered, imitate bundled reeds; but being undoubtedly the first attempt to copy tall, slender, free standing supports carrying a load of stone instead of wood, Imhotep cautiously attached them to the end of cross-walls (Plate xv–2). The capitals represent a binding sheath with three of the bundled reeds carried over it. These columns, which have no exact counterpart in subsequent Egyptian architecture, were not made of solid drums of stone, but were built up in stone courses, with two to six pieces of stone in each course, set around a central core and then carved to the circular and fluted exterior. At the very beginning of stone architecture we see how the Egyptian builders began to use the new material more imitatively than structurally. The ceiling, for example, of this hall is carved in imitation of the round beams of a timbered roof.

The roof of this processional hall rose higher than the top of the enclosing terrace. A little light was thereby introduced by small rectangular openings, producing, as the section shows (Plate xv–2), the earliest known example of the clerestory method of lighting. On the south wall, behind the last seven bays, is the carved façade of a *serdab,* decorated with the traditional small-wood paneling of the "palace-façade"; the central doorway (Plate xv–3) leads into a small sanctuary consisting of a chamber with a "false door" and a niche for offerings. This veritable mortuary chapel, in which were found fragments of statues, was incorporated into the colonnaded hall *after* a modification in the plans of the architect, and it may have been related to the well at P which descends 25 m. to a subterranean corridor, running directly under this *serdab.* At H was a brick chamber, perhaps for the guardian.

The second part of the processional hall has two rows of eight columns and terminates at the west end in a vestibule with what was probably thought of as two rows of four supports, but built with each pair of columns joined together by a wall (Plate xv–4). The outer face of the door which led from this columnar vestibule into the great open court to the south of the pyramid reproduces in stone an open door, swung on a pivot at the bottom, and set into a spool-like socket at the top (Plate xv–5). The back of the door is carved to imitate the small, round rungs which held the vertical planks of Egyptian doors together. The niche paneling on the wall at either side of the door is characteristic of all interior walls of the great courtyard.

THE GREAT SOUTH COURT. More or less in the center of the great south court are two B-shaped masses of stone which were probably altars, and at the north end are the remains of a rectangular platform ascended by steps. Flanking the court on the west side are the remains of three terraces, rising one above the other. Terrace I abuts the pyramid and was only 4.85 m. high; Terrace II, which is 25 m. wide and 400 m. long, was about 7.35 m. high; and Terrace III, which was part of the ancient walls, was still higher. Terrace II, which has galleries beneath it, probably had a curved top, like a vault, which reproduced the hooped roof of one of Zoser's long houses in his palace at Memphis. The subterranean passages cut in the rock beneath the terraces have small chambers opening off from them. Because of the large number of broken offering vases found in these passages it was suggested that the chambers may have been dummy burial places,

PLATE XV: STEPPED PYRAMID AT SAQQARA

1

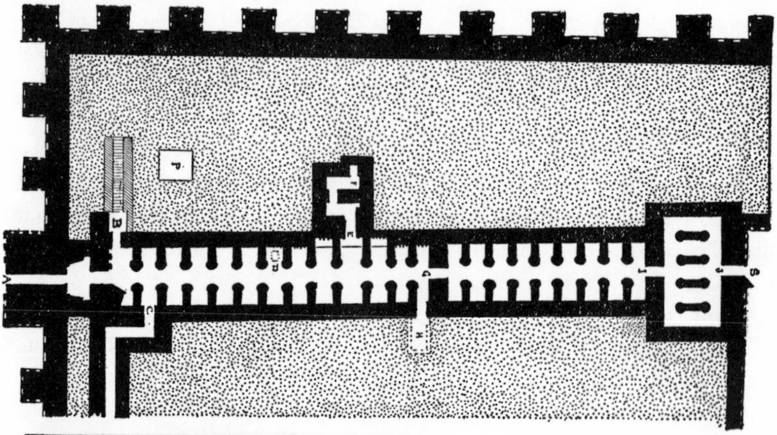

2

3

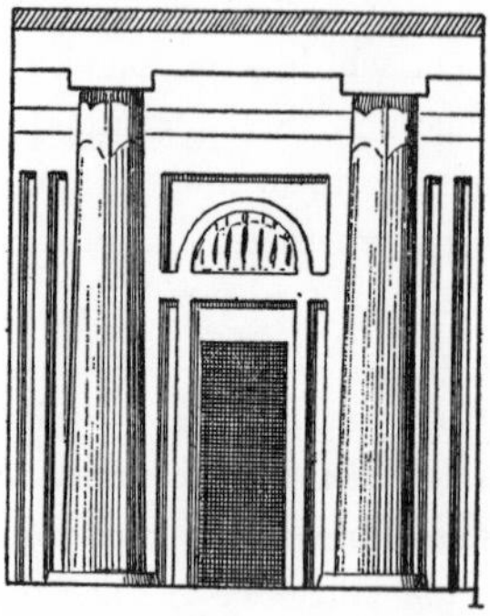

4

5

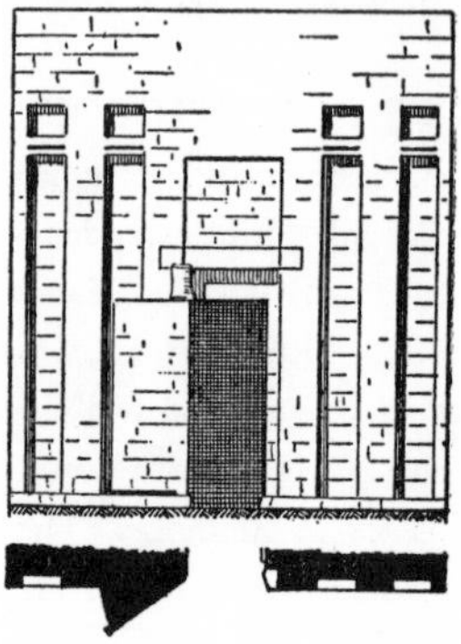

a survival from the time when large numbers of retainers were slaughtered at the tomb of the king.[11]

TEMPLE T., "THE OSIRIS TEMPLE." To the north of the Processional Hall and in a small court west of the Heb-Sed court, is a temple (Plate XVI–1). The temple, if such it was, is oriented north and south, and has two entrances, one with the door open in the center of the south wall, and the other with the door ajar at the south corner of the east wall. Both entrances open into a small hall of three columns; the columns, like all others at Saqqara, are attached to strengthening walls. The hall gives access to three interior courts on the west side and opens on the north into another court, off from which is the small sanctuary in which was a lintel, carved with the Osiris *dedu* pillars, and an offering niche. There were four or five windows in the west wall and perhaps two others in the north wall.[12]

The south façade of the temple (Plate XVII–1) is architecturally important, first, because it reproduces in stone a woven matting structure such as the prototype of the hut shrine of Anubis (Plate II–1), or of a shrine on a private tomb of the III Dynasty at Saqqara.[13] Imhotep in building this temple faithfully reproduced at the edges the round corner posts, or bundles of reeds, which formed the corners of the original structure, and then carved the smaller *torus* moldings in imitation of the edges of the mats which were lashed to the posts and stretched tight to form the walls of the house. Thus we have conclusive evidence of the origin and early use in stone of the *torus molding* at the edges of stone walls, to which the Egyptians religiously adhered during the whole history of Dynastic architecture. Even more important is the proof which this temple furnishes as to the origin of the persistent Egyptian *cavetto cornice*. The early pictographic representations of reed and matting structures show a parapet, or cornice, of reeds which bend forward over the walls. Such reed parapets, even to the curve and the vertical striations of the reeds, were stylized into the conventional cornice, used upon nearly all stone walls after the III Dynasty (Plate XLII–5, 7). At Saqqara, however, where the transition to stone was being made, there are no true cavetto cornices, but upon Temple T we have the intermediate step where the reed parapet is reproduced in block form and straight faces. The slabs of stone forming the flat roof of the

[11] C. M. Firth, *Annales du Service*, XXVIII, p. 83; Lauer, *op. cit.*, I, p. 181.
[12] Lauer, *op. cit.*, p. 150.
[13] M. A. Murray, *Saqqara Mastabas*, Pl. XXXIX, 44.

PLATE XV

1. Plan of Entrance Colonnade: *A* entrance, *B Porter's* lodge and stairs to terrace, *C* passage to Heb-Sed Court, *D* base of statue of Zoser, *E* & *F* Chapel with *serekh* façade, *H* chamber, *J* west porch, *P* well (Lauer, *op. cit.*, Pl. XXXVIII).
2. Section of Hall of Colonnades (*op. cit.*, Pl. XLIII).
3. *Serekh* façade of chapel in Hall (Lauer, *op. cit.*, Pl. XLII).
4. West porch of Hall of Colonnades.
5. Doorway to west porch of Hall of Colonnades (Lauer, *op. cit.*, Fig. 121).

PLATE XVI: STEPPED PYRAMID AT SAQQARA

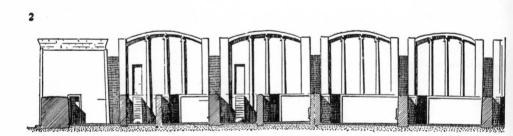

1

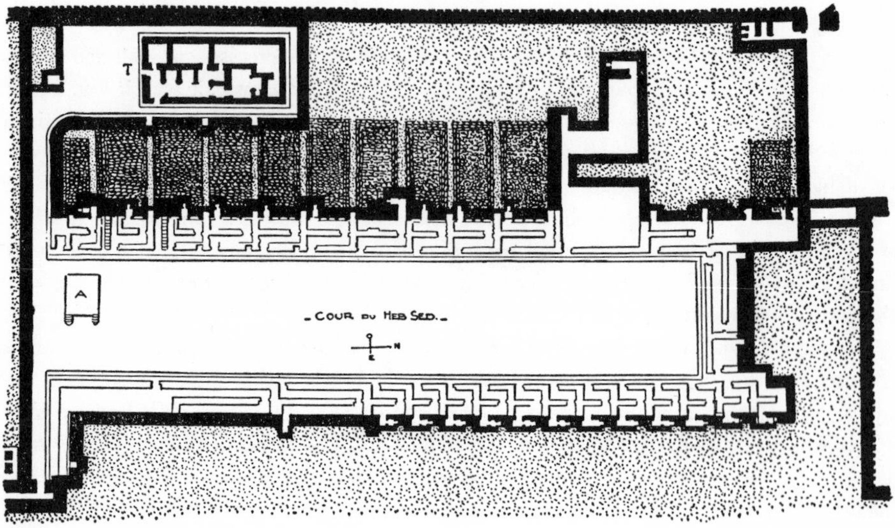

2

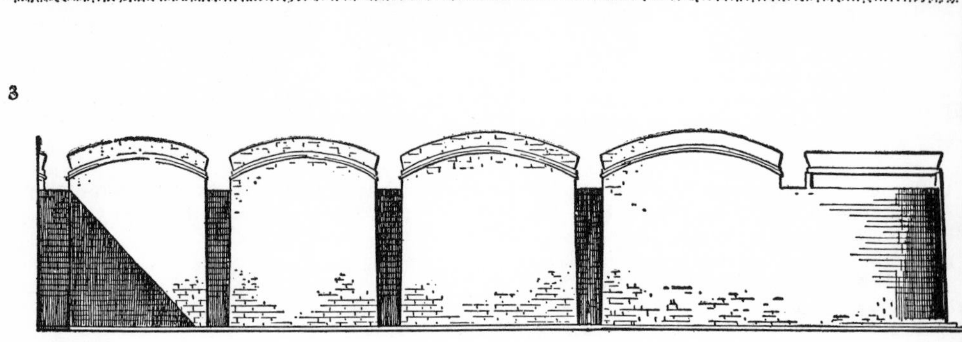

3

temple are carved on their under surfaces with parallel corrugations, painted red, to represent the round beams of contemporary roofs.

THE HEB-SED COURT. Temple T, which seems to have been the cult-house of Osiris, is ritualistically a part of the Heb-Sed court (Plate XVI–1), and the passage from the temple court passes around a unique curved wall enclosing the solid terrace in which the Heb-Sed shrines are reproduced. There are ten large shrines, each with its double forecourt, on the west side of the long court, and a large number of smaller shrines on the east side.[14] At the south corner of the west side the first shrine is of the same type as Temple T. Like all the cult buildings facing on the Heb-Sed court, this shrine has no real interior, but is a symbolic and ceremonial reproduction of the exterior of a contemporary cult-house. A recess in the heavy wall in front served as the theoretical chamber of the guardian, and an open door leads into a diminutive double court. At the side of the shrine is a small offering niche and in the east façade is a closed door (Plate XVI–2).

The next two shrines are the most interesting and exceptional. Both are in two stories, having a flight of steps leading up to a door, while at the side of these ramp-like steps a small, inner court protects the naos, or offering niche, which is set into the façade of the solid building. The most striking features of the façades are the curved roofs and the curious saddle capitals (Plate XVI–2). The chapels at first seem unprecedented, but actually their details provide further evidence of the literal intention of the architect to reproduce traditional and existing buildings. Each chapel (Plate XVII–8) has two courts, the entrance to the outer court having an open door swung back on pivots against the wall, while both flanking walls of the inner court are carved in relief with the representation of a wooden fence (Plate XVII–7), and the offering chamber has another replica of an open door which gives access to a wall niche with a curiously curved top.

Carefully carved in stone, then, are the characteristic features of the traditional tent-like hut-shrine, for the odd shape of the ceiling of the offering niche is the same double curve seen in the reproductions of the customary naos (Plate II–2, 7). If the shrine of Set (Plate II–2), and another hut-shrine from Meydum (Plate XVII–4), are compared with these stone details, it will be seen that both ideograms represent the forecourt by a wooden fence of three vertical bars. Without the evidence of Saqqara, we have already seen two types of venerated cult-houses, one with a flat roof and the other with the curved hoops covered with matting. Therefore these façades, as restored by the exca-

[14] The chapels surrounding the court suggest the chapels on the reliefs of the Sed temple of Osorkon II at Bubastis (E. Naville, *The Festival Hall of Osorkon II in the Great Temple of Bubastis,* Pls. VII, XII, XXIX). Lauer (*op. cit.,* I, p. 30) suggests that inasmuch as there are two groups of chapels to the east and west, as at Bubastis, they may represent the two confederations of Delta nomes.

PLATE XVI

1. Plan of Heb-Sed Court (Lauer, *op. cit.,* Pl. LV).
2. Chapels on west side of Heb-Sed Court restored (Lauer, *Annales du Service,* XXVIII, Pl. 8).
3. Back of the chapels (*op. cit.*).

PLATE XVII: STEPPED PYRAMID AT SAQQARA

1

2

3

4

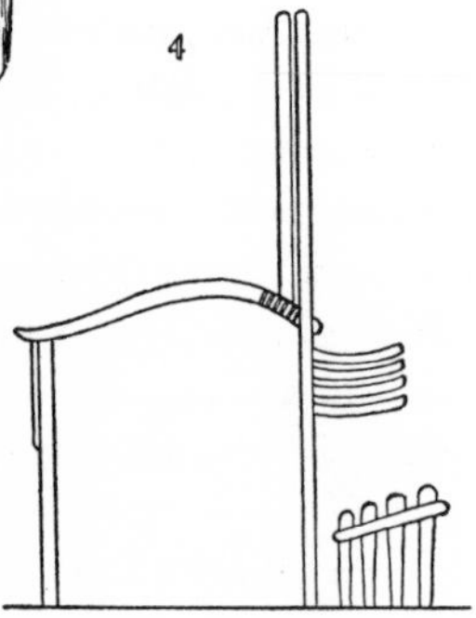

5

6

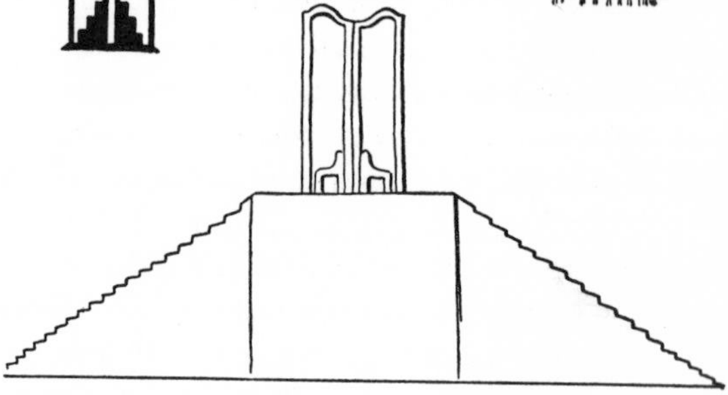

7

8

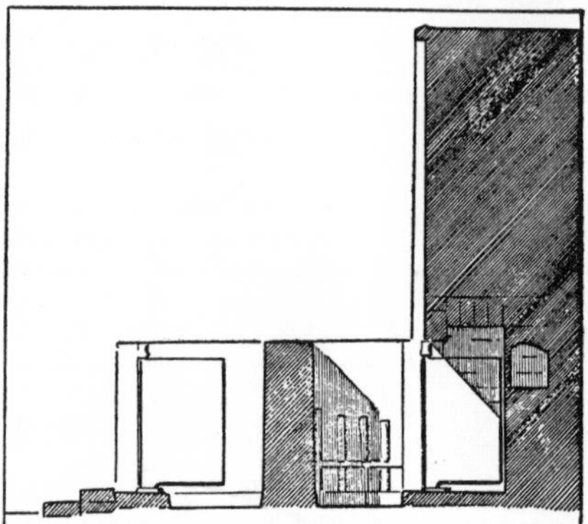

vators, merely help to complete the picture. They reproduce an obviously light construction with long slender supports of bundled reeds carrying the ends of small rafters set into their saddle capitals. But at this point the reader may wonder why such elaborate false architecture was built around the court.

The Heb-Sed ritual, from which came all the stage scenery that was here reproduced as part of Zoser's mortuary palace, went back to a primitive custom, common to many different agricultural societies,[15] and until recently in existence among those pagan tribes of the Sudan in whose tribal organization and religious conventions we have already seen so many primitive Egyptian survivals.[16] Because the magic of the chieftain, or king, was responsible for the engendering of the soil, the powerful one was ceremoniously killed after thirty years and his power transferred to a younger and more fertile leader. Just when such ceremonies ceased to be grim reality and became a royal ritual in Egypt it is impossible to tell. By the time of Zoser this reincarnation rite, supposed to take place after thirty years of reign, had become a Jubilee Festival. At the festival the king died as a mortal, but, like the fertility god Osiris, whose body was dismembered by his brother Set and was then reassembled and revived by the labors of his wife and son, the king was reincarnated as the embodiment of Osiris. In the course of Egyptian history the Pharaohs crowded the mourners and had several Jubilee Festivals at far less then thirty year intervals, and sometimes they preserved the essence of the rite by raising their heirs to joint power with them at the time of the Heb-Sed Jubilee.

We have no knowledge of how the many shrines of the Heb-Sed court were used. Each chapel may have represented a nome, or was a shrine for each regional divinity who had feudal dependence upon the Pharaoh. It is perhaps more likely that the shrines were for the whole pantheon of gods whom the king visited at the time of the festival, and represented on earth after his ritualistic deification. The exceptional feature at Saqqara is the reproduction of the Heb-Sed court as part of the sepulchral architecture. Its presence shows to how large an extent the whole arrangement was an imitation of the royal palace at Memphis, because the Jubilee Hall, or "House of Rejoicing," remained a traditional part of the royal and divine residence in later Dynastic architecture.

15 Frazer, *Golden Bough* (1890), I, p. 217 seq.

16 "The Shilluk Kings are (or were) killed in order to avoid those disasters which their senescence was thought to bring upon the State," (Seligman, *op. cit.*, p. 90); among the Dinka the great rain-maker, after his period of efficiency is over, is buried alive in ceremonial state upon his couch, while the custom of the Niel tribe is to strangle their rain-maker (p. 197); and in the Fung tribe the ceremonial king-killing was a recognized custom which took place during an annual festival, but later a dog was killed in place of the king (pp. 423-428).

PLATE XVII

1. South façade of temple T (Lauer, *La Pyramide à Degrés,* Fig. 157).
2. Capital from Heb-Sed Court (Lauer, *op. cit.*, Pl. LX).
3. Possible origin of bracket capital.
4. *Per-our* shrine from Meydum (Petrie, *Medum,* 1892, Pl. IX).
5. Hieroglyph for "Heb-Sed."
6. Heb-Sed platform on vase from pyramid (Lauer, *op. cit.*, p. 64, Fig. 43).
7. Fenced court of Heb-Sed chapel.
8. Section of Heb-Sed chapel (Lauer, *op. cit.*, Pl. LIX).

PLATE XVIII: STEPPED PYRAMID AT SAQQARA

1

2

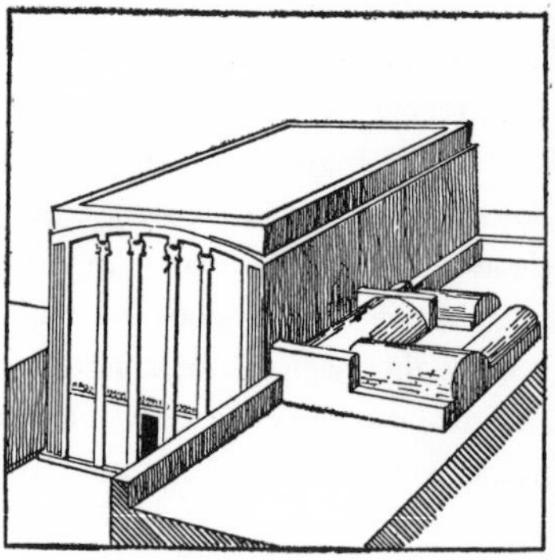

3

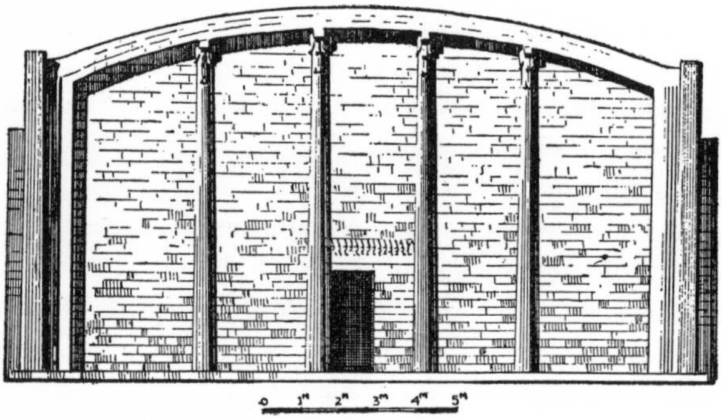

4

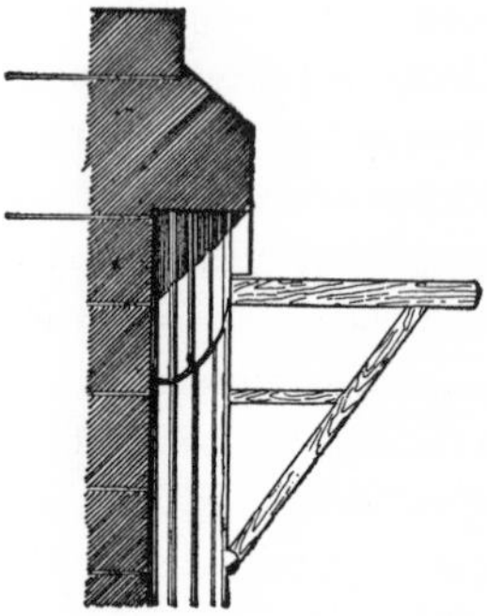

5

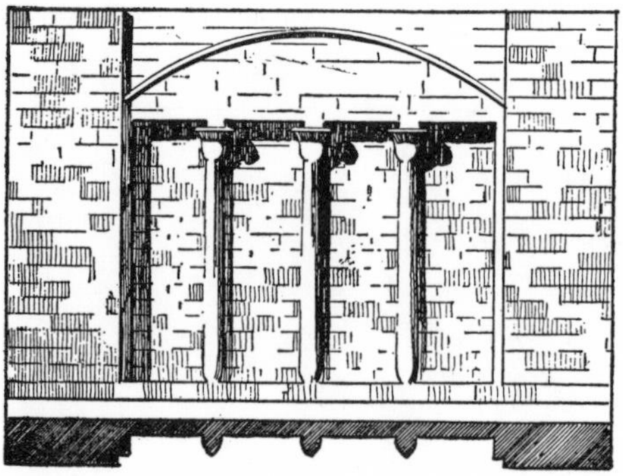

6

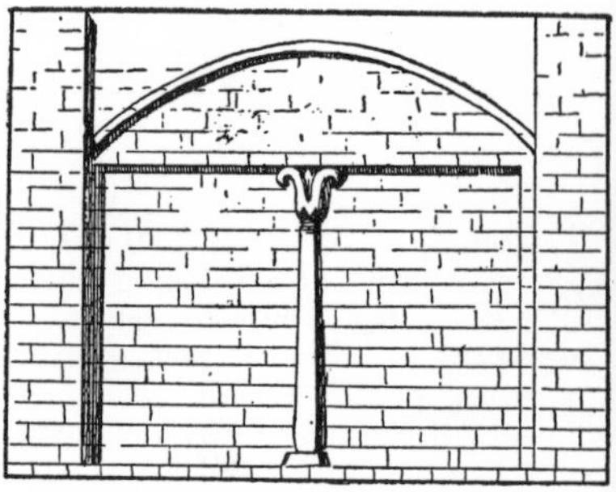

The sign for the Heb-Sed festival has two tent-like shrines on a raised platform (Plate XVII–5)—the two seats being for the king, either in his dual function of ruler of Upper and Lower Egypt, or for his appearance before and after deification.[17] At all events, in the southern end of the court are the remains of a large platform approached by two flights of steps. On this platform must have been two royal kiosks (Plate XVII–6) similar to the one beneath which we see Narmer seated for his Jubilee Festival (Plate I–4).

COURTS OF THE SOUTH AND NORTH PALACES. To the north of the Heb-Sed court are two smaller courts, each with the façade of a building at the north end. The two separate buildings, because they are solid rectangles of masonry, rising above their respective terraces, have been called the mastaba tombs of "the daughters of Zoser." This supposition, which has now attached the name of Princess Hetepher-Nebti to the south court and the Princess Intkas to the north court, is no longer tenable. The King of Egypt had a carefully observed dual function as the ruler of Upper and of Lower Egypt, and his palace was known as "the double façade." The evidence now indicates that the southern building at Saqqara, with its courtyard, was a reproduction of the Pharaoh's "White House," as King of Upper Egypt, while the northern building was his "Red House," as King of Lower Egypt.

Both palace-façades, especially in their ruined condition, have a simplicity and sculptural clarity of form which is misleading (Plate XVIII–1). The Southern Palace, usually called the chapel of Hetepher-Nebti, has four tall, slender columns attached to the wall, and pilasters of ribbed paneling at the corners, which represent reed or wooden uprights. There is no doubt that the roof line was curved, and there is the probability that the south palace had a rectangular parapet, or weight, to hold down the matting above the curved ends. If this were so, its roof was similar to the type of wooden house, with roof of matting, reproduced in the wooden sarcophagus from Tarkhan (Plate V–2).[18]

The applied columns have thirteen sharp arrises and are very tall and slender with a marked diminution. The capitals, which are the same as those on the Heb-Sed chapels, have no other counterparts in the history of Egyptian architecture (Plate XVII–1). Each capital has two curved and channeled leaflike pendants on either side of the rectangular rafters set between them. Below the capital are two square holes and two round bosses of stone. On the capitals of the Heb-Sed chapels there was only one hole and no bosses. The prototypes of these columns were undoubtedly made of a light ma-

[17] This sign is carved upon an alabaster vase of Zoser's from Saqqara, *Annales,* XXXIV, p. 58, Fig. 1; Lauer, *op. cit.,* I, Fig. 43.

[18] Page 23.

PLATE XVIII

1. Façade of Southern Palace.
2. Restoration of Northern Palace (Lauer, *Annales du Service,* XXIX, p. 113, Fig. 24).
3. Façade of Southern Palace restored (Lauer, *op. cit.,* Pl. LXXIII).
4. Totem bracket on columns of palace (Lauer, *op. cit.,* I, p. 161, Fig. 166).
5. Symbolic papyrus column façade in court of Northern Palace (Lauer, *op. cit.,* Pl. LXXXIII).
6. Symbolic lotus-column façade in court of Southern Palace (Lauer, *op. cit.,* Fig. 188).

terial, probably bundled reeds. The sharp arrises would then have come from the reed supports having been covered with mud plaster, and the channels formed by a thumb drawn down the grooves to lessen the thickness of the plaster.[19] That the pendants are "perhaps sepals of the white lotus reversed" as was at first suggested, is unlikely, for if they had represented the symbolic lotus flower, their form would have persisted in the subsequent architecture.

The "saddle" capital is one of the earliest types the world over, and the drawing (Plate xvii–3) shows how the bundled reeds of these Saqqara supports could have been spread to form a saddle support for roof beams. Being plastered with mud, the necessary binders at the base of the capital would not have been imitated in stone.[20] Firth successfully explains the holes and bosses by showing how the columns, in addition to being supports, were masts, veritable totem poles, on which were brackets, such as are common for Egyptian standards, to carry the totem (Plate xviii–4). The Meydum pictograph (Plate xvii–4) has two masts and horizontal lines at the top to represent the standards. According to this explanation, the two bosses were merely a support for the oblique bar of the bracket. The excavator points out that on the relief of a Hathor, or cow-goddess, shrine from Deir el-Bahari the façade has two high masts,[21] and four supports for the curved roof, each support having two horns and breasts projecting from the top. It is, however, impossible to agree with M. Lauer[22] when he explains the *ḳheḳher* ornament above the doorway as a stylization of the thongs which held the masts stretched in the panels of the façade (Plate xviii–3). The *ḳheḳher* pattern, as we saw, was a royal ornament originating as a parapet design, thereby helping to identify this building as the replica in stone of a king's palace.

On the east wall of the court, in front of the southern palace, is a sunken panel, badly ruined, in which the excavators restore the façade of a chapel, again with a curved roof, supported in the center by a single column with a lotus flower capital. (Plate xviii–6). Since the lotus was the emblem of Upper Egypt, it would here be the designating sign of the "White House" of the South. In the court is a horseshoe form, similar to one part of the B-shaped platform in the great court, which was perhaps an altar.

The palace-façade in the north court, which is called the tomb or chapel of the Princess Intkas, is a large rectangle of masonry rising above the surrounding terrace (Plate xviii–2). Instead of pilasters at the corners, it had vertical fluting in imitation of bundled reed uprights, which were probably imitated down the side of the building. Its actual façade was similar to the Southern Palace, but its cornice was flat[23] above the curved profile, and had a slight parapet around the edge. This was the "Red House" of Lower Egypt, and its prototype must have been a light, tent-like structure with bundled reeds stuck vertically into the ground, as the natives of Irak still build their huts. In view of

19 The concave arrises may have been imitated from bundles of "reeds split vertically, exposing the concave interiors, packed closely to avoid air spaces" (Firth and Quibell, *The Stepped Pyramid,* I, p. 13, 21).

20 Firth and Quibell (*op. cit.,* I, p. 21) say, "in every fluted column there is a band carved in relief about om. 75 from the ground as if to indicate the binding for fastening the split reeds together."

21 Naville, *Deir el Bahari,* IV, Pl. 103.

22 Lauer, *Annales,* XXVIII, p. 112; *La Pyramide à Degrés,* I, p. 166.

23 In his final study Lauer (*La Pyramide à Degrés,* Pl. LXXXI) restores this temple not with a flat, but with a curved, cornice, imitating a reed parapet.

all the evidence to show that such dwellings had hoop roofs, covered with matting, it is impossible to entertain the suggestion that these curved roofs represent brick vaults. Even the curious arrangement of apparent vaults which occurs to the east of the palace, on top of the solid terrace, is no indication of any intention to reproduce brick vaults. While brick vaulting was used to protect the tombs of the III Dynasty, there is no proof that any kind of true vaulting occurred on the brick dwellings of this period. Furthermore, the original form of the structural arch and vault is never ellipitical, while these figurative roofs, which had no practical purpose, have flat, elliptical curves, similar to the curve of bent hoops, such as was seen on the wooden cabin of a XII Dynasty boat (Plate III–2). In spite of the fact that these dummy wagon vaults are built with wedge-shaped voussoirs, laid over a rubble core, their presence is the result only of a desire to reproduce faithfully the curved matting roofs of the huts which flanked the king's great hall. Such vault forms suggest that true voussoir construction in cut stone may have originated here as an imitative, rather than as a structural, method of building. On the other hand, an ostracon of the III Dynasty from Seqqara proves that the Egyptian mason of this early period knew how to lay out a working diagram for a curve, by means of coördinates.[24]

Just as the identification of the Southern Palace was probably indicated by the façade of a little shrine, with a single, lotus column, carved on the east wall of the court, in the same way the Northern Palace is actually designated as the "Red House" of Lower Egypt by another shrine carved in the same relative position. This shrine, better preserved and again with a curved roof, has three *papyrus columns* with bell-shaped or campaniform capitals (Plate XVIII–5). The papyrus was the emblem of the Northern Kingdom, and these papyriform columns of triangular section are the earliest known examples of the type. The first appearance in architecture of the bundled papyrus stalk column, with a contracted capital, is in the temple of Neuserre at Abusir in the V Dynasty (Plate XXXIV–4). The spreading campaniform capital, such as appears here at Saqqara, does not occur as a monumental structural support until the XVIII Dynasty. Many years ago Borchardt pointed out how this kind of column, so popular in the great temples of the New Kingdom, must have originated as a bundle of papyrus stalks.[25] Its presence in the III Dynasty and the fact that it is not used architecturally until over a thousand years later, is strong proof of its symbolic significance here in the north court as the emblem of the Northern Kingdom and its royal palace. If the two courts and their palaces were associated with the dual personality of the Egyptian king, then the lateral wells at W, each in the same relation to the shrine façades in the courts, were presumably related ritualistically with this double personification, and were not actual burial shafts.

COURT OF THE SERDAB. In the court north of the pyramid is the *serdab,* an exceptional little structure built against the slope of the pyramid (Plate XIX–1). The *serdab* is a rectangular chamber of masonry, its front wall sloping parallel to the face of the pyramid, set in a small, walled enclosure.[26]

[24] Gunn, *Annales du Service,* XXVI (1926), pp. 197-202; Clarke and Engelbach, *Ancient Egyptian Masonry* (1930), pp. 52-53.

[25] L. Borchardt, *Die Aegyptische Pflanzensäule.*

[26] Firth and Quibell (*op. cit.,* I, p. 9) say that the enclosure was "a porch, or chapel." Its roof "was once of heavy limestone beams," but this seems most unlikely.

PLATE XIX: STEPPED PYRAMID AT SAQQARA

1

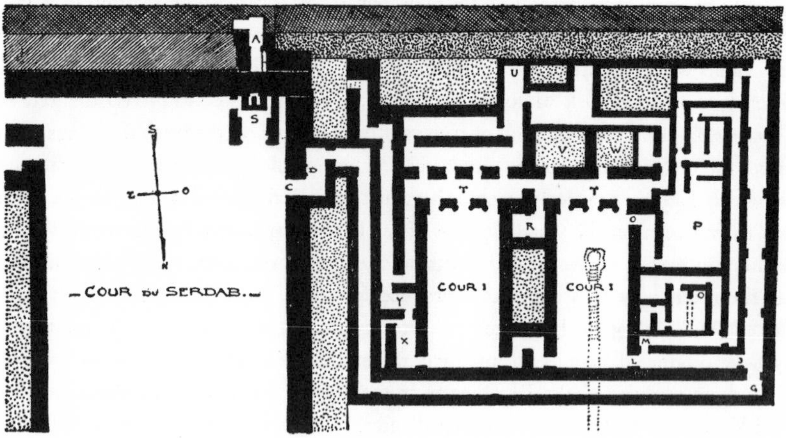

2

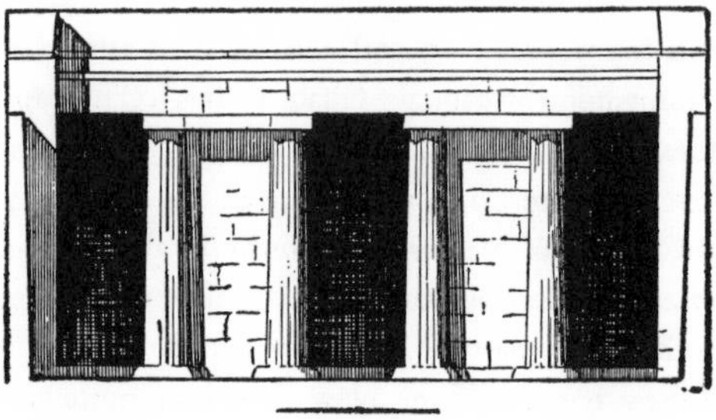

3

4

The entrance to the enclosure has the sculptural representation of two wooden doors swung back against the walls to give a full view of the *serdab* (Plate XIX–4).

On the face of the *serdab,* at the level of the eyes of the statue which stood within, are two holes. These holes, which were the only means of seeing into the otherwise sealed chamber, have been interpreted as openings through which to blow incense into the interior, and as peep-holes to look at the remarkable statue of Zoser with its eyes of rock crystals. Actually, however, these openings presumably were the "*serdab* squint"—the "Eyes of Horus," by means of which the *Ka* statue looked out upon the world of the living. Later *serdabs* have slits through which the statue might see, and on the sarcophagus of Mentuhotep (Plate IX–4) the openings are symbolized by the great, painted eyes of Horus. The exceptional features here at Saqqara are the isolation of the *serdab* and its conformity to the slope of the pyramid.

THE PYRAMID TEMPLE AND THE NORTH AREA. Close to the *serdab* is the entrance to the North Temple (Plate XIX–1), which was the actual mortuary chapel, here developed apparently for the first time into a mortuary temple. The fact that the offering temple is on the north side of the pyramid, while all subsequent mortuary temples are on the east side, may be explained by what has already been suggested, namely, that the early III Dynasty was a period of transition during which Zoser came under the influence of two different systems of funerary custom. In Upper Egypt, where he had built his mastaba at Bet Khallaf, the tomb entrance and offering chapel were on the north side. When he shifted his permanent residence to Memphis and began his tomb at Saqqara, he at first recognized the tradition of the nearby solar cult at Heliopolis with its emphasis upon the location of the mortuary chapel towards the rising sun. Then in the process of rebuilding he reverted to the Upper Egyptian and ante-Heliopolitan tradition of having the chapel on the north side of the tomb.

The entrance to the temple, near the *serdab,* where the statue of Zoser could watch and guard it, opens on a narrow corridor leading, mazelike, around the north periphery of the temple to the west side where its enters a court. Although there is little about this temple which conforms to the subsequent type of Old Kingdom temple, the length of the corridor suggests the long, covered causeway leading up at Gizeh from the entrance portico to the temple proper. The first court of Zoser's temple was possibly for sacrifices. It opens into two successive courts, each with a four-columned portico on the south side towards the pyramid (Plate XIX–2). Here again, because of the architect's reluctance to construct free standing columns supporting a heavy stone architrave, the columns are joined together in pairs by a piece of wall. The result is that these channeled supports of finely cut limestone, with sharp arrises, have a classic simplicity very different from anything else seen in Egyptian architecture.

PLATE XIX

1. Plan of mortuary temple (Lauer, *op. cit.,* Pl. XXII).
2. Façade of mortuary temple (Lauer, *op. cit.,* Pl. XXV).
3. Serdab looking west.
4. Serdab looking south.

The entablature on these porticoes has the blocked-in shape of the pseudo-cavetto cornice seen on the "Osiris temple." The roof of the temple had pieces of stone, painted red and cut to imitate beams of wood.

The inner courts, each with its columnar portico, suggest the dual personality of the Pharaoh as King of Upper and Lower Egypt, and the idea, already advanced, that the colonnade was a royal emblem. The two inner chambers behind the first colonnade may have been the chapels where the two name statutes of the king were worshiped, for at this time the king had only the two titles. In the IV Dynasty when the ruler was honored under his five names, there were an equal number of chapels. Beyond this possible explanation and the fact that the temple has no sanctuary for the royal stelæ, the rooms of Zoser's temple are not yet identified.[27]

The area to the north of the temple was a large terrace, with courts, which was perhaps never finished. Directly on axis with the center of the pyramid was a large rectangular block of stone, 15 m. square, cut out of the natural rock and faced with limestone, which was some kind of a sacrificial altar or offering table, with stairs leading up to it on the south side, and a depression, 8 m. square, cut into the top. At the northwest corner of the temenos were underground magazines, used for the storage of offering foods, and in them the excavators found grain and dried fruits. The entrance to the great pyramid started as a trench in this area, north of the temple, and then became a subterranean passage going under the temple.

THE PYRAMID. The stepped pyramid of Zoser is outstanding in the history of Egyptian architecture as the first pyramidal tomb, as the earliest stone structure of its kind, and finally, as supplying reasonable proof of how the pyramidal idea evolved naturally from the rectangular mastaba. In appearance the pyramid looks like a series of mastabas of diminishing size built one on top of the other. It is 413 feet by 344 feet at the base, rises 200 feet, and each stage is from 29 to 37½ feet high. Man, as we have already seen, never suddenly invents forms, but under the incentive of necessity adapts and recombines old ideas. The incentive, always driving the kings of Egypt to more ambitious sepulchral monuments, was the desire for everlasting protection for their divine bodies. The mastaba, which had taken shape both as an eternal dwelling and as a protection above the tomb, had one weakness; large as it might be made in mass and area, it was easily penetrated from the top. Therefore the next logical step was to build one mastaba on top of another, using the first as a terrace on which to gather the material and continue the work.[28] Zoser and his architect, Imhotep, however, did not arrive at the

[27] Lauer suggests the official use of the rooms (*Bulletin de l'Institut français d'Archéologie orientale,* XXX (1930).

[28] If the badly ruined pyramid of Zawiet-el-Aryan, which was built with oblique "accretion faces" and was probably finished as a step-pyramid, dates from the II Dynasty, as Reisner believes (*The Development of the Egyptian Tomb,* pp. 134-136), then the transition from the mastaba to the pyramid did not occur at Saqqara, and Imhotep cannot be credited with the idea. The Zawiet-el-Aryan Pyramid (Barsanti, *Annales,* II, pp. 92-94; Reisner, *Bulletin of the Museum of Fine Arts,* Boston, No. 54, 1911), seems never to have been occupied, and remains an undated monument. Its "accretion faces" and certain features of its construction recall Zoser's tomb, indicating that it was built at a later date. It is of course possible, as Reisner claims, that the step form of mastaba, built in oblique layers, went back to the I Dynasty when the tombs of Kings Zer and Zet at Abydos were perhaps covered with brick superstructures in layers. At present this possibility is too conjectural and contrary to the evidence of Petrie's excavation of the Abydos tombs to endanger Imhotep's claim to the idea. Lauer (*La Pyramide à Degrés,* I, p. 8) lists four probable step-pyramids, which he dates in the III Dynasty, but after Zoser.

pyramidal form by such simple reasoning. The idea was apparently forced upon them by successive enlargements of the original mastaba.[29] The steps in this development are buried under the great mountain of stone, but cuttings on the side prove that there were at least three enlargements of the original mastaba and then two pyramid structures, the last being an enlargement and casing for the first stepped pyramid (Plate xx). So much is certain, which is fortunate, for the rest of the evidence raises more problems than it answers.

On the east side underneath the two casings of the step pyramid the excavators have discovered by cuttings an addition to the original, central mastaba, which they call mastaba 3 (Plate xx–2). Vertical shafts descend from the top of this mastaba to a series of galleries. When mastaba 3 was finished these vertical wells were filled up and double stelæ were placed in front of the principal funeral wells —that is before 4 and 5 and perhaps in front of 2 and 3. Also beneath the pavement of the court in front of these stelæ the excavators uncovered a deep cutting which at one time formed the entrance to a winding passage leading down for 32 m. to the subterranean galleries beneath the mastaba.

The rock-cut galleries extending under mastaba 3 were found to contain pieces of alabaster sarcophagi, vases, and some blue tiles, also an inscription referring to Imhotep as the "first after the King of Upper and Lower Egypt." Galleries F and G were lined with a revetment of planks 2 to 3 cm. thick and 15 to 30 cm. wide, skilfully joined together to line the walls and ceiling. In chamber C were found the pieces of a wooden coffin marvelously constructed of six thicknesses of wood, each veneer only 4 mm. thick, and the outer surface covered with gold leaf.[30] These finds at least supply very definite proof of the early use of wood and the remarkable skill of the III Dynasty woodworkers.

But what was the purpose of these galleries and why were the grave stelæ on the face of mastaba 3 completely obliterated by the casings of the step-pyramid? There are the possibilities that mastaba 3 and the galleries beneath it formed the burial place of Zoser's wife and two daughters, or that they were prepared for the canopic jars, in which case it would be the first instance of the later Egyptian custom of preserving the entrails. The most reasonable explanation which, however, does not explain all the exceptional features, is that Zoser, after building his original tomb as mastaba 1, and before he and his architect had any idea of a stepped pyramid, came under the influence of the solar cult at nearby Heliopolis, and so extended his mastaba to the east with shafts, stelæ, entrance, and offering tables facing towards the rising sun. Later he abandoned this tradition and reverted to the custom in Upper Egypt of having the offering shrine above the entrance to the tomb on the north side. During this period of change the various enlargements of the original mastaba by rectangular additions, which were presumably not of the same height as the central mastaba, furnished the suggestion for the vertical extension by means of set backs and accretion faces. Hence in the end a step-pyramid was constructed which was once more enlarged and strengthened by a new casing, the final casing covering the original *serdab* on the north side and so necessitating the building of a new one.

[29] Lauer, *op. cit.*, p. 12, says there were six steps: first a square mastaba at the center (M^1), then a peripteral addition on all sides of the square (M^2), an addition of the east side (M^3), the first stepped pyramid of four steps (P_1), an enlargement of the pyramid to the north enclosing the original temple, making pyramid six stages high and locating the burial chamber in the center, and finally an enlargement of pyramid making seven steps (P_2).

[30] Lauer, *Annales*, XXXIII, p. 164.

PLATE XX: STEPPED PYRAMID AT SAQQARA

1

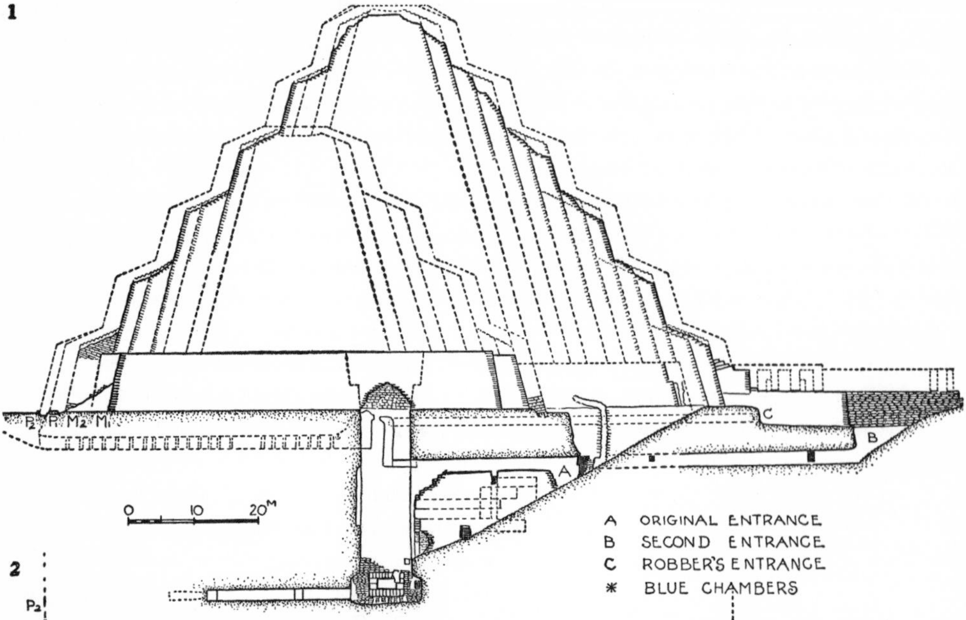

2

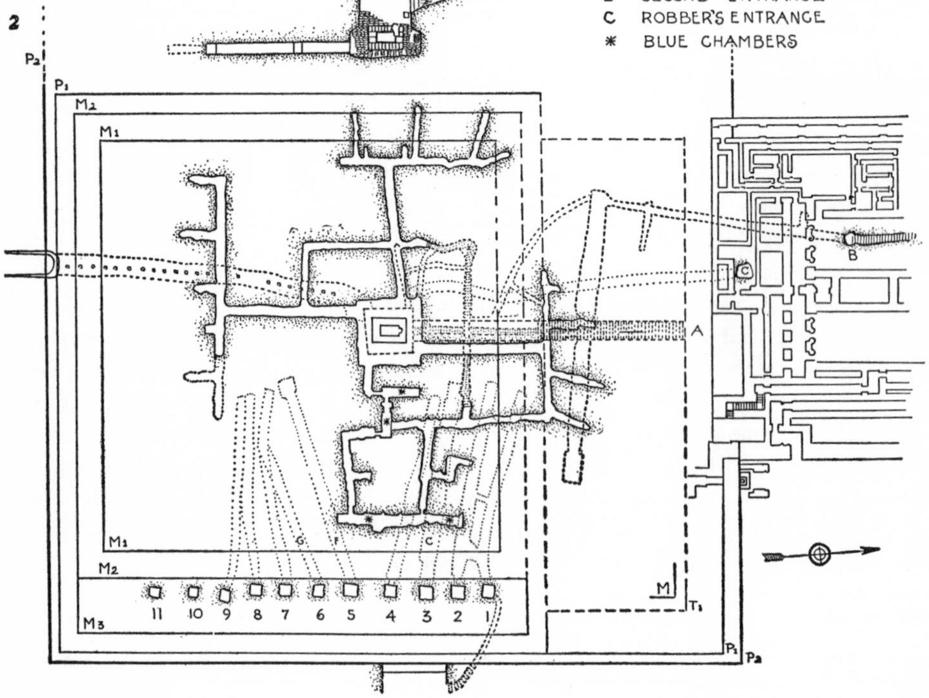

The pyramid, when built, was entered, as we saw, by a hidden and subterranean passage on the north side. Down its center is a shaft 25 m. deep and 8 m. wide, at the bottom of which is a granite sarcophagus chamber entered from the ceiling by a circular opening into which a stone stopper was lowered in order to close the entrance.[31] To the southeast of this central chamber are passages opening into corridors off from which are rooms lined with alabaster and inlaid with the same blue imitations of rush matting as were found in the south wall tomb. The pyramid, like all subsequent efforts to attain indestructibility, was successfully entered and pilfered during ancient times. In fact, Saïtic archæologists twenty-five hundred years ago left red lines on the walls where they squared up the designs preparatory to copying them. The futility of these elaborate preparations to attain a material immortality was never admitted by the Egyptians, although succeeding generations unscrupulously and skilfully succeeded in penetrating and robbing the greatest tombs of their predecessors. Each king went on building larger or more intricate tombs in the vain belief that his efforts would prove successful, but their very size and the riches hidden in them made such tombs an irresistible temptation. Therefore throughout Egyptian history the offensive ingenuity of tomb robbers kept pace with the defensive skill of royal builders.

THE MASONRY. The architectural forms at Saqqara complete the picture of the beginnings of Egyptian architecture, although much about them still seems vague and problematic. Even the forms which have hitherto been unknown in Egyptian architecture fit into a natural, although necessarily theoretical development of building tradition in the Egyptian environment. The building methods, including a type of masonry hitherto never found in Egypt, have made it necessary to revise the old views on the birth of masonry in Nilotic architecture.

At first sight this new masonry, with its simple and delicate surface and its carefully sculptural forms unconfused by hieroglyphic inscriptions, recalls Greek architecture, and therefore appears to be of superior quality to the masonry of the pyramids and temples which came later. To quote from the best and most recent study of Egyptian masonry, "the idea seems to be gaining ground that this form of masonry became, for some mysterious reason, a lost art. This is entirely erroneous. The Zoser masonry, generally speaking, is of much poorer quality than that of good mastabas and pyramid masonry of the IV and V Dynasties, and the structures, owing to the smallness of the blocks used, were not calculated to last any great time. . . . The more the III Dynasty small-block masonry is studied, the more clear it becomes that the megalithic masonry which followed is merely a development of it." [32]

[31] Mastaba M1 followed the tradition of Southern Egypt and had an open passage with stairs, descending from north to south, as at Bet Khallaf. At a depth of 5 m. the passage ceased to be open but was tunneled. Also as at Bet Khallaf there was a vertical shaft down to the burial chamber. All of this shaft, except a chamber directly above the sarcophagus room, and most of the descending passage, except a narrow corridor for the descent of the mummy, were blocked up after the digging was finished.

[32] S. Clarke and R. Engelbach, *Ancient Egyptian Masonry* (1930), p. 8.

PLATE XX

1. Section of Pyramid (Lauer, *op. cit.*, Plate XIX).
2. Plan of Pyramid (Lauer, *op. cit.*, Plates XV, XVI).

"The masonry of Zoser is inferior to the better examples of later times in that the fineness of the joints between adjacent blocks, which appears so good when viewed from the front, only extends inwards for at most a couple of inches; afterwards the joints become wider and irregular and are filled in with thick white gypsum mortar.... In the Zoser masonry, fineness of jointing at the face of the walls was obtained at the expense of solidity." [33] In fact, the methods of stone-cutting seen at Saqqara prove what the architectural forms have indicated, namely, that stone was here used for the first time on any monumental scale, as a sculptural means of imitating traditional forms which already existed in other materials. Because of the inherently sculptural character of this and all their subsequent stone-work, the Egyptians never learned the art of internal bonding and never saw the full advantage of using truly rectangular blocks of stone.

Before laying the blocks only the bedding face was cut smooth and flat; then the vertical joints were cut to fit the adjoining stones by a process of trial and error, for the joints are not always vertical, and the top face of the course was finished without preserving continuous horizontal lines of masonry. Finally, the face of the stone-work was not smoothed off until after the wall was otherwise finished. This sculptural treatment of stone started and then persisted because the Egyptian masons were always confronted with the problem of reproducing standard forms rather than developing a practical and sound method of building in cut stone. Before Imhotep and his apparently great innovations at Saqqara, there need not have been a long period of experimentation of which we are ignorant. Stone-cutting started in the I Dynasty with simple pavements such as were found in the tomb of King Den, but Clarke and Engelbach, who have made a thorough study of Egyptian building methods "believe that the art of laying finely dressed blocks may well have developed during Zoser's reign, the forms being translated from brick and vegetable forms."

The stone masonry at Saqqara was painted in imitation of wood and bundled reed construction. Floors were painted a red ochre; the exterior walls of the enceinte show traces of red, and red was found on the bottom course of the wall about the Great Court, in the Entrance Hall of the Colonnades, on the walls of the Heb-Sed court, on Temple T, and on many of the columns.[34] Inasmuch as red was the Egyptian color to signify wood, and a sign for a bundled reed shaft, dating from the III or IV Dynasties, has its base painted black and the rest red, save for a white line separating the two parts, there is reason to think that the columns at Saqqara were painted red.[35]

After Zoser there was one hundred years of the III Dynasty during which five kings reigned. Little or nothing is known of these rulers and their architecture until we come to Huni and Sneferu, at the end of the III Dynasty. Their pyramids, as the next examples of known masonry, are more closely related to the architectural efforts of the IV Dynasty than to the transitional architecture of the period of Zoser.

[33] Clarke and Engelbach, *op. cit.*, p. 97.
[34] Lauer, *op. cit.*, I, p. 227 *seq.*
[35] Lauer, *op. cit.*, I, p. 159; Petrie, *Medum*, Pl. XIII.

5. *DYNASTIC TOMBS*

The gods who were aforetime, Who rest in their pyramids,...
Those who built their tomb-temples, Their place is no more...
Their walls are dismantled, Their places are no more
As if they had never been.

"SONG OF THE HARPER," XI DYNASTY

THE MASTABA

THE IV DYNASTY stands forth from the obscurity of early Egyptian history as a period of amazing vigor. Its purposeful energy, directed by a short succession of capable rulers, brought Egyptian culture and art to a level which in many respects was never again equaled in the Nile valley and thereby fixed the mold in which the subsequent civilization was to take shape. Much of the creative force and organized resources were concentrated upon art as a preparation for the after life. The rectangular mastaba by this time was the standard type of tomb, although the kings had developed in the pyramid a more ambitious and symbolic form of sepulcher. Instead of being made of sun-dried brick, the mastaba was frequently constructed of limestone and its walls were decorated with finely carved and painted reliefs.

OLD KINGDOM. The typical stone mastaba built in orderly streets about the royal pyramids at Gizeh (Plate XXI) was a massive rectangular structure of large blocks of limestone. At times these mastabas were of solid masonry with only a single vertical shaft descending through them to the burial chamber deep underground, but more commonly they adhered to the method of construction first seen at Saqqara, having a cut-stone casing and a rubble fill. Attached to the east face of the solid superstructure was a small brick chapel with a vestibule, offering room and storerooms. These cult-houses had windows, tunnel-vaulted roofs in some cases, and in one instance a domical vault,[1] while the doorways were frequently round headed.[2]

After the IV Dynasty the tendency, begun in the brick tombs at the end of the III Dynasty, to move the chapel, and with it the *serdab,* into the solid core of the mastaba had resulted in opening up the interiors with a series of rooms and corridors. In spite of the elaborate interior arrangements of rooms, the essential features were the shaft with its tomb chamber underground, a chapel for the

[1] Uncovered by H. Junker (F. von Oppeln-Bronikowski, *Archäologische Entdeckungen,* 1931, Abb. 13).

[2] H. Junker ("Giza I," *Denkschriften Ak. d. Wissenschaften in Wien,* 69, 1929) thinks there was some association of ideas between the round top of the grave tumulus, and the round headed doorways of the Gizeh chapels. In view of the "house-stele" with a curved roof found at Saqqara (Plate XXIII-4) and the fact that the I Dynasty royal stelæ were house emblems, it seems more likely that the stele and the doorway both derived their round top from the hoop roof of the primitive shelter. The same idea is implied by Capart who writes, "The simple stele is probably the shrine which contained the statue" (J. Capart, *Egyptian Art,* p. 83.)

PLATE XXI: TOMBS

1

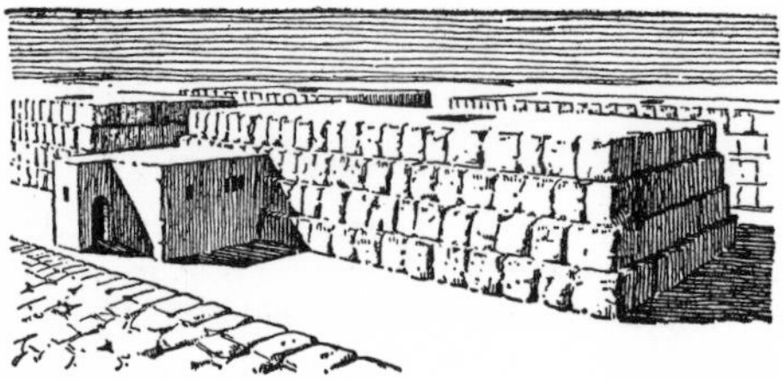

2

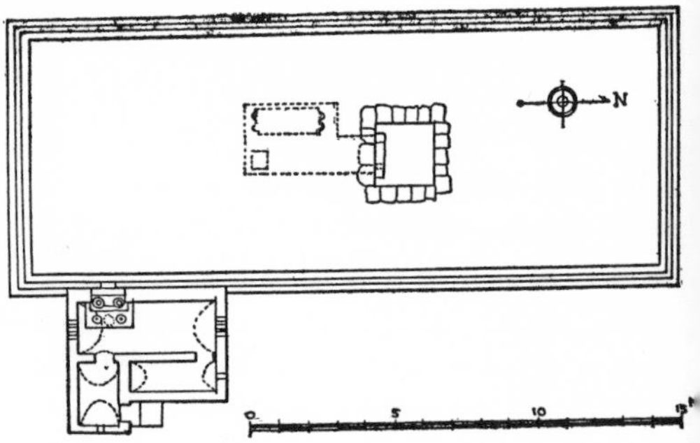
N
0
5
10
15

3

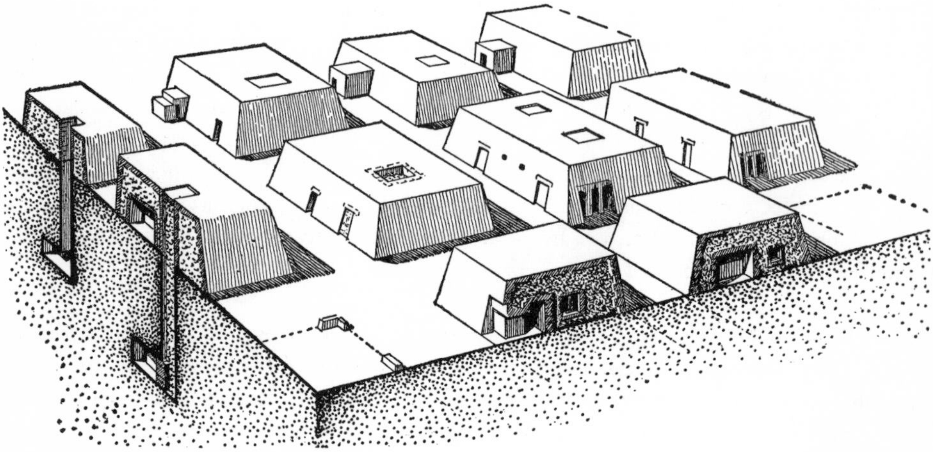

4

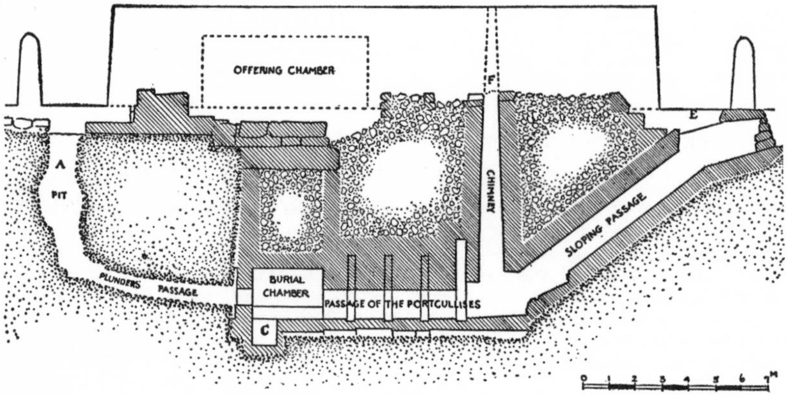
OFFERING CHAMBER
F
E
A
PIT
CHIMNEY
SLOPING PASSAGE
PLUNDERERS PASSAGE
BURIAL CHAMBER
PASSAGE OF THE PORTCULLISES
C
0 1 2 3 4 5 6 7M

5

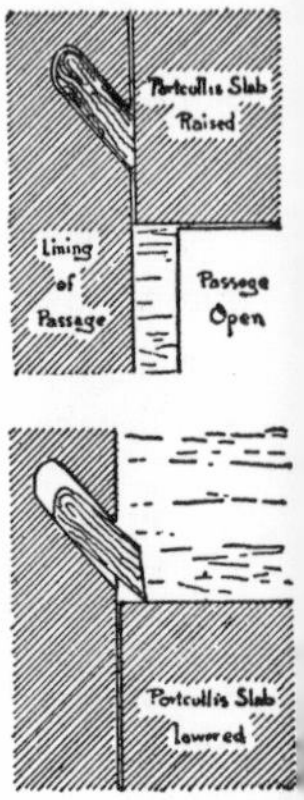
Portcullis Slab Raised
Lining of Passage
Passage Open
Portcullis Slab lowered

"false door" stelæ and offering table, and the *serdab* chamber. The *serdab,* which is a word taken from the Arabic for "cellar," was an inaccessible and sometimes secret chamber in which stood the statue, or embodiment, of the *Ka.* Usually there were small apertures opening from the *serdab* into the chapel through which the dead could look ou and enjoy the incense, prayers, and offerings of the living. By the V Dynasty, in addition to these essentials, the interior chambers of the mastaba were enlarged and multiplied as in a house, until there were corridors, chapels, halls, pantries, storerooms, and, before the end of the Old Kingdom, bedrooms and lavatories. The growth of the mastaba, therefore, was only a more ambitious and literal realization of the unaltered primitive instinct which considered the grave as the dwelling of the dead.

The finest mastabas of the V Dynasty are at Saqqara. Two of these are exceptional, not so much in size and in the complicated arrangement of their rooms as in the richness and quality of their painted reliefs. The mastaba of Ptahhotep [3] is a double one which this distinguished dignitary shared with his son, Akhethotep (Plate XXII–1). The entrance is on the north side and from it a corridor leads to a pillared hall, off which is the T-shaped chapel of Akhethotep and the long chapel of Ptahhotep with its two "false doors" (Plate XXII–3). The ceiling in this chapel, although made of slabs of stone, is painted red in imitation of the palm trunks which were the traditional method of roofing. All the interior walls are covered with remarkable reliefs, at once fascinating works of art and detailed representation of life in the Old Kingdom. Every important aspect of Ptahhotep's daily life is faithfully depicted: painted scenes show him dressing for the day, his diversions, his servants herding cattle through a crocodile-infested marsh, hunting and fishing, and all his poultry numbered to the last one, so that we know, for example, that he had 111,200 pigeon and 121,022 widgeon. Ni-ankh-Ptah, his "beloved and trusty" chief sculptor, was justly proud of his work, but we can well wonder why all this exquisite craftsmanship was expended upon a dark and relatively unvisited interior.

It does not lessen Ni-ankh-Ptah's achievement, or our own pleasure in the presence of these reliefs, to realize that the Egyptian, in such instances, did not think of art as something intended to give enjoyment, but instead expected from it a very practical return. Undoubtedly these scenes of the life and possessions of Ptahhotep were carved with remarkable precision and care because Ptahhotep fully believed in the magical efficacy of images. They represented to him the vital necessities of continued existence without which he would endure hunger and thirst. In a sense the reliefs were a substitute for the grain and wine stored in the earlier tombs, and even for the prehistoric custom of slaughtering

[3] N. de G. Davies, *The Mastaba of Ptahhetep and Akhethetep* (1900).

PLATE XXI

1. IV Dyn. Mastaba, Gizeh (H. Junker, "Giza I," *Denkschriften Ak. d. Wissenschaften in Wien,* 69, 1929, Abb. 6).
2. Plan of same (Junker, *op. cit.,* Abb. 3).
3. Mastabas, from model in Metropolitan Museum of Art, New York.
4. Section of mastaba of Senwosret-ankh, Lisht (A. Lansing, *Bulletin of the Metropolitan Museum of Art,* 1933, Sect. II, pp. 9-28, Fig. 19).
5. Portcullis locking device, mastaba of Senwosret-ankh, Lisht (*op. cit.,* Fig. 25).

PLATE XXII: TOMBS

1

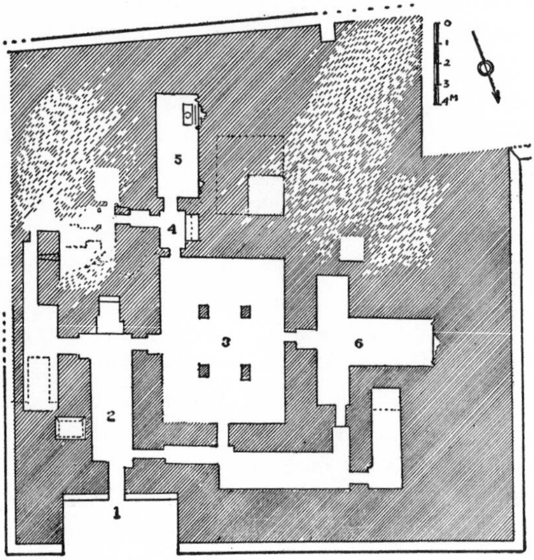

2

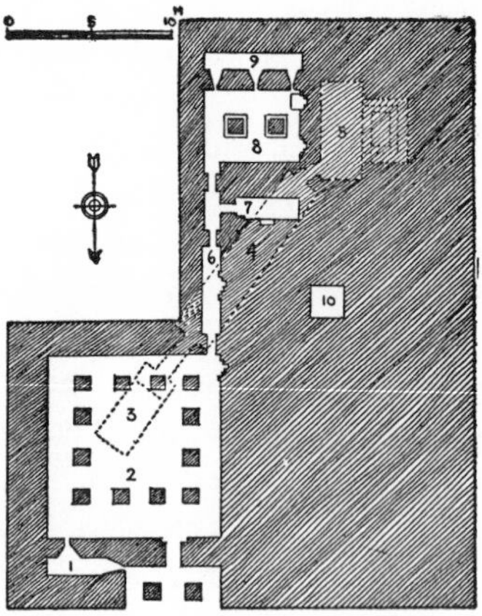

3

a household at the death of its master. Above all "they are the most conclusive evidence of a nation's passion for eternal endurance—a passion which has no parallel in the religious history of any other race on earth."

Finer even than Ptahhotep's is the mastaba of Ti,[4] another great noble of the V Dynasty who built his tomb at Saqqara. The plan of this mastaba with its two *serdabs* is illustrated and described on Plate XII. These rich lords of the Old Kingdom not only lavished their wealth upon their final resting place, but they endowed the future service at their tombs. Prince Nekure of the III Dynasty set aside the revenue of twelve cities for his sepulchral needs and attendance. How long after his death he continued to enjoy this provision is another question.

Any doubt as to the mastaba being a house-form in the Egyptian's mind is dispelled by the recently discovered brick tombs of the VI Dynasty at Saqqara, belonging to the period of the energetic Pepi II.[5] Many of these tombs are small rectangular structures of sun-dried brick, with two doorways on the long side, which imitate the hoop-roof type of dwelling (Plate XXIII–3). The same type of house is also reproduced in the stone "house-stelæ" (Plate XXIII–4) which were also found at the same site. Other tombs have more complicated arrangements of rooms with elliptical brick vaults. These vaults both reproduce the traditional curved roof and protect the chambers beneath them; they are "laminated" with their courses laid at an angle in order to do away with the necessity of centering (Plate XXIII–5). The existence of these vaults at Saqqara lessens the possibility that laminated vaulting, used frequently by the Egyptians in the New Kingdom, was introduced from Mesopotamia. Instead there is constantly increasing evidence to show that the Egyptians, perhaps as early as the Sumerians, were conversant with the structural possibilities of arch forms; in the necropolis of Pepi II there has been discovered a relieving arch which was of cut stone with roughly fitted voussoirs (Plate XXIII–6).

MIDDLE KINGDOM. The mastaba form of tomb survived the collapse of the Old Kingdom and the political and social chaos that followed, and during the Middle Kingdom, which was animated by a desire to reëstablish all the traditions of the past, it continued to remain a standard type. An excellent example of a Middle Kingdom mastaba is the XII Dynasty tomb of Senwosret-ankh, at Lisht

[4] G. Steindorff, *Das Grab des Ti* (1913).
[5] G. Jéquier, *Tombeaux de Particuliers Contemporains de Pepi II* (1929).

PLATE XXII

1. Plan of mastaba of Ptahotep, Saqqara:
   1) North vestibule, 2) corridor, 3) hall of Ptahotep, 4) ante-room, 5) chapel of Ptahotep with two "false doors," 6) chapel of Akhethotep (N. de G. Davies, *The Mastaba of Ptahhetep and Akhethetep,* Pl. 1).
2. Plan of mastaba of Ti, Saqqara:
   1) Serdab, 2) pillared hall, 3) shaft, 4) corridor, 5) sarcophagus chamber, 6) corridor, 7) larder, 8) chapel, 9) serdab, (G. Steindorff, *Das Grab des Ti,* 1913, Blatt. 1).
3. "False-door" stelæ, mastaba of Ptahotep, Saqqara (Perrot et Chipiez, *op. cit.,* Fig. 115).

PLATE XXIII: TOMBS

1

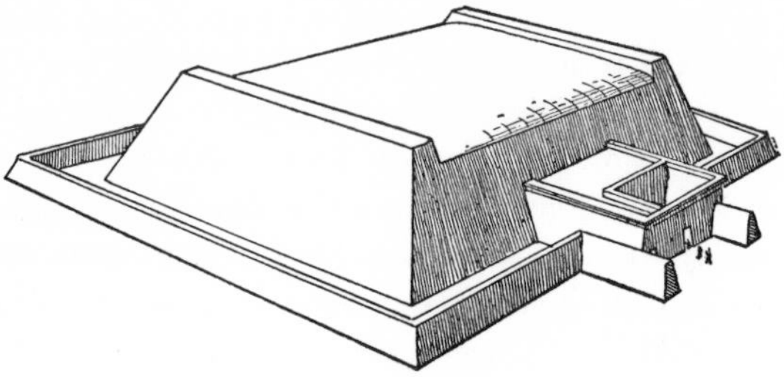

2

3

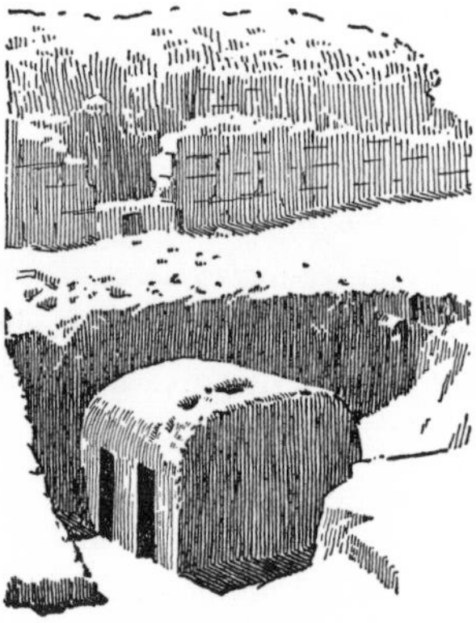

4

5

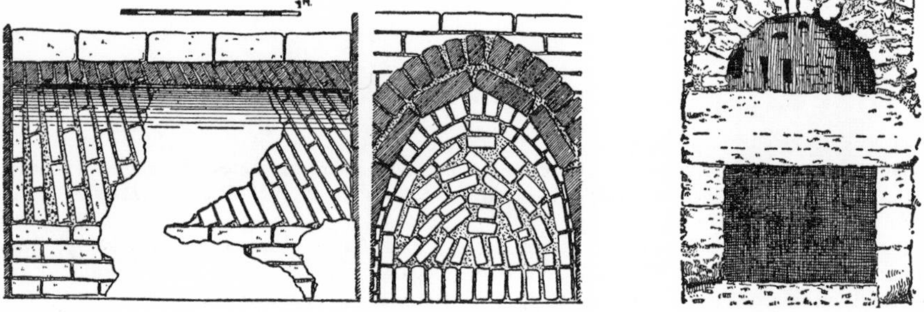

(Plate XXI-4). Senwosret-ankh, in addition to being a "Priest of Ptah at Memphis" was also the "Royal Sculptor and Builder" for his master, Senwosret I. His mastaba, made with a fine limestone casing, was decorated after the custom of the Early Dynastic period, with the schematic recesses of the "false-door" niches, and the wall about the enclosure was carefully cut in limestone to imitate the rounded top of primitive mud walls. Evidently Senwosret-ankh was a leader in the archæological revivals of his age, for his tomb shows how carefully he studied the earlier forms. The actual mastaba and the large mortuary chapel in front of it are too ruined to be considered, but the careful provisions assuring protection for his body, which Senwosret-ankh undoubtedly planned himself, are interesting as an ingenious improvement upon Old Kingdom structural methods.

The original passage down which his sarcophagus was lowered was on the traditional north side of the tomb and carefully concealed. The vertical shaft, which in Old Kingdom mastabas descended from the top of the tomb to the deep burial chamber, he put to a new use. This shaft he made like a chimney, small at the top and large at the bottom, filled it with loose stone and gravel, and had it open into the horizontal passage leading from the entrance to the tomb chamber. Its purpose, which proved effective with the excavators, was to discourage plunderers seeking to clear the passage by pouring an unending stream of stone and sand upon them. In addition, he built in this subterranean passage four ingenious portcullises, copied after similar devices in the great pyramids of the Old Kingdom, where the portcullis idea, first attempted in the III Dynasty, had been nicely perfected. Improving on the Old Kingdom device he introduced a wooden plug which slid down and locked the stones in place after the passage had been closed. His actual tomb chamber he had painted on three sides with the old "palace-façade" treatment, representing mattings hung in a framework of wood, such as was seen on the exterior of the tomb of Hesy in the III Dynasty (Plate VIII-5).

THE PYRAMID

OLD KINGDOM. The mastaba, from the IV Dynasty on until it went completely out of use at the end of the Middle Kingdom, ceased to be a form of royal burial, and its place was taken by the pyramid. There was no prototype for the pyramidal tomb before the III Dynasty and it was not in the conservative nature of man to invent it. Therefore its shape had to evolve from the

---

PLATE XXIII

1. Tomb of King Shepseshaf, South Saqqara (G. Jéquier, *Le Mastaba Faraoun,* 1928, Fig. 2).
2. Nubian house, Schellal (H. Ricke, *Der Grundriss des Amarna-Wohnhauses,* 1932, Abb. 11).
3. Brick tomb, VI Dyn. South Saqqara (G. Jéquier, *Tombeaux de particuliers contemporains de Pepi II,* 1929, Pl. VI bis).
4. "House-stele," tomb of Khoubaoui at South Saqqara (G. Jéquier, *La Pyramide d'Oudjebten,* 1928, Fig. 36).
5. Laminated vault, tomb of VI Dyn. at South Saqqara (Jéquier, *Le Mastaba Faraoun,* Fig. 19).
6. Stone relieving arch, tomb of Hebsed-Neferkara, Saqqara (Jéquier, *Annales du Service,* XXXIII, p. 144, Pl. II).

PLATE XXIV: PYRAMIDS

1

2

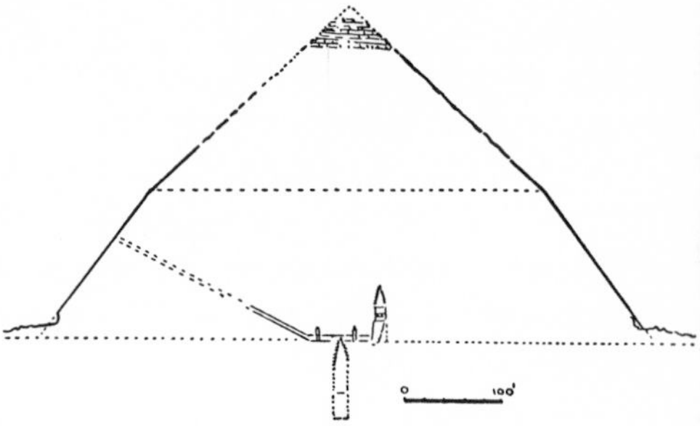

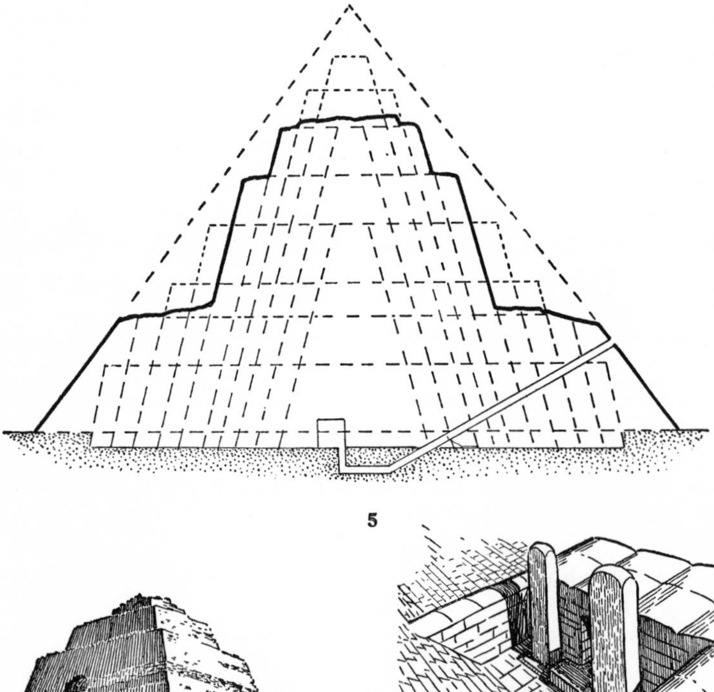

4

5

customary mastaba as the result of some special incentive and because of a certain association of ideas. The royal incentive was, of course, the desire for greater security, but this alone might not have made the mastaba into more than a stepped mastaba. After the experiment of King Zoser and his architect and before the end of the III Dynasty, the transitional form between this stepped mastaba and the true pyramid was built.

At Dashur (Plate XXIV–1, 2), which is within sight of Saqqara, stands the blunt or False Pyramid.[6] It is 188.5 m. square at the base and 99.04 m. high; its casing of cut limestone has a double slope, indicating that its builder, when he began to smooth off the surface of the stepped core by means of a casting, either had not planned the set-backs with the idea of a continuous and pyramidal slope, or was imitating the pyramidal *ben-ben* of Re-Atum at Heliopolis. Once the False Pyramid was finished by its builder, who was perhaps Huni, one of the last kings of the III Dynasty and the father of Sneferu, its divergence from a true pyramid became evident. Even then it undoubtedly required an ideographic transference of ideas to make the pyramid the established type of royal tomb.

When the early kings ceased to live in Upper Egypt, and in the III Dynasty established their permanent residence at Memphis, they came more and more under the influence of nearby Heliopolis, with its old prestige and its powerful cult of the Sun-god. The fetish of Re was the pyramidal stone, known as the *ben-ben*. By the IV Dynasty the Pharaohs were sun-worshipers and considered themselves to be the sons of Re and hence his incarnation on earth. Therefore they saw the obvious resemblance between the pyramidal tomb and the sun-symbol at Heliopolis: as the spirit and power of Re was in the pyramidal *ben-ben*, so would their divine spirit and body lie within the pyramidal tomb.[7]

This association was realized sometime in the III Dynasty, after Zoser, for it was at the end of the Dynasty that the offering temple was shifted, under solar influence, from the north to the east side of the pyramid. At this time the great Sneferu, who was probably the father of Khufu, built himself two pyramids in his dual personality as King of Upper and Lower Egypt. The

[6] Vyse and Perring, *The Pyramids of Gizeh*, III, 65; Lepsius, *Textband*, p. 208; Mariette, *Mastabas*, p. 575; Jéquier, *Annales*, XXV (1925), p. 71; Reisner, *op. cit.*, p. 197.

[7] The cap stone of a pyramid always had on it the name of the pyramid and two eyes, indicating the symbolic nature of the pyramid. At Lisht, the "Eternal dwelling" of Senwosret I, according to the foundation tablets, was called "Senwosret-surveying-the-two-lands" (A. Lansing, *The Bulletin of the Metropolitan Museum of Art*, April, 1933, p. 14). For the personification of pyramids see Carl Kilke, "Zur Personifikation von Pyramid," *Zeitschrift für Aegyptische Sprache*, LXX (1934), pp. 56-83.

PLATE XXIV

1. Blunt pyramid, Dashur.
2. Section of same (Vyse and Perring, *The Pyramids of Gizeh*, III, Pl. XV).
3. Section of pyramid at Meydum (A. Rowe, *The University of Pennsylvania, Museum Journal*, XXII, No. 1).
4. View of pyramid at Meydum.
5. Mortuary chapel, pyramid at Meydum (T. Dombart, "Der Zweitürmige Temple-pylon," *Egyptian Religion*, I, 1933, p. 90, Fig. 4).

PLATE XXV: PYRAMIDS

1

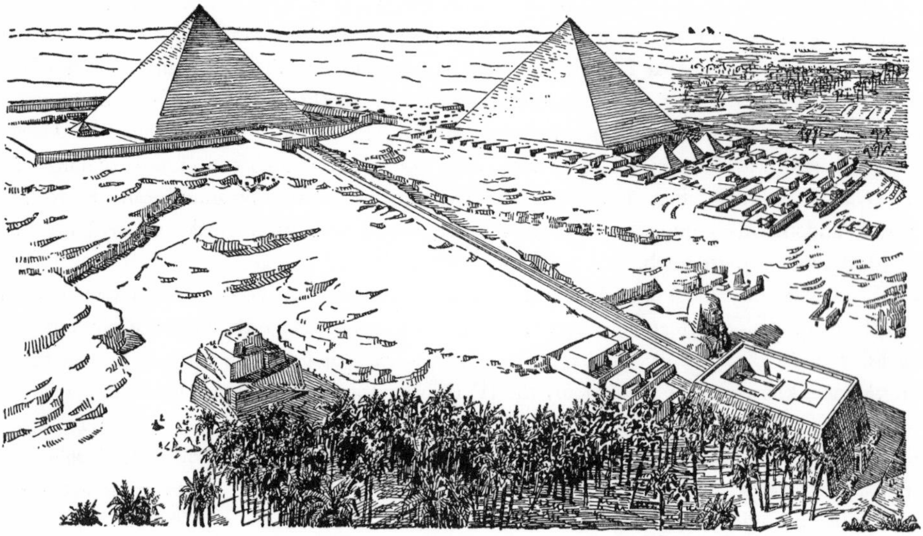

2

3

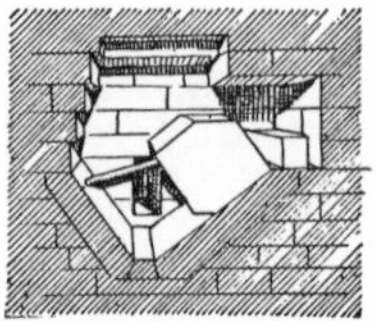

4

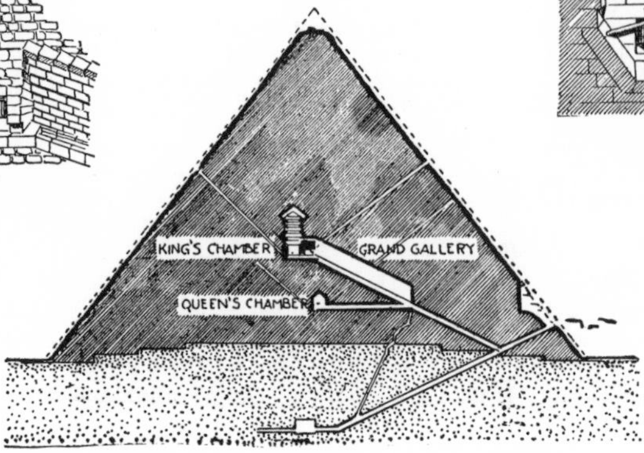

first he erected at Meydum,[8] which he apparently never used (Plate xxiv–3, 4); he began it as a stepped pyramid with "accretion faces," as is indicated by the mason's marks showing a stepped pyramid, and by the fact that the receding faces are finished in dressed stone. The work may have been continued throughout his reign by means of building successive casings and recessed stages. When this process had been repeated seven times he had what was a gigantic seven-stepped pyramid, for even in its present ruined condition its three remaining stages rise to a height of 214 feet. Before the end of his life, however, Sneferu had completed his tomb at Dashur as a true pyramid, and at Meydum had started to encase its stepped core of "accretion faces" with a smooth covering. The lower stage of this casing is still preserved, but there is no evidence to show that it was ever carried up to complete the whole pyramid.

The entrance at Meydum is a sloping passage, starting high up on the north side, which descends underground for a distance, then continues horizontally, and finally rises as a perpendicular shaft, giving access to the sarcophagus chamber, which is half below ground and half in the stone of the first mastaba-terrace. Over the burial chamber is a stone vault made by corbeling, which is the earliest stone vault known to have been used in Egyptian architecture, although this method of roofing was used in brick for sepulchral protection as early as the II and III Dynasties. A small chapel (Plate xxiv–5) on the east side is built onto the side of the pyramid in the same manner that offering chapels were added onto the III Dynasty mastabas at Bet Khallaf and the IV Dynasty ones at Gizeh. This little building with the two royal stelæ rising above the enclosing walls will be discussed more fully in the chapter on the temple. At Meydum there are indications of the great causeway leading up to the pyramid from the river, and around the tomb are grouped, like a city with streets, the mastabas of Sneferu's family and courtiers.

For some unknown reason the pyramid at Meydum was experimental, and if it took twenty years of Sneferu's reign of twenty-six years, as Borchardt estimated,[9] the king must have begun and perhaps finished his still larger pyramid at Dashur, before he started to encase the Meydum tomb as a true pyramid. His larger pyramid at Dashur ranks in size with the famous group at Gizeh, for it is still 709 feet wide at the base and 325 feet high. The three pyramids at Dashur and Meydum show only one technical advance over the pyramid of Zoser; this is their use of the corbel vault in stone masonry as a roofing construction for the burial chambers. The crude portcullis

[8] Petrie, *Medum;* Wainwright, *Medum and Memphis;* Allan Rowe, "Excavations at Meydum," *Pennsylvania Univ., Museum Journal,* XXII (1931); Reisner, *op. cit.,* p. 195; L. Borchardt, *Die Entstehung der Pyramide* (1928).

[9] L. Borchardt, *Die Enstehung der Pyramide* (1928).

PLATE XXV

1. Pyramids of Khufu (right) and Khafra, Gizeh (U. Hölscher, *Das Grabdenkmal des Königs Chephren,* 1912, Pl. 1).
2. Section of king's chamber, pyramid of Khufu (Perrot et Chipiez, *op. cit.,* Fig. 132).
3. Method of closing passage in south pyramid at Dashur (Perrot et Chipiez, Fig. 150).
4. Section of pyramid of Khufu (v. Bissing, *Ægyptische Kunstgeschichte,* Pl. xxiv).

method of closing the burial chamber after occupation, which was seen in the mastabas of the III Dynasty, is at Dashur worked out by accurate stonecutting as a very elaborate method of sealing up the chamber (Plate xxv–3). Once the sarcophagus and its accompanying wealth were in place, the workmen burned out the wooden prop and the gigantic stone slid down into position in front of the opening.

After Sneferu came the famous rulers of the IV Dynasty whose tombs at Gizeh (Plate xxv–1) still rank as one of the wonders of the world. The much illustrated and visited group consists of the three great pyramids of Khufu, Khafra, and Menkaura, with a cluster of much smaller pyramids and streets of mastabas making a large city of the dead under the supervision of the "Mayor of the Pyramids." Khufu (Cheops), who was the most powerful monarch of the Old Kingdom, began his pyramid with no modest intention of enlarging it as his reign progressed. Not only did he have the idea of a true pyramid from the start, but also he planned it to be what it has remained, the largest constructed mass of stone ever erected by man. Originally it measured 767 feet at the base and rose 479 feet. The core is built of Moqattam limestone, the casing and passages of finer limestone from Tura and Ma'sara, and the king's chamber cut from great blocks of hard granite. It is estimated that it contains 2,300,000 blocks of stone, totaling 3,277,000 cubic yards, the stones themselves averaging two and a half tons, while a few weighed as much as thirty tons. It helps a little in appreciating its size to know that the cathedrals of Florence, Milan, and St. Peter's, as well as Westminster Abbey and St. Paul's could all be grouped comfortably within the area of its base.

The section (Plate xxv–4) shows the vertical distribution of chambers, connected by long, sloping passages, which were intended to be concealed permanently in this stone mountain. The construction of the pyramid, however it is explained, was a remarkable feat: over the long corridors are corbeled vaults (Plate xxv–2), and above the king's chamber is an ingenious effort to lighten the pressure and divert the weight by means of a triangular stone arch and superimposed slabs of stone (Plate xxv–2). From this chamber two holes were pierced through the whole structure at an oblique angle, not for ventilation, as is sometimes suggested, but as exits for the spirit of the dead. In addition to the pyramid there was a large mortuary temple on the east side, the long causeway, used at first for the transportation of materials from the river and kept as a permanent approach across the inundated land during the flood season, and streets of mastabas, while nearby was a city for the priests, workmen, and storehouses which were all needed to perpetuate the service of the dead. The causeway leading down from the mortuary temple to the edge of the valley terminated in what has been called the "Valley temple" or landing pavilion. Its possible origin and use will be discussed in relation to the mortuary temple.[10]

The remarkable accuracy of nearly all the stonecutting in this pyramid furnishes astounding evidence of the technical skill of Old Kingdom stone masons. When laying out the plan of the pyramid, the workmen cleared the desert down to the solid rock, and on this floor laid a pavement with a core of natural rock rising up in the middle. Even though this outcropping of rock pre-

[10] Page 123.

vented any direct measurements, the masons were able to square the base so truly that between the north and south sides there is an error of only 7.9 inches in 9073 inches and between the east and west sides, an error of 0.3 inches in 9070.5 inches.[11] In the construction, stones weighing tons were set with joints a ten-thousandth of an inch, involving edges and surfaces, according to Petrie, "equal to opticians' work." Unfortunately the casing, which was originally highly polished and reflected, like the sun-symbol that it was, the rays of Re, has all been quarried away to be used for the houses and mosques of Cairo.

The measurements of the Great Pyramid have inspired more ingenious and purely imaginative speculation than any other monument in the history of the world. Many people, beginning with Herodotus, have been unable to believe that so much labor and such great accuracy had no other purpose than to protect a dried-up mummy. In much the same way as the Greeks thought of the mask-like Sphinx as the personification of wisdom, so the modern world has formed societies and written serious books to interpret the "pyramid prophecies" from the measurements of its stones. The reader of these expositions may be a little surprised to find how accurately the Egyptians thought in terms of English inches and feet, and he may wonder how it was that so much of this prophetic vision of the Old Kingdom dealt only with events important to the English people.[12]

Exactly how such a towering mass was built by Egyptian methods, without tackle and pulleys, is a reasonable question for which there is no reasonably certain answer. In the fifth century B.C. when the Greek historian Herodotus asked the same question, he was given some colorful information by one who was the ancestor of all modern dragomen and who pretended to get his information from the hieroglyphs on the stones. Herodotus was told that the equivalent of about a million and a half dollars was spent by Khufu on the radishes, onions, and garlic for the consumption of the workmen; "a hundred thousand men," he was informed, "labored constantly and were relieved every three months by a fresh lot"; that the causeway (1017 yards long, 60 feet wide, and 48 feet high at the highest point) was built first in ten years; and that the pyramid itself required another twenty years.

The construction of the pyramid Herodotus[13] describes as follows: "This pyramid was built in steps.... After laying stones for the base, they raised the remaining stones by machines made of short pieces of wood:... for the machines were equal in number to the ranges of steps.... The highest portion of the pyramid, therefore, was first finished." It is true that the earliest pyramids and the V Dynasty pyramids at Abusir were built "in the form of steps" by what are called "accretion faces" (Plate XXVI-1). There is no proof, however, that "accretion faces" were used in the Great Pyramid, and it is doubtful if this original method of building a pyramid by successive layers was kept up, because, as some writers believe, the Pharaohs wished to enlarge their tombs as their reigns continued. Clarke and Engelbach insist that the true pyramids were laid out to their

[11] R. Engelbach, *Annales du Service* (1925), p. 166.
[12] Piazzi Smyth, *Our Inheritance in the Great Pyramid;* D. Davidson, *Great Pyramid; Its Divine Message.*
[13] Herodotus, Book II, cap. 125.

PLATE XXVI: PYRAMIDS

1

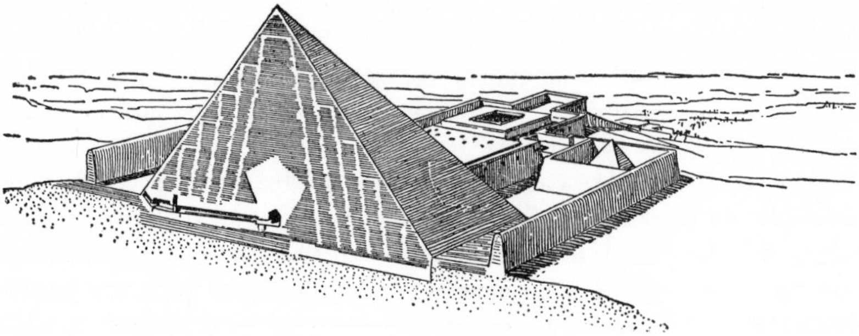

2

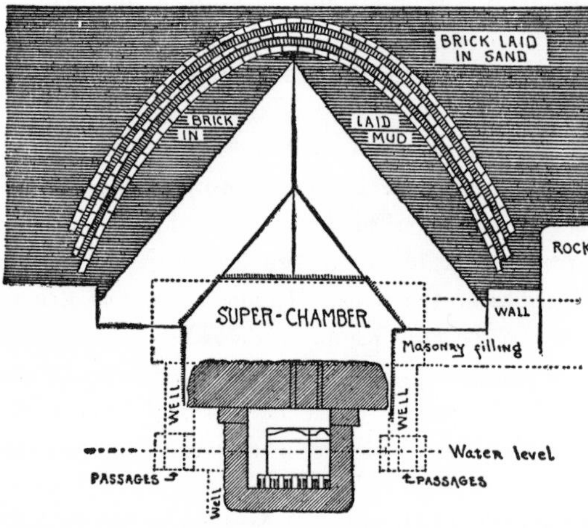

3

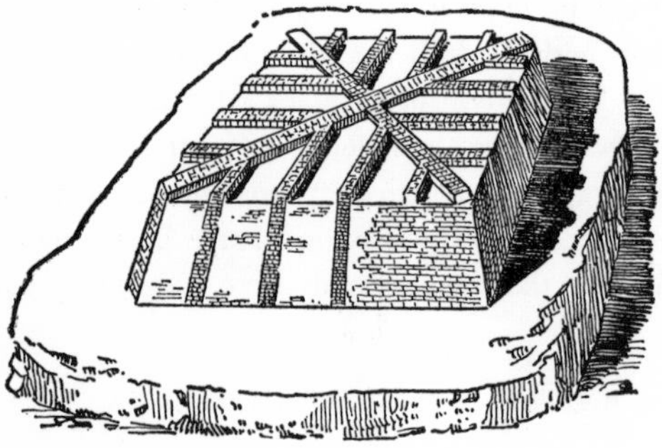

4

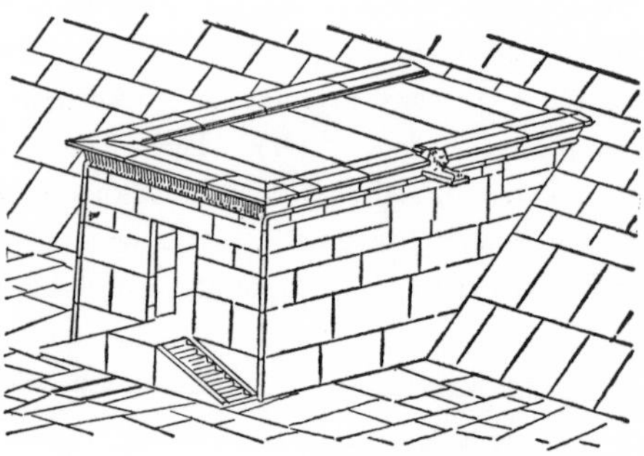

full size from the first and that the parallel skins of masonry were "considered by the Egyptians an aid to the stability of the structure" and a means, it might be added, of retaining the slope of the four faces. These authorities refuse to consider the possibility of wooden machines, other than sledges and levers, and deny the possibility of finishing the top of the pyramid first and then working down. The most satisfactory answer, then, to the question of how such pyramids were built, is to accept the simplest hypothesis for which there is the greatest evidence, namely, that the Egyptians used a series of embankments, made of brick and earth, on which they raised their stones by sledges and levers. The reader who is still puzzled by the mechanical and human difficulties of this laborious method, is referred to *Ancient Egyptian Masonry,* by S. Clarke and R. Engelbach. These writers cannot answer every question but they make the other theories seem unlikely.

The building of the Great Pyramid, however it was done, left a tradition in Egypt. Ages afterwards, the Egyptians believed that the gods slept in the pyramids in Gizeh, but by Greek times there was the legend, which Herodotous heard and believed, that Khufu had been a tyrannical slave driver who neglected the temples, forsook justice, and by means of the lash forced his nation to sweat at the building of his tomb. The Greek historian was about right in believing that it took 100,000 men twenty years to build the pyramid, and another ten to construct the causeway. The fact that modern computations sustain these figures does not prove Khufu to have been a self-centered and unintelligent tyrant, as Herodotus and Manetho thought. Unquestionably the king was an energetic and successful organizer, as any one seeing his tomb might suspect; and when it is surmised that he worked his vast army at full strength only during the slack months of the flood period, when labor was available, and, what is more important, when he could have the stones floated up to the end of the causeway, and for the rest of the year kept small contingents working in shifts of three months each, we see in Khufu an efficient administrator, and even a reconstruction expert, relieving unemployment during the dull season at the expense of the state. It is nearer the unknown truth, perhaps, to picture the pyramid rising "not to the sound of groans and sighs, but to the cheerful songs with which Egyptian workmen in all ages have been accustomed to lighten their burdens." The Egyptians thought long and seriously about death, but they were not a lugubrious, or even a cruel, race.

After Khufu, there was nothing which his successors could do to surpass him. Khafra (Chephren) built his pyramid alongside of his father's, but he was satisfied with a mass 707 feet in width and 471 feet high. Its particular distinction resides in the preservation of part of its original limestone casing

---

PLATE XXVI

1. Section of pyramid of Sahure, Abusir (L. Borchardt, *Das Grabdenkmal des Königs Sahu-re,* 1910, Pl. 7).
2. Section of burial chamber in pyramid of Amenemhet III, Hawara (Petrie, *Kahun, Gurob and Hawara,* 1890, Pl. IV).
3. Pyramid of Senwosret II, Lahun (Perrot et Chipiez, *op. cit.,* Fig. 131).
4. Entrance chapel to pyramid of Senwosret I, Lisht (W. C. Hayes, "The Egyptian Expedition 1933-34," *Bulletin of the Metropolitan Museum of Art,* XXIX, 1934, Sect. II, Fig. 17).

PLATE XXVII: PYRAMIDS

1

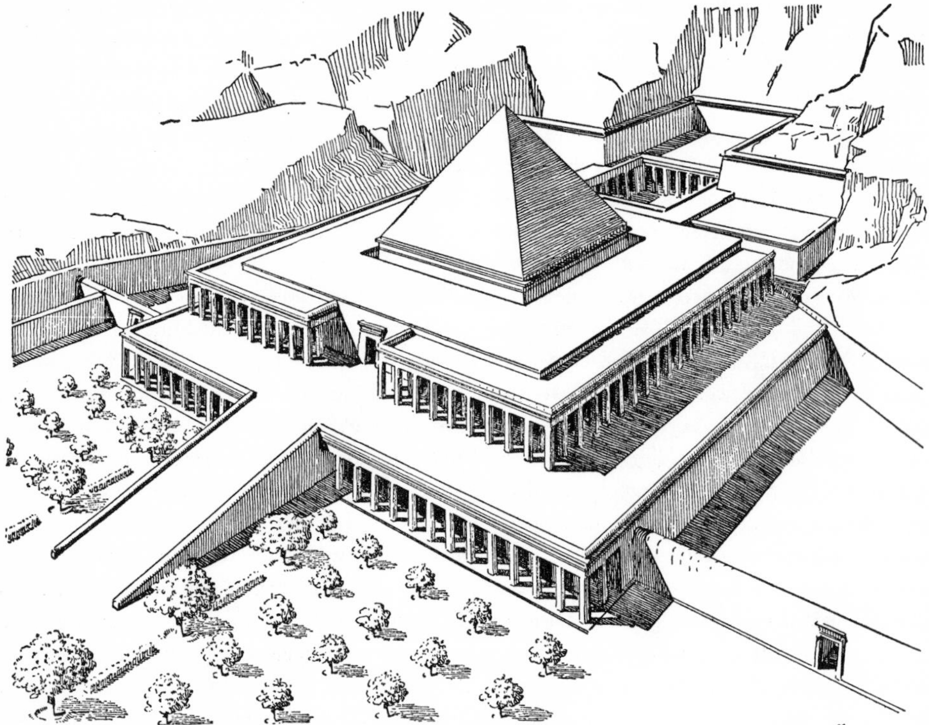

2

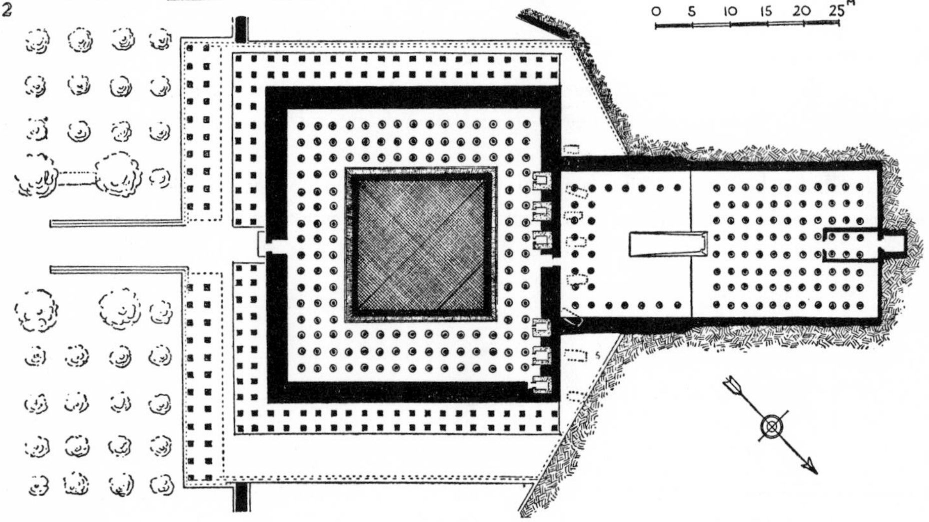

at the top and the use of red granite for the lower courses, which looks as if Khafra started out to finish his tomb in the harder stone. The last member of the sepulchral triad was built by Menkaura (Mykerinos) who was the successor and probably the brother of Khafra. His tomb, called "Divine-is-Menkaura," was inferior both in size and construction, being only 218 feet high. Southeast of the pyramid of Menkaura are the foundations of an unfinished pyramid which is of more importance to the history of the site and to the IV Dynasty than to architecture.[14]

After the III Dynasty, the pyramid was the regular mode of royal burial for a period as long as from Charlemagne down to the present. With one exception, each Pharaoh of the Old Kingdom from the IV Dynasty on, built himself a pyramid. The one king who did not build a pyramid was Shepseskaf, the last of the IV Dynasty, and in part the innovation was responsible for the termination of his line. His tomb, the "Shelter-of-Shepseskaf," at South Saqqara, known now as the Mastabat Fara'un,[15] or the "Seat of Pharaoh," looks like a rectangular mastaba made of large blocks of limestone of from 1.50 m. to 2 m. high. Originally it was cased in smoothly cut, fine limestone, and had the exceptional shape of a giant sarcophagus (Plate xxiii–1) with its top, at least, like the curved roof of the wooden coffin found at Tarkhan (Plate v–2). This wooden coffin, we saw,[16] was an early house-form, and the same type of "shelter," which Shepseskaf revived to be reproduced in stone upon a monumental scale, can be seen to-day in the houses of Nubia (Plate xxiii–2). The interior arrangement was very much like that of a pyramid, and it has a funerary temple on the east side. Such a radical departure could not have been, in Egypt, the result of a royal fancy; in fact, it was monumental expression of Shepseskaf's position in a bitter religious and political struggle for supremacy between the king and the priests of Re at Heliopolis—a struggle which was revived with tragic results centuries later by Amenhotep IV, when he tried to free the country from the tyranny of the priests of the Sun-god. While the great Pharaohs of the IV Dynasty admitted their descent from Re and built their tombs in the image of his fetish, Khufu saw the political dangers of religious intrigue and domination, for there is evidence that he dealt forcefully with some of the religious zeal, and at the end of the dynasty Shepseskaf, involved in what had become a desperate religious struggle, revolted against the growing power of the Heliopolitan theocracy by refusing to be buried under the *ben-ben* of Re. The result was apparently disastrous, for he was succeeded by the V Dynasty, the kings of which took the name of Re and were at first the puppets, if not the actual children, of the sun priests.

[14] G. A. Reisner, *Mycerinos* (1931).
[15] G. Jéquier, *Le Mastabat Faraoun* (1928).
[16] Page 23.

PLATE XXVII

1. Pyramid of Mentuhotep, Deir el-Bahari (*after* E. Naville, *The XIth Dynasty Temple at Deir el-Bahari,* ii, 1910, Pl. xxiii).
2. Plan of same (*after* Naville, Pl. xxi and H. E. Winlock, "The Egyptian Expedition 1920-21," *Bulletin of the Metropolitan Museum of Art,* xvi, 1921, p. 44, Fig. 20).

The pyramids built at Abusir (Plate xxvi–1) by the three usurpers of the V Dynasty who brought about the recrudescence of sun-worship, were never more than second-class in workmanship, and their funerary temples will be described in the next chapter. During the V and VI Dynasties the royal pyramids grew smaller and were built more economically by means of small stone, amounting to almost a rubble fill, within their casings. At the same time, the mortuary chapel increased in size and importance, while the north entrance to the pyramids, which in the late III and IV Dynasties had been high up on the face of the pyramids, came down to ground level and was in time marked by a small offering chapel above the entrance.[17]

MIDDLE KINGDOM. The Old Kingdom died away at the close of the VI Dynasty into the first Dark Ages of Egyptian history, during which, for over three hundred years, the country was laid waste by feudal anarchy and brigandage. As the admonitions of Ipuwer so dolefully tell us: "The doorkeepers say, 'Let us go and plunder.' The washerman refuseth to carry his load. Even the bird-catchers have to make themselves ready for battle.... Every town saith: 'Let us drive out the powerful from our midst.'... The land turneth round as doth a potter's wheel, and the robbers possess the riches." When unity is again restored at the beginning of the XI Dynasty by a new and warlike house, again from the South, the seat of power is for a time at Thebes but finally returns to Memphis. The rulers of the XI and XII Dynasties, anxious to prove their divine right to the throne, and therefore careful to revive and preserve the sacred traditions, continued to build pyramids, but they as vainly relied for their security upon structural ingenuity as had their predecessors upon sheer bigness and solidity.

The pyramids at Lisht, built by Amenemhet I, the founder of the XII Dynasty, and by Senwosret I, are badly ruined. Meri, the architect of Senwosret I, who built his master's mortuary temple, records, "to execute for him an eternal dwelling.... Its columns pierced heaven; the lake which was dug, it reached the river, the gates, towering heavenward, were of limestone of Troja,"[18] all of which seems a slight exaggeration when compared with the remains.

The most interesting architectural feature of Senwosret's pyramid is the entrance chapel which stood on the north side, directly over the concealed entrance to the pyramid.[19] Built directly against the casing of the pyramid, the chapel consisted of a single, rectangular room, the door in the north wall, and the stele, or "false door," set in the south wall, with the altar for offerings in front of it (Plate xxvi–4). Offering chapels situated on the north side of pyramids were the rule in the Memphite region from the VI to the XIII Dynasties. They were undoubtedly a survival of an early tradition before the influence of the solar cult shifted the offering chapel to the east side of the pyramid.[20]

The stone roof of the chapel sloped gently from east to west and was drained by a single lion-headed water spout set in the cavetto cornice on the west side. While it may seem curious to find

[17] Page 95.

[18] Breasted, *Ancient Records,* I, No. 509.

[19] W. C. Hayes, "The Entrance Chapel of the Pyramid of Sen-Wosret I," *Bulletin of the Metropolitan Museum of Art* (1934), Sect. II, p. 9 *seq.*

[20] Page 81.

such elaborate precautions to ensure proper drainage in a region where the rainfall was so light, "it must, however, be remembered that one of the torrential showers which occasionally fall in Egypt, carrying with it, through the roof of a building, streams of dirt-filled water, would be enough to ruin completely the painted reliefs on the interior walls; and that the roof of this particular building was required to shed not only the rain which fell on its own area, but also the wash from part of the north side of the pyramid." [21] Lion-headed water spouts, while not common in Egypt, because they belonged to that part of a building which would be first destroyed, are found from the V Dynasty to the Ptolemaic period.[22]

The tomb of Senwosret II at Lahun is an example of the easier method of pyramid construction adopted during this period (Plate XXVI–3). The solid mass of the pyramid consisted of a central core of natural rock on which was built a cross network of retaining walls to support the outer, limestone casing and to prevent the settlement of the interior brickwork. Here the traditional north entrance was abandoned and a carefully concealed access was built on the south side, while a curious passage was made almost all around the sarcophagus chamber.[23]

The most intricate brick pyramid of the Middle Kingdom is the one which Amenemhet III erected at Hawara (Plate XXVI–2). The sun-dried brick structure, built around a core of solid rock with a casing of limestone, offered little protection, and so the builder strained his ingenuity to construct an interior labyrinth of passages which would defy the tomb robber: there are blind passages and dummy chambers, gigantic sliding trapdoors in the ceilings which lead to other passages, and finally a sepulchral chamber without any door, which has a roof of three immense blocks of stone, one weighing about forty-five tons, that were lowered into place after the sarcophagus had been installed. For laborious effort and technical accomplishment, all of which were of no avail against the Egyptian plunderer, this chamber is remarkable: it is cut and polished accurately from one block of hard, yellow quartzite, over twenty-two feet long, eight feet wide and about two feet thick, which weighed about one hundred and ten tons; above this chamber, in addition to its forty-five ton slab, is a sloping roof of limestone beams, each one seven feet thick, which in its turn was covered by a series of brick arches.

PYRAMIDAL VARIATIONS

MIDDLE KINGDOM. The most impressive tomb of the Middle Kingdom was that of Mentuhotep III of the XI Dynasty at Deir el-Bahari, which is on the west bank, opposite to Thebes (Plate XXVII). Egyptian tombs, even in their pyramidal form, have up to this point been devoid of any architectural distinction other than structural impressiveness, but the builder of Mentuhotep was one of those architects, rare in Egypt, who produced a new and monumental type of tomb from traditional elements. Instead of merely adding together the customary mortuary forms, which was the usual architectural substitute for design in Egypt, he assimilated and unified the regular elements into an impressive

[21] Hayes, *op. cit.*, p. 17.
[22] Hayes, *op. cit.*, p. 16, note 36; Clarke and Engelbach, *Ancient Egyptian Masonry*, pp. 159-161.
[23] Petrie, *Illahun, Kahun, and Girob* (1889-90).

PLATE XXVIII: PYRAMIDAL TOMBS

architectural whole. The result bears witness to the lessening importance of the sepulchral tumulus and the growing significance of the funerary chapel, which by this time had become a temple. The tomb was approached on the east side by a paved avenue which ran from the edge of the cultivated valley, a half-mile away, to the limestone wall enclosing the forecourt. The court was two hundred yards long and one hundred yards wide and was planted with sycamore trees and tamarisks like a royal garden.[24] The east side of the great monument facing on this court had a long portico of two rows of square pillars; from the middle of the court an inclined ramp led up to the terrace above the portico, where deep colonnaded porches with octagonal piers formed an ambulatory around the pyramid rising out of the center. Beneath the west side of the encircling gallery were six earlier shrines for the queens of Mentuhotep II, whose tombs were in the courtyard behind the pyramid, these shrines having been incorporated into the structure of Mentuhotep III. The backs and sides of the little cubical shrines "were paneled to represent the great doors of the royal palace, into which the lady enters with the king, while the front showed the *harim* apartments with the lady in converse with her royal spouse or receiving the ministrations of her servants." [25] The inner court, cut back into the vertical cliff, was surrounded by piers and on the west side opened into a pillared hall in front of the chapel which was carved out of the solid rock. Mentuhotep III was entombed beneath the cliffs at the end of a passage sloping down from the center of the inner court. Later, in the XVIII Dynasty, after grave robbers had successfully plundered the tombs, a chapel to Hathor was added on the north side of the peristyle court. Although in its present ruined condition this monument is almost incomprehensible without the help of the restoration, it was architecturally the most impressive tomb ever built in Egypt, and as such, is evidence of the level to which Egyptian civilization had again risen after the long interim since the middle of the Old Kingdom.

Although the pyramid, by expense and symbolic significance, was a royal prerogative, the privilege of its use, even in the Old Kingdom, was extended to a royal wife, as in the case of Queen Wezebten,[26] the wife of Pepi II of the VI Dynasty, who was buried at Saqqara in a small pyramid with an

[24] H. E. Winlock, *Bulletin of the Metropolitan Museum of Art,* XVII (1922), Sect. II, p. 24 *seq.*

[25] H. E. Winlock, "Excavations at Thebes," Supplement of the *Bulletin of the Metropolitan Museum of Art,* XVI (1921), Sect. II, p. 44.

[26] G. Jéquier, *La Pyramide d'Oudjebten* (1928).

PLATE XXVIII

1, 2. Sections of tombs, Abydos (Perrot et Chipiez, *op. cit.,* I, Figs. 161, 163).
3, 4. Views of same (*op. cit.,* Figs. 160, 162).
5. Perspective, tombs 290 and 291, Deir el-Medina, Thebes (B. Bruyère, *Fouilles de l'Institut français du Caire,* I, 1921-23, Pl. XIX).
6. Section, tomb at Deir el-Medina (Bruyère, *op. cit.,* Pl. XX).
7. Tomb of Apis, Saqqara (Perrot et Chipiez, I, Fig. 190).
8. Painting from tomb of Amen-mes, Thebes (Petrie, *Qurneh,* 1909, Pl. XXXVIII).
9. Relief from Thebes (Perrot et Chipiez, *op. cit.,* I, Fig. 188).
10. Plan, tomb D-32, Abydos (Randall-Maciver and Mace, *El-Amrah and Abydos,* Pl. XXVI/4).
11. Plan, tomb D-8 Abydos (*op. cit.*).

PLATE XXIX: ROCK-CUT TOMBS

1

2

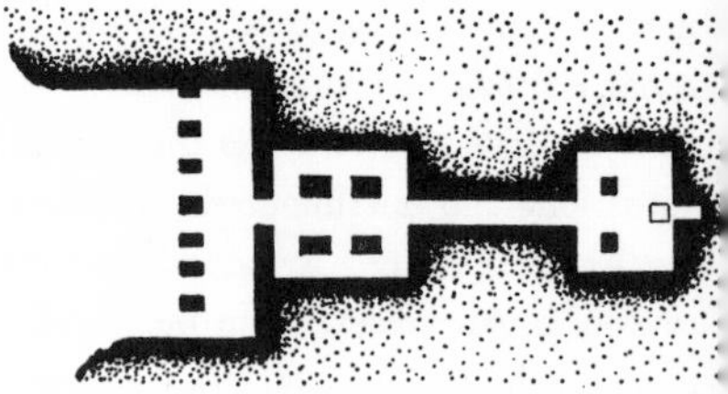

3

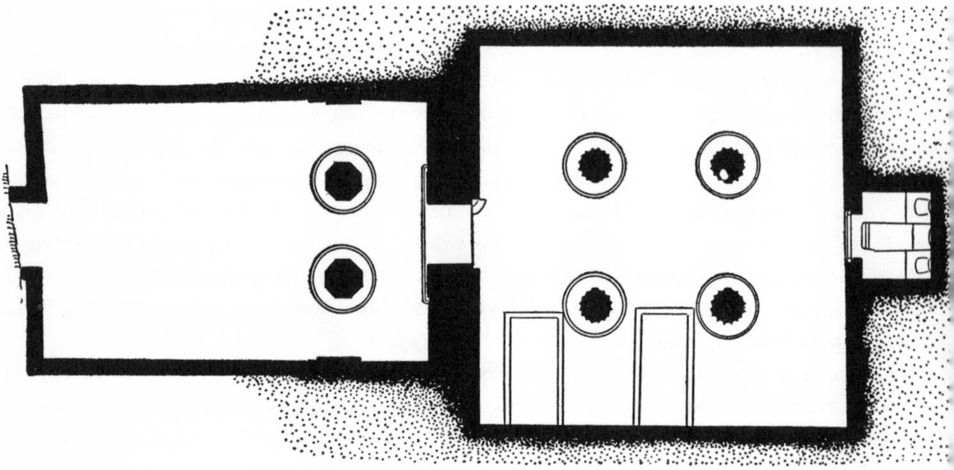

4

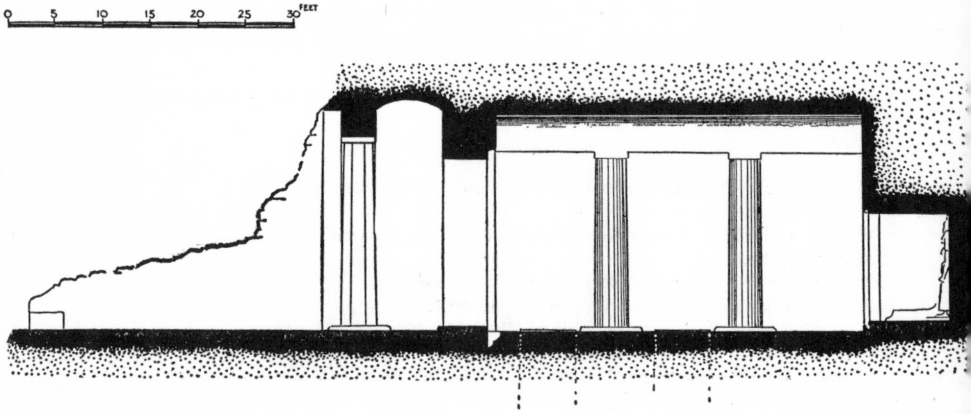

offering chapel on the east side. During the Middle Kingdom the pyramidal type of tomb, while still a royal form, lost some of its distinction when the Theban nobles began to adopt it for their sepulchral monuments and developed a modest combination of pyramid and mastaba. Examples of this combination type, attributed to the Middle Kingdom, are found in the necropolis at Abydos where the earliest generations of the Theban empire were interred.[27]

The Abydos tombs, carelessly oriented and only five or six meters high, are uniformly built of crude brick. They consist of a rectangular base surmounted by a pyramidal top made by stepping back the courses; the pyramid itself encloses a conical chamber of corbeled construction within which was the burial. In most examples they have no exterior chapel, the stele and services having been out-of-doors (Plate XXVIII–1, 3). A few, however, have a projecting chapel with a niche for the stele and a lower chamber which gave access by means of a small opening to the *serdab,* lying directly beneath the conical burial vault (Plate XXVIII–2, 4). Originally these tombs at Abydos were covered with a coat of mud-plaster which was whitewashed so that they must have looked like an encampment of tents.

During the XVII Dynasty, before the rise of the II Theban Empire, even the royal tombs were somewhat similar, consisting of crude brick pyramids with chapels on the east side, the chapels at times cut down into the rock, sometimes built against the side of the pyramid, and in some cases only a corridor extending into the pyramid, while in all examples the burial chamber is cut down into the rock beneath the chapel.[28] Very little remains of the superstructures of these tombs, but the XVIII Dynasty tomb of Apis at Saqqara (Plate XXVIII–7), and frequent representations of the type in Theban tomb paintings (Plate XXVIII–8, 9), give the general appearance of these sepulchral structures with their mastaba-like podiums and small pyramidal tops.

NEW KINGDOM. The painted representations show that in the New Kingdom at Thebes the combination type of tomb with the pyramidal top had become popular, presumably because the Pharaohs of the XVIII Dynasty had abandoned the pyramid for the greater security of the *speos,* or rock-cut tomb, hidden in the Valley of the Kings. At Deir el-Medina, one of the valleys in the great necropolis of Western Thebes, many of the tombs throughout the New Kingdom have the pyramidal shape.[29] It

[27] G. Maspero, *Manual of Egyptian Archaeology* (1902), p. 145; Mariette, *Voyage dans la Haute Egypte* (1879), Vol. I; *Abydos,* II (1880), Pl. 67.

[28] H. Winlock, "The Kings of the Seventeenth Dynasty at Thebes," *Journal of Egyptian Archaeology,* X (1924), p. 217.

[29] B. Bruyère, "Fouilles de Deir el Médineh," *Fouilles de l'Institut français,* 1923-1935; J. Vandier, "Tombes de Deir el-Médineh, *Mémoires de l'Institut français d'arch. orientale du Caire,* LXIX (1935).

PLATE XXIX

1. Plan of tombs of Sabni and Mekhu, Aswân (J. Baikie, *Egyptian Antiquities in the Nile Valley,* 1932, p. 728).
2. Plan of tomb of Sierenpowet I, Aswân (*op. cit.,* p. 737).
3. Plan of Amenemhat (Ameni), Beni Hasan (P. E. Newberry, *Beni Hasan,* I, 1893, Pl. IV).
4. Section of same.

has been suggested that this popularity of the pyramid in the vicinity of Thebes was due not to the general tendency of royal sepulchral customs to descend the social scale and become more universal, but was the result of a particular Theban symbolism whereby the pyramid was considered the high mountain of Thebes.[30] Whatever significance the pyramid may have had at Thebes, its adoption by the aristocracy was undoubtedly influenced by its previous social distinction and by its manifest association with the Sun-god.[31]

The Deir el-Medina tombs, as they develop in the course of the New Kingdom, are a further elaboration of an idea, seen in the Middle Kingdom, of combining pyramid and mastaba, with the difference that instead of a mastaba, the dwelling conception of the tomb is stressed by combining the pyramid with a traditional house-form. Also as a result of the popularity of the *speos,* the sepulchral chamber is cut underground at the bottom of a deep shaft. The type is illustrated by an example of the XIX-XX Dynasty, which consists, like a house, of a forecourt opening to the east, a colonnaded vestibule, a chapel or hall covered by a tunnel-vault and a pyramidal roof, with a niche for an adoration panel on its eastern face (Plate XXVIII–5, 6). The actual burial is in the courtyard, at the bottom of a shaft which opens by means of steps and corridors into a rock-cut and tunnel-vaulted chamber beneath the chapel. The superstructure of these tombs is partly built of either brick or stone and partly cut out of the side of the cliff.

ETHIOPIAN PERIOD. Because of the reverence which the kings of Ethiopia had for Thebes and the power of Amon-Re, the pyramidal tomb was adopted in the XXIII Dynasty by the Nubian rulers, and continued in use in Nubia from the eighth century down to Roman times. Nubia derived most of its culture from Egypt, and was incorporated into the Empire in the XVIII Dynasty. During the collapse of the Theban Empire this southernmost outpost of Egyptian culture asserted its independence and under a line of kings, established by Libyan mercenaries from the north, set up the Ethiopian Kingdom. In the eighth century the Ethiopians under Pianky conquered Egypt, set up the XXIII Dynasty, and in the XXV Dynasty vainly tried to hold the whole valley and withstand the Assyrian invasion.

The first capital of the Ethiopian Kingdom was at Napata where seven generations of rulers were buried. Their tombs show a progressive change; starting as round tumulus mounds, which were followed by the same type cased in limestone with brick chapels and surrounded by horseshoe-shaped, girdle walls, the tumulus gives way to the mastaba, and the series finally ends with the pyramid. Pianky was the first Ethiopian ruler to adopt the pyramidal form, and after him it became the mode, not only of all subsequent kings, but the standard type of upper-class burials after the capital of Nubia was moved to Meroë.[32]

[30] B. Bruyère, *Fouilles de l'Institut français,* II (1923-1924), Part II, p. 12.

[31] The large number of pyramidal stone caps from the destroyed brick tombs of the Memphite region indicate that pyramidal tombs continued to be used down to the New Kingdom in the region where the pyramid was first used, and hence suggest that their use spread from Memphis to Thebes.

[32] J. W. Crowfoot, *The Island of Meroë* (1911); J. Garstang, *Meroë* (1911); F. Cailliaud, *Voyage à Meroë* (1826); E. A. Budge, *Egyptian Sudan* (1907).

ROCK-CUT TOMBS

OLD KINGDOM. The chieftains of the clans and small states under the Double Crown had become, by the V and VI Dynasties, feudal barons who were buried near their own homes in rock-cut tombs, which perhaps went back to a remote time when their ancestors were buried in caves in the face of the cliffs. Although hewn out of the natural rock, such tombs nevertheless followed what has been seen to be the instinctive Egyptian habit, and sculpturally reproduced the regional dwellings. An excellent example of a rock-hewn tomb of the VI Dynasty is that of Mekhu (Plate XXIX–1) at Aswân, opposite to the island of Elephantine, at the first cataract. Mekhu was an Old Kingdom chief of the elephant nome who lost his life in an adventurous expedition into equatorial Africa. His son, Sabni, rescued his remains and gave them an honorable resting place next to his own tomb. The plan shows a door opening into a reception hall of eighteen columns, at the back of which is a recess with steps leading up to the stele. A closed shaft in the floor goes down to the burial chamber. This tomb, we can assume, reproduces the essential features of the kind of house in which the warlike leaders of the southern march lived. There are somewhat similar rock-cut tombs at Aswân and at other sites in the long valley, but the examples which are most important architecturally belong to the Middle Kingdom.

MIDDLE KINGDOM. In the XII Dynasty, again at Aswân, the tomb of Sirenpowet I, another Lord of Elephantine, has a courtyard in front of the cliff on which is carved a portico with six rectangular piers (Plate XXIX–2). From this porch a door opens into a small hall of four pillars which is decorated with painted stucco, and from it a long passage, its ceiling cut to a shallow curve, leads into the back chamber with the recess and shrine. Once more this tomb presents the essential elements of all Egyptian architecture: the courtyard, vestibule or portico, the pillared hall, and the private or sacred chamber.

Of the same general type, although much finer and magnificently decorated, are the famous rock-cut tombs at Beni-Hasan, where the rulers, princes, and nobles of the Oryx nome were buried. While some of the tombs of this region go back to the VIII Dynasty, the Oryx groups, beginning with the simple tombs of the XI Dynasty and ending with the elaborate ones of the XII Dynasty, are artistically the most important remains of the Middle Kingdom. The two best examples are those of Ameni (Amenemhet) and Khnemhotpe. Khnemhotpe (Khnumhotep) tells how the doors of his tomb were of cedar, seven cubits high, and records, "My chief nobility was: I executed a cliff-tomb, (for) a man should imitate that which his father does. My father made for himself a house of the *ka* in the town of Mernofret, of good stone of Ayan, in order to perpetuate his name forever and establish it eternally." [33] Originally a causeway led up from the river directly in front of the portico of Ameni. Ameni was a great man and a few of his many titles and duties recorded in his tomb give a reality to the nobleman and his position in the Middle Kingdom. He was "Treasurer of the King of Lower Egypt,"

[33] Breasted, *Ancient Records,* I, No. 635.

PLATE XXX: ROCK-CUT TOMBS

1

2

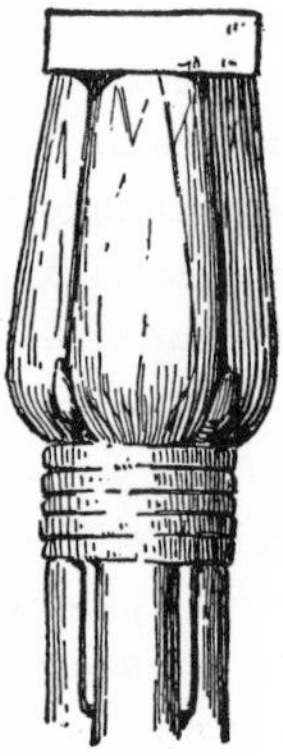

3

4

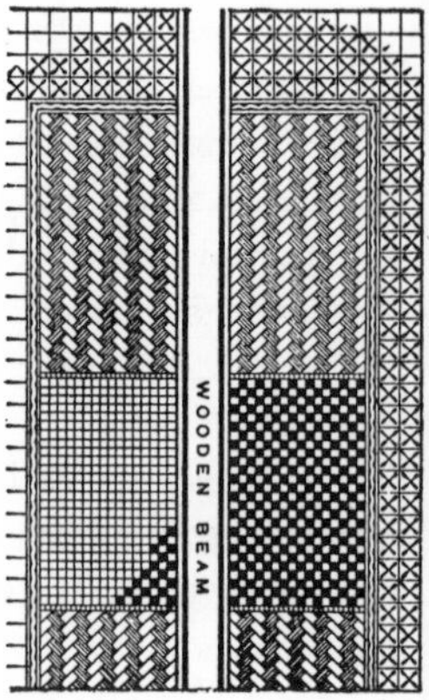

5

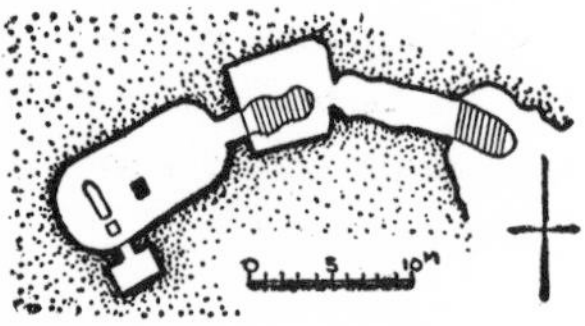

6

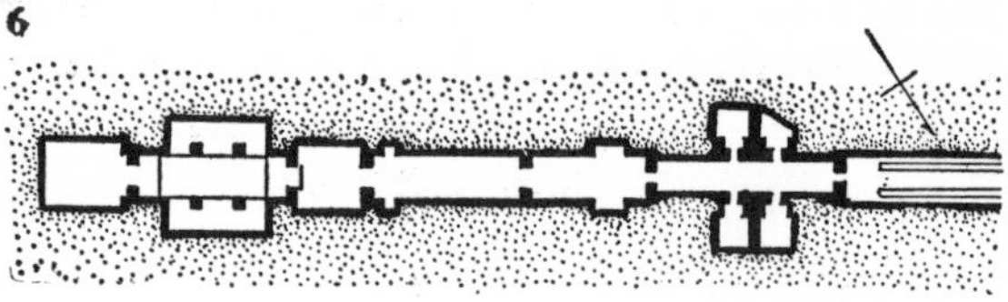

"confident and friend of the King," "great chief of the Oryx nome," "Regulator of the two Thrones," "Superintendent of the two (?) pools of sport," "Overseer of horns, hoofs, feathers and minerals," "Superintendent of all things which heaven gives and earth produces," "He who is in the chamber," "Superintendent of the temples," and "Consort in the house of the goddess Net."

Ameni's tomb had in front of it a court, partly built, and partly cut back into the face of the cliff (Plate XXIX–3). Its porch has two octagonal columns with simple abacus capitals, which appear to support the architrave. Within the portico the ceiling is twenty-three feet high and has an arched shape. The main chamber, entered by a large door 16½ feet high and 6 feet wide, is nearly square, and is divided into three aisles by two rows of sixteen-sided columns, two in each row. These polygonal columns, like those of the funerary temple of Zoser, are finished with concave flutings which give them the name of "Proto-Doric" columns, because of their fortuitous resemblance to Greek columns of the Doric order. The ceiling over each aisle is cut to the form of a flat arch and the surface decorated with diaper patterns imitated from the woven matting which covered the hoop-roofs of the Oryx dwellings (Plate XXX–3, 4). In the back wall, on axis with the central door and aisle, is the shrine, approached by a short flight of stairs; within the shrine, closed by double doors, stood the statue of the dead. The actual burial was in mummy pits cut down into the floor of the main hall, indicating that at some earlier period the dead in this nome had been buried in the floor of the house. The walls are still covered with the remarkable painted scenes of craftsmen, wrestlers, hunters, soldiers, and officials of the court of Ameni.

The columns in the reception hall of the unfinished tomb 18, instead of being polygonal, are quatrefoil in section, and their capitals represent four closed lotus flowers bound together (Plate XXX–2). The earliest example of this type of capital is found in the V Dynasty at Abusir (Plate XXXIV–2). By the Middle Kingdom this kind of column with the symbolic lotus capital was either imitated from Old Kingdom examples or copied from the contemporary supports used in the houses, which consisted of either four bundles of reeds, or four palm trunks, bound together and decorated at the top with lotus flowers. The faithful imitative character of the work is indicated by the care with which the sculptor reproduced not only the binding cords at the base of the capital, but even the little sticks wedged in between the curves of the palm trunks to assure a tight binding. The literal dependence of these tombs upon the traditional house of the region is also shown by the façades (Plate XXX–1), where, beneath the overhanging cornices, are reproduced the projecting ends of the little beams which formed

---

PLATE XXX

1. View of tombs at Beni Hasan.
2. Lotus capital, tombs 17, 18, Beni Hasan.
3. Interior of tomb of Amenemhat, Beni Hasan.
4. Painted matting pattern on ceiling of Tomb of Amenemhat (Newberry, *op. cit.*, I, Pl. 6).
5. Plan of tomb of Thutmose I, no. 38 Biban el-Moluk (W. C. Hayes, *Royal Sarcophgai of the XVIII Dynasty,* Fig. 1).
6. Plan of tomb of Ramses IX, Valley of the Kings, Thebes (Porter and Moss, *The Theban Necropolis,* No. 6).

PLATE XXXI: LATE TOMBS

1

2

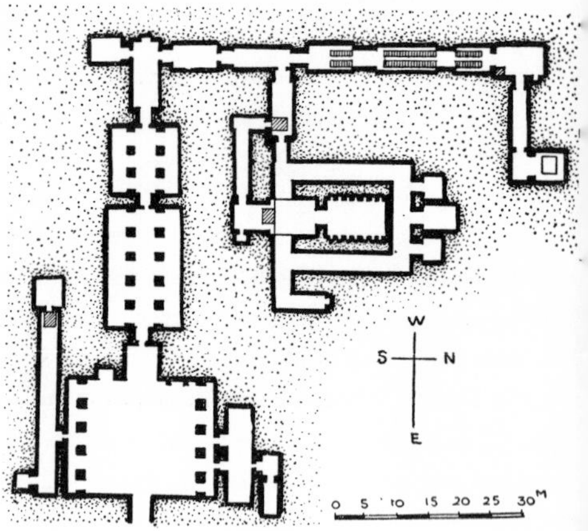

3

4

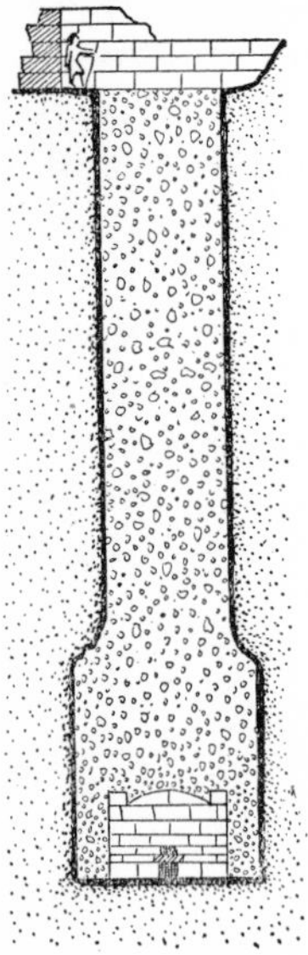

5

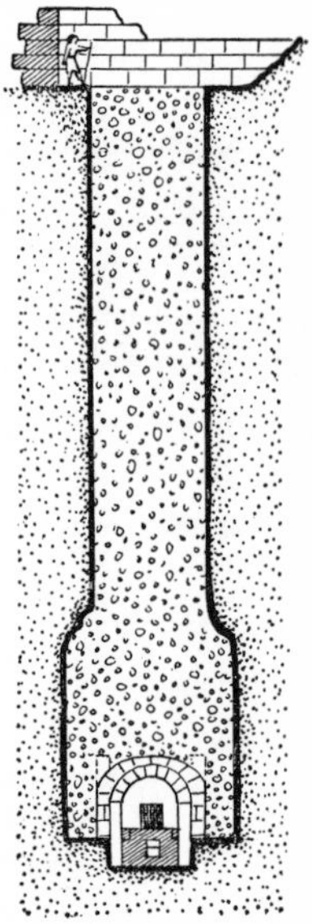

6

the roofs, and which, carved in stone, look like Greek dentils. Much has been written about the stone origin of the channeled columns at Beni-Hasan and the vaulting tradition preserved in the rock-hewn ceilings. In view, however, of the evidence found at Saqqara,[34] the opinion of competent Egyptologists,[35] and the obvious intention of the Egyptian mind to adhere to convention and reproduce architecturally the customary forms, there can be no doubt that these tombs were copied from the light wooden, and plastered reed structures of the region, which had curved roofs of matting and supports of wood or bundled reeds covered with stucco.

NEW KINGDOM. When the second long interim of Egyptian history was over and the hated Hyksos riders from the East had been expelled, it was another warlike Theban family which united the country, extended Egyptian dominion to Mesopotamia, and, from a material standpoint, made Egypt the richest and most powerful kingdom in the ancient world. From the beginning of the XVIII Dynasty the Pharaohs gave up all idea of constructing large tombs above ground and instead adapted the rock-hewn sepulcher to their needs. Still in search of protection, the rulers of the XVIII Dynasty trusted to concealment rather than to the massiveness of the Old Kingdom and the intricacy of Middle Kingdom tombs. They and their successors went off into the Libyan desert, back of Deir el-Bahari, and in the awesome desolation of the Valley of the Kings cut long corridors under the cliffs, hiding the entrances beneath the sand. There were innumerable minor, rock-cut tombs on the west bank at Thebes, dating back to at least the beginning of the XI Dynasty, but credit for this royal move may belong to Ineni, who was an important architect and clerk of the works under several of the kings of the XVIII Dynasty; he tells in his own tomb how "I attended to the excavation of the cliff-tomb of His Majesty (Thutmose I) alone, no one seeing, no one hearing" ... and goes on to prophesy, "I shall be praised for my wisdom in after years, by those who shall imitate that which I have done." The tomb he cut for his master was a very modest one (Plate xxx–5); in fact, all the royal tombs of the XVIII and XIX Dynasties were such simple arrangements of subterranean chambers as to have little architectural significance. The XVIII Dynasty tombs "contain the following essential elements: *a,* an entrance stair-well; *b,* an antechamber, lying between the entrance and the sepulchral hall; *c,* a pillared sepulchral hall,

[34] See page 76. Inasmuch as channeled columns with sharp arrises are reproduced in stone at Saqqara in the III Dynasty and in a small ivory colonnette of the I Dynasty at Abydos (Petrie, *The Royal Tombs,* II, Pl. XXXIV, 73), it is impossible to argue that they must have originated in stone, since the form antedates the use of stone in Egyptian architecture.

[35] G. Jéquier, *Manuel d'Archéologie Égyptienne,* I, p. 177; J. Capart, *Egyptian Art,* p. 111.

PLATE XXXI

1. Restored perspective and section, tomb of Pabasa, Asasif at Thebes.
2. Plan of rock-cut tomb of Pedamenopet, Asasif (Porter and Moss, *The Theban Necropolis,* No. 33).
3. Restored view of tomb of Pedamenopet (Perrot et Chipiez, I, Fig. 201).
4, 5. Shaft tomb, Saqqara (M. A. Barsanti, *Annales du Service,* II, 1901, p. 98).
6. Section of "Campbell's Tomb," Gizeh (Perrot et Chipiez, I, Fig. 200).

always placed at the inner end of the tomb, and one or more small storerooms opening off the sepulchral hall." [36] In the tombs of the series the sepulchral hall is cartouche-shaped, and in all cases is oriented with its long axis east and west. Beginning with Thutmose III the tombs are protected by a deep well, introduced into the corridor before the antechamber. While the rock-cut tombs throughout the New Kingdom increase in size and elaboration, even the later tombs of the time of the Ramesside kings (Plate xxx–6), while representing an astonishing amount of careful mining and stonecutting, are not architectural, being merely an extension of subterranean corridors with innumerable storerooms for the wealth and provisions which the kings tried to take with them into their other world.

The isolation of the royal tombs in the Valley of the Kings, and their concealment there without any superstructures either to mark the grave or provide a place for prayers and offerings, were, for Egypt, a radical departure from tradition, and the change had an immediate effect upon religious architecture. The result of this dissolution of the dual function of the tomb was that the Pharaohs of the New Kingdom continued to build mortuary temples near their palaces on the west bank opposite Thebes, where the heavily endowed services, which they still considered necessary for their eternal comfort, could be performed. At once the funerary chapel, freed from any dependence upon the tomb, became an independent, monumental structure which, as will be seen, set the mode and established a standardized temple concept by the end of the XVIII Dynasty.

Even during the XVIII Dynasty the royal conception of a mortuary temple influenced tomb designs, for there are private tombs at Abydos which were miniature temples, "consisting of a pillared forecourt, one or more outer courts, an inner court containing the pit, and a narrow, arched passage connecting with the inner court by three doors" (Plate xxviii–11). During the XIX and XX Dynasties at Abydos, the tombs were simplified into a walled enclosure,[37] the pit in the center, which opened into three small chambers at the back (Plate xxviii–10), very much like the Old Kingdom temple plan from the same region.

LATE TOMB TYPES

SAÏTIC PERIOD. During the New Kingdom there was an endless variety of tomb forms, most of which, however, were rock-cut versions of the houses of the living. The combination type of either mastaba or house with the pyramidal roof has already been described, and it is not until the Saïtic revival that any important innovations occur. The Kings of Saïs, who in the XXVI Dynasty gave Egypt a brief recrudescence of art, were all buried at their capital in the Delta. Their funerary architecture was entirely different from anything seen in the rest of Egypt, but may well have been an old Delta custom of which there are no records. Both *speos* and mummy pits were impossible in the marshy soil of Lower Egypt; stone, while used for the temples, had to be transported from Upper Egypt, and the preparation of solid foundations for it was difficult. Therefore, instead of

[36] W. C. Hayes, *Royal Sarcophagi of the XVIIIth Dynasty* (1935), p. 6.
[37] D. Randall-Maciver and A. C. Mace, *El Amrah and Abydos* (1902), p. 64.

building separate tombs and mortuary temples the Saïtic kings trusted for protection to the power of their gods, and built their small tombs inside the existing temples.

Herodotus says, "The Saïtes buried all the kings who belonged to their canton inside this temple (of Neith)." [38] "The tomb of Amasis, as well as that of Apries and his family," he describes as, "a chamber with folding doors" within the forecourt with its colonnade of palm columns. What the shape of this chamber was is unknown, but the presumption is that it was a free-standing sepulcher, suggesting the tomb of Emir Lagin which stands in the court of the mosque of Ibn Tulun at Cairo.

The private tombs show that the Saïtic builders outside the Delta went back with archæological enthusiasm and painstaking care to established forms in their effort to link themselves with the prestige of the past. While there was no one type of tomb there was a tendency to emphasize the residential character of the tomb, marking it by an imposing and temple-like superstructure, while at the same time excavating an elaborate palace complex in the rock beneath. At 'Asasif on the west bank at Thebes, in front of Queen Hatshepsut's mortuary temple, are the two largest tombs of this kind. One belonged to Pabasa (Pbes), who was chief Steward of Nitocris, the daughter of Psamtek I. During the Theban decline, before the Ethiopian domination, the civil power at Thebes was invested in a "Divine Votress or Consort of Amon," and Psamtek I, when he drove out the Ethiopians and established a new dynasty, gave this vice-regency of Thebes to his daughter.

The tomb of Pabasa had a temple-like superstructure of brick, plastered and painted, which consisted of two courts with pylons and was oriented to the east (Plate XXXI–1). Its inner court was cut down with great labor through the solid rock so that the actual forecourt of the underground palace might have its appropriate light. The *speos* has a pillared forecourt opening into a Hall of Appearances, off from which are the private chambers of the dead.[39] The actual entrance to the subterranean tomb was by a stairway, open to the sky, leading off to the north where it came to the surface at a small pylon. Pabasa, it appears, was careful to revive the Old and Middle Kingdom royal tradition of having the mortuary chapel face east, and the entrance to the north.

Nearby is the tomb of Pedamenopet, a Chief Lector, which is larger and more complicated but in a more ruined condition. It too had a temple superstructure of brick facing east, the walls paneled in imitation of the *serekh* façade (Plate XXXI–3). Its underground tomb (Plate XXXI–2) was entered from the temple court and consisted of a pillared court, chambers, stairs, and corridors, reproducing in schematic form the plan of an elaborate palace.[40]

More distinctive, and at the same time more archaistic, are the Saïtic tombs at Saqqara.[41] For security the builders took the ideas of a mummy shaft and a rock-cut tomb, and cut a great shaft straight down for about 25 meters (Plate XXXI–4, 5). At the bottom they built a burial chamber of

[38] Herodotus, *History,* II, 169.

[39] A. Lansing, "Excavations in the 'Asasif," *New York Metropolitan Museum Bulletin,* XV (1920), Sect. II, pp. 16-24.

[40] Dümichen, *Der Grabpalast des Patuamenap* (1884-85); Maspero, *Revue de l'Histoire des Religions,* XXXVI, p. 406; the perspective in Perrot and Chipiez's *History of Ancient Egyptian Art,* I, Fig. 191, based upon Prisse d'Avennes, is a composite of the superstructure of Pabasa's tomb and the *speos* of Pedamenopet.

[41] C. M. Firth, *Annales* (1929), p. 69; Barsanti, *Annales,* I, p. 161, 230; *Annales,* II, p. 97 *seq.;* V, pp. 69-83.

PLATE XXXII: CENOTAPH AND NAOS

1

2

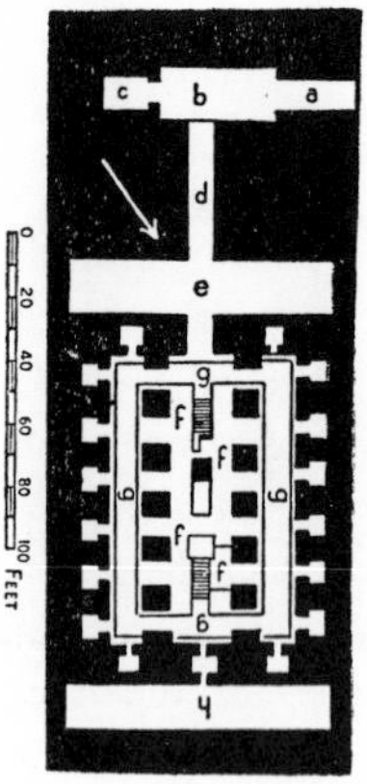

3

7

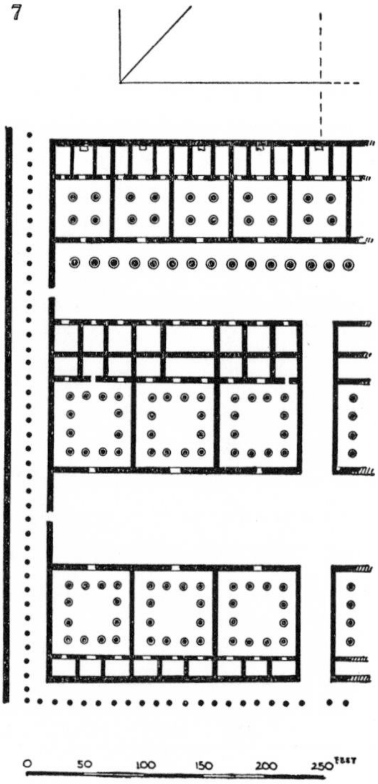

4

5

6

cut stone in the shape of a house-coffin such as was used in the Old Kingdom (Plate III–1). They made its curved roof of stone voussoirs, showing not only their mastery of the stone vault but again indicating that their vaulting efforts were for protection and intended to imitate an early house-form. Another example of this manner of burial was discovered at Gizeh and called Campbell's tomb (Plate XXXI–6). It dates from the reign of Psamtek I. At the bottom of the shaft, which is 54 feet, 4 inches deep, is a sarcophagus chamber with an elaborate system of vaulting to protect the dwelling from the weight of the loose gravel which filled the shaft. Other variations of this idea of building a vaulted chamber at the bottom of a pit have been found at Abydos.[42] All of these Saïtic shaft tombs had superstructures of which little remains.

With the return of the Saïtic period to a tomb-form imitating a primitive form of house, the history of sepulchral architecture in Egypt may be considered finished, for the Græco-Roman tombs merely combined Egyptian forms with classic details without establishing any new types, except those introduced from classic sources.[43]

CENOTAPHS

While the royal grave in the XVIII Dynasty ceases to have any particular architectural interest, the cenotaph which Seti I built at Abydos is and was a distinctive structure. With the growth of the cult of Osiris, many cities laid claim to being his birthplace, and during the Old Kingdom Abydos so successfully established its claim that the tomb of King Zer became honored as the burial place of the god. Because of Osiris' rule in the Kingdom of the Dead, and his embodiment of the resurrection myth, his shrine at Abydos became so venerated that every Egyptian desired to have his body taken there before it was interred in his own tomb. The Pharaohs of the XIX Dynasty, especially Seti I, were responsible for rebuilding the sacred place of Osiris which had been neglected during the Hyksos occupation. In addition to a great temple, which was as much in honor of Osiris as the priestly domination of Amon-Re would permit, Seti I also built what has been called the *Osireion,* or tomb of Osiris, but which was probably a symbolic cenotaph.

The structure in its unfinished state seems to resemble the so-called Temple of the Sphinx at Gizeh because of its square stone monoliths and its stern simplicity (Plate XXXII–1). Its architectural

42 Randall-Maciver and Mace, *El Amrah and Abydos* (1902), Pl. XXVII.
43 Ibrahim Noshy, *The Arts in Ptolemaic Egypt* (1937).

PLATE XXXII

1. Interior of Cenotaph of Seti I, Abydos.
2. Plan of Cenotaph of Seti I (Baikie, *op. cit.,* p. 307).
3. Naos of Rameses II with sun and moon gods, Abu Simbel (G. Roeder, *Naos,* 1914, Pl. 6).
4. Naos of Goldsmiths, XX Dyn., Abydos (*op. cit.,* Pl. 45).
5. Naos of Juf, XII Dyn., Abydos (*op. cit.,* Pl. 41).
6. Naos, temple of Horus, Edfu (De Rochemonteix-Chassinat, *Le Temple d'Édfou,* I, 1897, p. 9).
7. Plan of "Labyrinth," mortuary temple of Amenemhat III, Hawara (Petrie, *The Labyrinth, Gerzeh and Mazghuneh,* 1912, p. 29).

elements offer nothing new, for the general plan follows that of the royal tombs, having an entrance passage with anterooms, a pillared hall and a sarcophagus chamber (Plate XXXII–2). The sloping passage *a,* leading from the temple, opens into an antechamber at *b;* from this room another passage, forty-five feet long, leads at right angles to still another anteroom, running transversely the full width of the building, which was roofed with stone slabs cut to the tent-shape seen on the pavilions of the Heb-Sed festival.[44] The Great Hall is a three-aisled chamber, a hundred by sixty-five feet, surrounded by cells, or alcoves. Around the four sides of the room is a deep trench, leaving the central part an isolated platform, ascended by stairways cut at each end. The ten pillars on the platform are of rose granite, seven of which are monoliths and all intended to be sculptured. Two cavities cut into the pavement of the platform were perhaps intended for the ceremonial resting places of a symbolic coffin and canopic chest, while another long, transverse chamber, again with the traditional tent-roof, was probably some kind of a sarcophagus room. It is thought that the whole Osireion was intended to be buried under a mound, and that the pillared hall was the place where the builder intended to have his body exposed before its permanent entombment at Thebes. A recent theory,[45] dependent upon the assumption that water originally filled the space about the central, pillared platform, considers the Osireion to have been the expression only of a symbolic idea. This idea, according to the theory, was derived from the theology of Heliopolis, and so represented the Primeval Hill rising out of the Primeval Waters. At Heliopolis the hill was the place where death was vanquished and resurrection took place and, as such, it became one of the traditional burial places of Osiris. Therefore in ritualistic and ideographic terms Seti re-created the Primeval Hill by a platform approached by double flights of stairs on which Osiris was enthroned, or entombed, as the ruler of the dead.

A simpler explanation, which preserves the same basic symbolism, is to consider the structure not solely as a cenotaph, but as a Heb-Sed Festival Hall; the raised platform with the double stairs and canopy covering implied by the pillars and the tent-shaped roofs of the adjoining halls, as well as by the encircling niches which remind one of the niche shrines about the Heb-Sed court of Zoser, all suggest some relation to the Jubilee Festival at which time the king was reborn as Osiris. However doubtful these explanations may be, Seti I took a personal interest in the construction of the hall, for he had a palace built nearby so that he could watch the work progress. Even if all the elements of this building can be found in the Heb-Sed tradition and if we hesitate to agree with Dr. Frankfort's statement that Seti I was "the first and last king to have undertaken this extraordinary architectural expression of things religious," still it remains a remarkable example of Egyptian architecture.

[44] Page 71.
[45] H. Frankfort, A. de Buck, and B. Gunn, *Cenotaph of Seti I,* Abydos (1933); M. A. Murray, *The Osireion* (1904).

6. *DYNASTIC TEMPLES, I*

Thy house of a million of years. . . . .
A resting place for my father at all his feasts.
KING AMENHOTEP III, XVIII DYNASTY

THE GODS OF EGYPT, for whom by the New Kingdom a materialistically imposing religious architecture was erected throughout the valley, were such a confusion of regional survivals that their individual attributes, with a few exceptions, had very little influence upon the ultimate types of temples in which they were honored. They formed no established pantheon, save as the priests of Amon-Re succeeded in subordinating all other divinities to their Sun-god. When grouped according to their influence upon architecture, they divide into four classes, which conform to lines of social cleavage. At the top of this architectural and celestial hierarchy stood the king who, although he recognized the superiority of the gods by his lavish contributions and his prescribed observance of all propitiatory rites, was a divinity—the son of Re, the living Osiris, the Horus chief and, by extension, the incarnation of any and all the gods. During the Old Kingdom, as the Falcon triumphed over all the divinities and totems of the other clans, the king took unto himself their attributes. At first the royal chieftain was the high priest of his own protecting gods, and was assisted by laymen. When the unification of Egypt centered more and more of such unrelated communal worship in the person of the conquering Horus, the king delegated many of his priestly duties to nobles and members of his family, but remained the titular high priest of all gods. The regular service in the temples was a ritual of attendance based upon the daily needs of a powerful one living in his residence. Gradually, however, the religious offices and services were inherited by a powerful priesthood, who in the end overshadowed even the despotic will of the Pharaoh, so that during the XXI Dynasty the High Priests of Amon wore the Double Crown. It was the unlimited materialism of the ceremony of the dead, more than the ritual to the gods, which brought about a large priestly caste and put into its hands a tyrannical power.

Above the king, but unquestionably after him in architectural influence, were the Greater Gods, with Amon-Re acquiring an absolute ascendancy, and Osiris retaining his control over the all-important kingdom of the dead. Besides his peculiar relation to the Heb-Sed festival and its architectural embodiment, Osiris left his most evident mark upon the architecture in the Osiris pier (Plate XXXVIII–2). Temples were also built to the Lesser Gods, who retained at different times and places some of their original local prominence in their special capacities, but often their chapels and shrines were incorporated into the temples of Amon-Re. Of these Lesser Divinities the temples and chapels of the cow-goddess Hathor were distinguished by the head of the goddess as a capital (Plates XXXVII–2; LX–2), and the chapels of the matrimonial deity, Bes, during the Græco-Roman period,

PLATE XXXIII: MORTUARY TEMPLES

1

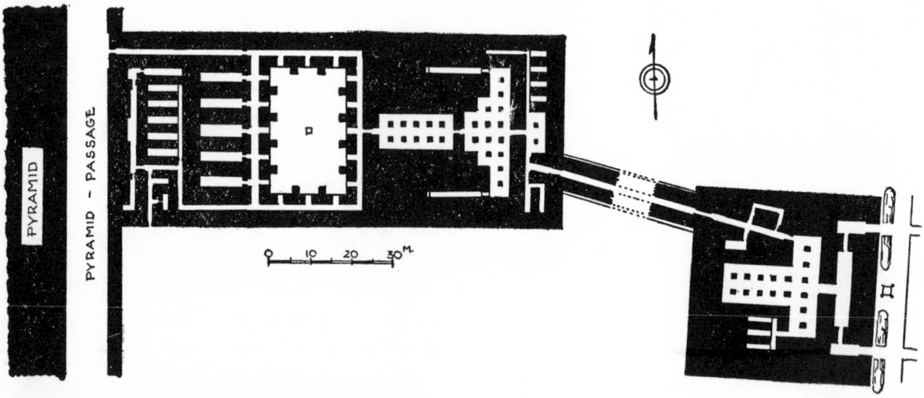

2

3

4

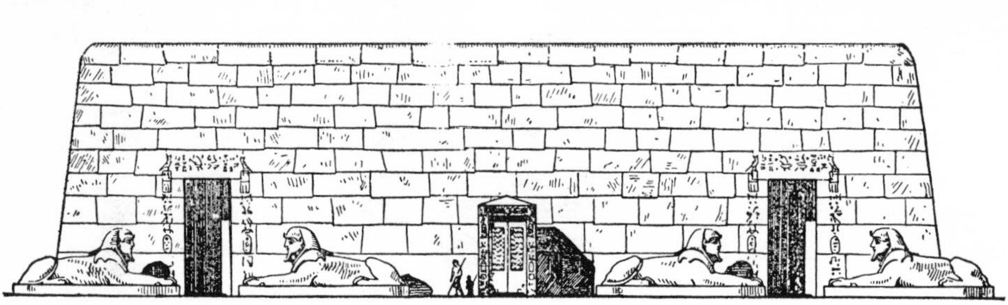

had his dwarflike figure attached to the pillars or carved upon the capitals (Plate LVIII–3). The Minor Divinities, to whom no temples were built, belonged to the people and were worshiped in the home or in the open.

THE SHRINE

At the beginning of the Dynastic period the temple, "the house called Shelter-of-the-Gods," and the usages which it embodied were in an undeveloped stage. The cult-house was little more than a venerated hut-shrine built, as it still is among the Dinka of the Sudan (Plate LXIV–1), in imitation of the primitive house. Many of these shrines are known, but none exist, and only a few are pictured in the hieroglyphs.[1] At Abydos was the shrine and tomb of Osiris to which the dead made pilgrimages before interment in their own distant tombs; at Hierakonpolis was the House of the Sacred Falcon; in the Delta was the temple of Re at Heliopolis and the sanctuary of the cat-goddess at Bubastis; and in the Fayum was the residence of the crocodile divinity. Nothing in Egypt was entirely forgotten, and the aboriginal shrine kept something of its basic form in the stone temples of the New Kingdom. In fact the primitive religious shelter survived in three ways: besides its fixation in pictographic writing and its persistence for ceremonial usages, it was preserved in the naos, or inner Holy of Holies, of the great temples.

The shrine of Ptah is pictured on the walls of the temple of Seti I at Abydos as a tent-like structure covered by a saddle roof, with the king officiating as high priest before the god in his naos (Plate II–7). Even after the temples became colossal monuments of stone, the traditional elements of the primitive sanctuary were conserved. In all the temples the shrine chamber is a simple and small rectangular stone room, with only one door, except in the case of the naos for Amon-Re which has a door at either end so that the sacred boat of the Sun-god could be dragged through the sanctuary. All the stone sanctuaries in the temple of Seti I at Abydos have curved ceilings in imitation of the hooped roof of the traditional hut-shrine (Plate LII–1). By the Ptolemaic period the naos of the god was frequently, as at Edfu (Plate XXXII–6), a stone monolith, hollowed out and carved to reproduce the tent or hut shelter which was then three or four thousand years old. All the earliest types of hut-shrine are preserved in the small portable shrines of stone, the conical hut in a naos of the XX Dynasty from Abydos (Plate XXXII–4), the *per-our* or tent-roofed house shrine

[1] Page 57. Rémy Cottevieille-Giraudet, "Note sur le Kiosque de Fête Sed," *Fouilles de l'Institut français d'Archéologie orientale du Caire,* IX (1933), p. 36 *seq.,* says the tent-roofed kiosk was the sanctuary of Upper Egypt, the primitive palace of the Southern Kings, the *per-our,* "the great house", and the hoop-roofed kiosk, in its turn, was the sanctuary of Lower Egypt, a palace type, the *per-nou* or *per-neser,* "the house of the flame."

PLATE XXXIII

1. Plan of temple of Khafra, Gizeh (U. Hölscher, *Das Grabdenkmal des Königs Chephren,* 1912, Pl. III).
2. Interior of "portico temple" restored (Hölscher, *op. cit.,* Pl. V).
3. Interior "portico temple," Gizeh.
4. Façade of "portico temple" restored (Hölscher, *op. cit.,* Fig. 5).

of the Southern Kings in a XII Dynasty naos (Plate XXXII–5), the *per-nou* or hoop-roofed sanctuary of the Northern Kings,[2] and the simple flat-roofed shelter with a reed parapet (Plate XXXII–3). A realization of this fixity of ancient Egyptian habit helps to make the architecture comprehensible.

THE MORTUARY TEMPLE

OLD KINGDOM. From the intricately interrelated beliefs regarding death and divinity, especially as they found expression at the hands of an all-powerful king, evolved two types of temple—one for the dead Pharaoh, and the other for the gods—which in the New Kingdom tended to combine into one architectural and religious concept. After the deified kings of the Old Kingdom began the struggle against oblivion they evolved the pyramid for protection and the funerary temple for offerings, prayers, and eternal service. Retaining the instinctive architectural dependence upon the house concept, they thought of the mortuary temple as an everlasting residence, a royal palace in which the *Ka* could enjoy the necessary care and attendance of subjects and servants. The transformation of hut chapels, with offering tables in front of them, into actual temples was a slow process. The development was not so much a matter of new needs as it was the result of the gradual substitution of an elaborate symbolic drama for the simplicity of primitive provisions. Just as the practical custom of renewing the effective fertility of the chieftain by slaying him after thirty years of rule was dramatized into the complicated, but no longer fatal, Sed festival, so the equally direct and efficient custom of providing kingly service in the hereafter by slaughtered attendants was remade into a ritual wherein living and endowed priests provided attendance in the Eternal Home.

The Thinite kings of the I Dynasty continued, with rapidly diminishing popularity, the practice of human sacrifice. Their tombs, surrounded by the graves of wives, concubines, and servants, required no elaborate symbolic residence and service. A simple thatched hut above the grave, with the stelæ and offering table, were all that was required.[3] By the III Dynasty the chapel for offerings was a small addition to the superstructures of the tomb, and at Saqqara the provisions of King Zoser reproduced in stone his palace complex at Memphis. The mortuary temple of Zoser (Plate XIX), while exceptional in many respects, undoubtedly reflected in its architectural arrangement some residential or ceremonial hall at Memphis which was distinguished by a columnar portico.

Immediately after Zoser there seems to have been a return to more simple sepulchral provisions regarding the tomb-chapel, for the pyramid of Sneferu at Meydum (Plate XXIV–5), dating from the very end of the III Dynasty, has a modest chapel, like those attached to mastabas, on the east side. It consists of a small court attached to the sloping sides of the pyramid, its stone walls rounded on top to imitate the earlier mud walls. At the end of the court is the chapel with two doors, and

[2] G. Roeder, *Naos,* Catalogue Général des Antiquités Égyptiennes du Musée du Caire (1914), Tafs. 4, 8, 16, 38.

[3] Dr. Reisner says (*op. cit.,* p. 320) that the mortuary shrines were at first "open air chapels." It is true that "all the chapels preserved to us from Dynasty I and the greater part of Dynasty II, whatever their forms, were open air chapels," but the lack of evidence, important as it may or may not be, does not preclude the possibility that early royal tombs had hut-shrines made of perishable materials, which would have left no archæological trace.

in front of them two stelæ, like the Sun-god's obelisks in front of the New Kingdom temples of Amon-Re.[4]

Since nothing remains of the pyramid-temple of Khufu except its basalt foundations, the mortuary temple of Khafra, his successor, furnishes the best indication of how large and important the tomb-chapel had become in the IV Dynasty (Plate XXXIII–1). The actual building is ruined beyond recognition by any casual visitor, but the plan shows a large, rectangular edifice, 110 m. long, situated on the east side of the pyramid. Its sole entrance was the enclosed corridor of the causeway leading down to the valley. To the right of the entrance was a chamber for the guardian and to the left was the vestibule with magazines leading off from it. From the vestibule a short passage gave access to a T-shaped hall, in which were square monolithic piers of Aswân granite, and at both ends of the horizontal arm of this reception hall were *serdabs*. After the hall came an open court surrounded by large rectangular piers, each one with a statue of the king, presumably as Osiris, in front of it. Off the west side of the court were five parallel sanctuaries where the Pharaoh was worshiped under his five official titles.[5] The public was not allowed beyond these chapels, and only the priests could penetrate to the inner storerooms and the holy of holies in which were two "false-door" stelæ.

The temple of Khafra somewhat resembled a mastaba in its construction: it was a low, rectangular mass of masonry with a flat roof and very solid walls, made of large limestone blocks faced with heavy granite ashlar, some of the stones weighing as much as 470,000 kilograms. The rose colored granite of the walls and pillars, the alabaster pavements, and the economy of reliefs and hieroglyphs must have given to it an impressive austerity. Some idea of its appearance can be formed from the "Portico" building, a quarter of a mile away at the edge of the fertile valley, with which the temple was connected by a covered corridor. The "Portico" is known as "the Granite Temple," "the Temple of the Sphinx," or just as "the Valley-temple." Inasmuch as the Pharaohs had their residences near their pyramids and funerary temples, and at Saqqara there was seen to be a definite relation between the royal residence and the sepulchral buildings, "the valley-temple" must have been in some way directly related to the palace. The practical purpose of the "Portico" structure was as a landing stage during the high water, but was also, perhaps, a reception hall or ceremonial portico, with a monumental façade, where "the ceremonies that were celebrated had without doubt a character more official than religious."[6] Its façade (Plate XXXIII–4), which was 12 m. high, had the edge of its flat roof rounded in imitation of the earlier tradition of brick and mud construction. The two doorways, symbolic of the North and South Kingdoms, were flanked by figures of the king in the form of a lion sphinx, "protecting his palace with his magical and divine power."

The interior is still impressive. The vestibule extends the full width of the building and from its center a door opens into a T-shaped hall with square monolithic piers of Aswân granite (Plate

[4] Allan Rowe, "Excavations at Meydum," *Museum Journal* (Penn. Univ.) XXII (1931), p. 30 *seq.*, Pl. XLI.
[5] A. Moret, *Mystères Égyptiens* (1922), p. 292.
[6] A. Moret, *Mystères Égyptiens*, p. 294.

PLATE XXXIV: MORTUARY TEMPLES

1

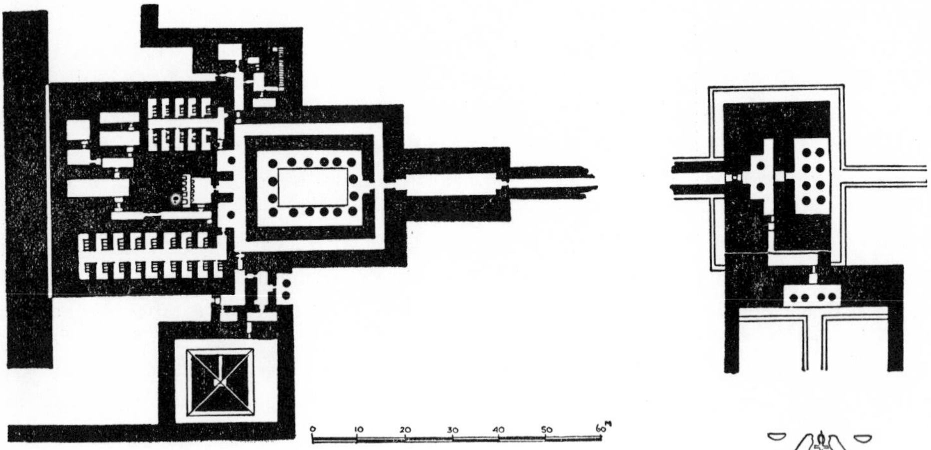

2

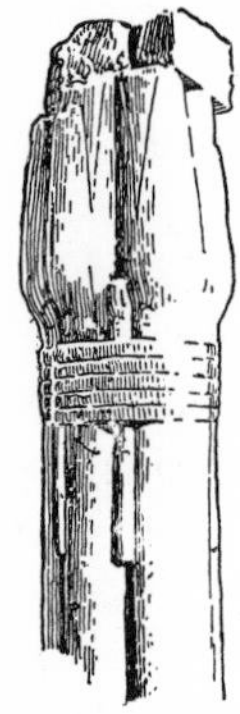

3

4

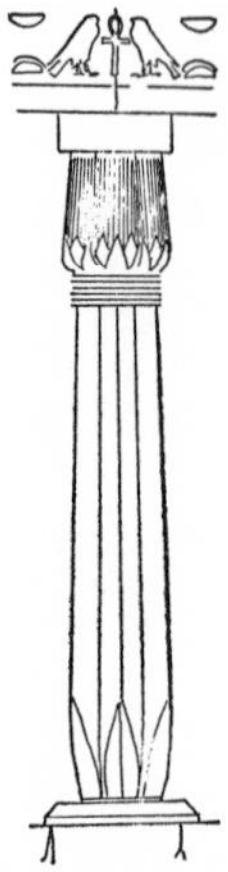

5

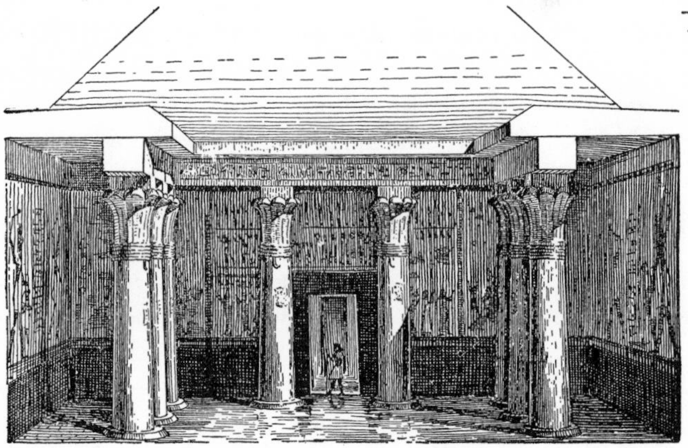

XXXIII–3). The T-shaped plan resulted from the combination within the stone terrace of two traditional house elements, the columnar hall and the royal portico in front of it. Around the walls of this hall were twenty-three seated statues of Khafra, each facing a pillar. The statues differed in their details and were carved in various fine stones, some of green diorite, others of white alabaster, and still others of yellow schist. They must have glowed dramatically in the half light of the polished and undecorated interior, lit only by oblique slits at the top of the walls,[7] which focused a spotlight on each figure (Plate XXXIII–2). A short corridor at the left leads to the storerooms for vestments, vases, lamps, etc., all necessary for the ritualistic ablutions and fumigations. At the right another corridor joins the covered causeway going up to the temple, and off this corridor is a guard-room on one side and an alabaster ramp to the roof on the other side.

Two features of Khafra's Portico are significant: in the first place, the absence of any painted or carved decorations emphasizes its massive proportions and differentiates it from the subsequent stonework covered with scenes and hieroglyphs; and in the second place it has the earliest known use of free-standing stone supports. The solid, lithic character of the architecture is very different in its simple massiveness from the small and imitative stonework at Saqqara. But even here it is impossible to say that the Old Kingdom masons developed the *square pier* directly out of stone construction. Wooden columns, perhaps squared, must have been common long before the IV Dynasty, and the use here in the Gizeh temple of peg dowels at the top of the stone piers and cramps of wood to bind together the architrave blocks indicates the influence of wood joinery which cannot be overlooked in explaining the origin of such piers.[8] In fact, these rectangular and monolithic piers may have originated in the Egyptian mind, not long before this time, from building either brick or stone walls pierced by a series of doorways, placed so close together as to make their common doorjambs suggest a rectangular pier.[9]

In the V Dynasty the funerary temple of King Sahure at Abusir is built in a different and more typical style of stone architecture (Plate XXXIV–1). Instead of the massive simplicity of the IV Dynasty it has walls and columns decorated with painted stucco and carved reliefs, and the columns are carefully sculptured in imitation of plant forms. While it was primarily a grave-temple for the king, the structure was also dedicated to the worship of Re, for among its decorations is the first use of the

[7] U. Hölscher, *Grabdenkmal des Königs Chephren* (1912), p. 48.
[8] Clarke and Engelbach, *op. cit.*, p. 112, Fig. 121.
[9] G. Jéquier, *Manuel d'Archéologie Égyptienne*, p. 152.

PLATE XXXIV

1. Plan of temple and "portico temple" of Sahure, Abusir (L. Borchardt, *Das Grabdenkmal des Königs Sahu-re,* 1910, Pl. II).
2. Lotus capital from V Dyn. mastaba of Ptah-Shepses, Abusir, in Cairo Museum.
3. Model of Sahure's portico temple, Abusir (Borchardt, *op. cit.,* Pl. III).
4. Papyrus column, Abusir (Borchardt, *op. cit.,* Pl. XI).
5. Forecourt of Sahure's temple restored (Borchardt, *op. cit.,* Pl. VI).

common sun-disk flanked by *uraei*. Sahure was one of the three kings at the opening of the V Dynasty who were either priests, or the sons of priests, raised to royal power in order to bring about a recrudescence of sun-worship.[10]

The Portico or Valley-temple at Abusir has a plan which recalls a royal residence (Plate XXXIV-1, 3). Its columnar portico is a feature associated during the Old Kingdom with palace architecture, while its interior reception hall has a T-shape, somewhat like the interior of the Portico at Gizeh. The temple proper, although it has the same essential elements as the IV Dynasty temples and preserves the basic characteristics of a dwelling—with vestibule, hall, and court—is much more elongated, in order to emphasize the professional ritual.[11] The long, narrow vestibule opens into a corridor extending around both sides of the inner walls. These inner walls form an open court, paved with basalt and surrounded by a peristyle of red granite columns whose sculptured capitals imitate palm fronds (Plate XXXIV–5). These are the earliest known examples of the *palm-leaf capital,* which seems to have gone out of fashion, except in domestic architecture, during both the Middle and New Kingdoms, and was revived in the Græco-Roman period. Beyond the court are *serdabs,* sanctuaries, and storerooms. In addition to the palm columns, there are two other types of columns at Abusir, imitated from the symbolic papyrus and lotus. Granite monolithic columns, 12 feet high, imitate *bundles of papyrus plants* bound together, the flowering heads standing erect instead of spreading into a campaniform capital (Plate XXXIV–4). After the Old Kingdom the space between the bundles on this type of column is filled by reeds, cut off short at the top and bottom. In the mastaba of Ptahshepses, also dating from the V Dynasty, are columns with a lotus-flower capital (Plate XXXIV–2) which are not found again in stone until the Middle Kingdom.

MIDDLE KINGDOM. The desire of the Pharaohs of the Middle Kingdom to strengthen their position as worthy successors of the divine kings of the Old Kingdom led them to revive old forms and scrupulously to preserve the formalized traditions. At Lisht, Amenemhet I and Senwosret I built pyramids with the customary temples. Further south, near the opening in the Libyan hills which gives access to the Fayum, is El-Lahun, where Senwosret II kept to the same sepulchral traditions. Nearby at Hawara, however, Amenemhet III, towards the close of the XII Dynasty, built himself a mortuary temple whose size so impressed the classical world that it lived on in man's memory as the great Labyrinth, one of the wonders of the ancient world. Little is known about this structure, for the enthusiastic descriptions of Herodotus, Strabo, and Pliny are evidently inaccurate and confused. Like all buildings of this period it suffered during the Hyksos interim; later its stones were used by irreverent builders of the New Kingdom; and finally its ruins served as quarries for all succeeding ages. Petrie says, "From the scanty indications of the levels of the ground, and the fragmentary accounts of

[10] "His Majesty caused that there be brought for him two false doors from Troja of stone, that they be laid in the audience-hall of the house (called): 'Sahure-Shines-with-Crowns' and that the two priests of Memphis and the artisans of the [........] be assigned to them, that the work on them might be done in the presence of the King himself. The stone work went on every day; there was an inspection of that which was done on them in the court daily. His Majesty had [color] put on them, and had them painted in blue." Breasted, *Ancient Records,* I, No. 239.

[11] In the vestibule of the mortuary temple of Neferkere at Abusir the doorjambs and lining of the walls were of wood (L. Borchardt, *Das Grabdenkmal des Königs Nefer-ke-re,* 1909, Figs. 42, 43).

ancient authors, it appears as if the Labyrinth were a peristyle temple with a central passage and two great crossways: the first crossway with courts or small temples opening on each side of it; the second crossway being a hall with a long row of columns, and with courts opening on the farther side of it, much like the temple of Abydos," [12] or, we might add, like a more monumental and developed version of such complicated mortuary provisions such as Zoser had at Saqqara. Petrie's restoration of one section of the labyrinth (Plate XXXI-7) shows a combination and repetition of house units, each with three chambers and a royal, porticoed court.

The suggestion that the Labyrinth was a peristyle temple recalls the sepulchral innovation of the Middle Kingdom. At Deir el-Bahari Mentuhotep III, in the XI Dynasty, combined the temple and the pyramid into an architectural unit, subordinating the tomb itself and making the temple an imposing colonnade about a pyramidal core.[13] Very little remains of this temple, and nothing exists of the temple complex of Osiris at Abydos which, if it was not an actual mortuary temple, was connected with the grave of Osiris and played an important rôle in the cult of the Dead. Several kings of the Old Kingdom added buildings to the shrine of Osiris. In the Middle Kingdom Senwosret I undertook to rebuild the sanctuary; and according to his vizier and master of works, "I conducted the work on the temple, built his house, and dug the (sacred) lake; I masoned the well, by command of the Majesty of Horus." Later Senwosret III sent officials to Abydos to adorn the temple with gold, and hew for the king a cenotaph in which his body could be exposed before it was interred in his pyramid at Dashur. The king's official has left inscriptions describing the passion-play of Osiris in which he was proud to take part, saying, "They brought Osiris, First of the Westerners, Lord of Abydos, to his palace (temple) and I followed the god into his house, to attend to his (needs), when he resumed his seat." [14] Otherwise the shrine of Osiris is more obscure than the other ruined buildings of the Middle Kingdom.

NEW KINGDOM. The continuity of Egyptian architecture can be more clearly presented if the social and political factors which made possible the grandiose architecture of the New Kingdom are discussed later in relation to the temples of the gods, for the mortuary temples of the Second Theban Empire conformed to the same architectural standards. The exception to such conformity was the funerary edifice which Queen Hatshepsut built in the XVIII Dynasty at Deir el-Bahari. Some time before the middle of the first Dynasty of the New Kingdom, the energetic queen ordered Senmut, the architect, to build a temple at the foot of the cliffs alongside of the temple-pyramid of Mentuhotep. The work was begun in the fifth or eighth year of the reign of young Thutmose III for whom the queen was acting as regent.[15] It was intended to be a mortuary place of worship for herself and her ancestors, for by that time the royal tombs were rock-cut and hidden in the Valley of the Kings, which lay back of the high cliffs at Deir el-Bahari.

[12] Petrie, *The Labyrinth, Gerzeh and Mazghuneh* (1912).

[13] Page 103.

[14] Breasted, *op. cit.*, I, No. 669.

[15] H. E. Winlock, *Bulletin of the Metropolitan Museum of Art,* XXIII (1928), Sect. II, pp. 26 *seq.;* XXIII (Sect. II), pp. 3*f. seq.*, XXVII (1932), Sect. II, pp. 4 *seq.;* W. C. Hayes, *Royal Sarcophagi of the XVIIIth Dynasty,* p. 146.

PLATE XXXV: MORTUARY TEMPLES

1

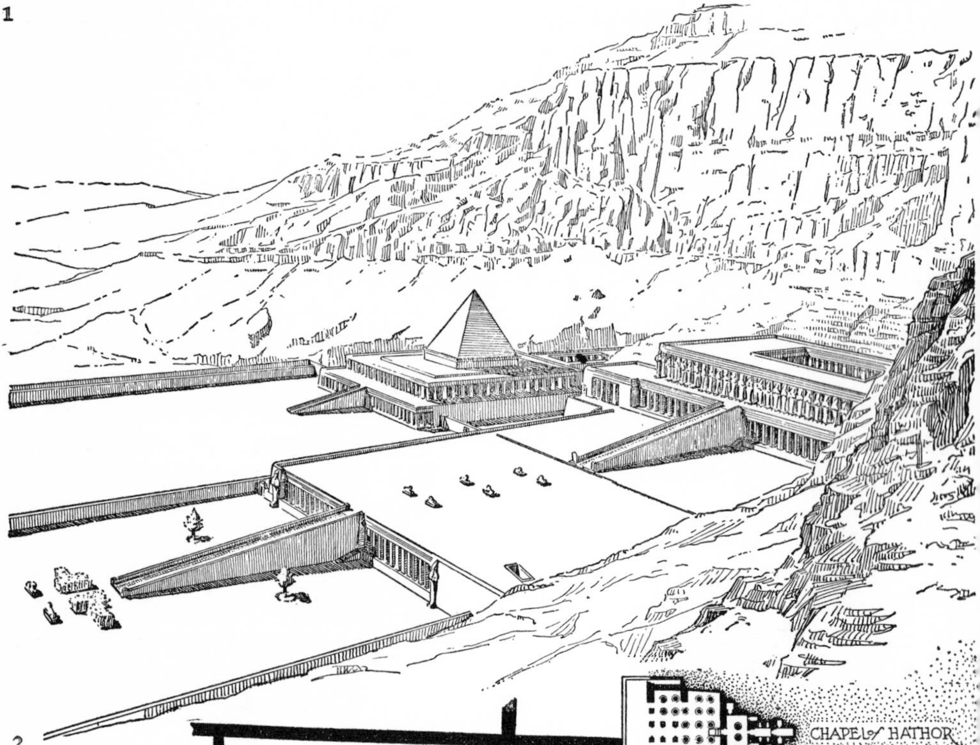

2

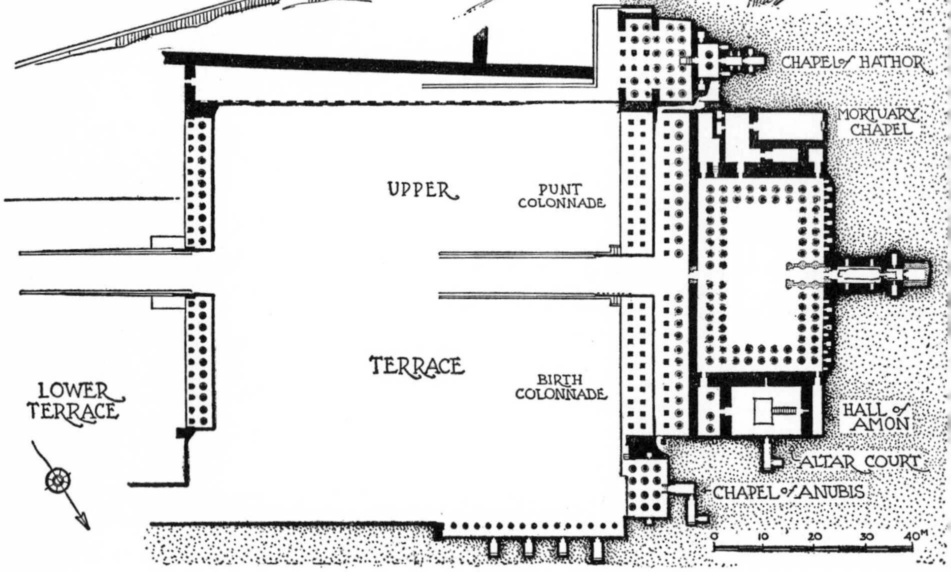

The queen's intention was to excavate the long, subterranean corridors of her tomb beneath the cliffs so that her burial chamber would lie directly beneath the temple. This plan was not carried out according to her orders because the quality of the rock forced the builders to mine the seven hundred foot corridor of her tomb in a wide curve which carried it away from the temple. There were also other motives behind the queen's intense interest in the building. At the time she was involved in a bitter feud with the Thutmoside men of her family, and in order to sustain her unprecedented feminine rights to the Double Crown, she wanted to show her people that she was the divine daughter of Amon-Re. For this reason her temple was more than an offertory shrine.

The queen was no ordinary woman and Senmut, her closest counselor, was no commonplace architect.[16] When she conceived the idea of building an earthly palace for the Sun-god, like the "myrrh terraces" of Punt, which was the legendary homeland of the gods, Senmut not only created an exceptional type of temple, but supervised sending the difficult expedition to Punt—probably at the southern end of the Red Sea—to get the myrrh trees for the terraced gardens of the "Paradise of Amon." Senmut, who was an architect worthy to rank in originality with Imhotep, was somewhat influenced by the neighboring temple-pyramid of Mentuhotep with its rising terraces of columnar porticoes approached by a ramp, but his mistress wanted a garden-villa for her god. In order to meet such a requirement, Senmut started with the perhaps not uncommon idea of a terraced garden and into its construction worked the portico motive (Plate XXXV).

The approach to the temple was originally an avenue of sphinxes leading up from the valley to the now vanished portal in the wall about the forecourt, before which were two sacred Persea trees. Inside the first court were carefully watered palm trees and papyrus beds. Still standing at its western end is a colonnaded portico, partly restored, which forms the retaining wall and the front face of the first terrace. The portico has two rows of columns, square piers in front, and sixteen-sided columns in back. An inclined ramp ascends to the top of the first terrace, and at the lower end of each parapet, flanking this ramp, was a beautifully incised lion, guarding the entrance. One of these lions is still in place (Plate XXXVI–4). The mortuary character of the temple is indicated by the traditional niche treatment, consisting of a row of large *serekh* façades, each surmounted by an Horus, carved upon the supporting wall at the south side of the terrace (Plate XXXVI–3).

At the back of the first terrace is another colonnade. The painted reliefs in these porticoes at either side of the second ramp, which goes up to the second terrace, are remarkable examples of Egyptian art and valuable documents as to the building of the temple. The Birth colonnade at the north side depicts the divine nativity of Hatshepsut in the presence of the gods, and the Punt colonnade at the

[16] Pages 238-239.

PLATE XXXV

1. Restored perspective of temples of Hatshepsut and Mentuhotep, Deir el-Bahari (after Winlock, *The Bulletin of the Metropolitan Museum of Art*, XXVII, 1932, Fig. 1).
2. Plan of Hatshepsut's temple (Naville, *The Temple of Deir el-Bahari*, VI, 1908, Pl. CLXXII).

PLATE XXXVI: MORTUARY TEMPLES

1

2

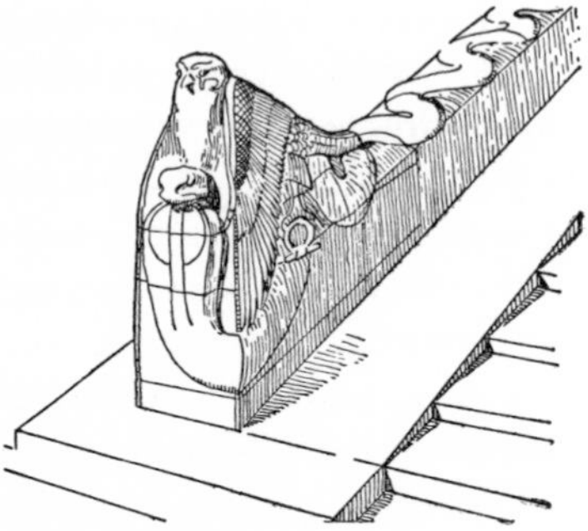

3

4

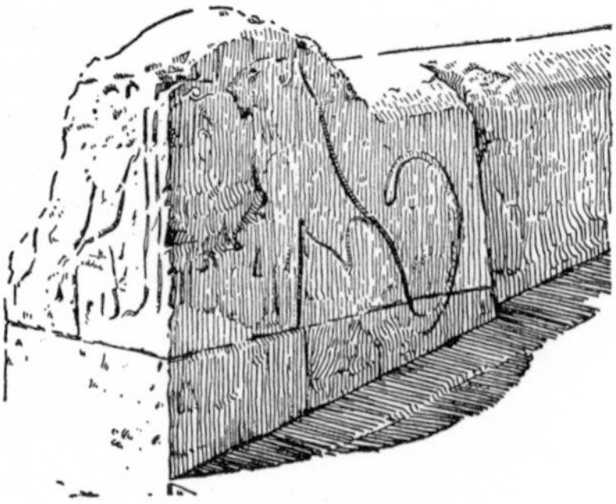

south side describes in pictorial form the famous expedition to Punt. In building her shrine the energetic queen had no intention of omitting anything which might find favor with her gods. To the right of the Birth colonnade is a sanctuary to Anubis (Plate XXXVII–1), the dog-headed god of the dead, and to the left of the Punt colonnade is a larger sanctuary to Hathor, the sky-goddess who at Thebes was the protectress of the necropolis.

The inner chamber of the Hathor chapel has a rock-hewn reproduction of the traditional curved roof of the primitive shrine, and in the two vestibules are Hathor columns (Plate XXXVII–2). These Hathor capitals illustrate the process, so foreign to the modern mind, by which the stone architecture of Egypt acquired its distinctive shapes. Hathor was an ancient and local divinity in Upper Egypt worshiped at Dendera as a cow, while in Lower Egypt, to the south of Memphis, she was thought to reside in a sycamore tree, and the sistrum was an object sacred to her worship. We may imagine that her ritualistic pillar was at first a wooden post on which was painted the sistrum; then, as Egyptian divinities were anthropomorphized, a female face with cow's ears was painted inside the top of the sistrum, whose curved sides came gradually to be represented as horns and finally as hair.[17] This symbolic sistrum post with a female head surmounted by an *uræus* frieze, was translated into stone as early as the Middle Kingdom.[18] By the New Kingdom the large block of stone above the head suggests a mastaba, perhaps because by that time the goddess was a protectress of tombs.

Across the front of the upper terrace was another colonnade, now destroyed, which served as a vestibule hall for the upper court. Originally the outer row of columns of this colonnade had carved upon them the Osiris images of the queen, but the figures were cut down to pillars by the relentless Thutmose III. Behind what was once the entrance hall is another large court surrounded by the fragments of a double peristyle of columns. Off the north side of the court is the altar, or sacrificial court, and the Hall of Amon, and on the south side is the queen's mortuary chapel, with a tunnel vault of corbeled construction (Plate XXXVII–3). Across the west side of the court are recesses, with the main sanctuary in the middle which is cut back into the cliff, imitating again a hoop roof.

The building was mutilated long before it was ruined. Thutmose III undoubtedly had cause to dislike his domineering relative, who was his stepmother, aunt, mother-in-law, and dominating regent, but mere royal spite is not enough to explain why he had every figure and cartouche of the queen hacked out of the temple after her death in 1479 B.C. He must have felt that she had set a dangerous precedent, as a woman, by usurping divine attributes. Later Akhenaten's effort to suppress the worship

[17] G. Jéquier, *Manuel d'Archéologie Égyptienne* (1924), p. 184.
[18] G. Jéquier, *op. cit.,* Fig. 109.

PLATE XXXVI

1. View of Hatshepsut's temple looking east, Deir el-Bahari.
2. Balustrade of upper stairway, Hatshepsut's temple (H. E. Winlock, *The Bulletin of the Metropolitan Museum,* XXVII, 1932, Sect. II, Fig. 21).
3. Balustrade of Hatshepsut's temple.
4. *Serekh* façade on retaining wall of Hatshepsut's temple.

PLATE XXXVII: MORTUARY TEMPLES

1

2

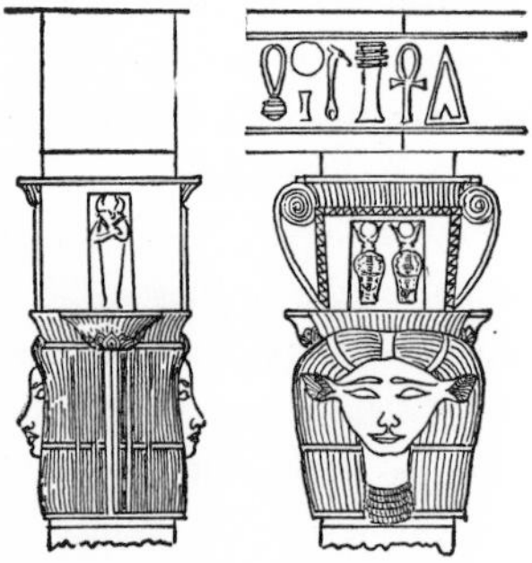

3

4

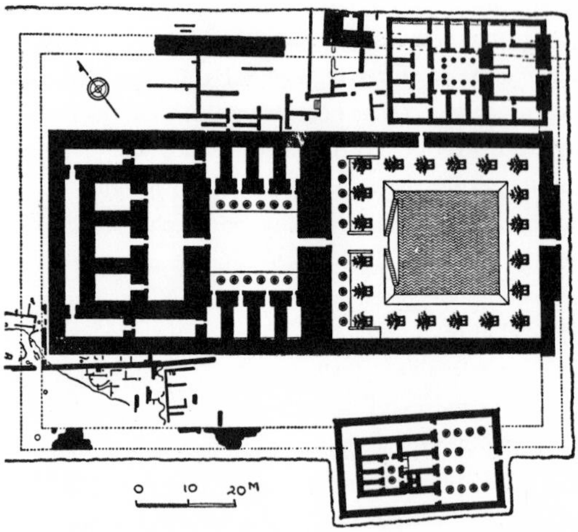

5

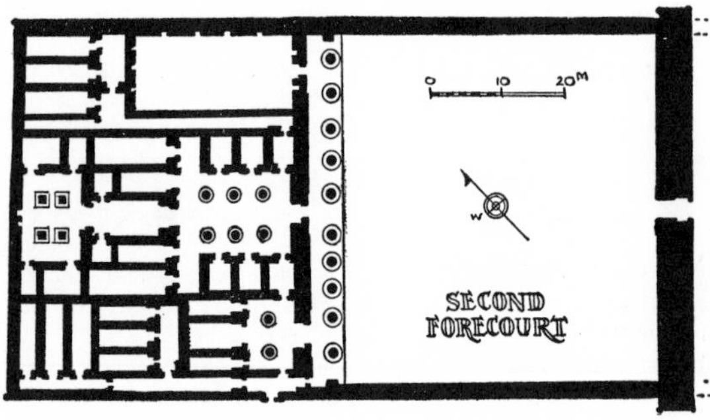

of Amon-Re resulted in more mutilations, while the restorations of Ramses II and a revived interest in the building during Ptolemaic times produced some alterations; but the architectural dissolution of the building began when a Coptic monastery was built on the upper terrace. To-day in its fragmentary and partially restored condition it is the finest building in Egypt from modern standards. While it lacks a sense of human scale, a deficiency of nearly all temples of the New Kingdom, it gives the impression of classic proportions and has a unity of design which is rare in Egyptian architecture (Plate XXXVI–1).

Books of criticism and appreciation on Egypt too frequently insist that the severe and flat horizontality of her stone architecture, so magnificently realized in Queen Hatshepsut's temple, was an inevitable result of environment working upon the architectonic imagery of man. Such imaginative environmentalism draws a parallel between the sharp horizontality of the limestone cliffs, cut with vertical erosions, and the equally flat, two-dimensional extension of Egyptian architecture, with its vertical supports and lithic solidity. The comparison is made to show how the Egyptian genius performed a self-conscious and reflective act of artistic creation when it chose stone as the natural material for building, and adhered to forms which were appropriate to the aspect of the environment.

Without depreciating Senmut's ability, and even admitting the possibility that he was the exceptional Egyptian architect who could realize critically the effectiveness of his design, the intentional æsthetic purpose of Egyptian architecture is in doubt. It does not require the evidence of these terraces at Deir el-Bahari cut with trenches for trees and papyrus beds and laboriously irrigated by water-carriers, to prove that the Egyptians valued a garden in their arid desert. On the other hand, the temple did not look as geometrically structural and modern in the XVIII Dynasty as it does to-day, because it had an enclosing wall around the forecourt which cut off the view, while painted statues, bonded into the piers, introduced a bizarre element into the tectonic simplicity.

The other mortuary temples of the New Kingdom extended along the west bank of the river at Thebes, the first rulers of each Dynasty building somewhere near to the entrance of the Valley of the Kings, and each successive king building his temple further to the north along the river, until, with a new Dynasty, the temples start once more at the southern end of the line, being forced in between the existing structures. With few exceptions so little of them remain that most of the temples can be disregarded: there are some fragments of the temples of Amenhotep I and II, but the large temple of Thutmose III was treated with so little piety by the Pharaohs of the XIX and XX Dynasties, who

---

PLATE XXXVII

1. Chapel of Anubis, Hatshepsut's temple, Deir el-Bahari.
2. Hathor capital from chapel of Hathor, Hatshepsut's temple (Naville, *The Temple of Deir el-Bahari*, III, Pl. LXVIII).
3. Mortuary chapel. Hatshepsut's temple.
4. Temple of Amenhotep, son of Hapu, Thebes (C. Robichon, "Quatre nouveaux Temples Thébains," *Chronique d' Égypte*, X, 1935, p. 237).
5. Plan of temple of Seti I, Qurna, Thebes (B. Porter and R. Moss, *Topographical Bibliography*, II, *Theban Temples*, p. 140).

PLATE XXXVIII: MORTUARY TEMPLES

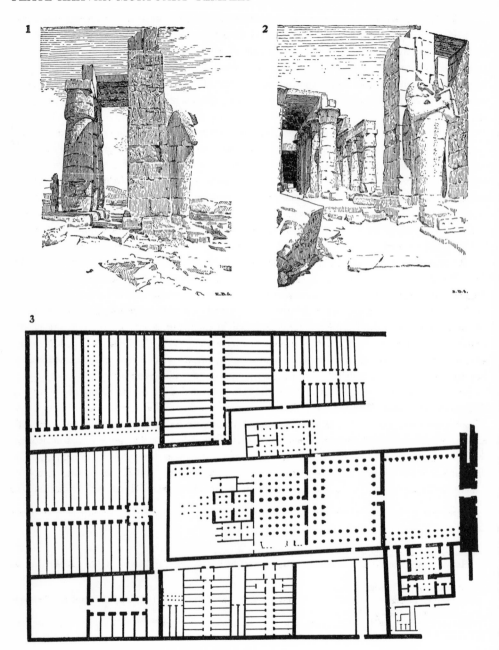

1

2

3

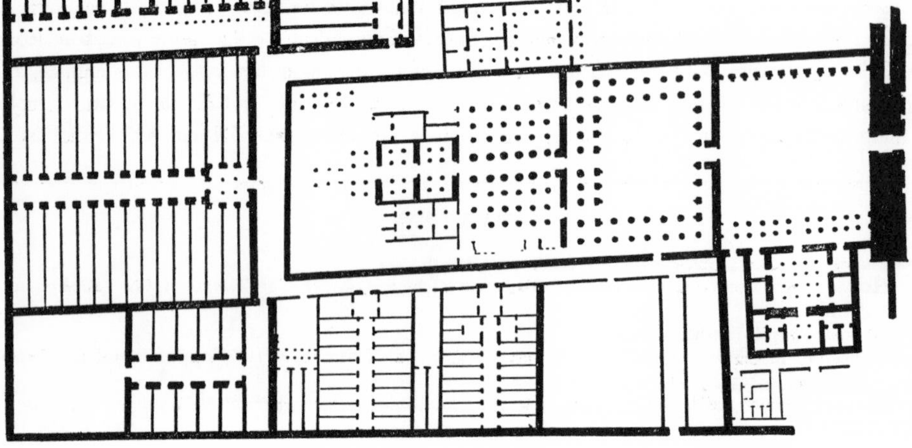

re-used its stones, that only an imprint of it has survived.[19] It was a retribution which must have satisfied the outraged spirit of Queen Hatshepsut. Ineni, the architect, says of the temple of Amenhotep I, "its doors were erected of copper made in one sheet; the part thereof were of electrum." [20]

Mortuary temples are usually considered a royal privilege, but at the end of the XVIII Dynasty Amenhotep, son of Hapu, the famous sage, great architect and counselor of King Amenhotep III, built himself at Thebes a temple of kingly proportions (Plate xxxvii–4). In the forecourt was a rectangular pool surrounded by trees and at the west was a monumental portico of eight columns on a raised platform, approached by three ramps, through which one entered the temple. Within the temple was a smaller court with a colonnade and chambers on each side, and at the west end a triple sanctuary preceded by a hall, or vestibule, covered, as reported, with a great tunnel vault.[21] Amenhotep, who in Ptolemaic times was elevated to divine worship along with Zoser's architect, Imhotep, was allowed royal privileges in his own life and, as far as we know, was the first to use the tunnel vault in something more than a utilitarian and protective manner.

Little exists of the mortuary temple of Amenhotep III, but his building inscriptions give some idea of its magnificence and indicate how an Egyptian Pharaoh looked upon his temple as an eternal dwelling and stronghold. "He made (it) as his monument for his father Amon, Lord of Thebes, making for him an august temple (called 'House-of-Amon-on-the-West-of-Thebes') on the west of Thebes, *an eternal everlasting fortress* [22] of fine white sandstone, wrought with gold throughout; its floor is adorned with silver, all its portals with electrum; it is made very wide and large, and established forever; and adorned with this very great monument (the stele which was in the back wall of the holy of holies and marked the station of the King).... Flagstaves are set up before it, wrought with electrum; it (the pylon) resembles *the horizon in heaven* [23] when Re rises therein. Its lake is filled with the great Nile, Lord of fish and fowl." [24] "Its storehouses contain all good things whose number is not known. It is surrounded with settlements of Syrians, colonized with children of princes, its cattle are like the sands of the shore, they make up millions." [25]

There are three other mortuary temples whose remains justify architectural consideration. All three, the temples of Seti I, Ramses II, and Ramses III, illustrate how closely the funerary temples of the XIX Dynasty resembled the regular cult-monuments, save for a few special provisions connected

[19] A. E. P. Weigall, *Annales du Service,* VII, pp. 125-141; VIII, p. 286 plan. For Temples of Amenhotep I and Thutmose IV see Petrie, *Six Temples at Thebes.*

[20] Breasted, *op. cit.,* I, No. 45.

[21] Clément Robichon, "Quatre Nouveaux Temples Thébains," *Chronique d'Égypte,* X (1935), p. 237, Fig. 1.

[22] Pages 139, 145, 211, 218.

[23] Page 153.

[24] Breasted, *op cit.,* II, No. 883.

[25] Breasted, *op. cit.,* II, No. 884.

PLATE XXXVIII

1. Interior of second forecourt looking north, Ramesseum, Thebes.
2. Interior of second forecourt, looking west.
3. Plan of the Ramesseum (U. Hölscher).

PLATE XXXIX: MORTUARY TEMPLES

1

2

with the service of the dead. By this time the Pharaoh was so identified with the gods that both types of structure served much the same purpose, and it is impossible to say whether one or the other set the standard for all religious edifices.

The first in chronological order is the funerary temple of Seti I, which was begun by his father, Ramses I, and finished by his son, Ramses II. The son had enough respect for his father's and grandfather's "august palace of eternity" not to appropriate it entirely to his own service, as he did so many temples begun by his predecessors. Ramses II, however, laid full claim in the inscriptions to this exceptional act of piety, which can be explained by the suspicion that he completely appropriated the so-called Ramesseum which may have been begun by Seti I for his own use. The temple, which is at Qurna, near Deir el-Bahari, is a typical axial temple of two forecourts with pylons in front of the vestibule halls and sanctuaries (Plate XXXVII–5). The inscriptions read, "Seti I, he made (it) as his monument for his father, Osiris—Ramses I [triumphant; making for him a house] of millions of years, the Temple-of-the-Spirit-of-Seti-Merneptah-in-the-House-of-Amon-on-the-West-of-Thebes."[26] It was originally 518 feet long, but to-day what remains is the main structure with the sanctuaries and part of the colonnade of papyrus bud columns which formed a raised portico leading from the second court into the actual temple. Three doorways, originally closed with doors "of real cedar, wrought with Asiatic copper, made high and large,"[27] lead from this colonnaded vestibule into the various halls. In the center is the main Hypostyle Hall, lit by a clerestory and flanked by alcoves after the tradition of royal residences, in which the painted reliefs show Seti I enthroned between both Amon-Re and Mut and between Ptah and Sekhmet, the respective patron divinities of Thebes and Memphis. The Hypostyle Hall, we are told, was "a wide hall, shining in the midst of his house, a place for the appearance of his august image at his beautiful 'Feast of the Valley.'"[28] Other reliefs depict the king as Osiris, the pacing off of the temple plan in the presence of Amon-Re, and the king performing certain ceremonies before himself as a god. Along the processional axis are two smaller, columnar halls, leading to the main naos, which has doors at both ends because it was dedicated to Amon-Re and still has the pedestals to carry his sacred boat. At the right of the Hypostyle Hall is the Altar Hall of Ramses II, and at the left is the chapel of Ramses I, in which are double stelæ, or "false-doors," on the end walls, and a dado of *serekh*-façade panels around the other walls. Nothing remains of the many storerooms and other brick structures which surrounded the temple, although the depression of the sacred lake of ablutions can still be located to the west of the sanctuary in what was once the temenos.

More important and better preserved is the mortuary temple of Ramses II, known as the Ramesseum and built during his reign from 1292-1225 B.C. Its sepulchral relation was recognized by Diodorus,

[26] Breasted, *op. cit.*, III, No. 212.
[27] Breasted, *op. cit.*, III, No. 217.
[28] Breasted, *op. cit.*, III, No. 218.

PLATE XXXIX

1. South side of Ramesseum, Thebes.
2. Brick storage vaults, Ramesseum.

who described it in the First Century B.C. as the Tomb of Osymandyas. Nearly all its material was pilfered in typical Ramesside fashion from earlier buildings. The temple proper, which covered 130,000 square feet, lay inside a large enclosure surrounded by brick walls and filled with long storage vaults and quarters for the army of priestly attendants and servants (Plate XXXVIII–3). The entrance was a double-towered gateway, called a *pylon,* at the east end towards the river. This solid pylon of masonry was covered with reliefs boasting of Ramses' campaign against the Hittites in Syria. It is still possible to make out on its ruins the scene of the Battle of Kadesh, a not too creditable engagement which the vainglorious Pharaoh portrayed on all his temples as an astounding victory due to his personal bravery. Within the First Forecourt are the battered fragments of the seated statue of Ramses. It was one of the largest blocks of stone ever handled by man. Standing 57 feet high, its index finger three and a quarter feet long, the nail seven and a half inches, and its weight estimated at a thousand tons, it was floated down river for a hundred and thirty-five miles from Aswân.

Along the south wall of this First Forecourt are the remains of a double colonnade, or monumental portico, forming the entrance vestibule to the king's private palace, which was connected with his temple. This direct relation between what was, of course, only one of the Pharaoh's private palaces and his mortuary temple was an association of tomb and palace which we have already seen in the dual meaning of the hieroglyph for palace and in the dependence of the Abydos tombs upon contemporary and traditional palace architecture. It was also seen at Saqqara in Zoser's reproduction of his palace for the service of his *Ka,* and during the IV and V Dynasties in the royal custom of building the palaces near the pyramids and perhaps representing the porticoed, royal residences by the so-called "Valley-temples" at the entrance to the causeways which led up to the tombs. The palace within the Ramesseum has nearly vanished, but a similar palace, in the same relation to the place of worship, will be studied later in the mortuary temple of Ramses III.[29]

The Second Forecourt has double rows of papyrus-bud columns on the north and south sides, and a single row of Osiris piers on the east and west sides (Plate XXXVIII–2). The pier, with the figure of the king in the form of Osiris carved upon the face of the support, was of symbolic origin connected with the beliefs and ritual of the Heb-Sed festival. In the great courts of the funerary temples of the Old Kingdom, the Osiris statues were not attached to the piers. In the Ramesseum the western row of Osiris piers are raised on a terrace which is ascended by three flights of stairs, each stairway opposite to a door leading into the main part of the temple. Behind the piers of this colonnaded portico is a row of papyrus bud columns (Plate XXXVIII–1). All three doors lead into the Hypostyle Hall with its two rows of tall papyrus flower, or campaniform, columns, thirty-six feet high, and its rows of shorter, papyrus-bud columns, twenty-five feet high. The difference in height of the columns forms a clerestory by which the interior was originally lighted (Plate XXXIX–1).

Beyond the large Hypostyle Hall, which should be called the Hall of Appearances, are three smaller columnar halls, the westernmost one and the sanctuaries beyond being entirely ruined. The plan of the temple, like all royal temples of the New Kingdom, seems complicated because of the multiplication of halls and rooms. Actually it is merely a monumental version in stone of the royal

[29] Pages 225-227.

palace, with its succession of columnar reception halls and inner chambers. What else could it have been? The primitive temple, it was seen, was a hut transformed into the dwelling of the divinity; its ritual was a routine based upon the daily service of cleansing, dressing, and feeding to which the Powerful One was accustomed in his abode; and the basic concept of a mortuary temple was that of a permanent residence for the eternal and divine spirit of the Pharaoh. The persistence of this dependence of the place of royal worship upon domestic architecture is clearly illustrated in the Ramesseum. If its First Forecourt is considered as an essential part of the private palace which opens directly from it on the south side, it is evident that both the palace and the temple have a similar axial arrangement of courts and halls of diminishing size. Architectural units may be multiplied and enlarged to colossal size in the temples of the New Kingdom, but the pattern of Egyptian architecture remains basically as simple and imitative as it was in the earlier periods.

On the north side of the Ramesseum, parallel to the Hypostyle Hall, is a small temple of Seti I which consists of a portico approached by two flights of stairs, a court surrounded by an interior colonnade, two halls, and three inner sanctuaries (Plate XXXVIII–3). Here again is a combination of elements which certainly reflect and probably imitate domestic architecture. Of the many long rows of brick vaulted storerooms which filled the temenos back of the temple, some are still standing (Plate XXXIX–2). They furnish interesting testimony to the Egyptian's skill in erecting brick tunnel vaults without the use of centering. The system of construction is called *laminated vaulting* and consists of laying the arched courses of the vault at such an angle, leaning against an end-wall, that the mortar will hold the individual bricks in place until the key brick is inserted and the arch-course completed. In this way the workman could work forward from the top of the vertical end-wall without any centering underneath the vaults.

Better preserved and more fully excavated than the Ramesseum is the mortuary temple of Ramses III, which was built early in the XX Dynasty, shortly after 1200 B.C., in imitation of the Ramesseum. It is situated on the west bank of the river, opposite to Thebes, at Medinet Habu. The temple and its original enclosure, which were finished early in Ramses' reign, made a symmetrical rectangle, the great solid pylon of the temple forming both the main entrance and part of the defensive walls of the enclosure (Plate XL–2). Like any royal residence, the space around the temple was protected by a massive brick wall, 6 m. thick, with protecting towers, which rose to about 18 m. (Plate XLI–1). The faces of both towers of the large first pylon are inscribed with scenes and inscriptions telling of the king's exploits. Although there is a more evident sense of symmetry and arrangement of scenes and hieroglyphs upon this pylon than on most Egyptian gateways, nevertheless, to our eyes, the great reliefs, painted in strong colors upon a white ground, would seem unfortunately emphatic, definitely out of scale, and as lacking in subtlety as most modern billboards.[30] Beyond the first pylon is the outer forecourt, flanked on the right by a colonnade of Osiris piers and on the left by a colonnade of papyrus-bud columns (Plate XL–1). This forecourt is also the ceremonial entrance to the royal palace, which opens from it on the south side.

[30] For a striking and accurate restoration in color of this façade see U. Hölscher, *The Excavations of Medinet Habu* (1934), I, Pl. 23.

PLATE XL: MORTUARY TEMPLES

1

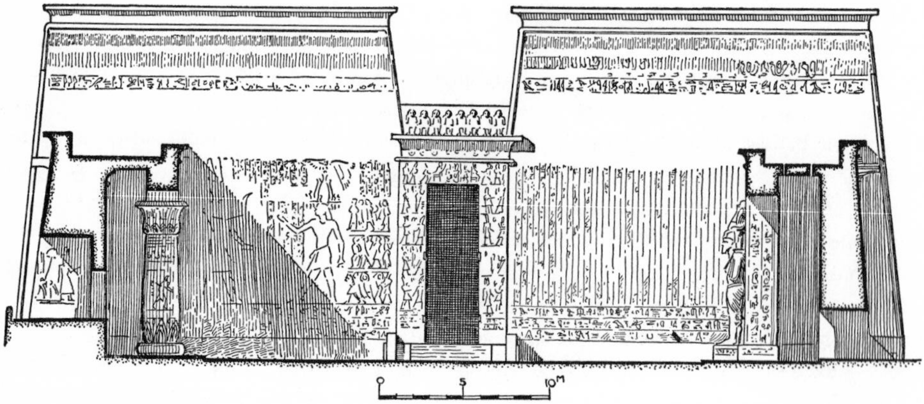

2

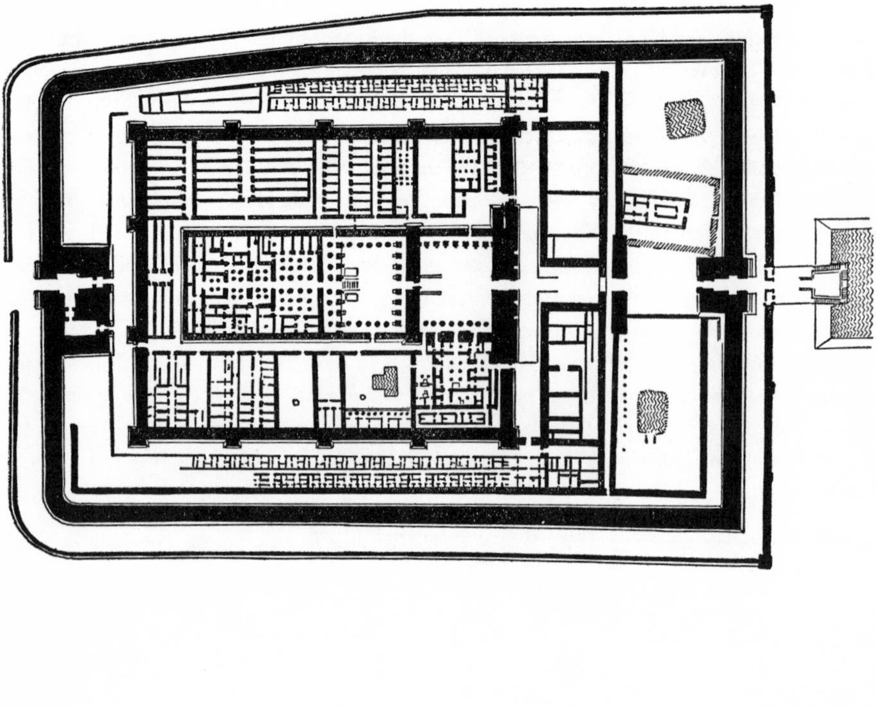

Of his temple-palace Ramses says, "I made for thee an august house of millions of years, abiding upon the mountain of 'Lord-of-Life,' before thee, built of sandstone, grit stone, and black granite; the doors of electrum and copper in beaten work. Its towers were of stone, towering to heaven, adorned and carved with the graver's tool, in the great name of thy majesty. I built a wall around it, established with labor, having ramps and towers of sandstone. I dug a lake before it, flooded with Nun (celestial water), planted with trees and vegetation like the Northland (the Delta)." [31]

While the actual palace is discussed in a subsequent chapter,[32] certain features of this royal residence show to what extent the Egyptian ruler considered his mortuary temple a permanent abode. The palace itself was only one of many, his principal residence being in the Delta. It was therefore intended to be used during his lifetime only for visits at the time of the temple festivals. The front of the palace, opening directly on the forecourt of the temple, is marked by a columnar portico, and on the first pylon an inscription reads, "Erecting for him a colonnade at the double façade (palace) of his house, its [roof] of real electrum." [33] There are three openings from the palace into the aisle behind the royal portico of the forecourt of the temple. Two of these openings are doors and the center one is a large Window of Appearances (Plate XLI-2), 2 m. above the floor, where "the Sun in the Horizon" sat in his window, and then, after a rebuilding, in his projecting wooden balcony, to behold the captives and plunder which he was presenting to his place of worship after a campaign. From this balcony "of fine gold" the Pharaoh amused himself with the dancing and gladiatorial combats which were a part of the temple festivals, and here he stood to reward his faithful followers by throwing down chains of gold. The reliefs on the walls of the forecourt depict these scenes, accurately recording the ceremonies once celebrated in front of the palace and temple of the divine representative of Amon-Re.

From the court an inclined ramp leads up to the doorway of the second pylon, on which is depicted the triumph of the king in the eighth year of his reign against the Peoples of the Sea who attacked Egypt (Plate XL-1). The Second Court, which in the Christian period was converted into a church, is almost an exact production of the second court of the Ramesseum. Beyond this court is the "Hall of Appearances," its roof formerly supported by twenty-four columns, and beyond are a series of smaller halls and sanctuaries dedicated to various divinities, with Amon in the place of honor and Osiris next in importance. The small chambers to the left of the Hall of Appearances were the treasury of the temple, and the scenes on their walls depict the more important gifts.

Around the temple, inside the fortified enclosure, were the quarters for the priestly retinue, the slaves of the temple, and the great storerooms (Plate LXXIII-5). The account of the temple preserved in the *Papyrus Harris* says, "It (the temple) was surrounded with gardens and arbor areas, filled with

[31] *Papyrus Harris*, Breasted, *op. cit.*, IV, No. 189.
[32] Pages 225-227.
[33] Breasted, *op. cit.*, IV, No. 16.

PLATE XL

1. Section of first forecourt, temple of Ramses III (U. Hölscher, Excavations of Medinet Habu, I. 1934).
2. Plan of temple of Ramses III, Medinet Habu (*op. cit.*).

PLATE XLI: MORTUARY TEMPLES

1

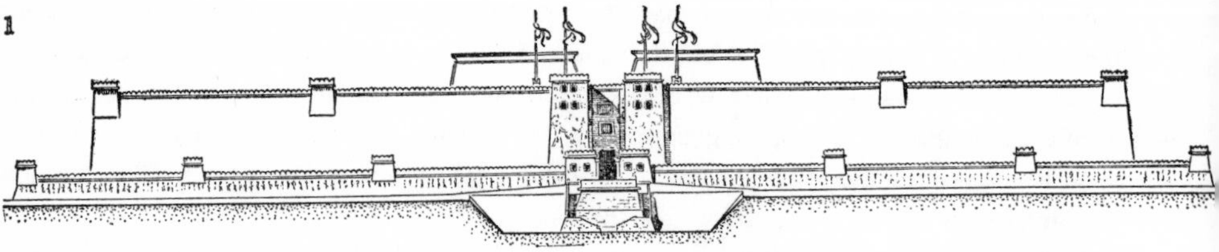

2

3

4

fruit and flowers for the two serpent-goddesses. I built their [châteaux] having [windows]; I dug a lake before them supplied with lotus flowers," [34] but most of the space, except in the front part of the temenos, was filled with long-vaulted storerooms constructed in brick. Inasmuch as there was no medium of exchange, gifts and revenue had to be in kind; therefore there were separate magazines for grain, oil, wine, beer, leather, metals, and all that a royal and everlasting residence might need in the way of supplies.

Three entrances in the east wall gave access to the divine residence, the one at the left leading directly into the palace, the center one opening through the pylon into the first court, and the right-hand gateway providing access for the revenue. This was brought into a court in front of a three-aisled hall where scribes recorded the contributions and distributed them to the various magazines.

During the second half of his reign, Ramses enlarged the enclosure about his temple, rebuilt his palace, and strengthened the defenses. First of all he built a tremendous outer wall of brick, 10 m. thick and estimated to be 18 m. high which probably had straddle-towers as the restoration shows (Plate XLI–1). This wall had square corners at the east, but at the west its corners were rounded both inside and out. The Fortified Gate in the center of the east side of this wall is one of the most interesting structures in Egypt, but it has no particular association with either mortuary or temple architecture and so will be discussed fully in another chapter.[35] Inside the wall was a wide street, 1 to 3 m. higher than the enclosed space, running around the walls, which was used for circulation and the prompt movement of troops. Along the inner wall, flanking this street, were quarters for priests, craftsmen, and slaves. In the center of the west wall, opposite the Fortified Gate, is a ruined core of brick which was originally a western gateway.

Ramses was undoubtedly preparing for trouble at the end of his reign, for, in addition to the great wall, he built a low girdle-wall, which was also crenellated and strengthened by straddle-towers. In front of the Fortified Gate there were sentry towers flanking the entrance. Outside the gateway was a rectangular quay, its sides sloping, and with steps leading down to the water level. The quay itself was at the end of a canal, which was the ceremonial approach to the temple, leading in across the cultivated fields at a right angle from the river. Hölscher, in describing the quay at Medinet Habu, suggest that similar quays and canals gave navigable approach to the "Valley-temples" which formed the landing stages for the causeways leading up to the mortuary temples of the Old Kingdom.[36] Inas-

[34] Breasted, *op. cit.*, IV, No. 194.

[35] Pages 225-227.

[36] U. Hölscher, "Excavations at Ancient Thebes 1930-31," *Oriental Institute of Chicago University, Communications,* No. 15, p. 7.

PLATE XLI

1. Exterior from east restored, temple of Ramses III, Medinet Habu (Hölscher, *op. cit.*, 1, Pl. xxx).
2. South colonnade of forecourt with "Window of Appearances," temple of Ramses III.
3. Interior looking east, temple of Ramses III.
4. South sides of temple, showing ruins of palace and "Window of Appearances."

PLATE XLII: TEMPLES

1

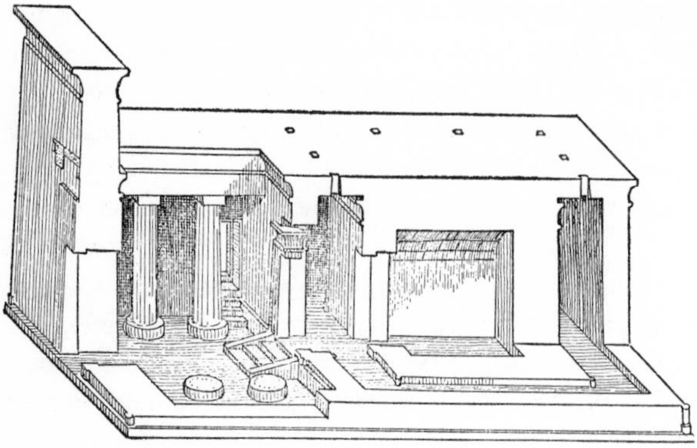

2

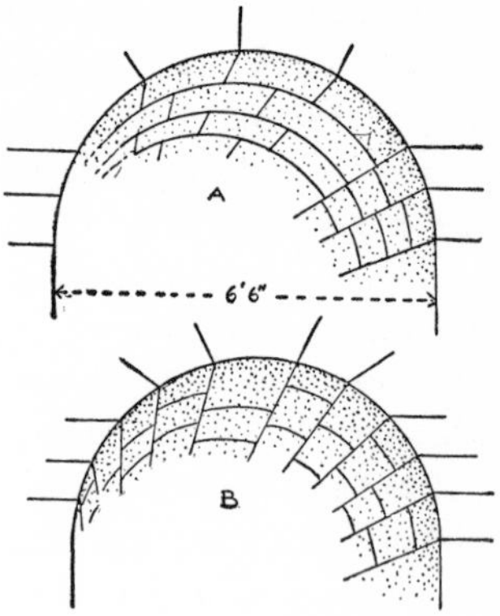

3

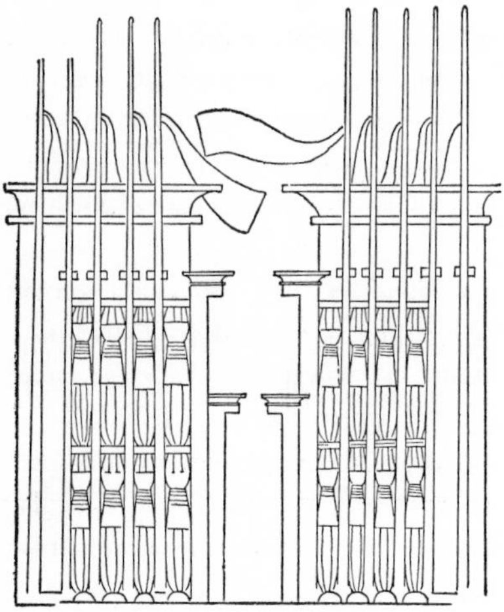

4

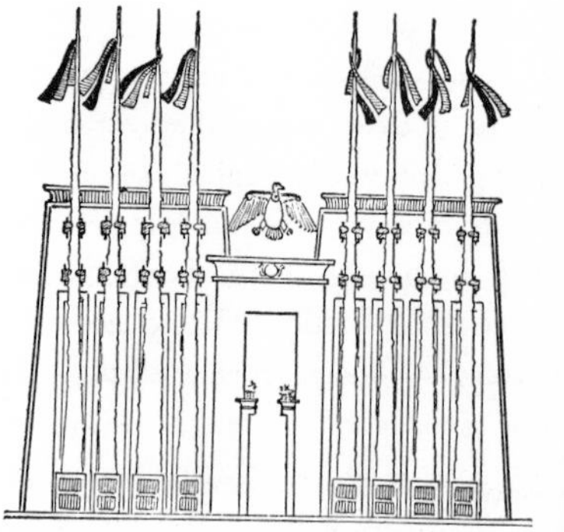

5

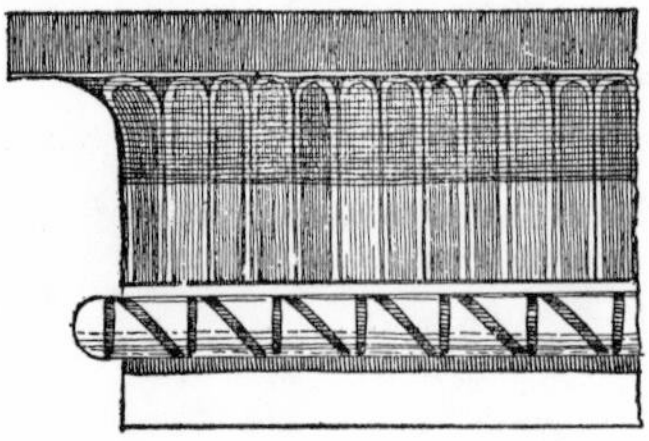

6

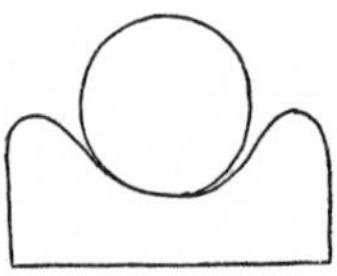

7

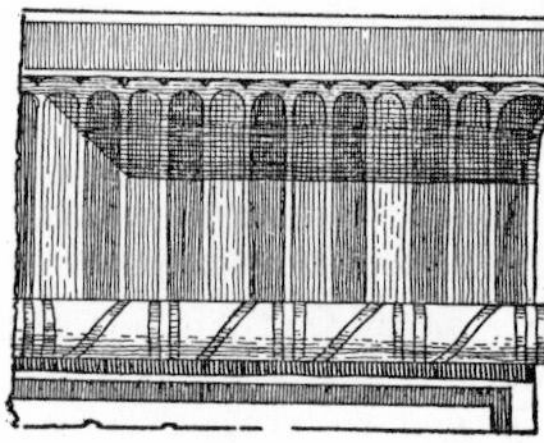

much as the canal leading across the fields from the river would have been necessary to transport the heavy stones, Hölscher believes that the quay, like the causeway to a pyramid, was part of the first construction at Medinet Habu.

The reader must not judge the proportions and workmanship of Egyptian architecture by this building which happens to be so well preserved. By the XX Dynasty Egyptian craftsmanship, like the Empire itself, had lost its vigor and some of its assurance. Much of the stone carving is careless in execution and weak in its imitation of previous monuments. After Ramses III Egypt went into a long and monotonous decline. Although the Pharaoh had leveled "the Hill of the Lord of Life" as a site for his perpetual place of worship, fortified it with the greatest care, and endowed it with all the riches and splendor of his reign, the effort was futile, for shortly after his death all service in the temple ceased and it became a refuge filled with a welter of cheap hovels. In leaving Medinet Habu, the reader should look again at the plan of the temple, and note the narrow passageway that runs around the temple, separating it from the surrounding storerooms. While it is impossible to describe the reliefs which decorated the Egyptian buildings, it will help in the final analysis if the reader realizes that here at Medinet Habu, as with all temples of the later period, the high exterior walls of the temples were covered from base to cornice with historical reliefs, telling of Ramses' great exploits, which must have been seen by very few people and by those few in a very inadequate fashion, because of the narrowness of the passage around the temple.

Moreover, the plan of Ramses' temple is a key to Egyptian temple architecture. The building with its fortifications is a veritable *"château dieu,"* an enlarged but none the less literal survival of the primitive protected village with the dwelling of the god and priest-chieftain at the center. The royal palace and the divine temple are, architecturally, interchangeable ideas, except that the temple is made permanent in stone. Ramses, therefore, like Zoser at Saqqara, built as his mortuary temple a fortified city and eternal palace where slaves, craftsmen, and storehouses would assure the royal dead of service and protection in the long hereafter.

After Ramses there are no more visible remains of royal mortuary temples, although Ramses IV, at a time when kingly power was on the wane, began at Thebes a mortuary temple intended to eclipse all others.[37] Without the slightest regard for either the sanctity or appearance of his

[37] H. E. Winlock, "Excavations at Thebes," *New York Bulletin of the Metropolitan Museum,* IX (1914), p. 20, plan Fig. 11; A. Lansing, "Excavations at Thebes," *op. cit.,* Section II, XXX (1935).

PLATE XLII

1. Mortuary chapel of Amenirdis I, Medinet Habu (U. Hölscher).
2. Cut-stone vaults in mortuary chapels, Medinet Habu (Clarke and Engelbach, *Ancient Egyptian Masonry,* 1930, Figs. 222, 223).
3. Pylon of temple of Aten, as depicted in tombs at Tell el-Amarna (N. de G. Davies, *The Rock Tombs of El Amarna,* I, Pl. XXVII).
4. Pylon depicted on temple of Khons at Karnak (Prisse d'Avennes, *Histoire de l'art Égyptien,* 1879).

5, 7. Egyptian cornices (Prisse d'Avennes).

6. Hieroglyph for "horizon of heaven."

predecessors' monuments, he set his gigantic temple in the narrow valley in front of Deir el-Bahari, directly upon the avenue of approach to Mentuhotep's pyramid; his plan he copied from the mortuary temples of Ramses II and III, but laid it out on a scale intended to be half as large again as the previous structures. Apparently his only innovation was to continue the colonnade of the first court around three sides in the manner which is only found in Ptolemaic temples. Unable to complete such an ambitious scheme, his successors Ramses V and VI both appropriated his start and went on with the work, pilfering material, cutting away existing tombs, and yet leaving it still unfinished. As retribution, nearly every stone of this last mortuary temple went into the lime kiln. After these late Ramessides the royal dead disappear into an oblivion which the Egyptians dreaded. By the Saïtic period the kings were buried in the existing temples of their Delta cities and we have only Herodotus' description of the tomb of Amasis.[38]

At Medinet Habu, however, within the great girdle-wall, lies a group of late chapel-tombs, dating from the Seventh Century B.C., which, while not mortuary temples, are a modified survival of the same idea. The most interesting and the one most indicative of the change which had gone on is the combination mortuary chapel and tomb of the "god-wife," Amenirdis I, sister of the Ethiopian Pharaoh Shabaska, and a high priestess of Amon. The chapel-tomb of Amenirdis, which is similar to other tombs of the Saïtic period, is a small, traditional temple with its sanctuary transformed into a vaulted sepulcher (Plate XLII–1). Its vault, and the others like it, are still the oldest known examples of true voussoir construction in stone. Two examples of these XXV Dynasty vaults at Medinet Habu (Plate XLII–2) show the persistent Egyptian tendency to imitate their stone forms from brick construction. As in the brick vaults of the Ramesseum, the first three courses of the vaults are corbeled, while the upper courses which complete the span are actual voussoirs.

[38] Page 115.

7. *DYNASTIC TEMPLES, II*

I will make a work, namely a great house for my father Atum . . . My goodness (nefer) *shall be remembered in his house . . . Eternity is that excellent thing which I have made.*

AMENEMHET I TO HIS SON, SENWOSRET I, XII DYNASTY

Let your hands build, ye people. Let us do the pleasure of this official in restoring the monument of his Lord in the house of his father Amon. His name is upon them, abiding, permanent, for both æons of years.

VIZIER RAKHMERE, IN REIGN OF THUTMOSE III, TO THE BUILDERS

WITH THE NEW KINGDOM the temple proper emerges as an architecturally important and monumental structure in stone. Regardless of how one feels about the effectiveness of the New Kingdom temples, the buildings themselves are evidence of a megalomania impelling the royal builders to outdo their predecessors. This urge for measurable bigness which characterizes so much of the architecture of the period was the natural result of many influences working upon the Egyptian mind. In the main it was still the same primitive quest for certainty, now intensified by the materialistic ideals of a prosperous and despotic age.

The organization of Egyptian resources under the energetic Pharaohs of the XVIII and XIX Dynasties made the architecture possible. With a strong line of militant rulers the second Theban Empire spread to Mesopotamia, where it came into contact with eastern ideas and oriental despotism, and from its conquests gold, slaves, and tribute of all kinds poured in to make it the richest and most powerful country in the Mediterranean world. The Pharaoh was more absolute in his power than ever before. The land was his and was worked by his serfs. The old class of feudal and hereditary nobles had disappeared, and in its place a new official class existed as the instrument of the Double Crown. In addition to this servile bureaucracy, the professional soldiers now formed a new and influential group in control of the Empire. The reorganized society, therefore, offered position, wealth, and professional advancement to middle-class minds which were obsequiously obedient, conventionally efficient, and materially ambitious.

It was a period in which public opinion was trained to expect and appreciate physical bigness, efficient organization of labor, and the manifestations of power and wealth. From the Pharaoh down, with the exception of the ill-fated Amenhotep IV, it was an age of doers rather than dreamers, ritualists rather than religious thinkers. Hence it built numerous and large temples, not because it enjoyed them æsthetically, but because it considered them necessary and useful. Temples propitiated the gods

PLATE XLIII: TEMPLES

1

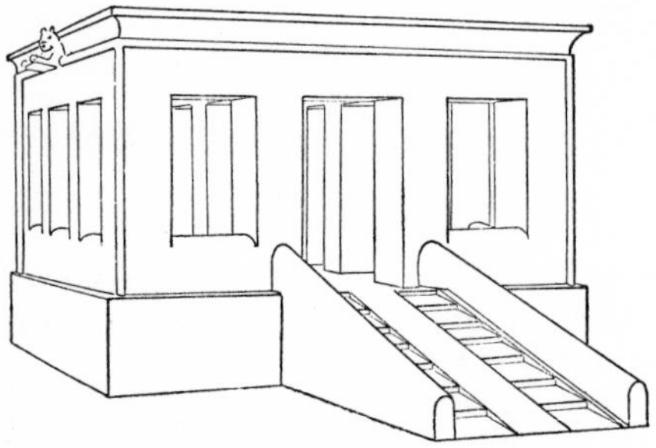

2

3

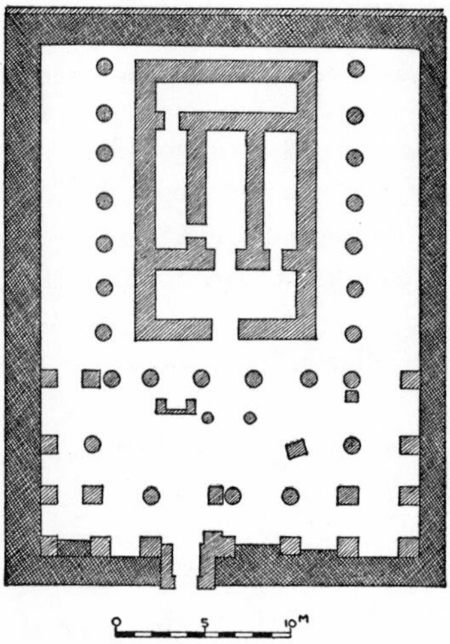

4

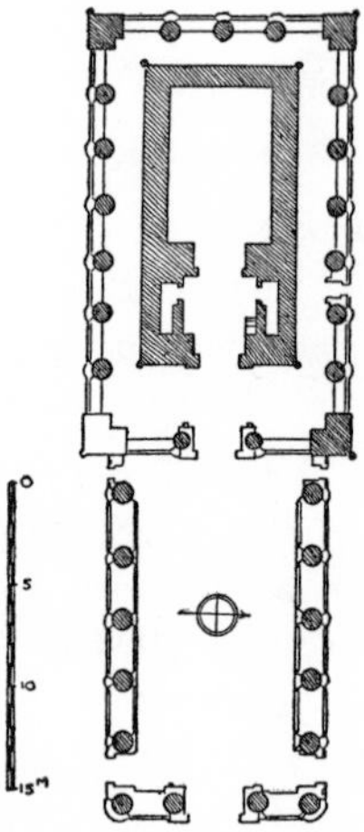

5

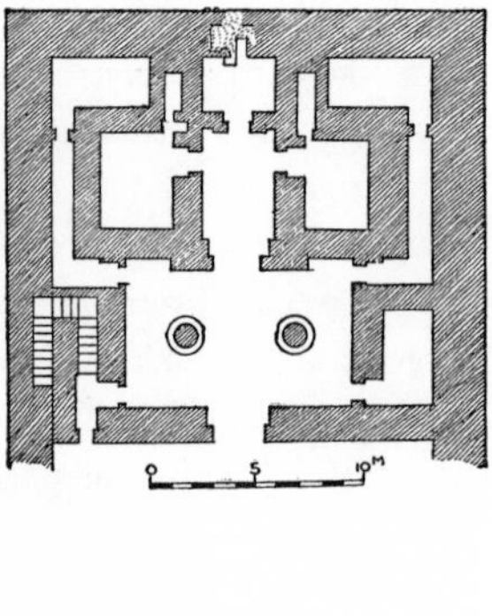

6

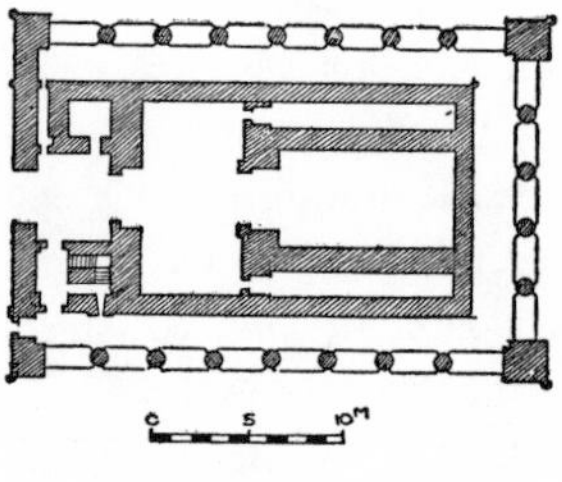

and were everlasting sanctuaries for the spirit of the divine and royal builder. There was every reason to make the temples as large as possible. Megalithic forms, to the Egyptian mind, were indestructible; they were measurable evidence of devotion; and their surfaces furnished big areas on which the glories of the Pharaoh could be carved.

By this time the priesthood had acquired unlimited wealth and power, for like the army and the government it was made up of a highly organized professional class. As in the temple of Khonsu, "the lay priests were children of great men whom I (Ramses III) trained." The state religion placed Amon-Re of Thebes, the divine father of the Pharaohs, above all other gods. The accumulated wealth of the Sun-god gave his priests an ability to mold the religious, social, and even the political life of Egypt to the rigidly conservative will of Amon-Re. The priests made and unmade kings, as Amenhotep IV learned to his sorrow when he undertook to defy them. Like all wealthy and despotic theocracies this priesthood knew the value of impressive ceremonies, material splendor, and stupendous bigness as awesome preservers of the established order. More than any ease of life and monotonous regularity in the order of Egyptian living, it was this sacerdotal despotism which kept the Egyptian mind and its form of expression in the established groove of time-honored and stultifying conventions.

PERIPTERAL TEMPLES

The peripteral temple first appears in the Middle Kingdom, the idea, at least, being fully developed on a monumental scale by Mentuhotep III around his pyramid at Deir el-Bahari. It also survives in the small stone shrine of Senwosret I, the fragments of which were recently discovered, re-used in the third pylon at Karnak. This little temple of the Middle Kingdom consisted of an open loggia of rectangular piers upon a rectangular platform (Plate XLIII–1), the space between the piers closed by a low parapet with a rounded top, and approached at both ends, as a naos for the bark of Amon-Re, by a ramp. Like the pyramid-chapel of Senwosret I, it had a lion-headed waterspout projecting from the cornice.

This type of shrine, the prototype for the peripteral temples and Amarna chapels of the XVIII Dynasty, should have been a common form of cult-house during the Middle Kingdom. Theoretically it must have developed from primitive open shelters of posts, covered by a roof. Unfortunately the remains of Middle Kingdom temples, other than mortuary chapels, are so ruined and rebuilt that it is

---

PLATE XLIII

1. Peripteral chapel of Senwosret I, Karnak (M. H. Chevrier, *Annales du Service,* XXXIV, p. 172).
2. Peripteral temple of Amenhotep III, Elephantine.
3. Plan of the peripteral temple of Hatshepsut, Buhen (D. Randall-Maciver and C. L. Woolley, *Buhen,* 1911, Plan D).
4. Plan of the Ptolemaic Birth House, Edfu (G. Jéquier, *Les Temples Ptolemaïques et Romains,* 1924, p. 5).
5. Plan of temple of Apet, Karnak (Jéquier, *op. cit.,* p. 2).
6. Plan of the Birth-House of Augustus, Dendera (*op. cit.,* p. 8).

PLATE XLIV: TEMPLES

1

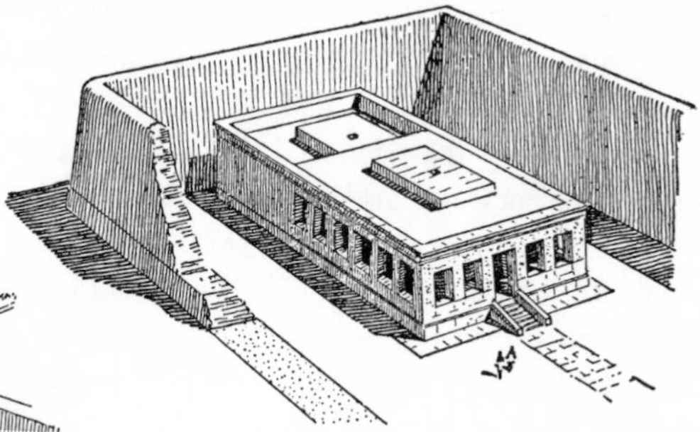

2

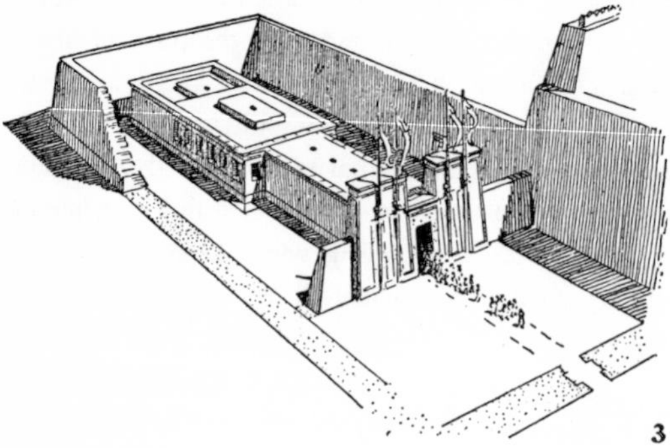

3

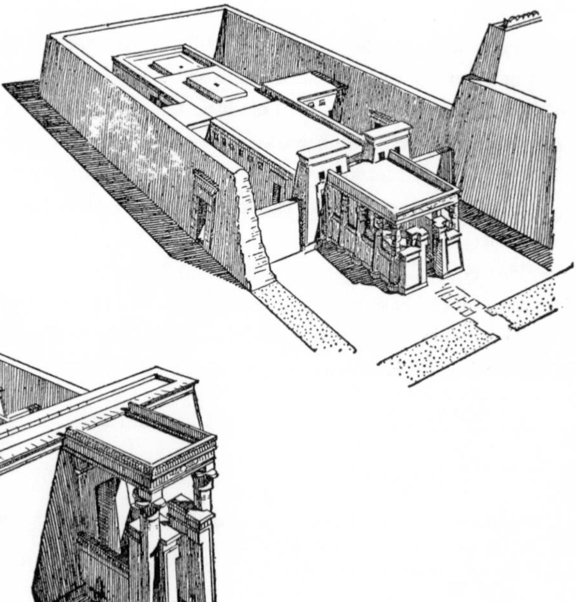

4

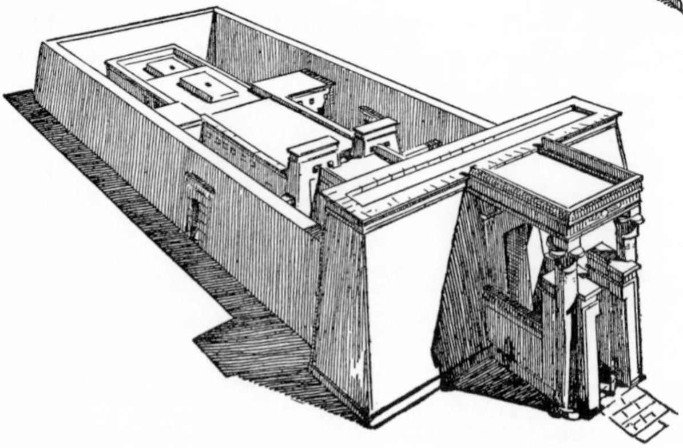

only from the persistence of the type at the beginning of the New Kingdom that we have any indication of its earlier prevalence. The fashion in which the New Kingdom temple of Amon-Re at Karnak grew around the original Middle Kingdom foundation suggests that it too had originally been peripteral. Petrie's restoration of the Labyrinth at Hawara (Plate XXXII–7) and the remains of the temple of Senwosret III at Abydos[1] also indicate the importance of peripteral courts and porticoes during the Middle Kingdom.

During the XVIII Dynasty the peripteral temple was perhaps the prevailing type before the more palatial form was developed. There remains the plan of a small, peripteral temple in the complex at Karnak which was built by Thutmose III (Plate XLVIII–2G). The same Pharaoh and Queen Hatshepsut built similar temples at Buhen (Plate XLIII–3), near Wadi Halfa, and Amenhotep III erected still another in honor of Khnum, creator and god of the cataract, on the Island of Elephantine. The Elephantine temple was only forty feet long by thirty wide, thirteen feet high, and must have been very effective in its simplicity (Plate XLIII–2). Although drawn and described by the French Expedition, it was entirely destroyed early in the Nineteenth Century to furnish stone for the palace of a local governor.

Therefore the best preserved example of a peripteral structure is the small temple built by Queen Hatshepsut at Medinet Habu, which Ramses III preserved and incorporated inside the precinct of his great mortuary temple (Plate XLIV–1). It was built to hold the sacred bark of the Sun-god, and it might be thought that the peripteral design with the open porticoes on three sides was used so as to permit visitors to view the emblem of the god. Egyptian temples, however, even when as fine as this little building, were not designed for either decorative effect or public enjoyment. The brick wall which surrounded the temple area shut it off from all except the privileged few.

Like so many temples, the small temple of Medinet Habu underwent various enlargements, none of which improved its appearance. In the XXV Dynasty, under the Ethiopian kings, a narrow hall, ending in a pylon, was stuck onto the front of the peripteros (Plate XLIV–2). Later in the Fourth Century B.C., while Egypt was under Persian domination, the narrow hall was replaced by a three-aisled hall and two wings were added at the sides of the original structure. Later Nectanebo I built an open porch in front of the pylon to serve as a reception vestibule (Plate XLIV–3). Finally in the Ptolemaic period the Greek Pharaohs added a stone pylon, out of all scale with the temple, and finished it with another reception pavilion (Plate XLIV–4).

[1] D. Randall-Maciver and A. C. Mace, *El Amrah and Abydos,* Pl. XX.

PLATE XLIV

1. Peripteral temple of Hatshepsut, XVIII Dyn. Medinet Habu (U. Hölscher, "Architectural Survey," *Oriental Institute of the University of Chicago, Communications,* no. 19, 1931, Pl. I).
2. The same temple with additions of the XXV Dyn. (*op. cit.,* Pl. II).
3. The temple with additions of the IV century B.C. (*op. cit.,* Pl. III).
4. The temple in the Ptolemaic Period (*op. cit.,* Pl. IV).

After the XVIII Dynasty the peripteral temple type appears to have gone out of use, only to be revived in the Ptolemaic period. In its revived form it is always a small, free-standing sanctuary within the precinct or even forecourt of a larger temple. These Ptolemaic examples are called Birth Houses, or *Mammisi,* because they were usually dedicated to the worship of a maternal deity, such as Isis, and frequently have on their capitals representations of the dwarf-divinity, Bes (Plate LVIII-3), who was the patron deity of women in labor.[2]

THE STANDARD NEW KINGDOM TYPE OF TEMPLE

Since there are so few remains of XVIII Dynasty temples, other than mortuary, it is probable that the change from the Middle Kingdom type of temple, possibly peripteral, to the standard, New Kingdom form, took place towards the close of the XVIII Dynasty. The standard type of temple was essentially the same as the mortuary temples, and therefore, like them, was an adaptation to his religious purposes of the palatial dwelling of the divine Pharaoh. The reigning incarnation of Amon-Re considered every temple as an everlasting palace which he would share with the other gods in the long hereafter. Therefore each successive Pharaoh during the New Kingdom, with curiously little sympathy for the divine needs of his predecessors, was inclined, if he had the resources and initiative, to appropriate the temples of his fathers, enlarge them, and carve his name and attainments on their walls. Hence many of the temples are the result of successive additions whereby each king sought to outdo the greatness of his ancestors. The result is that most New Kingdom temples at first appear to be lacking in any unified sense of design or even in any standard arrangement of elements.

In spite of the apparent diversity and confusion of plans, the actual elements and their arrangement followed rigid conventions. The basic parts of the temple were the traditional and essential house elements which underlay all Egyptian architecture. They consisted of the forecourt, porticoed vestibule, great hall, and private chamber of the great one. No matter how large and complicated a temple might be, it consisted of a multiplication of these essential parts, usually along a horizontal axis. The extension of parts in length was both a naïve and natural method of building and the result of the ritual which required a corridor-like plan because of its preoccupation with processionals.

Like palaces, which were the private retreat of the most high ruler, the temples were often placed outside the cities within a sacred enclosure, surrounded by high and protective brick walls. Each one was a self-contained and sumptuous stronghold of the god in the center of his city. The entrance of the temenos was a stone gateway, as a rule facing the river, approached by a processional way, lined on either side by guardian spirits in the form of lions, sphinxes, and rams. Inasmuch as the Nile was the one great highway, the approach to the temple began either at the river or at the quay of a canal which led in from the river. The fact that the mud walls of the sacred domains have for the most part disappeared has left a few of the stone gateways standing, as at Karnak (Plate LII-2), like Roman triumphal arches over the road, and so given rise to the misconception that these gateways were *propylons.* Within the walls were the brick storerooms and quarters for the priests and slaves of the divine estate, which in the case of the temple of Amon-Re at Karnak formed a city in itself.

[2] Pages 187, 189, 195.

From the gateway of the temenos wall the avenue, in some cases still lined with symbolic beasts, led to the front of the actual temple, which was usually of sandstone. The façade, which was the only visible and architectonic feature of the exterior, consisted of two towers with a doorway between them. Taken together, these towers formed the *pylon*. The stone pylons of Egyptian temples show their dependence upon an earlier prototype, probably towers of matting construction strengthened by a core of solid mud, because their sides are always sloping; their edges are carefully protected by torus moldings, which even in stone continued to be carved and painted to imitate bundle reeds (Plate XLII–5, 7), and their tops are crowned with the typical cavetto cornice, which in its turn was a reproduction of the reed parapet upon the primitive house. The pylons, in addition to the moldings and laudatory reliefs carved and painted upon their flat sides, had deep grooves cut into their battered bases, and at the top, sockets for stone or wooden brackets, so that flag poles could be stood vertically in front of them. These flagstaves, as seen on an Egyptian painting of a pylon from Tell el-Amarna (Plate XLII–3), were great masts of cedar or cypress wood, from which floated divine and royal banners. In the gateway of the pylon were double doors of cedar, elaborately covered with bronze, gold and electrum. Before the temples of Amon-Re it was customary for the Pharaoh, on the anniversary of a Jubilee Festival, to erect two obelisks, as sun symbols.

Although the pylon façade only appeared as an established temple form in the stone architecture of the New Kingdom, it must have had a long evolution in the more primitive methods of construction, and behind its use must have been an association of ideas which gave it a very specific significance. In Mesopotamia the ceremonial and processional entrance to palaces, temples, and cities was marked by a towered gateway, the protective dwelling and receiving threshold of the guardian spirit.[3] A similar belief was in some way embodied in the Egyptian towered pylon. While the pylon may have originated as a copy in stone of one section of a traditional defensive wall in brick, with two towers and a gate between, as several Egyptologists have insisted,[4] it is certain that behind the form is an old ideographic convention, perhaps remotely connected with the legendary and royal towered *serekh* façade seen on the grave stelæ of the I Dynasty. The ceremonial façade of what was probably a divine abode on the symbolic boats painted in the Predynastic tomb at Hierakonpolis shows a towered gateway, while the entrance to Zoser's mortuary stronghold must have been distinguished by flanking towers.

The inscriptions sometimes designate the temple-pylon as the "Horizon of Heaven." This comparison indicates that the Egyptians imagined the flanking towers of the pylon as representing the boundary limits of north and south, between which, as in the sign for "horizon of heaven" (Plate XLII–6), the Sun rises and sets. Such cosmic symbolism made the door of the pylon the gate of heaven through which, from the East, in most temples, emerged the shining one and his divine and equally resplendent representative on earth.[5] This imagery explains why "the shadow," or

[3] W. Andrae, *Das Gotteshaus und die Urformen des Bauens im Alten Orient*, p. 24.

[4] U. Hölscher, *Das Hohe Tor von Medinet Habu* (1910), p. 27; Petrie, *Egyptian Decoration*, p. 96; Jéquier, *Manuel d'Archéologie Égyptienne*, p. 66.

[5] Theodore Dombart, "Der Zweitürmige Tempel-pylon altaegyptischer Baukunst und seine Religiöse symbolik," *Egyptian Religion*, I (1933), pp. 87-98; p. 135.

PLATE XLV: TEMPLE OF AMON-RE, LUXOR

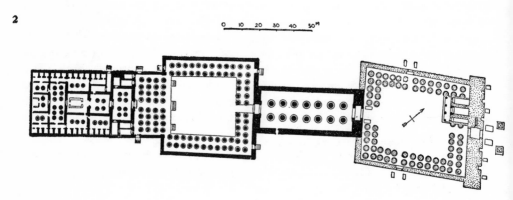

1

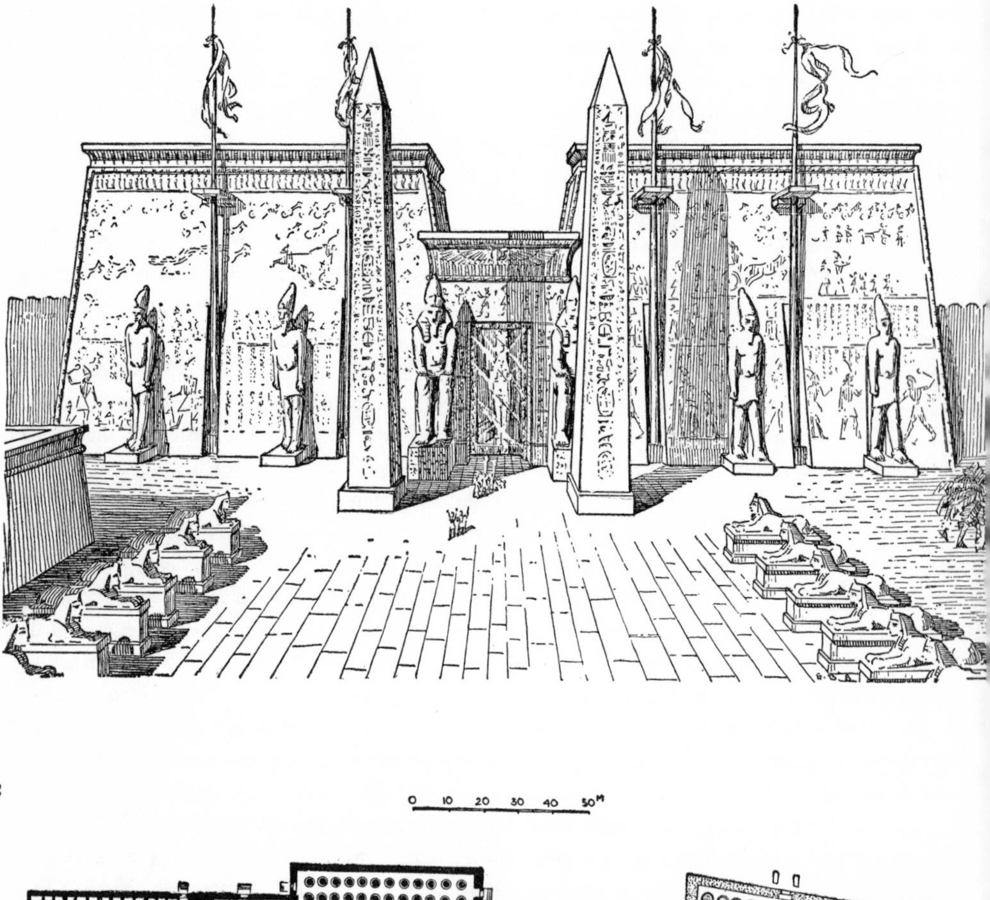

2

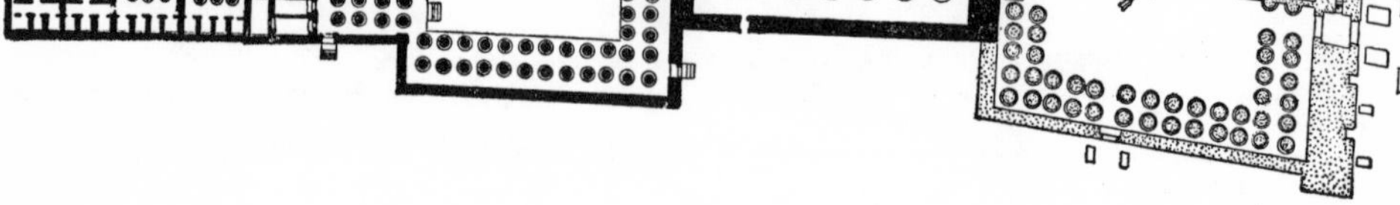

image, of the divinity was wrought in burnished metals upon the doors of the pylon (Plate XLV–1), for it was the representation of the sun coming forth from his house in the east. It also explains the inscription on the pylon at Karnak, built by Amenhotep III, which reads, "making for him a very great portal over against Amon-Re, lord of Thebes, wrought with gold throughout. The *Divine Shadow,* as a ram, is inlaid with real lazuli, wrought with gold and many costly stones; there is no instance of doing the like. Its floor is adorned with silver; [towers] are over against it. Stelæ of lazuli are set up, one on each side. Its towers reach heaven like the four pillars of heaven; its flagstaves shine more than the heavens, wrought with electrum." [6] The picture also becomes clear when Amenhotep describes his temple of Soleb in Nubia as, "thy house of a million years.... A resting place for my father at all his feasts.... Two great obelisks are erected, one on each side. When my father rises between them, I am among his following." [7]

Within the pylon came the *forecourt* of the temple, like the inner court of a palace. Along one or more sides of the court was a covered colonnade, the royal portico and palace symbol. In very few temples were these colonnades extended around all sides of the forecourt, while in the earlier temples, like that of Seti I at Abydos and his smaller temple alongside the Ramesseum, the colonnade, like a long porch, was on a raised platform approached by steps, directly in front of the great hall of the temple. The public part of the festivals and ceremonies of the temple took place in the forecourt, for beyond lay the private residence of the god. The "wide" columnar hall of the divine palace is usually called the *hypostyle hall,* but to the Egyptians it was the *Hall of Appearances* where the dweller of the palace came forth among his court. During the New Kingdom the Hall of Appearances was characterized by a clerestory raised upon the two central rows of columns. Its form and method of lighting were copied in stone from the central hall of the New Kingdom palaces, with their columns of wood and their raised, central clerestory which gave light and ventilation. In the temples these hypostyle halls, with their forests of gigantic columns, served only as a traditional element in a divine residence, and interposed a veil of darkness and mystery between the inner abode of the god and the bright, outer world.

Beyond the great hall might be other, smaller, columnar halls, but finally, still on axis with the entrance, came the small, private chamber of the godhead. This inner sanctuary, the *sekos,* was always a rectangular room, preserving the proportions and isolation of a primitive shelter. As a rule the *sekos* had only one doorway, but in the temples of the Sun-god, where the sacred bark of Amon-Re had to be dragged through it, there were doors at both axial ends of the chamber. In temples where more than one god was worshiped, there was a *sekos* for each divinity. Frequently temples were dedicated to a triad such as Osiris, Isis, and Horus. Around the *sekos* was a periphery of rooms including the

[6] Breasted, *op. cit.,* II, No. 889.
[7] Breasted, *op. cit.,* II, No. 890.

PLATE XLV

1. Façade (restoration).
2. Plan of the temple (*after* Jéquier).

PLATE XLVI: TEMPLE OF AMON-RE, LUXOR

1

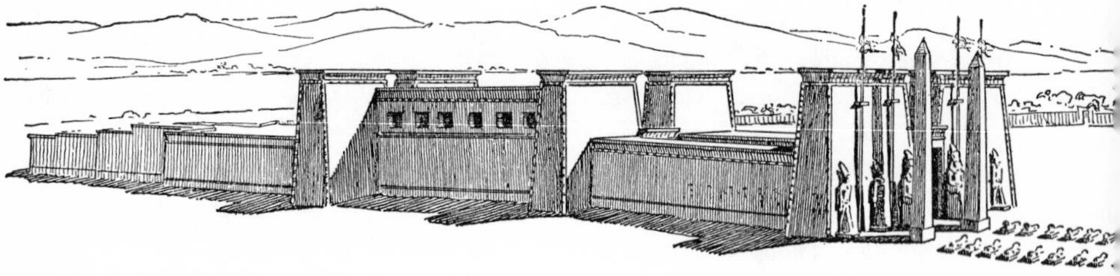

2

treasury and various offices and storerooms connected with the daily ritual of cleansing, feeding, purifying, and dressing the divine master of the house. As a part of every temple was a slaughter room or court, where the sacrificial food of the divinity was prepared. Such were the essential architectural elements of all temples. Even when a temple, like Amon-Re's at Karnak, was progressively enlarged and rebuilt during more than a thousand years, the elements remained the same and were merely repeated along the same horizontal axis.

TEMPLE OF AMON-RE, LUXOR. Chronological sequence in the study of New Kingdom temples does not reveal any logical growth, for every important temple was so frequently enlarged that the sequence loses all significance. The Temple of Amon-Re at Luxor, which was ancient Thebes, is, however, the earliest and one of the best preserved of the large temples of this period.[8] The temple was built by Amenhotep III (1412–1376 B.C.) on the site of an earlier sanctuary, and was dedicated to Amon, his wife Mut, and their son Khons, the Moon-god. The original temple of Amenhotep, exceptionally oriented north and south in order to connect it directly by a straight avenue with the temple of Karnak to the north, consisted of a large forecourt (148 x 184 feet) surrounded on three sides by two rows of bundled, papyrus-bud columns (Plate XLVI–2), and preceded by the traditional pylon; beyond the court came the "Hall of Appearances" (Plate XLVII–2), followed by smaller halls and the sanctuary of Amon with the chapels of Mut and Khons at the sides (Plate XLV–2).

It was "of fine white sandstone, made very wide and large and its beauty increased. Its walls are of electrum, its floor is of silver, all the portals are wrought with [ ], its towers reach heaven, and mingle with the stars. When the people see they give praise to his Majesty."[9] The main sanctuary with its two doors was rebuilt by Alexander the Great as a chapel to "his father Amon-Re." To the east of this central sanctuary is the Birth Room of Amenhotep III where the reliefs explain one of the Pharaoh's reasons for building the temple. Amenhotep, it seems, did not have a perfectly clear title to the throne because of his foreign mother. The reliefs, however, make it clear that Amon, in the absence of his father, loved his Mitanni mother and so established beyond any priestly question the divine origin of the Pharaoh. The priests of the Sun-god apparently accepted this evidence, especially since it was incorporated in such a magnificent and richly endowed temple to their god. What the original endowment of the temple was is not known, but by the time of Ramses III, 2623 slaves were servants of the shrine.

Before his death, Amenhotep was not satisfied with the temple, and built a double colonnade of gigantic columns with spreading, campaniform, papyrus capitals which led up to the entrance pylon

[8] L. Borchardt, "Zur Geschichte des Luqsortempels," *Zeitschrift für Aegyptische Sprache*, XXXIV (1896), p. 122 *seq.*
[9] Breasted, *op. cit.*, II, No. 886.

PLATE XLVI

1. Perspective of temple (*after* Perrot et Chipiez, *op. cit.*, Fig. 218).
2. Forecourt of Amenhotep III from northeast.

PLATE XLVII: TEMPLE OF AMON-RE, LUXOR

1

2

(Plate XLVI–2). This avenue of fourteen columns, each 52 feet high, has been attributed to various later Pharaohs, but there seems to be very little question as to Amenhotep having started the construction.

It may have been his intention to build a great hypostyle hall, but before his death he finished only the two central rows; Engelbach, however, believes that Amenhotep intended these columns as an open processional avenue.[10] In either event, one of his successors, either Tutankamun or Harem-hab, enclosed the columns with walls and so made an exceptional type of approach to an Egyptian temple (Plate XLVI–1). About a century after the death of Amenhotep, Ramses II appropriated the temple by adding a second forecourt (Plate XLVII–1) at the end of the corridor and finishing the temple with a great pylon, before which he erected two obelisks and six colossal granite figures of himself, four standing and two seated (Plate XLV–1). In order to keep the entrance through the pylon alongside of an existing chapel of Thutmose, which had been overrun by the court, the axis of the temple was twisted to the side. By this time the temple was 835 feet long, and, in spite of the coarse work of Ramses, it is picturesque and impressive.

TEMPLE OF AMON-RE, KARNAK. The power and weakness of New Kingdom ambition are most evident in the temple of Amon-Re at Karnak,[11] the largest columnar structure ever built. Karnak lies about a mile and a half to the north of Luxor, and it was there that Amon, the god of Thebes, had his most sacred domain. There were twenty temples, shrines, and sacred halls to various divinities in the religious complex at Karnak (Plate XLVIII), but the greatest was the palatial temple of the Sun-god. The fortunes of Amon had risen with the power of the Theban chieftains who had made themselves masters in the valley at the beginning of the Middle Kingdom. After the expulsion of the Hyksos invaders, the Theban war lords raised their local god, Amon, into a supreme divinity, and his sanctuary at Karnak was made to reflect his new wealth and omnipotence. Next to the Labyrinth in the Fayum, it was the largest monument in Egypt, and since the total destruction of the Labyrinth, it has remained the largest religious edifice in the world. It is not so much a single unified temple, as it is a continuous repetition and aggregation of traditional architectural elements which represent the efforts of successive Pharaohs to propitiate both the god and his powerful priests. It is a history of two thousand years of Egyptian architecture from early in the Middle Kingdom to nearly the end of the Ptolemaic period.

The detailed history of this monument is as confusing as a survey of its ruins tends to be. Both the history and the remains have to be simplified. Otherwise the unending records of building and

[10] Engelbach, *Ancient Egypt* (1924), p. 68.

[11] G. Legrain, *Les Temples de Karnak* (1929); H. Chevrier, "Plan d'ensemble de Karnak," *Annales du Service,* XXXVI, pp. 77-87; "Rapport sur les traveaux de Karnak" by M. M. Pillet and H. Chevrier in *Annales* from 1923-1935.

PLATE XLVII

1. Forecourt of Ramses II from north.
2. "Hall of Appearances" from west.

PLATE XLVIII: TEMPLE OF AMON-RE, KARNAK

1

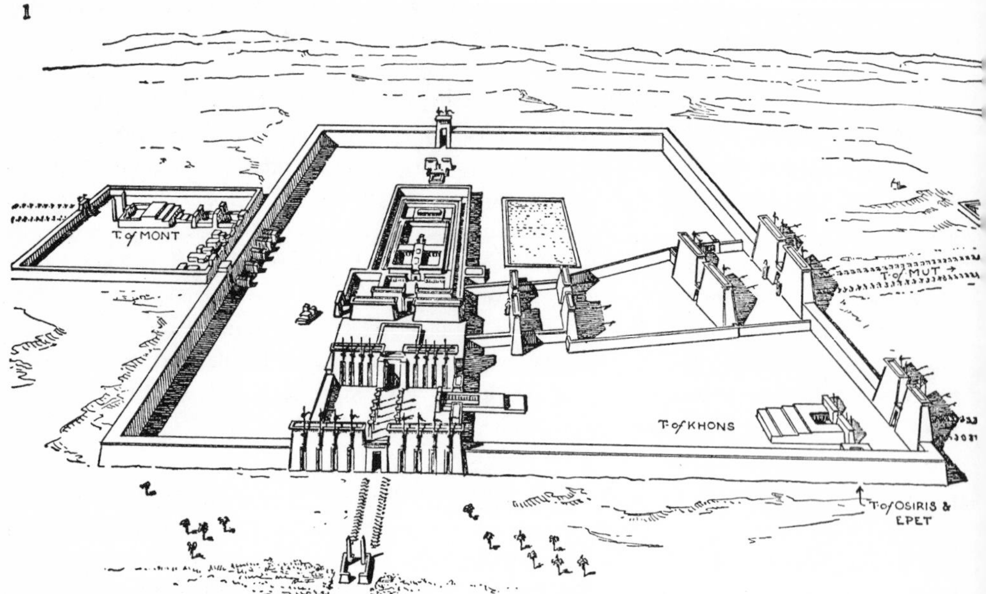

2

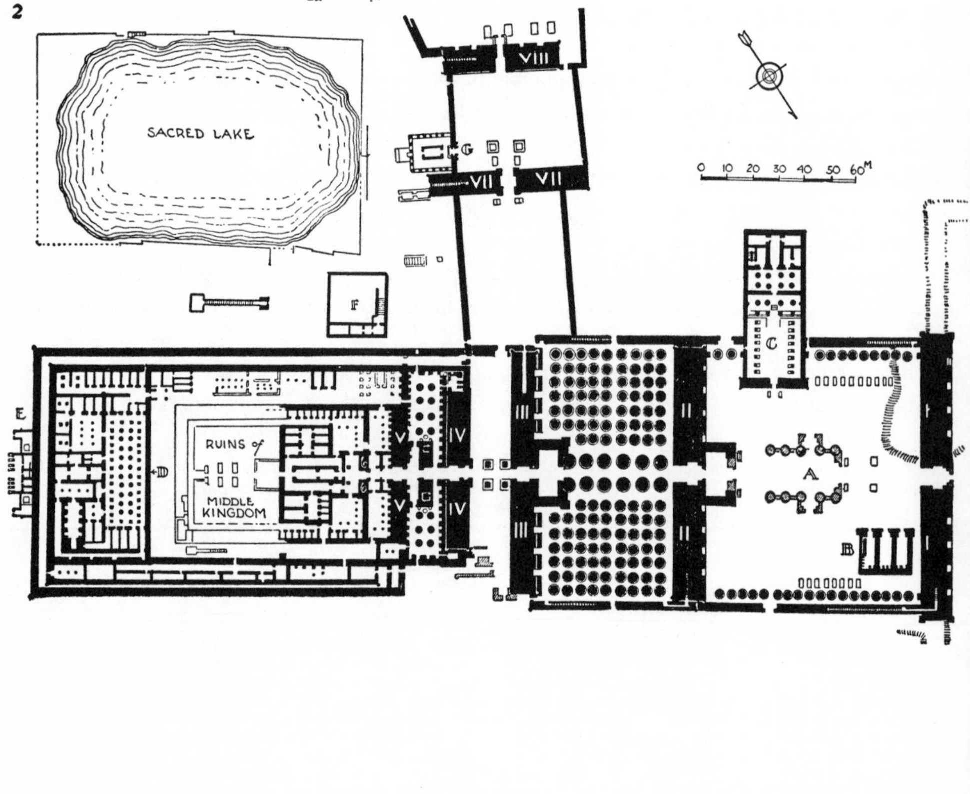

re-buildings, additions and enlargements, rising steadily in a crescendo of colossal size, becomes overpowering and incomprehensible. Its outstanding characteristics are its size and its lack of unity. Before its size is measured and compared, it may help the imagination of the reader to gauge the greatness of Amon by his material possessions.

In the time of Ramses III the estate of Amon at Thebes, including his various temples, of which Karnak was the most important, possessed 86,486 slaves, 421,362 head of cattle, 433 gardens and orchards, 691,334 acres of land, 83 ships, 46 workshops, 65 cities and towns, all in addition to the unestimated riches of gold, silver, incense, and tribute which were pouring into its treasuries. With such wealth it is easy to see how Amon's power became greater than the Pharaoh's. The sacred enclosure covered 61,775 acres, and the temple itself, after the final extensions were made, was 1220 feet long and 338 feet wide, which was space enough to accommodate the cathedrals of St. Peter's, Milan, and Nortre Dame of Paris.

Although its growth was along the processional axis, the temple had no design. Its unorganized extension by accretions is clear proof that the royal builders who enlarged it were motivated by something other than a desire to improve its appearance. There was a temple to Amon on the site during the Middle Kingdom which was incorporated into what are now the ruins of the east end. Some work was done under Amenhotep I, probably by his famous architect Ineni, but it was not until Thutmose I made Thebes the capital of his empire that the old shrine was incorporated in the new structure. He not only built a colonnaded court, with Osiris statues, around the Middle Kingdom temple, but he built two pylons to the west and between them constructed a hall with columns of cedar.[12] Regarding the use of wooden columns it is recorded at Karnak how Thutmose III "found the temple (of Ptah) built of brick and *wooden columns,* and its doorway of wood, beginning to go to ruin."[13] Queen Hatshepsut made some alterations on the interior, unroofing the central part of the hall with the cedar columns, and in the space erected two obelisks which must have looked very crowded for space as they towered above the surrounding colonnade. Although she records with great pride the task of having her architect, Senmut, cut and transport the obelisks from Aswân to Karnak, the queen does not mention why she chose such an unfortunate place for them.

After the queen's death, Thutmose III expressed his dislike for Hatshepsut by encasing her obelisks to a height of eight feet, and remade the hall, leaving the top of the obelisks projecting above

[12] Breasted, *op. cit.,* II, No. 601.
[13] Breasted, *op. cit.,* II, No. 614.

PLATE XLVIII

1. Bird's-eye view (*after* Perrot et Chipiez).
2. Plan:
   A kiosk of Taharqa, *B* temple of Seti II, *C* temple of Ramses III, *D* Festival Hall of Thutmose III, *E* building of Thutmose III, *F* building of Taharqa, *G* peripteral chapel of Thutmose III, pylon I Ethiopian, pylon II of Ramses I, pylon III of Amenhotep III, pylons IV and V of Thutmose I, pylon 6 of Thutmose III, pylon VII of Thutmose III, pylon VIII of Hatshepsut, and pylon IX of Haremhab (H. Chevrier, *Annales du Service,* XXXVI, Pl. I).

PLATE XLIX: TEMPLE OF AMON-RE, KARNAK

1

2

3

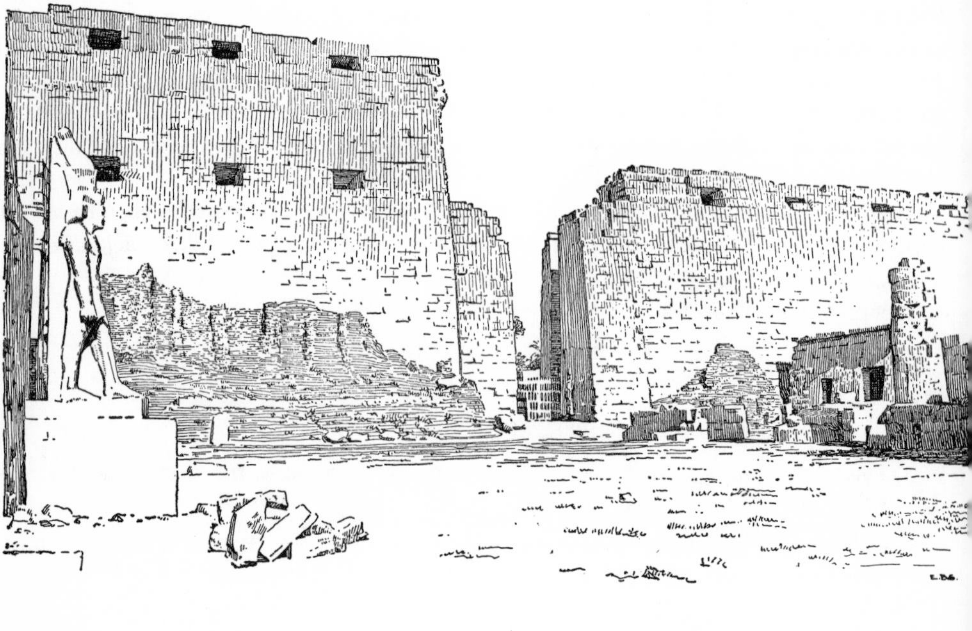

the roof. He also made two Halls of Annals between pylons V and VI; and then about twenty years later he extended the temple eastward by building a Festival Hall. Amenhotep III, who was under obligations to Amon and his priests, added a forecourt to the west, erected an entrance pylon, built an avenue of ram-sphinxes, and left the temple, as he considered it, finished.

About sixty years later, Ramses I, stirred by a desire to outdo all others in his concern for the comfort of the god, erected pylon II, and probably started the great Hypostyle Hall in between his pylon and that of Amenhotep III. The task of completing the largest columnar hall in the world was left to his son, Seti I. The relation between a hypostyle hall and a royal palace is shown by the inscriptions, which call this hall, "the great divine palace of the spirit of Seti I Mer-en-Ptah in the temple of Amon." One hundred years later Ramses III made the mistake of thinking the temple was finished, and so concentrated his interest upon building a complete temple partly in front of the entrance pylon. Two hundred years later, the Libyan Pharaohs of the XXII Dynasty took a new interest in the temple and started to build the final forecourt, called the court of the Bubastides, which was laid out to be larger than any other part of the temple. Like everything this Dynasty undertook, the construction was not finished, and it was the effort of an Ethiopian Pharaoh of the XXV Dynasty, with contributions of several Greek Pharaohs, which completely finished the work. The Ethiopian king, Taharqa, built the last, and largest pylon, which, although never finished, has remained the entrance façade of the temple. In front of the temple was a landing quay and a canal leading to the river, as was seen in front of the mortuary temple of Ramses III at Medinet Habu.

The pylon of Taharqa is a mountain of stone, 370 feet wide, 49 feet thick, and 142½ feet high (Plate XLIX–3). Against its inner face are remains of the brick compartments, filled with sand, which formed the platform for its construction. As it stands, it is impossible to grasp its proportions. The same is true of the Court of the Bubastides, which covers 93,000 square feet, is 276 feet deep and 338 feet wide. Place in it the Duomo of Florence and there would be a comfortable 10,000 square feet left for tourist purposes. This court overran the temple of Ramses III and a small sanctuary of Seti II, which were spared and included without any crowding.

The most famous achievement of Egyptian architecture is the Hypostyle Hall (Plates XLIX and L). Its superhuman size still connotes greatness, power, and magnificence, just as it did to the royal Egyptian mind. It is not the time to ask if these columns are beautiful, or if their sheer bulk reflect a drying-up of Egyptian imagination. They are undoubtedly grandiose, and since they represent the greatest material effort of ancient man to mold stone to his desires, they deserve respect and study.

The Hypostyle Hall alone covers 54,000 square feet and is divided into aisles by fourteen rows of stocky papyrus-bud columns and two central rows of mammoth columns with full-blown papyrus

---

PLATE XLIX

1. View down central aisle of Hypostyle Hall, looking west to pylon I.
2. From roof of Hypostyle Hall, looking north.
3. Court of the Bubastides, looking west, temple of Seti II at right and temple of Ramses III at left.

PLATE L: TEMPLE OF AMON-RE, KARNAK

capitals. These twelve columns of the middle aisles are sixty-nine feet high, eleven and three-quarters feet in diameter, and have a circumference which five men cannot embrace. It is estimated that one hundred men could stand on their campaniform capitals; but the estimate leaves some doubt as to whether the men on the edge would be comfortable. The hundred and forty-two columns of the side aisles are only forty-two and one-half feet high, with a circumference of twenty-seven and one-half feet. When it is realized that these columns supported stone architraves of sixty and seventy tons, and that the central columns carried the roofing blocks seventy-nine feet in the air, it is little wonder they are thick and close together. The construction was accomplished by the effective, but not time-saving, Egyptian method of gradually building up the interior with brick compartments, filled with sand, which made a rising terrace onto which the stones could be dragged by means of inclined ramps. When the stonework was finished, the interior fill of earth, as it was cut away, served as platform for the carving and painting of the six acres of interior surface. The decoration, however, was not finished by Seti I, for the southern part of the hall was decorated by Ramses II and some of it was not completed until the time of Ramses IV.

The creation of this mammoth room with its clerestory windows filled with stone grilles involved no imaginative thought. It was only a copy, blown up to great size in stone, of the great hall of a New Kingdom palace with its wooden columns and clerestory windows filled with wooden grilles. As a result, its interior has no scale, and it is only when one climbs to the roof and looks down into the canyons between the columns that its size begins to be evident. Wonderful as it is to think of men accomplishing such a task, the modern mind, in contemplating this forest of columns, senses a certain futility, for in addition to not revealing their size, the very bigness of the columns has endangered the life of the structure.

The Festival Hall of Thutmose III illustrates the same imitative instinct. It was erected for the celebration of his Heb-Sed festival, and its columns are apparently something new (Plate LI–1). Their shafts taper down instead of up, and their capitals look like campaniform papyrus capitals inverted. Actually these columns were copied in stone from the type of wooden post, with a tenon top, which had been used in Egypt from primitive times as the supports for the canopy above the king in the Heb-Sed festival (Plate II–6, 7). In fact, as we have seen, the kiosk with these tenon poles was the actual symbol of the Heb-Sed festival in hieroglyphic writing.

Egyptian stonework, even though it looks so permanent and was intended by its builders to be everlasting, was curiously careless, especially in the matter of foundations. The foundations of the Hypostyle Hall, in addition to being inadequate, were further weakened by the infiltration of water during the flood season and by the action of saltpeter, with the result that during the interval be-

---

PLATE L

1. From roof of Hypostyle Hall looking north at clerestory windows.
2. From floor of Hypostyle Hall looking south at clerestory windows.
3. Clerestory windows of Hypostyle Hall.

PLATE LI: TEMPLES

1

2

3

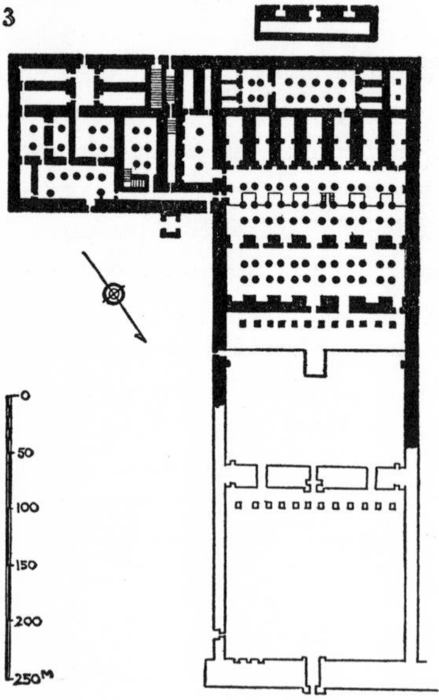

4

tween the beginning of the reign of Ramses II (1292) and the reign of Herhor (1090) the work began to disintegrate. Some restorations were made at that time, but it was during the Ptolemaic period that the two last columns in the central row were rebuilt and their rough blocks left unfinished (Plate XLIX–1). It was the weight of the roof, more than the foundations, which kept the structure stable and erect. Now that the roof has fallen, the problem of reërecting the fallen columns and keeping the standing ones from falling is a task of great engineering difficulty, which the Egyptian Department of Antiquities has undertaken.

The reader who is interested in a more detailed investigation, not only of the Temple of Amon, but of the other temples at Karnak, should turn for guidance to the Baedeker of Egypt, which is clear and accurate. To the south of the great temple is a series of smaller shrines and pylons stretching out towards the interesting temple of Mut. The last pylon in this southern avenue was built by Haremhab (Plate LI–2), and in its ruins again shows the tendency of Egyptian building methods, going back to the first ambitious stonework at Saqqara, to carve an impressive skin of cut masonry and then fill it with loose and careless stonework. In spite of their longing for indestructibility, the Pharonic builders never seem to have benefited from the experiences of the past and realized that a fine veneer of ashlar was not as solid and permanent as it looked.

TEMPLE OF SETI I, ABYDOS. The most exceptional, and in many ways the most interesting temple of the New Kingdom is the "House of Men-ma-re" (Seti I) which that energetic ruler built at Abydos, and his ubiquitous son, Ramses II, finished.[14] The temple, which Seti I calls "an august palace of eternity," and which is also the *Memnonium* of Strabo, is exceptional for two reasons. Unlike other temples, it was laid out in a curious L-shaped plan, and was dedicated to seven divinities: Seti I, Ptah, Harakhte, Amon, Osiris, Isis and Horus (Plate LI–3).

Its two large forecourts, each entered through a pylon, are badly ruined, but the raised portico of twelve square pillars, leading from the second court into the temple, makes an impressive façade. Originally seven doors led from this outer vestibule into the first columnar hall, but Ramses II closed all except the central opening. The first hall, wide and shallow, has two rows of twelve papyrus-bud columns, arranged in pairs so as to make seven aisles leading to the seven doors of the second hall. The second hall has three rows of twelve supports, the first two rows being papyrus-bud columns; then the floor rises by means of ramps, and the last row are "tree-trunk columns" with cylindrical

[14] A. St. G. Caulfield, *The Temple of the Kings* (1902); J. Capart, *Abydos, le Temple de Seti I* (1912); M. Calverley, *The Temple of King Sethos I at Abydos* (1933).

PLATE LI

1. Festival Hall of Thutmose III, temple of Amon-Re, Karnak.
2. Pylon IX of Haremhab, temple of Amon-Re, Karnak.
3. Plan of temple of Seti I, Abydos (Caulfield, *The Temple of the Kings*, 1902).
4. Looking west along aisle in front of sanctuaries, Temple of Seti I, Abydos.

PLATE LII: TEMPLES

1

2

3

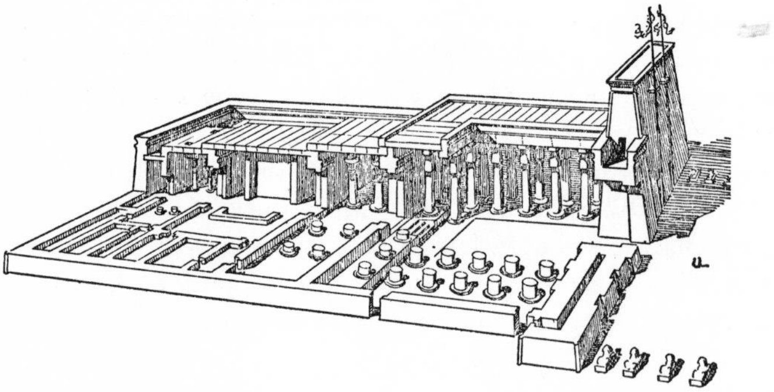

4

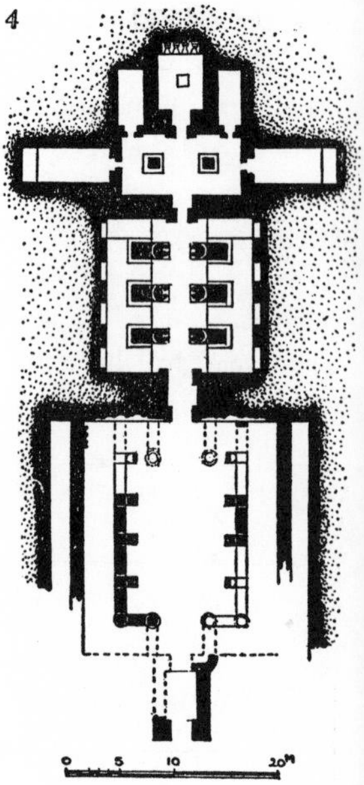

5

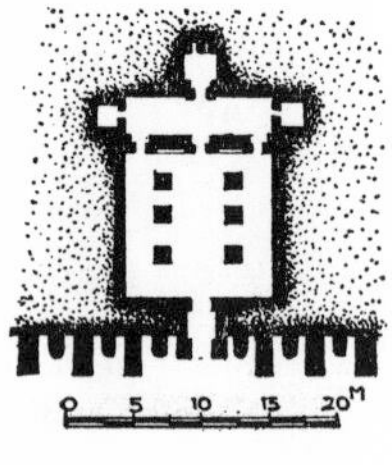

6

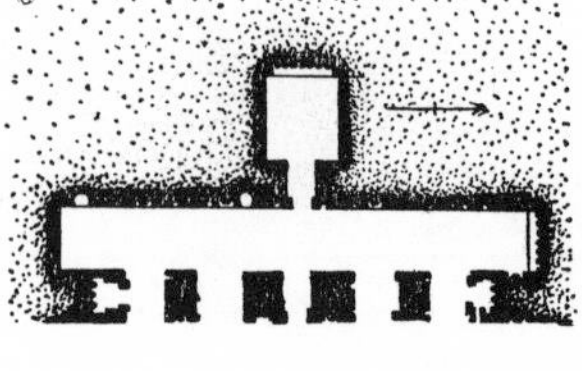

shafts and no capital save a square abacus block. In other words there is a raised portico at the end of this hall, directly in front of the long row of seven sanctuaries.

Although the sanctuary of Amon has the central place of honor, the temple was actually built and arranged for the mysteries of Osiris, whose grave and temple were at Abydos, and for this reason the *sekos* of Osiris leads into a large hall, running north and south, with smaller chapels for Isis, Osiris, and Horus. Where the sanctuary of Osiris opens into rooms of deeper mystery, the other sanctuaries have closed "false doors" carved at their west walls (Plate LII–1). Furthermore all these holies of holies imitate the curved roof of the primitive hut-shrine, and hence are roofed with corbeled slabs of stone cut to the appearance of a hoop roof.[15]

At this point, the temple, instead of continuing to the west, turns at a right angle to the south. A long passage, known as the "Gallery of the Kings" because of the remarkable list of kings inscribed upon its walls, leads from the great hall to the sacrificial slaughter room and its adjoining complex of service halls. From this gallery another passage runs west, and was used in all probability for ceremonal processions to the tomb of Osiris and the Osireion of Seti I, which lay directly behind the temple. This passage also had a curved ceiling carved in the overlapping slabs of the roof.

Many explanations have been advanced for the curious break in the plan. Largely on the authority of Strabo, who mentions a spring connected with the *Memnonium,* some have said the spring endangered the foundations of the temple at the west end; others insist it was a sacred spring, either connected with the Osireion or the tomb of Osiris, which made a western extension impossible. The existence of the cenotaph, known as the Osireion,[16] of Seti I, directly behind the temple, sufficiently explains the plan of the temple, especially if the site of the cenotaph was in some way sacred to Osiris.

The temple is both impressive for its architecture and interesting because of the finely carved and brilliantly colored reliefs upon nearly all its walls. These reliefs are themselves a pictorial record of the complicated ritual of an Egyptian temple, for they depict Seti I in nearly every imaginable relation to the gods, himself performing most of the services of dressing, feeding, perfuming, and decorating the divine family, of which he was no less divine a member.

TEMPLE OF KHONS, KARNAK. The small temple of Khons which Ramses III built at Karnak is so outstandingly typical that it is exceptional (Plate LII–3). Although the decorations were finished

[15] M. Calverley, *op. cit.,* Pl. 1 B.
[16] Page 117.

PLATE LII

1. Sanctuary, temple of Seti I, Abydos.
2. Ptolemaic gateway, temple of Khons, Karnak.
3. Temple of Khons, Karnak (after Perrot et Chipiez, *op. cit.,* I, Fig. 208).
4. Plan of rock-cut temple, Garf Husein (Baedeker).
5. Plan of small rock-cut temple of Ramses II, Abu Simbel (Baedeker).
6. Plan of rock chapel of Haremhab in quarries of Sisila (Baedeker).

PLATE LIII: TEMPLES AT ABU SIMBEL

1

2

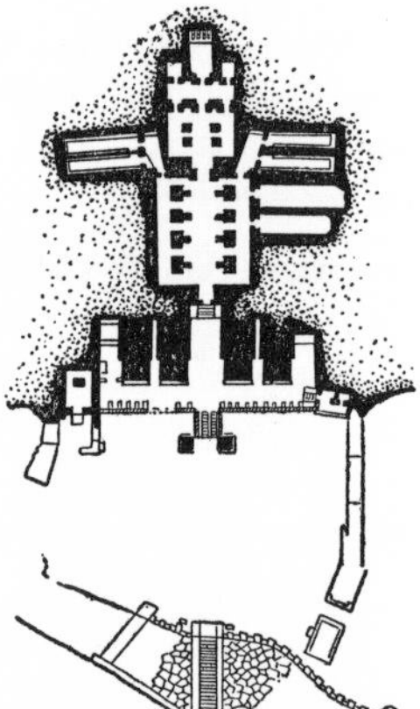

3

by Ramses IV and XI, and Herikor, Ramses III built it to the Moon-god, the son of Amon and Mut, and it was never enlarged or changed. Therefore it has only the standard and essential elements of an Egyptian temple. The stone gateway in front of it, which was originally the entrance through the precinct walls, was built in the Ptolemaic period (Plate LII–2).

ROCK-CUT TEMPLES

TEMPLE OF HARAKHTE, ABU SIMBEL. Ramses II recognized no limits to his pride and ambitions. One hundred and sixty-six miles south of Aswân in the land of Nubia, this prodigious builder had two temples carved out of the solid rock on the west bank of the Nile. The site, known as Abu Simbel, was sacred long before Ramses II to "Hathor of Absek," but in the thirty-fifth year of his reign, 1257 B.C., the Pharaoh had the great temple made, ostensibly in honor of Harakhte of Heliopolis, but actually to the glory of Ramses himself. Between the river and the face of the cliffs is the forecourt, bounded on the north and south by brick walls. Before the façade is a rock-cut terrace, approached by a flight of steps with an inclined plane in the middle, and enclosed by a balustrade behind which stand a row of hawks, and statues of the king in various forms (Plate LIII–2).

The façade, carved into the face of the cliff, represents the front of a pylon preceded by four colossal figures of the seated Ramses (Plate LIII–1). This bold piece of aggrandizement is one hundred and nineteen feet wide, and one hundred feet high, while the colossi are sixty-five feet in height, the ear of each seated Pharaoh measuring three and one-half feet. Above the cornice at the top of the façade is a row of dog-headed apes, who, as "Watchers of the Dawn," were sacred to the worship of the rising sun. As if the colossi and the smaller figures of his family around their legs were not enough identification, the royal egotist worked his own name onto the façade by a neat pictographic conceit. In the recess on the façade is the figure of Re-Harakhte, hawk-headed one, to whom the temple was dedicated, but at one side is carved the jackal-headed User, and on the other side the figure of Maet, so that the whole reads User-Maet-re, which was the prenomen of Ramses.

The actual temple is cut back into the living rock for one hundred and eighty feet. The first hall, which really represents the traditional forecourt of a typical mortuary temple, is fifty-four feet wide and fifty-eight feet deep, and has two rows of Osirid figures of the king, each thirty feet high, the row on the south side wearing the Double Crown, and the row on the north wearing the White Crown of Upper Egypt. On the walls of this chamber are carved the usual Ramessid scenes, with the customary emphasis upon the fictitious victory at Kadesh. At the west end are three doors, the side ones leading into lateral chambers, and the central one opening into the main hall, which has four square

---

PLATE LIII

1. Façade of Great Temple of Ramses II.
2. Plan of great rock-cut temple of Ramses II (Baedeker).
3. Façade of small temple of Ramses II.

pillars. Beyond the hall is an antechamber preceding the *sekos* in which the four gods, Ramses, Ptah, Amon, and Harakhte are seated in hieratic dignity.

TEMPLE OF HATHOR, ABU SIMBEL. Nearby is another rock-cut temple (Plate LII-5), again executed for Ramses II, and dedicated to the local divinity, Hathor of Absek. It was "a house hewn in the pure mountain of Nubia, of fine, white and enduring sandstone, as *an eternal work*."[17] Although the façade is only thirty-nine feet high, it is an interesting and striking monument, for carved in deep niches are three standing colossi, two of the great Ramses and one of his chief wife, Nefertari, who is also represented in deified form (Plate LIII–3). Rock-cut tombs and chapels go back to the Old Kingdom, but it was Ramses II, apparently, who had the idea of carving a great temple in the cliff. Modern visitors of speculative imagination have been intrigued with the problem of how the stone-cutters dug out these caverns and decorated them in the unsanitary ventilation and inadequate illumination of oil lamps and smoking torches. It has even been suggested that the Egyptians must have had electricity in order to account for their subterranean carving, but we may safely assume that Egyptian stone-cutters could work long and skilfully under what we would consider impossible conditions.

TEMPLES OF SEBUA AND GARF HUSEIN. Two other rock-cut temples were executed in honor of Ramses II on the banks of the Nile between the First and Second Cataracts. The temple of Sebua, called the "House of Amon" by the Egyptians, was dedicated to Amon and Re-Harakhte by Ramses II. The walls of the forecourts and pylons were built of brick and stone, but the great hall and inner sanctuaries were cut into the cliff. The plan is much the same as that of the temple of Garf Husein (Plate LII–4), the "House of Ptah," which was executed in honor of Ptah of Memphis, Ramses II, Ptah-Tenen, and Hathor with the cow's head.

"SPEOS ARTEMIDOS." Among the possible examples from which Ramses II may have gotten his idea of rock-cut temples is the shrine of Pasht at Beni-Hasan. Pasht was a variant of the cat-goddess Ubastet, and was one "who traverses the valleys in the midst of the east land, whose ways are storm-beaten." Her sanctuary at Beni-Hasan was probably an old quarry which Queen Hatshepsut and Thutmose III adapted by carving into a speos. It consists of a portico with two rows of pillars, four in each row, and a chamber behind it. The Greeks, who considered it a grotto of Artemis, gave it its name of the Speos Artemidos.

THE HERETICAL TEMPLES OF ATEN

When Egypt's one outstanding religious thinker and heretical Pharaoh, Amenhotep IV, defied the power of the priests of Amon-Re, dedicated himself and his Empire to the service of Aten, the one and only god, changed his name to Akhenaten, "He in whom Aten is satisfied," and, abandoning Thebes,

[17] Breasted, *op. cit.*, III, No. 500.

constructed a new capital at what is called Tell el-Amarna, he built a new type of temple to Aten, the giver of life and light. At first Aten was not a jealous god, as he became, and Akhenaten was not an unqualified monotheist; so the Pharaoh built shrines to such great predecessors as Amenhotep II and Thutmose IV; he also erected small temples to Tyi, the queen-mother, to Princess Baktaten, his sister, and to his dear, eldest daughter, Meryt-aten; but his great effort, and in the end his whole interest and resources, was devoted to adoration of the one god, the "living Aten, beginning of life." For him he built a *Great Temple,* a *River Temple, Hat-Aten, Per-Hai-Aten,* the "House of Rejoicing," connected with *Gem-Aten, Maru-Aten,* the garden precinct of Aten, and the semi-sacred chapels and kiosks of the Southern Pool, besides many great altars, either free-standing or in pavilions.

Maru-Aten is described in the next chapter,[18] but before we look at the new sun-temples and gauge their originality, we must have some estimate of Amenhotep and his religion. This estimate is hard to form because Amenhotep was a religious enthusiast, a youthful reformer, a pacifist, and a pathetic martyr to his ideal. All these qualities are dear to the Anglo-Saxon imagination, with the result that a great romance and spiritual awakening have been read into the life and ambitions of this distinctive individual who, by contrast with all other figures in Egyptian history, stands forth as a creative dreamer and tragic personality. He was an abnormal man, as the shape of his head and body in the Amarna scenes shows. What deductions can be made from the elongated cranium, the long neck and chin, the delicate and sensuous features, and the protruding stomach, it is for physiologists and psychologists to say. In fact the Amarna phenomenon, its art and its creator, are remarkable and lovely, but like any deviations from the normal it requires trained mental and medical diagnosis before we can be sure of our analysis. Akhenaten was unquestionably a delicate and sensitive dreamer, physically prevented by his body from being a man of action. But in how far did his deformities and sensitive nature make him a pacifist, a lover of flowers, nature, and the pleasant warmth of the sun, and in the end leave him an indulgent and beauty-loving recluse, feeding his vanity in an artificial paradise where he would not listen to bad news from his representatives in an Empire which was falling to pieces because of royal neglect? His motto "Living in Truth," and the references in the hymns and inscriptions to the "Heat" and "splendour which is in Aten" read as if he were a seeker after the spiritual force which lies behind the sun and its great powers, but some writers have questioned whether Akhenaten sought a more spiritual conception of divinity than had been followed before. Beautiful as the hymns to Aten are, they contain no ethical references, and the picture they paint of the Sun-god is still a materialistic, though picturesque and charming account of his marvels. Aten, save as we read the Hebrew spiritualism of the Psalms into the translators' versions of the Sun-god's hymns, was not a new and original divinity, and it was the physical sun which Akhenaten still worshiped. Aten was Re, softened to the temper of the gentle, nature-loving, and sensitive neurotic, for Akhenaten may have lived true to his creed, but his creed was the unconscious creation of his own temperament.

Whether we consider him a great religious thinker or a delightful and yet pathetic sensualist who wanted only to live happily in a Paradise of his own creation, it makes little difference to our inter-

[18] Page 213.

PLATE LIV: TEMPLES OF TELL EL-AMARNA

1

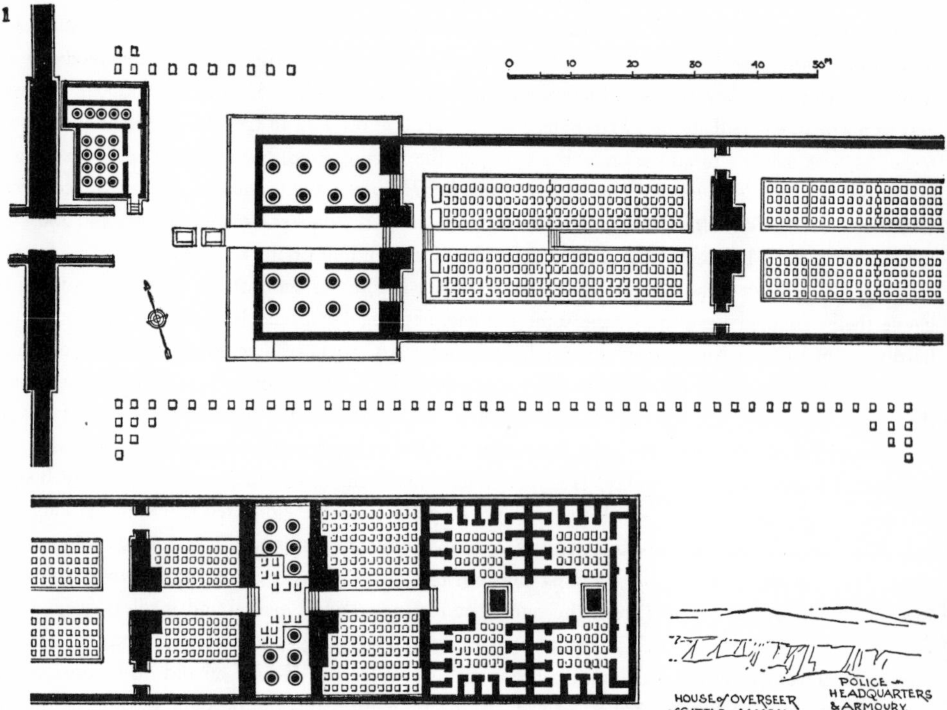

2

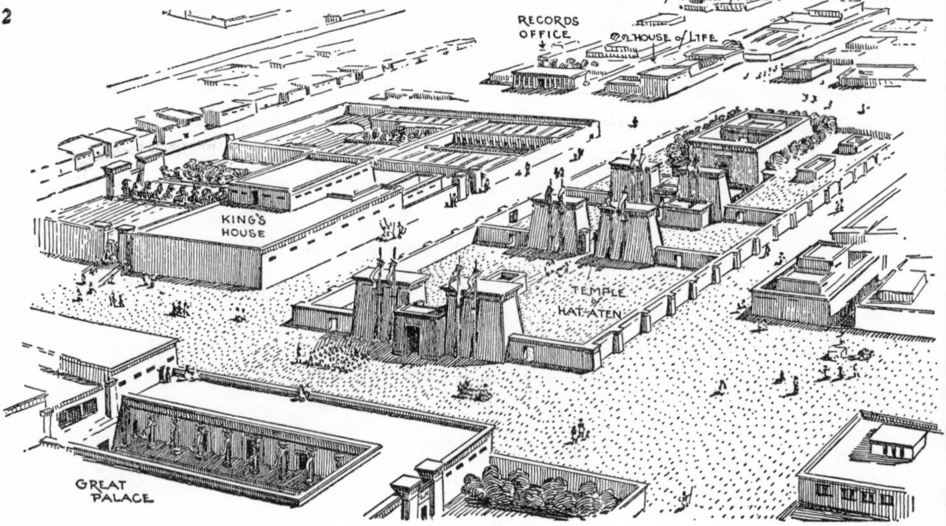

pretation of the architecture. The temples are all new in type, but lacking in any marked originality. They were all built of brick or rubble, and whitewashed. The largest and most important of Amarna temples was the Great Temple of Aten with its series of courts and sanctuaries along one continuous axis. It differed from the usual Egyptian abode of the gods in the fact that it had no covered sanctuary in which the image of the divinity was worshiped. Instead of dark and mysterious halls, inner chambers, and dim recesses, it consisted of a series of courts, open to the light of the sun, in which were offering tables and great altars. While the form of the temple is unique, the idea went back to the earliest temple of the Sun [19] where the services took place in front of the *ben-ben* of Re. While the excavators believe they have discovered the actual form of the structure,[20] the remains are so fragmentary and their restoration so problematic, there is still doubt as to whether we should fully accept the excavators' restorations, or follow the plan of Mr. Davies [21] which he worked out from the Egyptian representations of the temple in the tombs at Tell el-Amarna. The temple complex is represented with great detail and completeness in the tombs of Merya [22] and Panehesy,[23] and the pictures, while varying somewhat in the details and proportions, are so consistent as to make it certain that the craftsmen worked from their memories of the actual buildings. In the chapter on Egyptian methods of drawing is a schematic plan of the temple (Plate LXXV–4) based upon the evidence of these tomb pictures.

The Great Temple consisted of a long walled precinct divided by a cross-wall into two sections, and surrounded by an open corridor or ambulatory. According to the inscriptions the temple included four essential parts, the Temple of Aten proper, the House of Rejoicing, and the "Sun-Shade of Tyi," which were all presumably in the first section of the precinct, and, finally, the Sanctuary of the *Ben-Ben,* which was in the smaller precinct at the eastern end. The main temple was preceded by an open court entered through a gateway. At either side of the gateway, according to the Amarna representations, was a villa, belonging to officials of the temple, and at the extreme left of this gateway was the slaughter house. The excavations show a pavilion (Plate LIV–1) immediately to the left of the entrance, and then the porticoed façade of *Per-Hai-Aten,* "The House of Rejoicing," which in its turn is followed by *Gem-Aten.* It is difficult to believe that the craftsmen depicting the Aten temple in the tombs could have been wrong when they represented this unique portico in front of the pylon as eight columns wide and two rows deep (Plate XLII–3),

19 Page 58.

20 J. D. S. Pendlebury, "Excavations at Tell El-Amarnah," *Journal of Egyptian Archaeology,* XIX (1933), pp. 113-116; XX (1934,) pp. 129-133.

21 N. de G. Davies, *The Rock Tombs of El Amarna,* II, p. 20 *seq.*

22 Davies, *The Rock Tombs of El Amarna,* I.

23 Davies, *op. cit.,* II.

PLATE LIV

1. Plan of the Per-Hai-Aten and Gem-Aten (*after* Lavers, *Journal of Egyptian Archaeology,* XIX, 1933, Pl. XIII).
2. Restoration of a part of Akhetaten showing temple of Hat-Aten (*after London Illustrated News,* Sept. 15, 1930).

PLATE LV: TEMPLES OF TELL EL-AMARNA

1

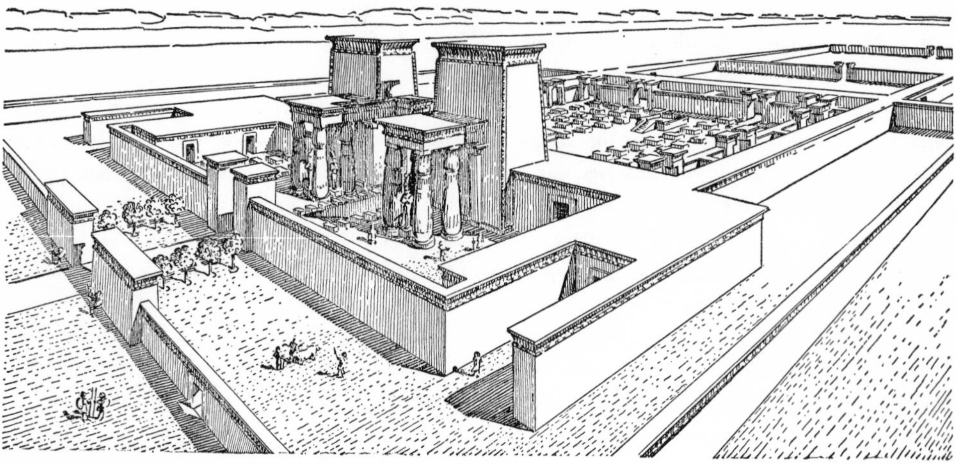

2

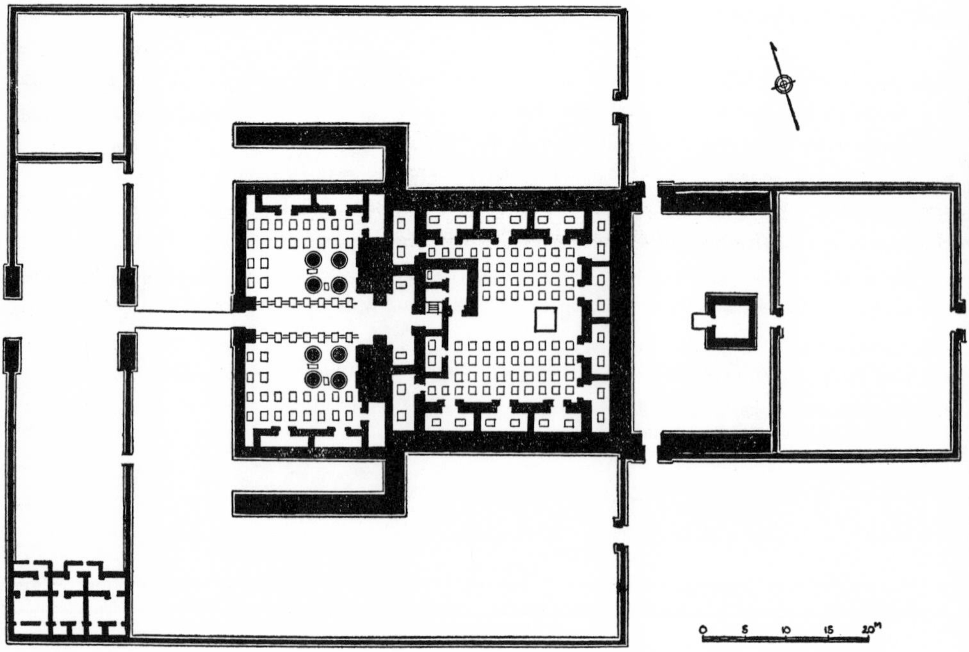

and then carefully depicted the pylon of the last sanctuary as having a portico only four columns wide [24] and two deep; but the excavators have reversed the arrangement, making the portico four columns wide and eight rows deep. In the restoration the entrance is a sunken passage between two columnar halls; beyond these halls the processional path descends into a court where on either side are rows of small offering tables; then the passage ascends to a raised causeway which continues through a second and third court, each filled with rows of offering tables. At what point in this endless repetition *Per-Hai-Aten* turns into *Gem-Aten* is uncertain; but the division probably came at the point where the causeway enters a columnar hall and descends into a sunken area filled with offering tables. Beyond this hall the causeway passes through still another court before entering the double sanctuary at the east end in which there are two large altars and rows of offering tables. Some one of the colonnades in this part of the temple was presumably the "Sunshade of Tyi," for the inscriptions make it evident that "her sun-shade" was the equivalent to "her colonnade." [25]

The smaller precinct at the eastern end of the complex was the "Sanctuary of the *Ben-Ben,*" according to pictorial representations, or the Great Temple of Aten, according to the excavators. The Amarna pictures make it clear that within the forecourt and to the left of the entrance was a stele, or *ben-ben,* on a pedestal; also in the court was a slaughter house and a villa for the priest. The restoration of the façade of the temple (Plate LV–1) shows what is graphically represented on the Amarna frescoes as an open portico of two rows of two columns on either side of the pylon gateway. In front of each column, or between the columns, was a statue of the king, with smaller statues ascribed to his favorite daughter Meryt-aten, who had a shrine in the temple. The curious arrangement of corridor-like recesses on either side of the pylon is accurately depicted in the Egyptian drawings. The corridor at the right was probably for the choir led by a harpist. The circuitous passage through the pylon into the inner court of the sanctuary is again verified by the Egyptian drawings in the tombs, although the picture in the tomb of Panehesy [26] shows a more circuitous approach than the restoration. Around this court were a series of chapels, and in the open space were rows of offering tables with the great altar in the center.

Beyond the main court was a second court in which there was a brick altar of an earlier period. It must be kept in mind when trying to straighten out the confused evidence as to the form of this exceptional temple that there was much hasty building and rebuilding at Amarna, with the result that the Egyptian representations may represent a different period in the construction from what appears as most evident in the excavations. Although we do not expect Egyptian drawings of archi-

[24] Davies, *op. cit.,* Plates XI, XXV; II, Pl. XIX.
[25] Davies, *op. cit.,* II, p. 27.
[26] Davies, *op. cit.,* II, Pl. XIX.

PLATE LV

1. Restoration of the Great Temple of Aten (*after* Lavers, *op. cit.,* XX, 1934, Pl. XVI).
2. Plan of Great Temple of Aten (*op. cit.,* Pl. XIV).

tecture to be absolutely consistent, it is unfortunate to find inconsistencies between modern plans and elevations.

Besides the Great Temple of Aten there was at Akhetaten a smaller temple, called Hat-Aten, or the "Castle of Aten," situated east of the great palace and next to the King's House (Plate LIV–2). This stronghold and dwelling of the god consisted of a series of three courts, entered by pylons, an altar in the outer court, a priest's house in the second court, and the sanctuary in the last court. The sanctuary, with its walls of rubble faced with masonry, was surrounded by an ambulatory of trees; a ramp led into its outer court within which was an altar; from this court an ante-room gave access to the inner chamber which had a narrow corridor around it.[27]

These temples built for the devotion of Aten may be striking variations from the standard type of temple, and hence suggest a more attractive form of worship, but they must have been reminiscent of earlier forms of which we have little or no remaining evidence. Certainly they show the primitive tendency to feel conviction and truth in endless repetition, as if by saying or doing a thir three times, or better a hundred times, it must be proved true. In spite of his religious revolt, Akhenaten still had implicit faith in Egyptian habits of formalized repetition.

[27] At the so-called Third Cataract is the Temple of Sebesi, built inside the fort of Gem-Aten, which is the only Aten temple of Amenhotep IV to survive.

8. *LATE DYNASTIC TEMPLES*

Let my name abide in your house, let my Ka be remembered after my life, let my statue abide and my name endure upon it imperishably in your temple. XXVI DYNASTY.

ARCHITECTURE IS ALWAYS DEPENDENT upon peace and prosperity. After the death of Ramses III Egypt enjoyed very little of either one. For three dynasties, beginning with the XXIII, the country came largely under the rule of the Ethiopian kings of Nubia, who fought bravely but ineffectively to prevent its becoming tributary to the Assyrians. By the XXVI Dynasty the Assyrians were expelled, Psamtek (Psammetichos) of Saïs usurped the power, and, as a result of the growing trade relations with the Greek world, Egypt had a brief recrudescence of prosperity and art from 663-525 B.C. Even under the energetic Delta kings there was no significant architectural revival. The Saïtic period was terminated by the Persians, under Cambyses, who dominated the valley until 332 B.C., when Alexander the Great incorporated Egypt into his new Hellenistic Empire. At his death Alexander left Egypt to be ruled by his general, Ptolemy Soter, whose descendants continued to rule down to Ptolemy XVI, the son of Cleopatra and Julius Cæsar, when in 30 B.C. Augustus annexed Egypt as a Roman province.

During the Græco-Roman Period there was a revival of monumental building as a result of the increased revenue which came from trade and a systematic exploitation of the country. In spite of the foreign domination the Nile continued to assimilate the invaders, and the architecture, although distinctive, still adhered to the native traditions. The most evident characteristics of late dynastic temples in the Ptolemaic and Roman periods are the more florid richness of the decoration, the abandonment of the clerestory method of lighting the Hypostyle Hall, and the use of a columnar *vestibule,* with a *screen wall,* as a pronaos between the forecourt and the Hall of Appearances.

Although there are no existing stone prototypes for the screen wall between the columns of an entrance portico, the idea itself went back to those primitive barriers of matting between reed uprights, such as were seen copied upon the façade of Zoser's mortuary palace at Saqqara, where the screen has a cresting of *khekhers* (Plate XVIII–3). In the XVIII Dynasty the palace of Akhenaten had a light, entrance pavilion, a kiosk of appearances or a royal vestibule, which is frequently represented in the paintings of Tell el-Amarna (Plate LVI–2). This royal portico had screen walls capped with a cornice of cobra heads, and was therefore the same type of vestibule as that which the Ptolemaic builders revived and copied in stone.

When the late builders abandoned the clerestory method of lighting they reverted to the early custom of illuminating their interiors by means of small hypæthral openings cut through the stones

PLATE LVI: GRÆCO-ROMAN TEMPLES

1

2
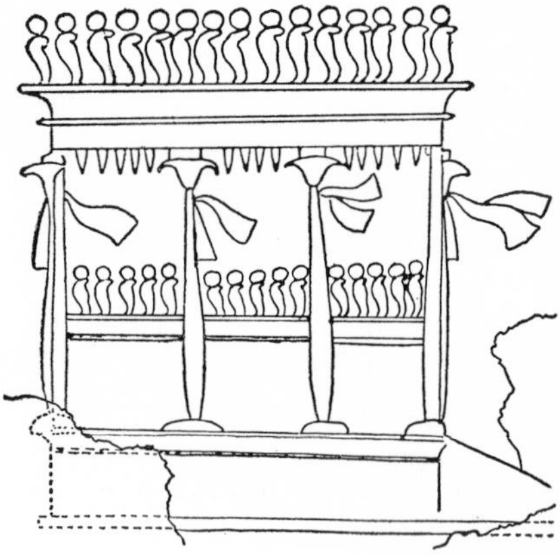

3
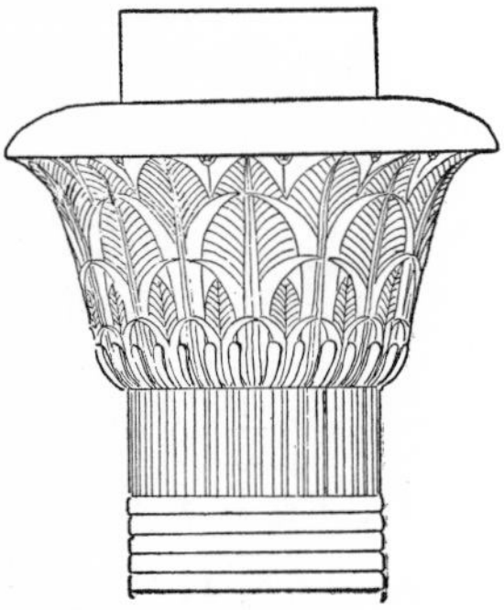

4
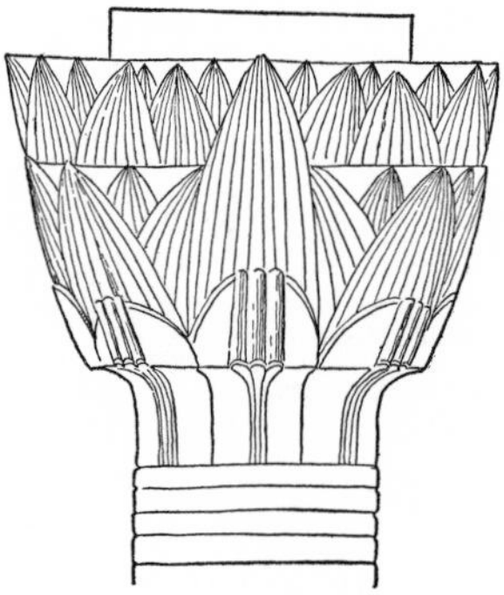

5
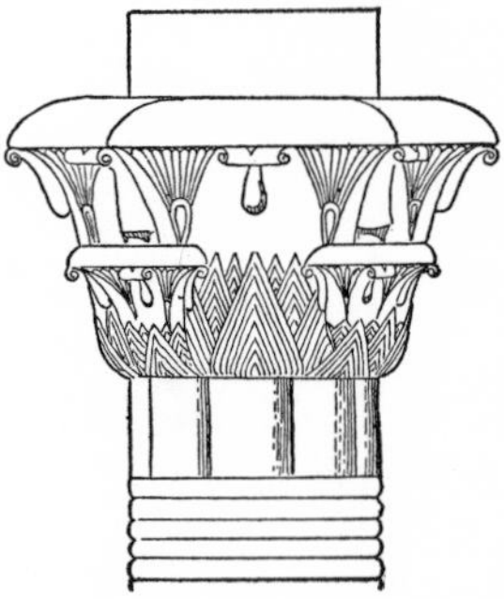

6
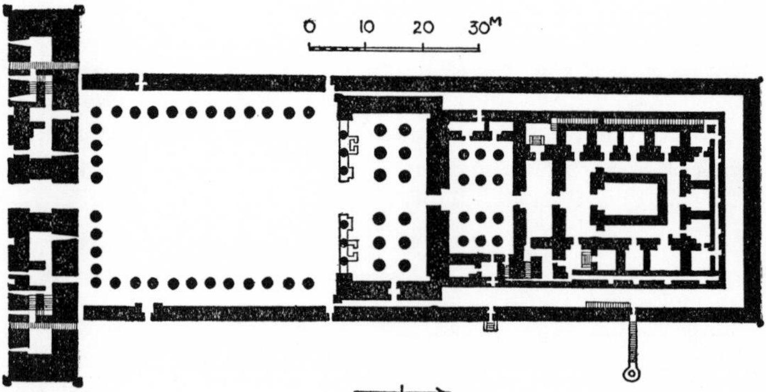

of the roof (Plate LX–1). Thus they were able to direct theatrical shafts of symbolic sunlight into the dark interiors, in much the same way that the Old Kingdom builders lit the interior of Khafra's "Valley-Temple" by means of overhead beams of light focused upon the statues of the king (Plate XXXIII–2). The screen walls across the façades of Ptolemaic temples, however, were not for lighting the interiors, because the Hall of Appearances was cut off from the vestibule by a solid wall pierced only by a single doorway.

Another persistent feature of Ptolemaic and late dynastic temples, which also went back to an earlier prototype, common in the domestic architecture of Tell el-Amarna, is the so-called broken-lintel doorway. This feature is not the bizarre creation which it appears to be, but had a reasonable origin, presumably in the domestic architecture of the XVIII Dynasty. The gateways to the Amarna villas were small pylons with doorjambs capped with pieces of cavetto cornice attached to them on the inside, which, when open, have much the same effect as the Ptolemaic doorways. This type of doorway is not only depicted upon the walls of the Amarna tombs (Plate XLII-3), but it exists as a free-standing stone shrine in an Amarna house (Plate LVI–1), showing that it had special ritualistic significance.

In their temple construction the Ptolemaic architects took exceptional pains with the drainage of the flat roofs, and seem to have revived, if revival it was, the use of the lion-headed waterspout.[1] Rain was probably no more common at that time than it is to-day; but when it did occur it was a terrifying experience to the Egyptian, endangering his painted reliefs and threatening the very permanence of his structures.[2] It is nevertheless curious to find the Græco-Roman period providing for an occasional downpour when the New Kingdom appears to have disregarded such phenomena. It is more reasonable to assume that waterspouts were always a necessary provision for palaces built of crude bricks, and that the Græco-Roman period continued to reproduce royal dwellings as abodes for their gods. If the walls and roofs of the New Kingdom temples were as well preserved as the later ones, we would undoubtedly find that waterspouts and drainage troughs on the flat roofs continued in use through the whole history of stone architecture in Egypt.

The persistent traditionalism of Ptolemaic architecture is proof that the methods of construction followed established usage. While the late temples exhibit a few new decorative features and some variations in plan, they still faithfully adhere to convention. Because of the inherent conservatism of the culture and the desire of a new dynasty to strengthen its position before the native population, the architects went back, whenever possible, to prototypes sanctified by a venerated past. No age, how-

[1] Page 103.
[2] E. A. W. Budge, *A History of Egypt*, VII (1902), p. 37.

PLATE LVI

1. Shrine in house of Panehsy, Tell el-Amarna (*Journal of Egyptian Archaeology*, XIII, 1927, Pl. XLVII).
2. Royal kiosk, Tell el-Amarna (N. de G. Davies, *The Rock Tombs of El Amarna*, I, Pl. XXXI).
3, 4, 5. Ptolemaic capitals (G. Jéquier, *Manuel d'Archéologie Egyptienne*, 1924, Figs. 135, 157, 171).
6. Plan of temple of Horus, Edfu.

PLATE LVII: TEMPLE OF HORUS, EDFU

1

2

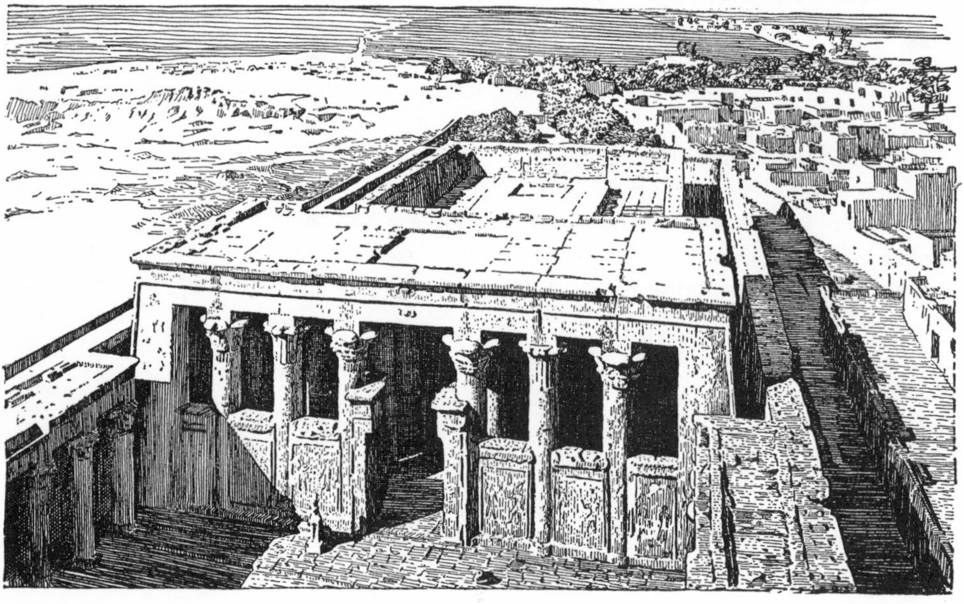

ever, can artistically conceal its instinctive tendencies in a revival, and the most expressive manifestation of late dynastic taste is the decorative character of the temples. In place of the standard papyrus capitals, so universally used during the New Kingdom, the Ptolemaic stone-masons carved a variety of complicated, *lobed campaniform capitals* (Plate LVI–3, 4, 5), which have a semi-naturalistic and picturesque appearance.[8] These fanciful creations were not a revival of older forms, unless they were adapted to architecture from pictorial sources. Often the quatrefoil capitals have globular pendants which are seen on earlier wall paintings. At the same time the sculptors revived the *palm capital* with its spreading fronds (Plate LVIII–1), and made monumental use, whenever possible, of the human-headed *Hathor capital* (Plate LIX–3).

It has been suggested that the revival of the palm capital and the development of complicated papyrus forms were a reflection of the naturalistic taste of Hellenistic culture, coming into Egypt with Greek influences. It is also claimed that the smaller, and hence better, scale of the temples shows an improved sense of proportion due to Classical inspiration. Even though the Greek and Roman domination left an imprint on the Nile civilization, it is difficult to believe that these assumptions are true. Greek interest in Egypt was in the beginning purely commercial, and localized to a few Delta cities. Later, when the Greeks were the most powerful foreign element, their influence on architecture was largely limited to such cities as Alexandria, Ptolemais, and Naucratis, where Hellenic tastes set the mode. The Ptolemaic rulers were at first hardly representative of Greek refinement, and in the end they became more Egyptian than Greek. Moreover, they were studiously desirous of propitiating native tradition, and were dependent upon Egyptian craftsmen. In fact, when we do see in the pictographic reliefs an effort to combine Classic modeling and naturalistic anatomy with Egyptian conventions, the result is usually unfortunate. If the Egyptians could do no better than they did with the proportions of Greek figures, it is difficult to believe that Classic refinement had much influence on their architectural proportions. The real distinction of Ptolemaic buildings is their smaller size, their obviously intended decorative effect, and the fact that they are not only better preserved, but that each of them was built over a relatively short term of years.

On the other hand, it is true that in all late phases of artistic expression, at a time when forms tend to lose their ideographic significance and craftsmen begin to enjoy objective nature as a more complicated manifestation of technical dexterity, art becomes more consciously decorative and naturalistic. Egyptian architecture by Ptolemaic times is consistently picturesque. The capitals in a colonnade are no longer uniform; wall surfaces are more ornately carved with pictorial reliefs, cut deeply, and frequently crudely, in order to produce a more striking effect; and at the same time there is a studied

[8] A detailed discussion of the different types of Ptolemaic capitals is given by G. Jéquier, *Manuel d'Archéologie Égyptienne,* I.

PLATE LVII

1. Forecourt and pylon, looking south.
2. Looking north from top of pylon.

PLATE LVIII: TEMPLE OF HORUS, EDFU

1

2

3

regularity to the rich, all-over, wall reliefs which suggests a desire for pictorial pattern. It all indicates that even Egypt, given plenty of time and a sufficient dislocation to undermine some of its faith in traditional ideology, could gradually acquire, without Classical influence, an objective interest in decorative effect and the picturesque forms of nature.[4]

TEMPLE OF HORUS, EDFU. Of the many Ptolemaic temples, that of Horus at Edfu is the best preserved.[5] Situated on the west bank, not far above Thebes, it was begun in 237 B.C. by Ptolemy III, on the site of an early temple dedicated to the sun-god Horus, to Hathor of Dendera and to Horus, "the uniter of the two lands." Horus of Edfu was identified with Apollo by the Greeks and the Romans. The actual construction was finished by 212 B.C., the decoration was almost done by 147 B.C., the vestibule was completed by 122 B.C., and the final touches were added by 57 B.C.

The temple is oriented north and south, and part of the mud-brick walls about the precincts are still standing (Plate LVI–6). In front of the entrance pylon at the south end of the temple are two large falcons carved in dark granite. While the temple is not very large, the pylon has a total breadth of nearly 250 feet and rises to a height of about 145 feet. It is complete except for the crowning cornice (Plate LVII–1), and is full of chambers opening off the stairway leading to the roof. From the top one can look down at the forecourt and the rest of the temple extending to the north (Plate LVII–2). The forecourt is surrounded on three sides by colonnaded porticoes, the columns decorated with foliate and palm capitals. The vestibule, or pronaos, which was built after the temple was completed, is an excellent example of a Ptolemaic screen wall (Plate LVIII–1). The ceiling of the vestibule is decorated with astronomical scenes, and at either side of the broken-lintel doorway are two small chapels, one a "consecration chamber," and the other a room for the official library of the temple.

The Hall of Appearances is small, having three rows of four columns to carry its flat ceiling, through which small apertures let in light. Beyond this main hall are two antechambers, first the "Hall of the Altar Offerings," from which a stairway leads to the roof, and second the "Hall of Repose of the Gods." The sanctuary, which opens off from this last antechamber, is a single, isolated chamber, illumined by three small openings in the ceiling. Within it are a granite shrine (Plate XXXII–6), a relic of the original pre-Ptolemaic temple, and a small pedestal, intended to support the sacred boat. Surrounding the sanctuary is a passage or ambulatory from which open various storerooms.

[4] G. Jéquier, *Les Temples Ptolémaiques et Romains*, has excellent photographic reproductions; Ibrahim Noshy, *The Arts of Ptolemaic Egypt* (1937).

[5] Émile Chassinat, *Le Temple d'Edfou* (1897-1934).

PLATE LVIII

1. Vestibule looking east.
2. Passage between the walls.
3. Peripteral Birth-House.

PLATE LIX: TEMPLE OF HATHOR, DENDERA

1

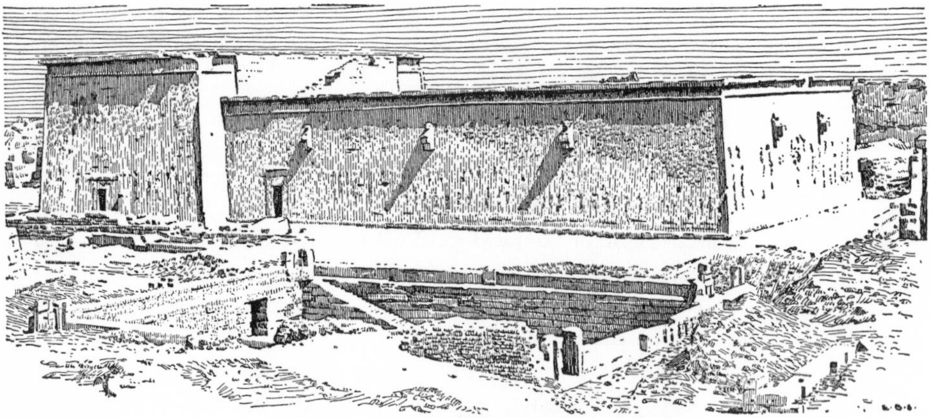

2

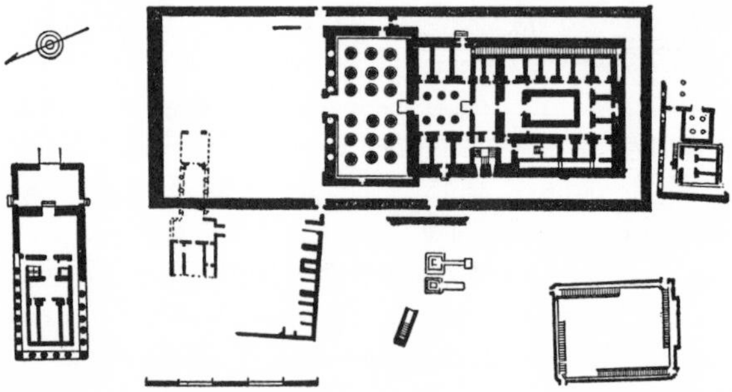

3

Beneath the temple are elaborate crypts. The roof is drained by lion-headed waterspouts, which project out over the narrow passageway separating the temple proper from its outer wall (Plate LVIII–2). Both sides of this open corridor around the temple are carved from base to cornice with elaborate pictographic reliefs. To the west of the main pylon is a small, peripteral Birth House, or *Mammisi,* with elaborate capitals and the figure of Bes, the gnome-like god, carved upon the abacus blocks (Plate LVIII–3; XLIII–4).

TEMPLE OF HATHOR, DENDERA. North of Thebes at Dendera, is the temple of Hathor,[6] a goddess closely associated with Horus of Edfu. Dendera got its name from the primitive pillar-cult of the locality, for it means "She of the Goddess-pillar." Although Hathor had many forms and attributes in different parts of Egypt, here at Dendera she was a divinity of love and joy, and hence identified with the Greek Aphrodite. Her temple was built between 116 B.C. and 34 A.D., though some of the reliefs were finished as late as 117 A.D. It was erected upon the site of an older edifice which may have dated back to the Old Kingdom. In the XI Dynasty, under the interested supervision of Queen Nefru Kayt, consort of Mentuhotep II, the old temple was the repository for a large and famous library.

The Ptolemaic temple is oriented north and south (Plate LIX–2). It has no entrance pylon, but originally the forecourt was formed by a plain, enclosing wall which extended southward around the inner temple, leaving, as at Edfu, a narrow corridor between the outer and inner walls of the temple. This forecourt was entered on both the east and west sides. The vestibule with its screen wall, which now forms the façade of the temple, is impressive and distinctive, for it has twenty-four *sistrum* columns, capped with Hathor heads (Plate LIX–3). The screen wall has the usual uræus cresting and broken-lintel doorway. On the cornice is the late inscription of the time of Tiberius which reads, "...the inhabitants of the capital and nome dedicated the pronaos to the great goddess Aphrodite and her fellow gods." The interior of this "pronaos" is richly carved from floor to ceiling with painted reliefs, and has a bizarre effect with its twelve great columns crowned by the battered features of the cow-goddess (Plate LX–2).

The "Hall of Appearances" is small, having only two rows of two columns with foliate capitals and an abacus block decorated with the head of Hathor. It is illumined by eight apertures in the roof (Plate LX–1), and its walls are covered with reliefs, some of which depict the foundation of the temple. The three chambers on either side of this hall were for the treasure and stores of the temples.

[6] Émile Chassinat, *Le Temple de Dendera* (1934-1935).

PLATE LIX

1. Exterior from west side.
2. Plan of temple:
   A Birth-House of Augustus, *B* Birth-House of Nektanebos, *C* sacred lake, *D* temple of Isis (*after* Baedeker).
3. Façade.

PLATE LX: TEMPLE OF HATHOR, DENDERA

1

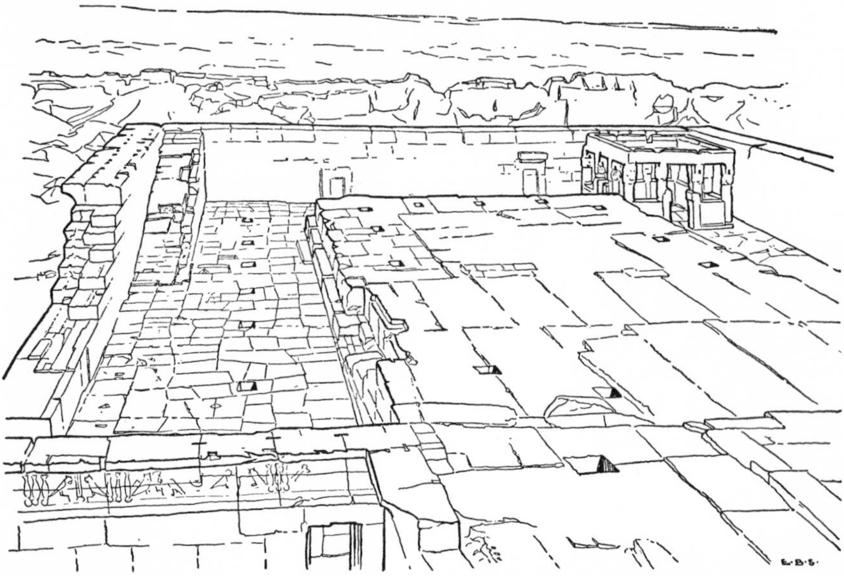

Back of the hall is the first antechamber, "the Hall of the Altar," again lit by square apertures in the ceiling. From this room passages to the right and left give access to stairways leading up to the roof. The east stairs are straight and dark, while the west stairs are a rectangular spiral of ten turns, lighted by small windows, their sides decorated with symbolic representations of the inflowing rays of the sun. Both stairways have continuous reliefs of priestly processions ascending to the roof at the time of the New Year festival when Hathor was united with the beams of her father Re.

The second antechamber, called the "Hall of the cycle of the Gods," opens at the left into a room for the perfumes and garments of the Goddess. At the right it leads to a small court illumined by an hypæthral opening (Plate LX–3), and having at the end a kiosk, approached, like a dais or audience chamber, by stairs, where "The Day of the Night of the Child in her Cradle" was celebrated. Also off from this antechamber is the sacred "Dwelling-place of the Golden One," her sanctuary doors shut and sealed, to be opened only once a year by the king or his representative. Around the *sekos* is an ambulatory with small chambers, chapels, and storerooms,—variously named the "Throne of Re," "Union of the Two Lands," "Flame Room," "Birth Room," and "Room of Resurrection." Beneath the temple are twelve separate crypts for mystical rites, storerooms, and treasuries.

The lion-headed waterspouts around the exterior of the temple are more evident than at Edfu because the brick girdle-wall, enclosing the forecourt and stone walls of the actual temple, is gone (Plate LIX–1). The roof of the temple, which shows the provisions for draining it by gutters, is interesting because of its different levels, rising from the back to the front, and because of its provisions for special rituals (Plate LX–1). At the southwest corner is a small, open kiosk, supported by twelve Hathor-headed columns; on the high terrace is a shrine of Osiris and a room carved with the famous Zodiac of Dendera, the only circular representation of the heavens in Egypt. From the roof one can look out over the great precinct with its massive mud-brick walls built in the Egyptian fashion by sections; sections with the brick courses arching up in the middle alternate with sections where the courses curve down in the middle. At the side of the temple is the sacred lake for ablutions, with stairways leading down into it from the four corners; in back of it is a small temple of Isis, and in front are the two Birth Houses of Nektanebis and Augustus (Plate XLIII–6).

KOM OMBO. Halfway up the river between Edfu and Aswân is the double temple of Kom Ombo.[7] There had been an earlier temple, the "House of Sobk," on the site, dedicated to the much feared local divinity, the crocodile, known as Suchos or Sobk; but the city had no real importance until Ptolemaic times when the double temple to Suchos and the falcon-headed Haroeris was built. The temple is

[7] J. J. M. de Morgan, *Kom Ombos.*

PLATE LX

1. Roof, looking south.
2. Interior of vestibule.
3. Chapel of the Birth-House of Hathor.

PLATE LXI: TEMPLE, KOM OMBO

1

2

3

oriented to the river (Plate LXI–3) with its façade facing the southwest. Its impressive isolation, which strikes the visitor coming up the Nile, is due to the disappearance of the high wall which formerly enclosed the forecourt, and to the erosion of the river which has cut away all the original enclosure except the forecourt, leaving the temple on a terrace at the very edge of the river. In addition to the brick wall surrounding the whole precinct, there was also an inner wall of brick, instead of stone, around the forecourt and temple which was entered through a stone gateway with two doors. The columns around the court are largely destroyed. The reliefs of the temple were mostly executed under Philometor, Euergetes II, and Neos Dionysos, although some of the carving in the court and on the outer walls was added under the Roman emperors.

Being a double temple constructed for two separate rituals, it is bisected by a central axis and has on either side a complete sequence of doors, halls, and sanctuaries. The vestibule has the customary screen wall, capped with the uræus-cornice, between the columns with their richly decorated papyrus and palm capitals (Plate LXI–1). The hypostyle hall, which is entered by two doors, contains ten columns with spreading capitals, its ceiling being lower than that of the vestibule (Plate LXI–2). Behind the hypostyle hall are three antechambers, each of which lies at a slightly higher level, and an ambulatory extending around the double sanctuaries. Between the sanctuaries is a narrow chamber on the axis of the temple. Here a movable stone gave access to a hidden passage beneath the dividing wall, which opened on a series of hidden corridors and crypts, one above the other, thus allowing the priests of the temple to work their convincing magic. At the back are seven chambers entered from the open corridor which runs around the inner temple. On the front terrace is a ruined Birth House built or restored by Euergetes II. To the south of the temple is a small chapel of Hathor, probably built under the Emperor Domitian. All the sculptures of the temple, while interesting and richly decorative, are soft and lifeless in their forms and execution.

ESNA. At Esna, not far up the river above Thebes, are the remains of the Ptolemaic temple dedicated to Khnum, the ram-headed divinity of this locality. All that remains is the seven-aisled vestibule which corresponds in arrangement to the vestibule of the temple of Hathor at Dendera (Plate LXII–3). While built in the Greek period the inscriptions on the entablature refer to Claudius and Vespasian.

Above Aswân there are numerous Ptolemaic temples in Nubia: at Debod, ancient Ta-het, meaning "the Dwelling-place," is the shrine of a double cult; at Tafa are the remains of a small temple; at Dendur[8] is the small sanctuary dedicated to two brothers who were drowned, their importance

[8] M. Henri Gauthier, *Le Temple de Kalabschah* (1911).

PLATE LXI

1. Façade.
2. View from southeast.
3. Plan (Baedeker).

PLATE LXII: GRÆCO-ROMAN TEMPLES

1

2

3

4

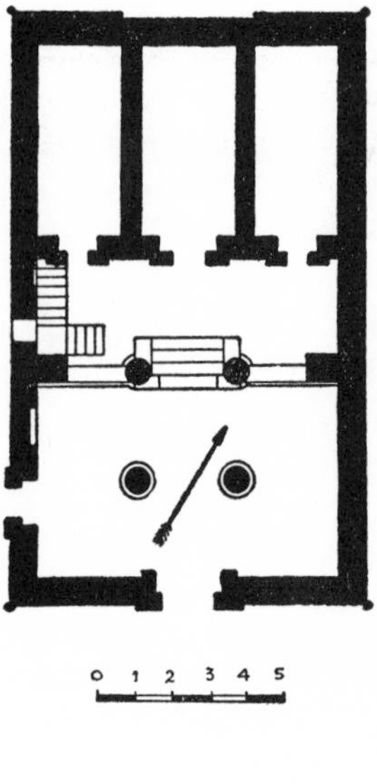

being that in their death they were the personifications of the king who thereby died to increase the fertility of the land. At El Maharraka, Dakka, and Kalabsha there are other Ptolemaic temples.[9]

DER EL-MEDINA. Of the many small temples of the Græco-Roman period, the most historically interesting is the shrine at Der el-Medina, near Deir el-Bahari, on the west bank at Thebes.[10] This temple, although principally dedicated to Hathor, goddess of the dead, and to Maat, goddess of truth, was also a tribute to two great architects, the deified Imhotep of the Old Kingdom, and the venerated Amenhotep, son of Hapu, of the New Kingdom. The cult of Amenhotep, who had been a builder, sage, physician, and magician under Amenhotep III, had begun shortly after his death, but reached its height during the Ptolemaic period. The sculptures of the temple show that he shared his position with the revered Imhotep.

The brick wall of the precinct is built in a continuous, wavy line, which was a common Egyptian method of making very thin brick walls stable. The stone temple (Plate LXII–4) has a vestibule separated from the three inner sanctuaries by a screen wall with its two columns and pillars capped with the heads of Hathor. Within the screen a staircase, illumined by a window, led up to the roof (Plate LXII–2). The triple division of the west end recalls the early temple at Abydos (Plate XII–6) and various tomb and house plans. During the Ptolemaic period the triple sanctuary became popular, due to the Egyptian tendency to group their divinities, especially Isis, Osiris, and Horus, into a family triad.

PHILÆ. Architecturally, the most important center of the Isis cult, which in time spread over the Roman empire, was the small island of Philæ in the river above Aswân (Plate LXIII–1). Because of the Aswân dam this delightful island with its various temples is now under water for the greater part of the year. The worship of Isis gave Philæ its distinction in Ptolemaic and Roman times, but it must have had some associations with an earlier and indigenous mother-goddess, for the priests of Isis practically ruled Lower Nubia.

At the southwest corner of the island is the porch of Nektanebis, originally built as an entrance hall to an earlier and now destroyed temple of Isis. This porch opens on the so-called outer court of the temple (Plate LXIII–2); along the east and west sides of the court are long, colonnaded porticoes with richly variegated foliate capitals, no two alike. The columns are tall, slender, and with-

[9] M. H. Gauthier, *Le Temple de Ouadi es-Seboua* (1912); *Le Temple d'Amada* (1913); M. G. Roeder, *Der Tempel von Dakke* (1930); *Debod bis Bab Kalabsche* (1911); M. G. Maspero, *Les Temples immergés de la Nubia* (1911); A. E. P. Weigall, *Antiquities of Lower Egypt* (1907); A. M. Blackman, *The Temple of Derr* (1913), *The Temple of Dendur* (1911), *The Temple of Bigeh* (1915).

[10] É. Baraize, "Compte Rendu des Traveaux Éxecutés à Déîr-el-Médineh," *Annales du Service,* XIII, pp. 19-42, Pls. I-X.

PLATE LXII

1. "Pharaoh's Bed," Philæ.
2. Interior of temple at Deir el-Medina.
3. Plan of temple at Deir el-Medina.
4. Façade of temple at Esna.

PLATE LXIII: ISLAND OF PHILÆ

1

2

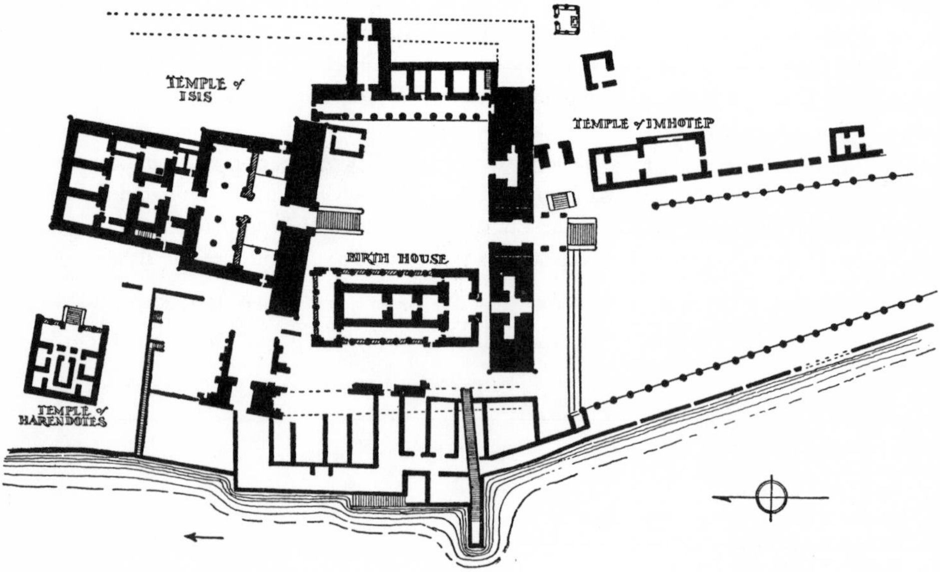

out entasis, undoubtedly dating from the Roman period. These long columnar porticoes were very much like classical stoas surrounding a public square, and were probably used for much the same purposes. Opening off from the eastern colonnade are a temple of Eri-hems-nufer, a chapel to the Nubian god Mandulis, and a well preserved shrine to the divine architect, Imhotep, who by this period was identified with Æsculapius as the god of medicine.

The temple of Isis, begun by Ptolemy II and almost wholly finished by Euergetes I, has a large outer pylon in front of the forecourt. The court is flanked on the east side by a long building, with a colonnade, which was occupied by the priests, and on the west side by the peripteral Birth House, dedicated to Hathor-Isis and to the memory of the birth of her son Horus. At the north end of the court a second pylon forms the façade of the actual temple and gives access to a very small court, covered probably with an awning, which has a little portico of two intercolumniations at each end. Beyond the court is the vestibule with eight columns which was originally separated from it by stone screens between the first row of columns. Between the vestibule and the triple sanctuaries are small antechambers from which stairs led up to the roof.

There are many other ruins of shrines and temples on the island, but the only one of architectural significance is "Pharaoh's Bed" (Plate LXII–1), a stone kiosk which was never sculpturally finished. It is a rectangular, open pavilion of fourteen columns, with screen walls between the columns. The columns have intricately lobed papyrus capitals with impost blocks which were intended to be carved with Hathor heads. It is entered by three doors, two large ones on the east and west, and a smaller door on the west side. It was intended to be covered with awnings. Another similar kiosk is preserved at Qertassi, near Philæ, which is reported to have had a wooden lining.[11] The unfinished reliefs of "Pharaoh's Bed" show Trajan making offerings to Isis and Osiris. The clue to the origin of this type of structure is furnished by the tomb paintings at Tell el-Amarna where Akhenaten and his wife are frequently represented holding audiences in a royal kiosk of light wooden construction with decorative capitals and a screen-wall capped by a cobra-cornice, and entered through a "broken-lintel" doorway (Plate LVI–2). Presumably the stone kiosks of Philæ and Qertassi were not "introduced by Romanized architects," as has been suggested, but are another example of how an old and traditional form of royal shelter, presumably built of wood and light materials, was imitatively reproduced on a larger scale in stone, and put to a specific religious use. The audience pavilion of Philæ is therefore a fitting monument, dating as it does from the time of Trajan and the end of Egyptian history, with which to close a survey of the religious monuments of Egypt, for it shows how the origin, character, and purpose of Nilotic architecture had remained astonishingly consistent for so many thousand years.

[11] M. A. Murray, *Egyptian Temples* (1931), p. 193.

PLATE LXIII

1. View.
2. Plan of temples (Baedeker).

PLATE LXIV: HOUSES

1

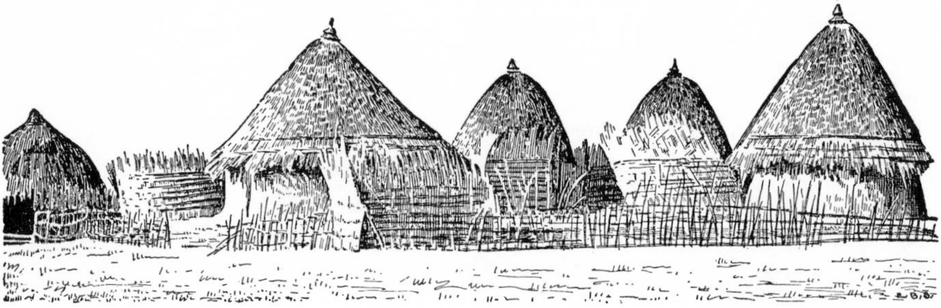

2

3

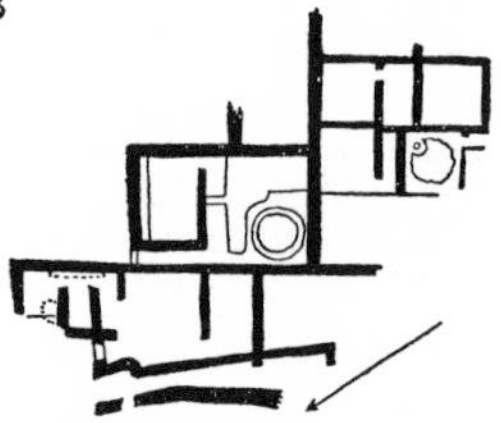

4

5

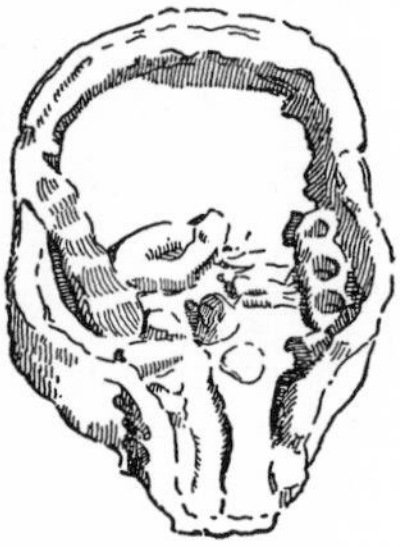

6

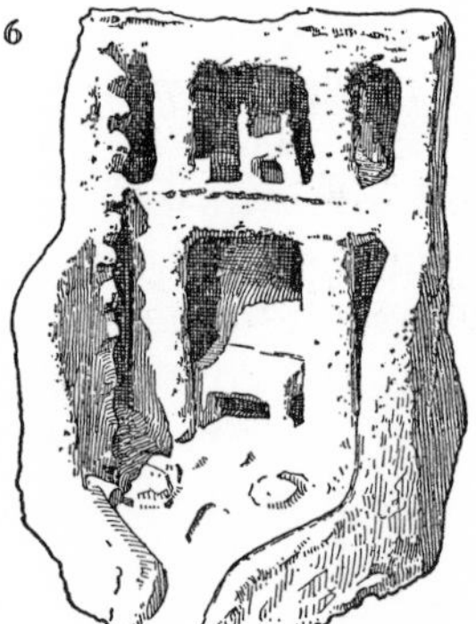

7

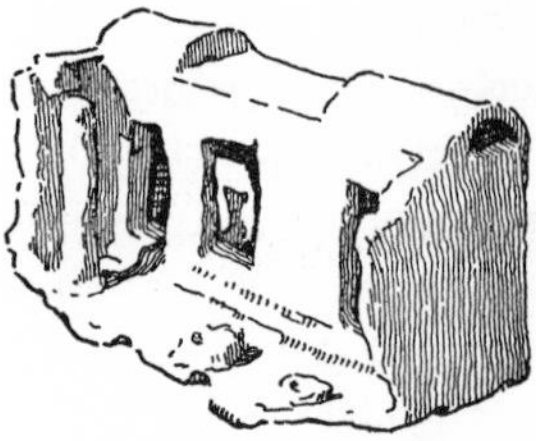

8

9

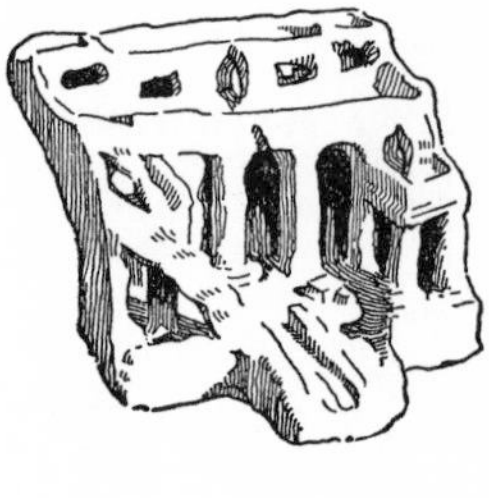

10

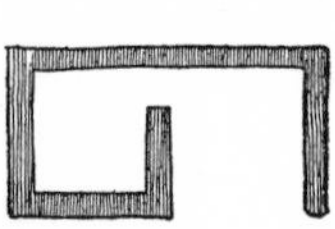

9. *HOUSES, CITIES AND PALACES*

As for those who build houses, their place is no more; Behold what hath become of them.—XII Dynasty, "Song of the Harper" of King Antef.

LIKE THE XII DYNASTY HARPER of King Antef, the Egyptians thought of their houses as transient; yet the house, impermanent as it was, supplied the fundamental forms of all Egyptian architecture. The basic types of primitive dwellings, it has been seen,[1] were the tent, the round hut, the hoop-roofed house,[2] and the rectangular house with either a *khekher* or reed parapet. All were at first built of pliable materials, and it was only gradually that plastered mud, brick, and rigid timbers were introduced into the construction. Each one of these Predynastic types persisted, in one way or another, throughout Egyptian history, but as actual dwellings they sank lower and lower in the social order as more commodious abodes were developed for the prosperous and ruling classes. There is conclusive evidence of the persistence of these simple, prehistoric forms of shelter, such as a clay model of an oval hut (Plate LXIV–5) from the Old Kingdom, and representations of round, thatched huts (Plate LXIV–2) and hoop-roofed shelters (Plate I–7) in the Nile scenes from the Roman period.

The embryonic house was a single-roomed shelter, constructed of perishable materials, in which the domestic life was of a communal simplicity. The subdivision and multiplication of these primitive units are an early indication of the rising level of culture with its need of separate quarters for the more important functions of private life. The architectural provisions for these social requirements at first evolved naturally in two ways, one by repeating the separate house units, and the other by subdividing the traditional communal shelter. The duplication of several free-standing, single-roomed huts was an easy and hence early means of acquiring separate accommodations for

[1] Pages 15-19.
[2] Pages 22-23.

PLATE LXIV

1. Shrine of Nyakang, Fenikang in Nilotic Sudan (Seligman, *Pagan Tribes of the Nilotic Sudan,* Pl. VII).
2. Circular Nile house, terra-cotta, Museo Nazionale delle Terme, Rome (*Alinari* 28363).
3. Houses, Hierakonpolis (J. E. Quibell, *Hierakonpolis,* II, Pl. LXVIII).
4. Soul-house, Rifeh (Petrie, *Gizeh and Rifeh,* Pl XVI/1).
5. Soul-house, Cairo Museum.
6. Soul-house, Rifeh (Petrie, *op. cit.,* Pl. I).
7. Soul-house, Rifeh (Petrie, *op. cit.,* Pl. XVI/10).
8. Soul-house, Rifeh (*op. cit.,* Pl. XVII/35).
9. Soul-house, Rifeh (*op. cit.,* Pl. XVII/128).
10. Hieroglyph for "house" (F. L. Griffith, *Hieroglyphs,* 1898, no. 146).

sleeping, cooking, servants, and women. This method of making a homestead is common to most primitive cultures at a certain stage in their development, surviving down to the present time in different parts of Africa (Plate LXIV–1), and persisting among the traditions of Egyptian domestic architecture (Plate LXV–7, 9).

It was, however, the method of providing special spaces by subdivisions which had the greater effect upon the growth of architecture. Even though little remains of early Egyptian houses, the evolution of the tomb,[3] as a house-form, shows how the single-roomed dwelling, around the opening of Dynastic history, had begun to be subdivided into rooms. At first the divisions, such as a bedroom for the head of the family, were made by light lattice partitions, then by hangings, and finally by walls of brick. The chambers were little more than alcoves along one or more sides of the common room. This type of house, enlarged by a periphery of alcoves as a feudal stronghold, has been described by Sir Flinders Petrie.[4]

Once the idea of subdivisions was initiated the character of domestic architecture at once began to be more and more complex and varied. Early plans of brick houses, dating from the beginning of the Old Kingdom, have been uncovered at Hierakonpolis (Plate LXIV–3). They consist of a simple arrangement of either two rooms, or a room and a court. In their outer space is a round pit for the storage of fodder, indicating that the average Egyptian family lived, as it does to-day, on intimate terms with its domestic animals. These plans have a striking resemblance to the hieroglyphic sign (Plate LXIV–9), usually translated "courtyard" but probably representing a house and court. Later the royal tombs at Abydos and the mastabas of Old Kingdom grandees at Tarkhan and Saqqara (Plate VI–1) illustrate something of the progressive elaboration of upper-class dwellings by means of alcoves and chambers, while the so-called "forts" at Abydos (Plate VI–4, 7) show how the defensive strongholds of the first two Dynasties were sufficiently complicated in their arrangement of rooms and courts to have become palaces under more stable conditions.

PORTICOED HOUSE WITH COURT. By the Old Kingdom the essential features of an Egyptian house must have been fully established. Of these features, next to the courtyard the most important is the columnar portico. Instead of being an architectural element added onto the existing house form, it fits the evidence better to consider the portico as a direct and, for a time at least, an independent evolution from the primitive tent-shelter,[5] which by the Old Kingdom had combined with the rectangular house. A house-model, or "soul-house," of the Old Kingdom from Rifeh (Plate I–1) resembles a Bedawin tent, its front supported by two posts driven into the ground and opening, like a portico, upon a mud-walled court. Other "soul-houses" from Rifeh indicate how this generic type of open tent presumably developed into a rectangular shelter, still open on the front and without chambers behind its portico. The model (Plate III–8) best illustrating this stage in the evolution has a pool in the court, covered by an awning supported by four poles, while around

[3] Page 47.
[4] Page 33.
[5] Page 24.

the edge of its roof is a parapet. The actual evolution of the portico must, however, have taken place at an early date, for it was a symbol of royal power in monumental architecture and hieroglyphic writing from at least the III Dynasty (Plate III–7), and by the Middle Kingdom had become a common characteristic of prosperous, middle-class houses.

If we can rely on the literal character of Egyptian representations, another model (Plate LXIV–4) illustrates how the portico shelter combined with the single-roomed house. From the IV Dynasty the rock-cut tombs[6] show that this combination of an open shelter and an enclosed house was an established tradition, with the result that the porticoed house continued to be common throughout the history of the country. At least by the Middle Kingdom this type of house had ventilators (Plate LXIV–7) projecting above the flat room in order to lead refreshing breezes down to the hot interiors.

Also by the Middle Kingdom the porticoed house had developed a second story (Plate LXIV–6). The vertical extension began in the Old Kingdom, or earlier, with the erection of light pavilions of wood upon the roof.[7] One Rifeh model (Plate LXIV–8) has a roof loggia with ventilators, and another (Plate LXIV-9) of the same period has the parapet divided into three parts in which there are four ventilators, while on the front of the house are two small, columnar porches and an exterior staircase ascending to the roof.

These "soul-houses," which supply so much accurate information regarding the external features of Middle Kingdom houses, are libation and offering plates placed upon the graves, and used in the service of the dead. Their literal adherence to house-forms is a survival of the primitive custom of making offerings before a shelter above the actual grave, while their prevalence at Rifeh and at other sites implies that the house-forms, which they reproduce, must have been fairly typical of the middle-class dwellings of the period.

During the Middle Kingdom the porticoed house was still the traditional dwelling of provincial chieftains, if we can judge by their rock-cut tombs. The tombs at Beni-Hasan are certainly replicas of the houses of the rulers and nobles of the Oryx clan (Plate XXIX–3, 4). These houses must have been built of light wooden frames, reeds, and latticework, covered with mud plaster, and arranged with the essential house features of courtyard, portico, columnar hall, and private chamber.[8] They were roofed with bent hoops covered with woven mattings.

MULTIPLE AND PARALLEL HOUSE UNITS OPENING ON A COURT. A derivation of the primitive custom of building separate house units inside an enclosure is seen in house models where three units are parallel and contiguous at one side of the court. Early evidence of this type of house is suggested by the plans of a I Dynasty temple at Abydos (Plate XII–6) and by a II Dynasty tomb at Mahasna (Plate X–7). In the Middle Kingdom, and undoubtedly before, the parallel chambers were frequently under one flat roof (Plate LXV–3), although some models from Rifeh (Plate

[6] Pages 109-113.

[7] There seem to have been houses of two stories as early as Menes, for the Egyptologists consider the sign with the *ḳheḳher* cornice (Pl. III-9) to represent a two-storied house.

[8] Pages 109-113.

PLATE LXV: HOUSES

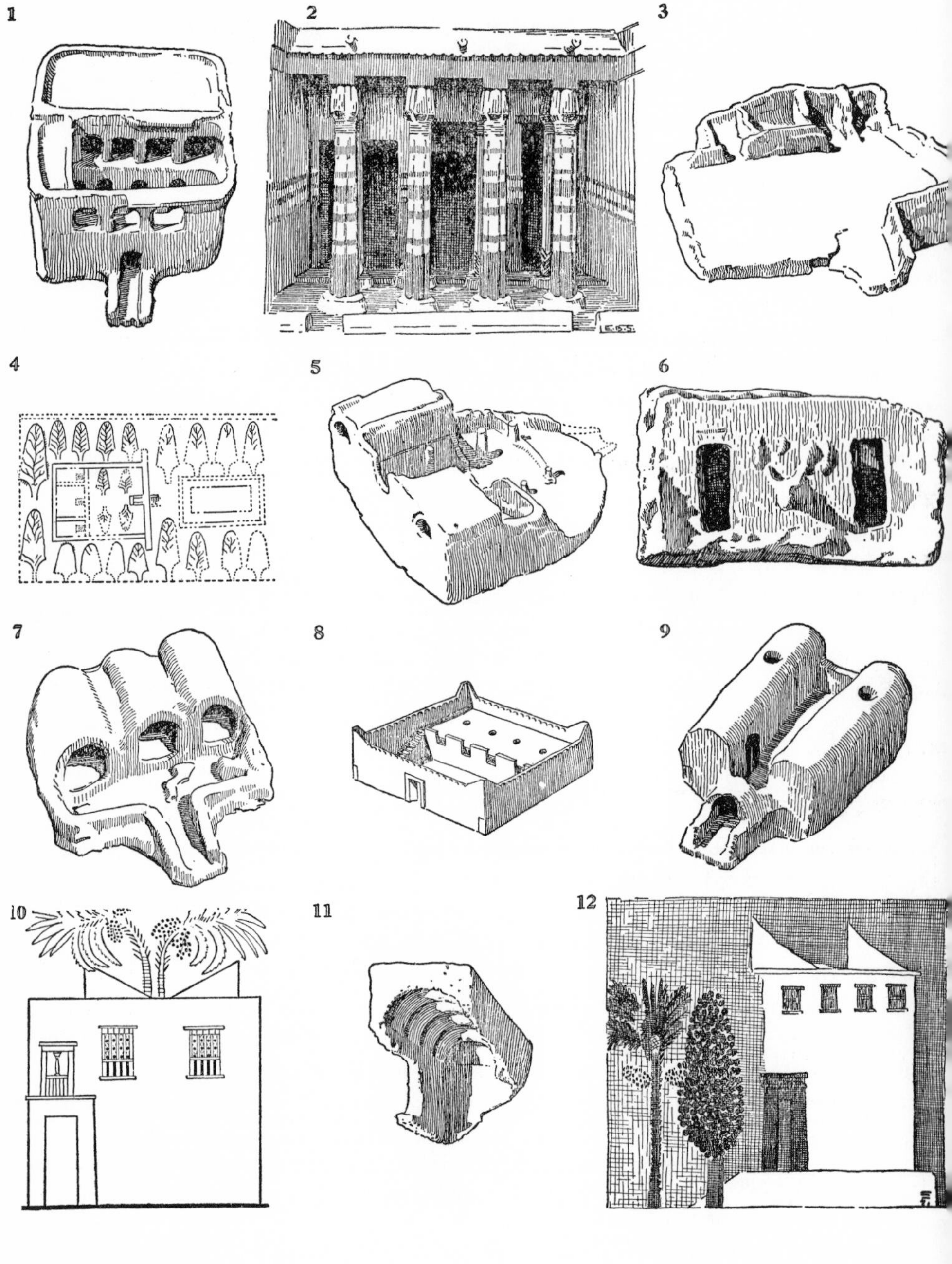

LXV–5) have each adjacent chamber under a separate curved or flat roof. A model in the Cairo Museum (Plate LXV–7) has three long chambers, each covered with a curved roof, while another variant of the same idea shows two long halls on either side of the open court (Plate LXV–9). Houses of this type are frequently seen in Nubia to-day, where they are usually tunnel-vaulted.

When he published the "soul-houses" of Rifeh, Sir Flinders Petrie singled out one fragment (Plate LXV–11) to prove how the Middle Kingdom houses were vaulted. Actually, however, the corrugations on the under side of this apparent vault represents bent hoops upon which the woven mattings were stretched. Although the Egyptians used the vault in their tombs as early as the III Dynasty, enough evidence has already been advanced [9] to establish more than a presumption that a curved roof does not by necessity imply vaulting.

VENTILATED HOUSES. By the Middle Kingdom, it has been seen, houses frequently had ventilators on the roof. In the New Kingdom the house of Neb-Amun, which he had painted in his tomb at Thebes (Plate LXV–10), has a pair of these ventilators on the roof. Davies insists that on the actual house these ventilators must have pointed in the same direction in order to catch the prevailing breezes from the north.[10] He cites the pictures of another New Kingdom house, on the papyrus of Nakhte (Plate LXV–12), to show how they pointed in the same direction. The Rifeh models, however, make it clear that it was customary to have the ventilators at opposite ends of the building, just as Neb-Amun's house shows them, so as to ensure a flow of air through the interior.

URBAN HOUSE. At an early date the Egyptians began to use the flat roofs of their houses for domestic purposes, erecting thereon light canopies and loggias as protection from the sun. The roof was at times called the "upper house," [11] and it was natural that the light, roof pavilions should have

[9] Pages 22-23.
[10] N. de G. Davies, "The Town House in Ancient Egypt," *Metropolitan Museum Studies,* I (1928-1929), p. 10.
[11] Breasted, *Ancient Records,* I, No. 784.

PLATE LXV

1. Soul-house, Cairo Museum.
2. Model from Theban tomb of Meket-re, Metropolitan Museum of Art, New York.
3. Soul-house, Rifeh (Petrie, *op. cit.,* Pl. XVII/95).
4. Plan of house or garden temple from tomb 324, Thebes (N. de G. Davies, "The Town House in Ancient Egypt," *Metropolitan Museum Studies,* I, 1929, Fig. 9).
5. Soul-house, Rifeh (Petrie, *op. cit.,* Pl. XVII/69).
6. Soul-house, Rifeh (*op. cit.,* Pl. XIX/58).
7. Soul-house, no. 3270, Cairo Museum.
8. House model, Louvre (Perrot et Chipiez, *op. cit.,* I, Fig. 268).
9. Soul-house, no. 3273, Cairo Museum.
10. Painting of house of Neb-Amun, tomb 90, Thebes (N. de G. Davies, *The Tombs of Two Officials of Tuthmosis Fourth,* Pl. XXXIV).
11. Fragment of soul-house, Rifeh (Petrie, *op. cit.,* Pl. XX/160).
12. Picture of a house, papyrus of Nakhte, British Museum.

PLATE LXVI: HOUSES

1

2

3

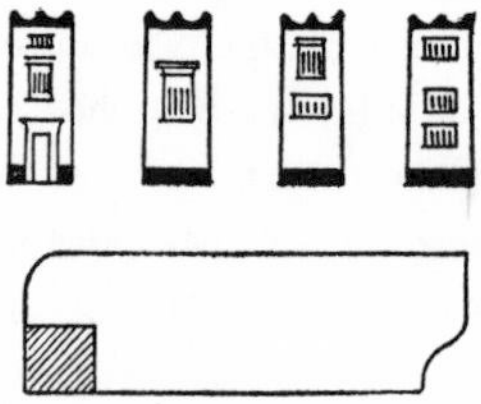

4

5

4

6

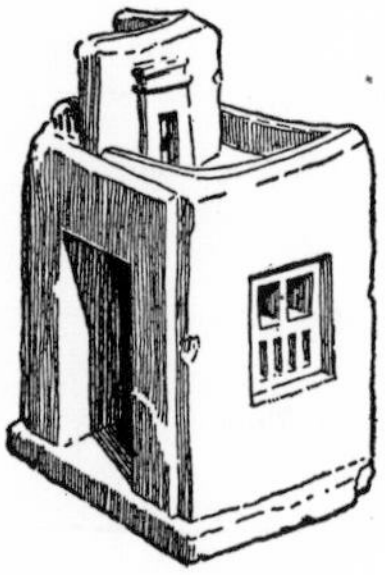

7

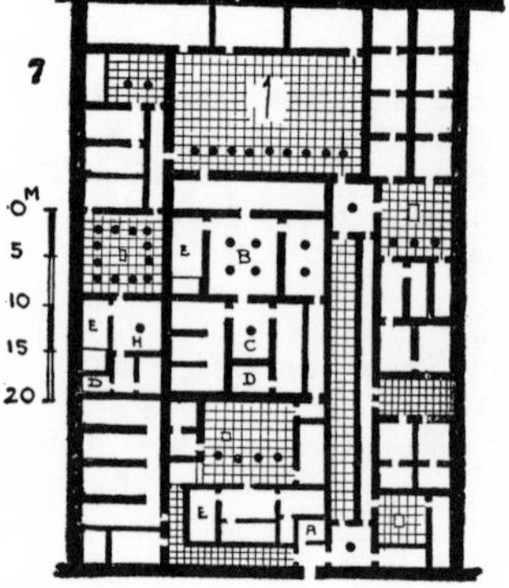

8

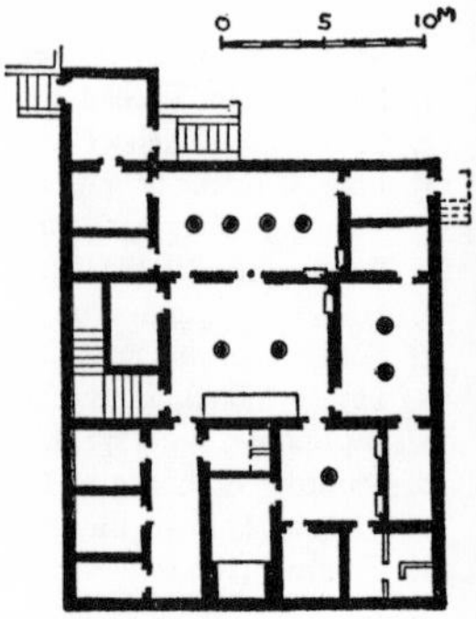

developed into second stories, especially under urban conditions when a vertical extension became necessary. The Neb-Amun and Nakhte houses depict dwellings of two, or perhaps three, stories, which are different from the provincial bungalow-type of house illustrated by the Rifeh models. The porticoed, one-story house, with possibly a loggia on the roof, was, during the New Kingdom, the customary villa-residence outside the crowded urban centers. A model of the painted house of Meket-re (Plate LXV–2), found in his tomb at Thebes, is of this type, and has a columnar porch opening on an enclosed garden with a small pool in the center.

In the large cities, especially in Thebes, where congestion, at least by the New Kingdom, had imposed a new condition on domestic architecture, an urban type of house developed, characterized by its vertical extension. A small, town house, still with space enough for a garden, either at the side or in back, is represented on a tomb-painting at Thebes (Plate LXVI–2). It depicts a three-storied house, ventilated by grilled windows on the second and third stories, and entered by a flight of steps leading to the front door. The flat roof is surrounded by a latticed parapet of interwoven palm ribs. These light parapets, which have been seen as a characteristic cresting of Egyptian houses from the I Dynasty,[12] are still used to-day in Nubia and on the mud houses of the oasis of Kharga (Plate LXVI–1). The urban tendency to verticality must have begun before the New Kingdom, because a model from el-Bersha (Plate LXVI–3) shows a compact, three-storied house of Amenemhet, who was mayor and superintendent of priests in the XII Dynasty.

More information as to the appearance and interior arrangements of a city house is furnished by the wall painting of a New Kingdom tomb. Thutnufer, the Theban owner of the tomb, had both the façade and interior section of his house reproduced. The façade is simple, as urban houses usually are, and the horizontal lines, which seem to suggest stone coursing, must represent a banded decoration, perhaps derived from strengthening the mud-brick walls with balks of wood, such as were indicated in so much Egyptian mud-brick architecture.[13] In fact, the house

[12] Page 21.

[13] Horizontal banding, such as the red lines upon "soul-houses," and rows of circles (L. Borchardt, "Friesziegel in Grabbauten," *Zeitschrift für Ægyptische Sprache*, LXXX, 1934, pp. 24-35) are presumably architectural decorations derived from structural forms in which either horizontal or transverse timbers were used to strengthen the brick walls. There is conclusive

---

PLATE LXVI

1. Village in oasis of Kharga.
2. Picture of house, tomb 254, Thebes (Davies, *Metropolitan Museum Studies*, I, Fig. 6).
3. Plan and elevation of a house model of Amenemhet, El-Bersha (Ahmed Bey Kamal, *Annales du Service*, II, p. 31).
4. House of Thutnufer, tomb 104, Thebes (Davies, *op. cit.*, Fig. 1).
5. Græco-Roman house model (Engelbach, *Annales du Service*, XXXI, p. 129).
6. Stone model, Cairo Museum.
7. Plan of house, Kahun:
   A porter's lodge, *B* central hall, *C* living room, *D* bathroom, *E* bedrooms, *H harim* (Petrie, *Illahun*, 1889, Pl. XIV).
8. Plan of house, Tell el-Amarna.

models from Rifeh are painted on the exteriors with red bands, which Petrie inadvertently described as brick coursings, even though the Egyptian brick was always mud-colored, and red usually represented wood. The interior of Thutnufer's house (Plate LXVI-4), presumably a typical Theban house of the official class, shows the ground floor occupied by the servants at their various duties, the second floor reserved for the master and his family, and the top floor and roof used for the kitchen and granaries, thereby keeping the coolest and most protected sections of the house for the family.

What has been called the house of Neferhotep (Plate LXXV–5), an under supervisor, is now considered to be the *harim* of King Ay.[14] This is perhaps fortunate because it is almost impossible to interpret a logical structure from the pictographic conventions of the artist. According to Davies it represents a somewhat free combination of the Amarna bungalow with the higher town house. Later representations of the urban house are less confusing, for there remain several accurate models from the Græco-Roman period (Plate LXVI–5). These Ptolemaic and Roman examples[15] still follow the old custom of laying brick in sagging courses, but the houses probably had light-wells instead of ventilators. Among the models from the last period of Egyptian history are some one-story structures with a small ædicula on the roof (Plate LXVI-6). Whether the penthouse was a covering for the stair well or only a more permanent form of roof pavilion, it is impossible to say. The best preserved Ptolemaic houses have been uncovered at Soknopaiou Nesos[16] in the Fayum. Several of them must have had more than two stories. House II–201 was constructed with heavy brick walls strengthened and decorated by wooden blocks laid transversely in the wall at regular intervals, its exterior corners protected by wooden uprights set into the brickwork.[17] The bricks were laid in the Old Egyptian method of sagging, concave courses. This house had a basement in which the rooms were covered by barrel-vaults and on the first floor its rooms were carefully paneled with small pieces of wood.[18] Other Ptolemaic houses of more than one story have been found at Philadelphia.[19] At Karanis in the Fayum the excavators[20] uncovered houses of Græco-Roman period in which bricks were laid in concave courses, vaults were common in the lower stories, and wood was extensively used for bonding, decoration, stair facing, window sills and grills, and doorways.

KAHUN AND AMARNA HOUSES. The customary Egyptian dwelling of prosperous officials and landowners in the villages and smaller towns was a one-story structure with some variety in the arrangement of the rooms, but always preserving the characteristic features of court, reception

evidence that the Egyptians used balks of timber for bonding and strengthening in all brick walls subject to a heavy load; in addition to the evidence of this type of construction at Tell el-Amarna, the consistent use of timbers in the military walls (p. 230), and their frequent use in the houses of Karanis (p. 204) and Soknopaiou Nesos (p. 204), show that this method of building must have been a persistent tradition in Egyptian architecture.

14 N. de G. Davies, "The Town House in Ancient Egypt," *Metropolitan Museum Studies,* I (1928-1929), Fig. 3, p. 241.

15 R. Engelbach, "Four models of Græco-Roman Buildings," *Annales du Service,* XXXI, p. 129; N. de G. Davies, *op.* cit., Fig. 14; I. Noshy, *The Arts in Ptolemaic Egypt* (1937), pp. 54-61.

16 A. E. R. Boak, "Soknopaiou Nesos," *University of Michigan Studies,* XXXIX (1935).

17 *Op. cit.,* Pl. XVI.

18 *Op. cit.,* p. 11, Pl. XV.

19 F. Zucker, *Archäologischer Anzeiger* (1909), p. 179; 1910, p. 246.

20 A. E. R. Boak and E. E. Peterson, *Karanis* (1931).

hall, common room, and private quarters. Two sites, the XII Dynasty town of Kahun and the XVIII Dynasty city of Tell el-Amarna, furnish the principal evidence for this form of house. It has been suggested that the residences of these sites are not typical, inasmuch as both towns were hastily built and abandoned in less than a generation; but considering the conservative habits of the Egyptians, and the hurried construction and temporary character of both places, it is more likely that the houses reproduce easily built and traditional arrangements of rooms.

El-Lahun, or Kahun, was a temporary town of the Middle Kingdom, built in the desert by Senwosret II for the officials and workmen engaged in erecting his pyramid. The houses for the supervising officials were large and complex structures. Each of these important dwellings was built in a compact block, about 138 by 198 feet (Plate LXVI–7). The only entrance was a small door on the street, opening into a narrow passage where it was overlooked by the room of the doorkeeper. From this entrance an open passage led to the left and right, the left corridor leading to the offices, guest rooms, and business section, and the right corridor going down the length of the building to the *mandara*. This reception room, in its turn, gave access to a square living-room, with four columns supporting a flat roof, and probably lit by a clerestory. North of the central living-room a long, narrow room, perhaps a loggia, opened on the columnar portico of the courtyard which was also connected with the women's quarters on the west side of the house. These few, large houses at Kahun seem a little like labyrinths, as if the owners were trying to get as many rooms as the prescribed area would permit. What is architecturally significant in the plan is the persistence of the central living-room, like an embryo around which the rest of the house had grown, and the complex arrangement of rooms and corridors to provide private quarters for the family, women, servants, and business activities of the establishment. In addition to clerestories over the principal rooms, there must also have been ventilators, for the heat upon the flat roofs and small courts must have been terrific during much of the year.

The workmen's houses (Plate LXIX–1) at Kahun are simple, and vary somewhat in design, but all have small courts with one to three narrow chambers opening off from them. Petrie believes that many of the houses had tunnel-vaulted roofs because of the scarcity of wood, but the actual evidence for such vaults is only one room which shows the remains of a vault. Somewhat similar groups of workmen's houses will be seen later on under planned towns.

At present the best site for the study of domestic architecture is Akhetaten, the city of Aten, known to-day as Tell el-Amarna. Unlike Kahun, where there was a great variety of plans, considering the limited size of the town, all the dwellings of Amenhotep's city, regardless of size and class, have a marked similarity. This uniformity, consisting of a rectangular plan (Plate LXVI–8), modified only by the size and number of special chambers arranged around a square living-room, shows a firmly established type of bungalow house, for there was little organized planning when Akhetaten was so hastily built. The construction was largely of sun-dried brick, stone being used rarely for thresholds and the frame of outer doors, and wood was limited to columns, ceiling beams, bonding for the walls, supports of stairs, and some inlay work. The floors in the poorer houses are of stamped mud, and in the richer houses they are of brick, whitewashed, and at times painted.

PLATE LXVII: HOUSES OF TELL EL-AMARNA

1

2

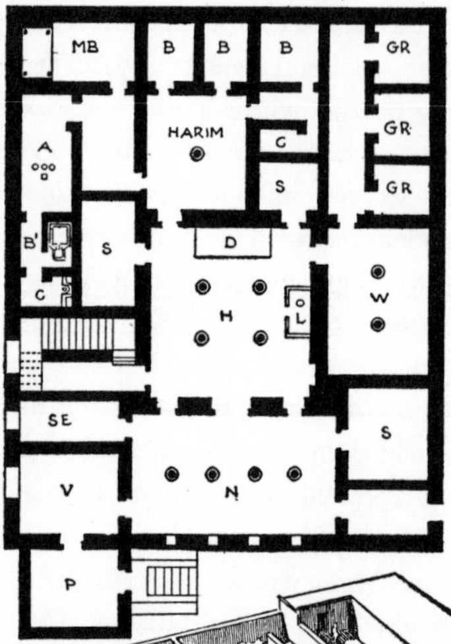

3

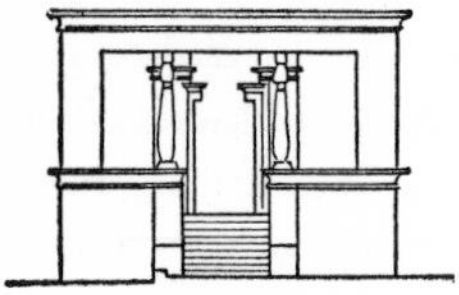

4

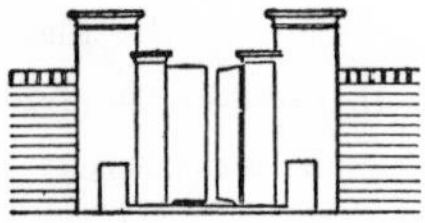

5

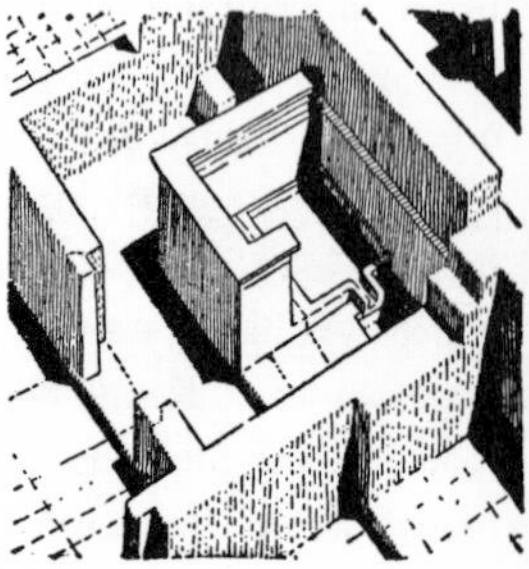

6

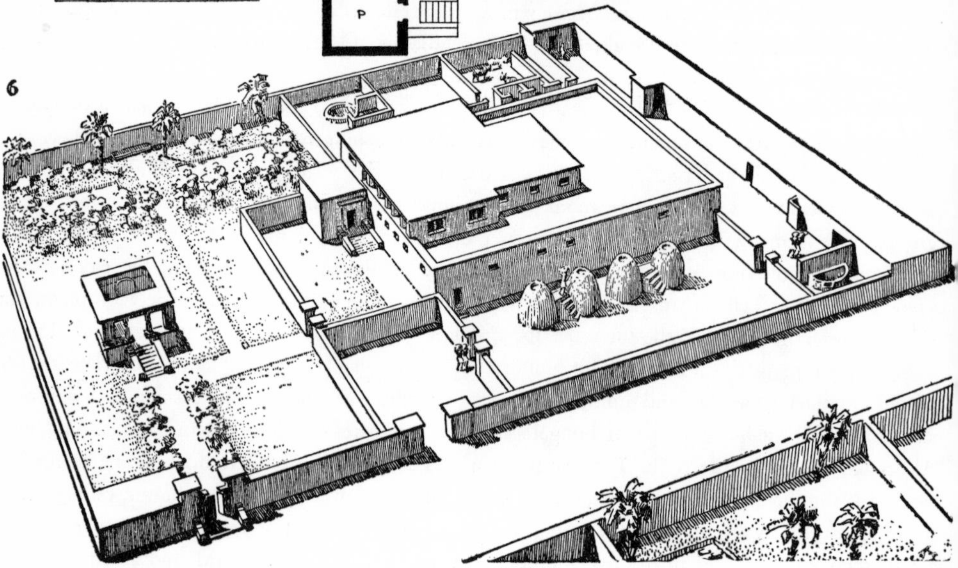

All the houses tend to be square with a central living-room, again a survival of the primitive one-room shelter, enlarged by various, special chambers added around it (Plate LXVII–2), the number and size of these rooms depending upon the social position and prosperity of the owner.[21] Always present are a living-room, sleeping-room, kitchen, and stairs to the roof. The larger houses have one or two reception halls, or "loggias," opening into the central hall. In fact, the Amarna houses may be classified as (1) without loggias, (2) with one loggia, and (3) with two loggias.

The mansions are all situated in large, enclosed plots of ground (Plate LXVII–6). The houses are entered on either the north or west, or on both sides, by stairs or ramps rising parallel to the house. The door is in the side of a protruding vestibule, which in turn opens into the "Reception Room" on the north side of the house (Plate LXVII–1, 2). When Petrie first excavated the Amarna houses, he thought that these long reception rooms on the north and west sides were like open verandas, with either a screen wall or a large central window. So he called them "loggias." Subsequent excavations have proved that they had only a row of very small windows, high up, near the ceiling. As reception rooms, they served two purposes, one, to connect the central communal hall with the kitchen and outside servants' quarters, and, second, to provide formal and informal entrance to the main living-room by means of a double door and small doors at either side. In some of the finest houses there is also a west hall which was more private. Both the north and west halls were decorated with a painted band at the level of the windows, which repeated a false, grilled window as a decorative motive in the painted pattern. At times, festoons of flowers were painted on the walls, and brightly colored niches faced the doorways in the opposite walls.

The central hall (Plate LXVII–1), its flat roof supported by four wooden columns painted red and with palm leaf capitals, rose above the surrounding rooms to provide clerestory light by means of small, grilled windows. As part of the fixed furnishings, this room had a lustration slab, a low dais, and, at times, a pottery-hearth or brazier sunk in the floor. Its roof consisted of large, painted beams supporting smaller rafters on which were laid mats of reeds covered with stamped mud. In the largest houses the master's suite consisted of a bedroom with a raised dais for the bed, a bathroom (Plate LXVII–5), a

[21] Petrie, *Tell el-Amarnah* (1894); T. E. Peet and C. L. Woolley, *The City of Akhenaten*, I (1923); H. Frankfort, *ed.*, *The Mural Painting of El-'Amarneh* (1929); Seton Lloyd, "Model of a Tell el-'Amarneh House," *Journal of Egyptian Archæology*, XIX (1933), pp. 1-7; Herbert Ricke, *Der Grundriss des Amarnawohnhauses* (1932); H. Frankfort and J. D. S. Pendlebury, *The City of Akhenaten*, II (1933).

PLATE LXVII

1. Section of house T 36. 11 (*after* S. Lloyd, "Model of a Tell el-Amarnah House," *Journal of Egyptian Archæology*, XIX, 1933, Fig. 3).
2. Plan of house T. 36. 11:
   P porch, *V* vestibule, *N* north room, *W* west room, *S* storerooms, *H* central hall, *C* closet, *B* bathroom, *A* anointing room, *MB* master's bedroom, *B* bedrooms, *L* lustration slab, *D* raised dais.
3. Private chapel (Lloyd, *op. cit.*, Fig. 2).
4. Gateway (*op. cit.*, Fig. 2).
5. Bathroom (H. Ricke, *Der Grundriss des Amarna-Wohnhauses*, 1932, Fig. 32).
6. Model (Lloyd, *op. cit.*, Pl. IV).

PLATE LXVIII: TOWNS

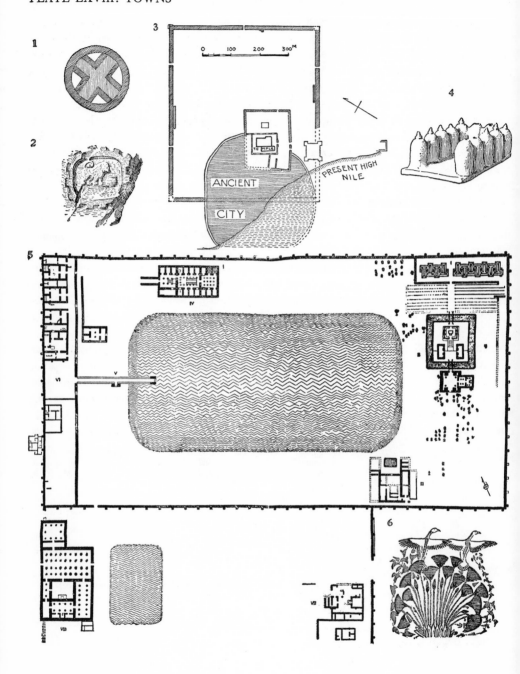

1

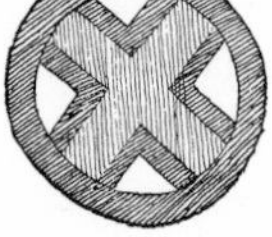

2

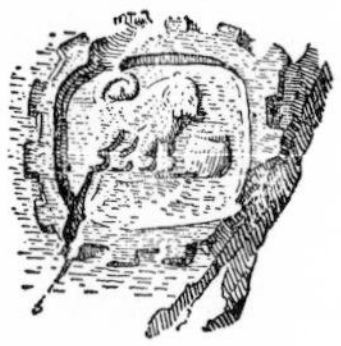

3

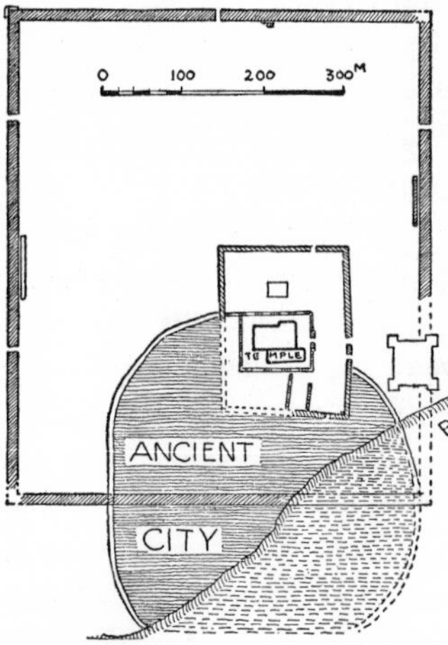

4

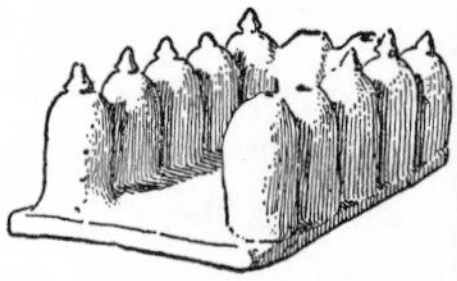

5

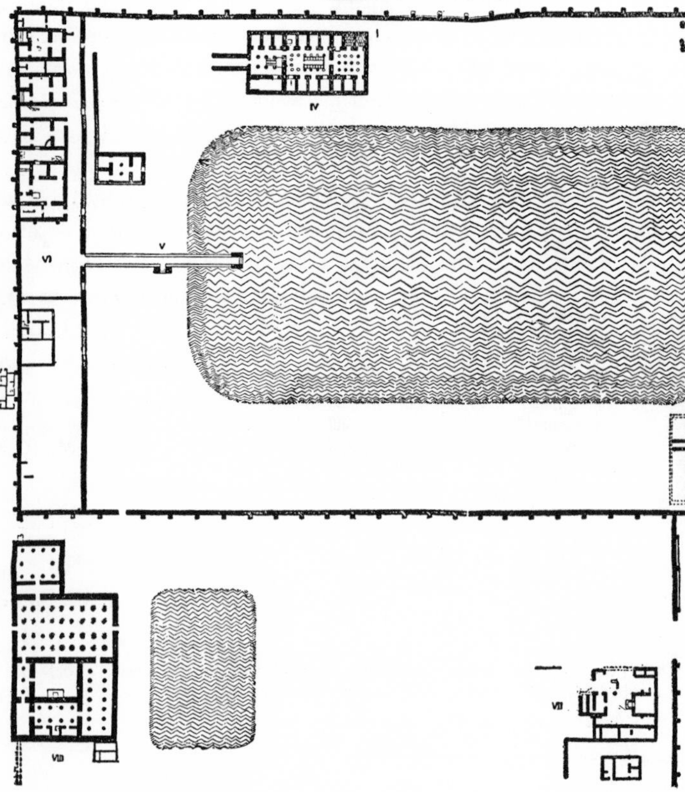

6

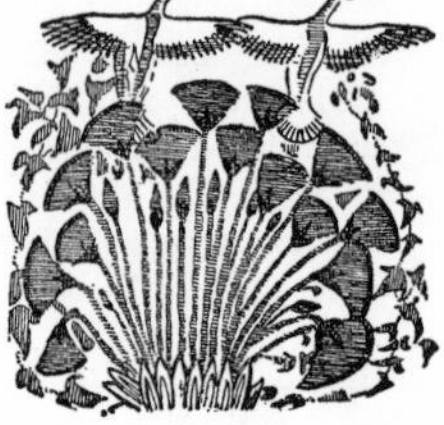

toilet, a reception room and in some cases an anointing room. The kitchen was commonly outside in a separate building. As a rule the houses were of only one story, but in at least a few examples they had a covered pavilion, or true loggia, above the north reception room, where the family could enjoy the refreshing breezes (Plate LXVII–1). All the exteriors were plain and undecorated, the dark gray brick being whitewashed only on the front of the house.

The grounds of an Amarna mansion were entered by a gateway (Plate LXVII–4) which was possibly the prototype of the later Ptolemaic "broken-lintel" doorway. At one side of the pillared gateway was the porter's lodge, and from the entrance a path led either to the house or to an out-of-doors chapel (Plate LXVII–3, 6) which was certainly open in front and may very likely have been peripteral like the chapel of Senwosret (Plate XLIII–1) and the XVIII Dynasty temple of Queen Hatshepsut at Medinet Habu (Plate XLIV–1). It was in these open-air pavilion-like chapels that the wealthy inhabitants of Amarna gave evidence of their obedience to the will of Akhenaten by proclaiming their devotion to Aten. Within the enclosed estate were kitchens, quarters for the servants, byres for the cattle, and granaries, consisting of domical, bee-hive structures with exterior steps going up to the openings in the top.

The Amarna dwellings of the official class were comfortably furnished with wooden and ebony chairs, rugs, vases, and a profusion of flowers. While all the workmanship shows the hasty character of the construction, there was a lavish use of painted decoration on the interiors which was executed in a bold and rather impressionistic technique. One house had a vaulted cellaret, consisting of a rectangular compartment for storing wine, which was covered by a laminated tunnel-vault.[22] The wooden columns, which supported the ceilings, were plastered before being painted,[23] red being the usual color for the lower part of the shafts.

Outside the Ptolemaic cities where Greek influence was so strong, the Egyptian house preserved its traditional forms down to Roman times. The plans of Ptolemaic houses uncovered at Medinet Ghoran [24] in the Fayum are of two customary types: one a square bungalow of five rooms, recalling the poorer workmen's quarters at Kahun, and a second type, like the Amarna dwellings, with the

[22] Frankfort and Pendlebury, *The City of Akhenaten,* II, p. 53, Fig. 6.

[23] Frankfort and Pendlebury, *op. cit.,* p. 98.

[24] Pierre Jouguet, "Fouilles du Fayoum." *Bulletin de Correspondance Hellénique,* XXV (1901), p. 391, Fig. 5, and p. 395, Fig. 10.

PLATE LXVIII

1. Hieroglyph of walled city (Griffith, *Hieroglyphs,* no. 142).
2. Walled city on slate palette, Louvre (Capart, *Primitive Art in Egypt,* 1905, Fig. 182).
3. Plan of El Kab (S. Clarke, "El Kab and the Great Wall," *Journal of Egyptian Archaeology,* VII, 1921, Pl. X; Quibell, *El Kab,* 1898).
4. Model of granary or village (Quibell, *op. cit.,* Pl. VI/2).
5. Maru-Aten, the Precinct of the Southern Pool, Tell el-Amarna (Peet and Woolley, *The City of Akhenaten,* I, Pl. XXIX).
6. Painted pavement motive from Maru-Aten (*op. cit.,* Pl. XXXIX).

rooms grouped about a central hall. The central hall, instead of being covered by a clerestory roof as at El-Amarna, appears to have been open to the sky, at least in the center. It is dangerous, however, on such limited and doubtful evidence to assume that a hypæthral method of lighting the main living room was common in Ptolemaic houses, and that it was introduced into Egypt from Greek lands. The Egyptian knew the hypæthral method of lighting interiors before he came into contact with the Greek; also we know too little about the different types of Pharaonic house more than to classify the evidence which have been uncovered.

TOWNS AND CITIES

Ancient Egyptian cities and towns, in spite of their ruined, rebuilt, and buried remains, are important evidence in the history of urban architecture, first, because they illustrate many of the natural stages in the early development of communities and, second, because they show the first systematic and geometric town plans. It must not be inferred, however, that the use of geometrically arranged streets was a natural and inevitable stage in the development of urban life, or that the ordinary Egyptian city was laid out in any prearranged fashion. Except under very specific conditions there was no conscious town planning in Ancient Egypt.

In general, as the forces of communal interest, such as hunting, defense, and the necessity of subjugating the Nile, bound men together into communities, the evolution of the town tended to conform to an instinctive pattern. This pattern was much the same in Egypt as it was in Mesopotamia, where relatively similar environmental conditions prevailed. Somewhat as the house started as a single cell, a round unit, became rectangular, then was enlarged by an agglomeration and agglutination of parts around a focal center, and thus finally developed into a complex arrangement of specialized rooms, so the town underwent a comparable evolution.

The embryonic town in Egypt was a casual grouping of clan, tribal, or more frequently communal, huts around the totem house of the high priest and chieftain. When defense became necessary these huts were enclosed within a roughly circular stockade and undoubtedly resembled homesteads and small villages to be seen to-day in various parts of Africa (Plate LXIV–1). A small model from El Kab (Plate LXVIII-4) shows a group of conical huts arranged around three sides of a square. While this Old Kingdom model may actually represent a granary, it also suggests the layout of an early homestead.[25]

The usual defensive town at the opening of Dynastic history was roughly circular,[26] a grouping of dwellings around the palace-temple of the king.[27] The circular form is indicated for Egypt by the hieroglyph designating city (Plate LXVIII–1), which is a circle with two lines, or streets, intersecting at the center. The representations of a walled town on the palette of King Narmer [28] and on the frag-

[26] F. Oelmann, "Das Kornspeichermodell von Melos," *Athenische Mitteilungen,* I (1925), p. 21.

[26] In Abyssinia, where cultural survivals have evident relations with ancient Egyptian civilization, there are, as at Adua, circular strongholds (Oelmann, *Haus und Hof im Altertum,* I, abb. 64).

[27] A potsherd of the I Dynasty from Abydos (E. Naville, *The Cemeteries of Abydos,* I, 1914, Pl. VIII), shows a *serekh* palace in the center of an oval fortification.

[28] J. E. Quibell, *Hierakonpolis,* I, Pl. XXIX.

ment of a palette in the Louvre (Plate LXVIII–2), show a towered or crenellated wall in a curved plan. The remains of the sacred high-place, the oldest part, of Hierakonpolis (Plate XII–4), have a curved, retaining wall. At El Kab,[29] another important city in Upper Egypt under the Thinite Kings, there are three sets of walls, the earliest being a double wall, oval in plan, which surrounded the ancient city (Plate LXVIII–3). A much later wall, rectangular in plan, cuts through the old town, enclosing a very large and apparently open area, 580 m. by 515 m., which must have been occupied in times of war by the peoples and their herds from the surrounding country. Finally there is an innermost wall, also rectangular in plan, which formed the sacred precinct about the temple, the divine palace and stronghold of the protector of the city.

Only important and probably royal towns were fortified; but this natural, and primitive conception of the town as a stronghold, a *château dieu,* around which the community gathered for protection and spiritual guidance, persisted in Egypt, as it did in the temple city-states of Mesopotamia, and thereby influenced both urban and temple architecture. The two palace-forts at Abydos (Plate VI–4), with their great walls enclosing an open space for the huts, tents, and possessions of their retainers, and with the residence of the king at the center, are the first actual remains which show this idea of a community. The same concept, however, was transferred to the cities of the royal dead, as at Saqqara where Zoser's eternal abode was a modified copy in stone of his walled stronghold at Memphis.

By an association of ideas it has been seen how this stronghold concept was literally preserved in all religious establishments. The walled domains of the great gods were fortified towns in which the temple proper was an eternal palace dominating the surrounding storehouses and dwellings for the priests, slaves, attendants, and craftsmen. Seti I spoke of his temple at Abydos as "the stronghold,"[30] and had it written, "another good thought has come into my heart, at command of the god, even the equipment of a town, in whose august midst shall be a resting-place, a settlement, with a temple."[31] It is only necessary to look at the restoration of the mortuary temple of Ramses III (Plate LXXIII-5) to get some idea how a fortified town of the New Kingdom must have appeared.

While specific proof evades us, it is possible to argue, from this analogy between temple domains and the fortified town of a great chieftain, that important royal cities at the opening of Dynastic history had a processional avenue extending from the palace down to the gate of the city and thence to the nearby landing quay on the bank of the Nile. Processional ways, which are characteristic features of Egyptian temples, are also a persistent tradition of early cities, especially in ancient Mesopotamia. In Babylonia they ran from the temple to the city gate, and in modern Irak they are the main highway, lined with bazaars, running from the great mosque to the city gate. At the time when great fortified towns were uncommon, and yet very important, in the life of the district, the city gate had symbolic significance in men's minds. If for no other reason, the importance of the monumental defensive gateway is proved by its influence on subsequent architecture in so many parts of the ancient world. In Egypt the pylon entrance of the stone temples was undoubtedly derived from the towered gateway

[29] Somers Clarke, "El Kab and the Great Wall," *Journal of Egyptian Archaeology,* VII (1921), p. 54.
[30] J. Breasted, *Ancient Records of Egypt* (1906), III, No. 174.
[31] Breasted, *op. cit.,* III, No. 172.

of the royal city; in Mesopotamia the temple façade was also a replica of the flanking towers of the defensive walls; and in Greece the traditional approach to a sacred high-place, the dwelling of gods and heroes, was a propylæa. Gateways, like doorways, had a deeply rooted ideological significance in primitive thought.[32] They were the openings through which the miraculous Great One appeared, and the place where both spiritual and natural enemies were kept out. Many rituals and customs undoubtedly grew up around these important entrances.

Towns, however, originated in different ways: a few were strongholds, others were merely enlarged homesteads, and the majority were little more than casual grouping of agriculturists along the border of the cultivated area, as they still are to-day. Describing the village of Lisht, which grew up in the ruins of Amenemhat's pyramid of the Middle Kingdom, Mace says, "Nothing in this world is quite so conservative as an up-country Egyptian village"; [33] it follows no plan, obeys only the individuality of the peasant's whim and requirements.

Many environmental conditions entered into the gradual development of Egyptian towns. Nothing in Egypt could get away from the Nile, for it was the one great highway, the source of all water, and the life-giving fertilizer of all agriculture. Towns had to be near the water, and yet they could not encroach upon the scanty and valuable strip of fertile land bordering the river. Hence, they had to spread along the edge of the cultivated area, being unable to extend very far into the desert. All the villages and most of the towns of Egypt were therefore long and narrow, running in a rambling fashion roughly north and south, parallel to the river. Orientation was of less rigid significance in Egypt than in most early cultures, because there the demanding conditions of the Nile were of more importance than the position of the heavenly bodies in the disposition of cities.

The city of Tell el-Amarna is our only well-preserved example of a long, narrow and casual type of undefended Egyptian town. Towards the close of the XVIII Dynasty, when Amenhotep IV built his sacred city of Akhetaten as a refuge from the priestly domination at Thebes, there was no necessity for a walled city, for Egypt ruled the eastern end of the Mediterranean, the country was firmly administered, and Amenhotep was a physical and intellectual pacifist. His city of Aten followed no plan, and rambled along the course of the river for several miles. The king marked out its limits in the sixth year of his reign, and chose for it the name Akhetaten, meaning "Aten is satisfied." Three main streets traversed the city from north to south and were crossed irregularly by smaller streets leading down to the river, but there was too much haste in the construction for any systematic plan. Apparently the nobles, as soon as they heard rumors of the intended abandonment of Thebes as the capital, laid out generous claims for their estates at Akhetaten. In many cases they were probably unable for financial reasons to develop all the land. Therefore, as the city grew, the rabble closed in around their houses, explaining why "high priest rubs shoulders with leather-worker, and vizier with glass-maker."

The city, even to most of the temples, was built of sun-dried bricks. In the northern section was the North City, two palaces and a "custom-house"; in the central portion was the main palace, the "Castle of Aten," the Great Temple area and the "Hall of Foreign Tribute" (Plate LIV–2); in the

[32] W. Andrae, *Das Gotteshaus und die Urformen des Bauens im Alten Orient*, p. 24.

[33] A. C. Mace, "The Egyptian Expedition," *New York Metropolitan Museum Bulletin*, Sect. II, XVI (1921), p. 11 *seq.*

southern suburb was Maru-Aten, the "Precinct of the Southern Pool." A large Egyptian city had many specialized buildings,[34] such as police headquarters, "records office," tribute hall, storehouses, and official meeting places, but none of these apparently had any striking architectural significance. Also at Amarna was a "university," quite different, however, from our conception of a place of learning.[35]

Maru-Aten, while actually a summer palace, gives us an insight into what Akhenaten wanted to make of his ideal refuge from the outside world: this "precinct of Aten" was a private, royal garden, —an Egyptian Versailles,—consisting of two separate enclosures, where the Pharaoh could enjoy the flowers and artificial lakes, could bask in the warmth and beauty which emanated from Aten, and under serene conditions could offer up praise to the celestial giver of light and happiness. The southern enclosure (Plate LXVIII–5), 160 m. long by 80 m. wide, had a large entrance hall with pillared rooms in which the palm capitals were made of faience inlays, and the hasty workmanship was covered with bright paint. Beyond this hall was an artificial lake, flower beds and shrubbery. The northern enclosure, immediately adjacent to the southern one, was 200 m. long and 100 m. wide. Across its western end was a row of gardeners' and workmen's houses concealed by a high wall; in the middle was a large, shallow lake with a stone quay at one end, from which the royal family could embark on its peaceful boating parties; and at the northern side of the lake was a two-storied audience hall, or summer-house, where Akhenaten probably kept his *harim* on the upper floor and his fine wines beneath. In the northeastern corner of the precinct was the "Aquarium," or perhaps lustration hall. It was a long, narrow building with a single row of square piers down the center, and in the floor was a row of T-shaped tanks fitted together around the piers. Both the floor of the ambulatory and the low parapet surrounding the tanks were decorated with a continuous pattern of richly painted flower panels (Plate LXVIII–6), of which the best preserved are in the National Museum at Cairo. The painting is brilliant and somewhat impressionistic, but it shows "a poverty of imagination" in the persistent repetition of identical patterns. South from this water court a path led between rows of flower beds and across a moat to a square, artificial island on which were two kiosks flanking a stone altar pavilion, or chapel, on axis with the entrance to the island. The formal approach to the island was from the south, where a rectangular court, with pylons at either end, formed a propylæa before the bridge leading onto the island.

In these gardens and chapels the delicate and pathological Akhenaten, "happy in the Queen and her children," could enjoy his family and the serenities of an artificial world. At first Queen Nefertite presided officially over the precinct, but for some reason her name was erased from the inscriptions, just as it was in the palace,[36] and the lovely gardens were transferred to the favorite daughter, Meryt-aten.

The architecture of Tell el-Amarna must have presented a festive appearance in its bright paint, faience and colored glass. In the city were two large glazing works and numerous glass factories. Whole statues were at times glazed, and the brilliant cloisonné work of the jeweler was enlarged and

[34] H. W. Fairman, "Topographical Notes on the Central City, Tell El-Amarnah," *Journal of Egyptian Archæology,* XXI (1935), p. 136.

[35] *Journal of Egyptian Archaeology,* XX (1934), p. 134.

[36] Page 223.

PLATE LXIX: TOWNS

1

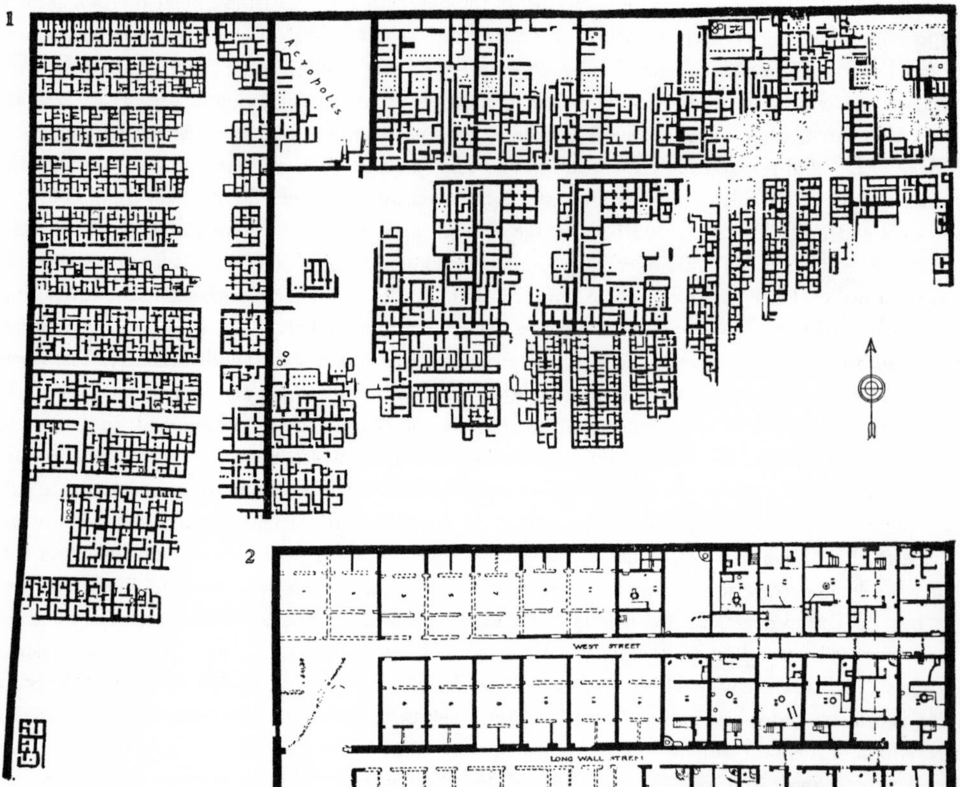

2

transferred to architecture, with the result that capitals were frequently cut witn compartments in which faience and colored glass were inlaid. It all may have been a little gaudy and in time a bit tawdry, for the excavations indicate that the architects relied upon brilliant paint to conceal careless workmanship, and that technical facility was combined with a lack of originality. The death of Akhenaten in 1358 B.C. was a premature and tragic end to his heresy, but it was archæologically fortunate that the city was so quickly abandoned, for otherwise the repeated rebuildings of subsequent ages would have left far less of it than we now have to study.

Thebes, which by the New Kingdom was the most important city in the ancient world, is buried and obliterated in its own débris. According to a poem on Thebes, written in the XIX Dynasty, "more orderly (?) is Thebes than any city; the water and the land were in her in the beginning of time, and the sand came to the tillage (?) to create her ground upon the highland, and the land came into being." [37] Ramses III says, "I planted thy city, Thebes, with trees, vegetations, isi-plants, menhet flowers for thy nostrils." [38]

Memphis, which was chosen by Menes as the capital of unified Egypt, and had had a far longer history than Thebes, was an agglomeration of various villages, precincts, and defensive towns, which gradually merged together, like London, into a large city. According to Diodorus, it was 150 stadia in circumference. As interpreted by Petrie,[39] and verified by his excavations on the site, these dimensions made it about eight miles long and four miles wide. This whole area, however, was not all lined with streets and houses, but "consisted largely of gardens and fields belonging to various villages," and precincts which only in time merged into a more or less continuous city. There are references to the temples of nineteen gods in the city: of these, Apis, the bull, was the oldest, and his temple stood upon the site of the primitive settlement. In time, Apis was eclipsed by Ptah, whose sacred domain was larger than Amon-Re's at Karnak. The plan of the city, however, lies under too many layers of rebuilding ever to be recovered in more than a few small pieces.

The oldest cities of Egypt must have been in the Delta. King Merikere, at about the beginning of the Middle Kingdom, was formally instructed by his father to "Build towns in the Delta. A man's name will not be small through what he has done, and an inhabited city is not harmed." [40] The Delta cities, because of the flat, marshy soil and the yearly floods, were gradually built up on mounds. Herodotus, in describing the city of Bubastis, writes, "Among the many cities which thus attained to a great elevation, none, in my opinion, was raised so much as the town of Bubastis." The temple of the goddess Bubastis, he says, "stands in the middle of the city and is visible

[37] A. Erman, *The Literature of the Ancient Egyptians,* p. 295.
[38] Breasted, *Ancient Records,* IV, No. 213.
[39] Petrie, *Memphis I* (1909), p. 1.
[40] A. Erman, *op. cit.,* p. 81.

PLATE LXIX

1. Plan of Kahun (Petrie, *Illahun, Kahun, and Gurob,* Pl. XIV).
2. Plan of workmen's town, Tell el-Amarna (Peet and Woolley, *The City of Akhenaten,* I, Pl. XVI).

on all sides as one walks around it; for as the city has been raised up by embankment, while the temple has been left untouched in its original condition, you look down upon it wheresoever you are"; "the entrance to it is by a road paved with stone for a distance of about three furlongs, which passes straight through the market-place with an easterly direction, and is about four hundred feet in width. Trees of an extraordinary height grow on each side of the road." [41]

Kantir is thought to have been the Delta residence of Ramses II and the subsequent Ramesside kings, from which they could govern their domains in Egypt and Palestine.[42] An account, presumably of the city, reads, "His Majesty hath builded him a castle called Great-of-Victories. It lieth betwixt Palestine and Egypt, and is full of provisions and victuals. It is like unto Hermonthis (an ancient city near Thebes), and its duration is that of Memphis. The sun ariseth in its horizon, and setteth within it (meaning that the king abides in it day and night). All men forsake their towns and settle down in its territory. Its western part is a temple of Amun, its southern part a temple of Sutekh. Astarte is in its Orient, and Buto in its northern part. *The castle which is within it is like unto the horizon of heaven* (a temple). Ramesses-Beloved-of-Amun is in it as god; Month-in-the-Two-Lands as herald; Sun-of-Princes as Vizier; Joy-of-Egypt, Beloved-of-Atum, as mayor, to whose dwelling the world goeth down." [43] The description may be bombastic and omit much that we would like to know, but it pictures a walled city dominated by the palace-temple of the divine king.

GEOMETRICALLY PLANNED TOWNS

The geometrically planned and surveyed town, with rectangular blocks of houses and regular streets at right angles, was an intellectual concept, rather than any natural evolution of the primitive village, and as such it tended to disregard environmental limitations and the unsystematic accretions of social communities. It therefore could only be realized either when there were no existing urban conditions, or when the human elements involved were subject to the plan and power of one man. Curiously enough, these conditions appear to have obtained from the beginning of Dynastic history, when the Egyptian kings began to lay out the earliest known ordered and regular towns. At first the idea and realization of town planning was limited to the cities of the royal dead, built in the desert, constructed more or less at one time, and subject to the command of the king and his surveyors. The simplest beginning of the ordered plan was apparently initiated by the Thinite Kings of the I Dynasty at Abydos, who had their eternal abodes constructed with hundreds of rectangular graves for the sacrificed retainers arranged in a large rectangle about the royal tomb, like a defensive wall about the palace and stronghold of their chieftain (Plate IV–6). By the IV Dynasty, when the primitive custom of forcibly providing the king with henchmen and servants in the hereafter had long since been abandoned, the king still expected his courtiers to be buried about him, and so had their stone mastabas, as at Gizeh (Plate XXV–1), arranged in regular streets about his pyramid.

[41] Herodotus, *History,* II, 137 and 138.

[42] W. C. Hayes, "Glazed Tiles from a Palace of Ramesses II at Kantir," *The Metropolitan Museum of Art Papers* (1937).

[43] A. Erman, *op. cit.,* pp. 270-271.

In the XII Dynasty when Senwosret II constructed his city for the dead around his supposedly impregnable pyramid of Il-Lahun, he had a regular and planned town, compact, efficient, and controlled, built for the workmen. Il-Lahun, or Kahun (Plate LXIX–1), was a walled enclosure divided by a cross-wall into eastern and western sections; on the north side was a raised knoll on which was a large house, apparently reserved for the king when inspecting the work on his tomb, and below it was a guard-house; also along the north wall was a row of five houses, and opposite to them, across a straight street, were three other large residences for officials, with storehouses back of them; down the western wall of the large section was a row of smaller dwellings, probably for foremen, and in front of them were five streets of workmen's quarters. In the walled-in eastern section were eleven streets of workmen's quarters, the houses more or less standardized by streets.

A smaller planned and controlled town was built in the XVII Dynasty by Akhenaten, to house the stone-cutters at work on the tombs outside of Tell el-Amarna (Plate LXIX–2). This "eastern village" was a perfect square surrounded by high walls, controlled by a limited number of exits, and laid out with uniform houses on parallel streets. As at Kahun, the quarters were divided by a wall into two sections, which suggests a racial or social distinction; but either because of proximity of the city or the character of the work, there was only one large house, situated in the corner of the enclosure near the exit, for the supervisor.

There are two other planned towns for workmen which have been excavated. One is the town of Aahmes I,[44] constructed for the men employed on the different monuments erected in connection with the tomb (Plate LXX–1). It was inhabited about ten years between 1580-1570 B.C. and then abandoned. The other town was also built early in the XVIII Dynasty by the king for the men working on the Necropolis of Der el-Medina,[45] and it was in use down to the end of the Ramessides.

In how far the economy of space and the efficiency of a surveyed arrangement of streets was applied to the ordinary towns of Egypt, before such Hellenistic cities as Alexandria were built, we do not know. It is customary to credit the Hellenistic Greeks and the Pre-Roman builders of such towns as Terra-Mare and Marzabetto with having been the first to develop rectangular town plans, but Egypt anticipated the idea by hundreds of years.

PALACES

As the palace gradually developed from the house, the royal residence in each period so far excelled the ordinary dwelling that it in time gave rise to new and more elaborate ideas of domestic architecture. At the opening of Dynastic history we know something about the wooden strongholds of the ruling class in the Delta,[46] and at Abydos we have the plans of two brick, defensive palaces of the early Thinite kings.[47] The plan of the "Middle Fort" palace at Abydos (Plate VI–7) appears, in the simplicity of its arrangement of rooms, to be merely an enlarged version of the type of house seen in

[44] E. R. Ayrton, C. T. Currelly, A. E. P. Weigall, *Abydos,* III, p. 37, Pl. LIII.
[45] B. Bruyère, "La nécropole de Deir el Médineh," *Chronique d'Égypte,* XXI (1936), p. 329 *seq.*
[46] Page 33.
[47] Page 40.

the XII Dynasty as workmen's quarters at Kahun, for it has only a court, vestibule, and long hall; and the Shunet-ez-Zebib palace (Plate VI–4) is basically the same, but with a larger number of private chambers opening off from the general living-room. Again, the so-called fort at Hierakonpolis (Plate LXX–2), which also dates from this early period, was probably a similar royal residence. Its remains, square in plan, still preserve the inner and outer walls of the defensive enclosure, which was oriented with the corners to the cardinal points. At its eastern corner was a projecting gate which presumably had a towered treatment. But nothing remains of the actual palace of the commanding chieftain or king.

In the III Dynasty Zoser's sepulchral arrangements at Saqqara [48] furnish the best indications of what a royal palace and its defensive walls were like. It suggests that inside the protecting walls of such strongholds as those at Abydos and Hierakonpolis were long halls, ceremonial buildings, and storage places, all built of bundled reeds and mattings, perhaps plastered with mud, and therefore destroyed, which were grouped around the actual dwelling of the king. After the III Dynasty there are no remains of royal residences until the new Kingdom. During the Old Kingdom the palaces were all in the neighborhood of Memphis, and the only picture which we can form of the dwellings of the Pharaohs of the IV and V Dynasties is based on the assumption, already discussed, that the mortuary temples and "Valley-temples" of this period reflect, or even imitate, the contemporary palace architecture. The royal residence was known as the "Great House," and at times was referred to as the "Double Front," usually interpreted to mean that the palace had two gateways; although Zoser's mortuary palace indicates that "Double Front" may refer to two separate ceremonial halls, which served for the functions of the Pharaoh in his dual capacity as King of Upper and Lower Egypt. In the XII Dynasty Amenemhet described his palace, "I made a [palace] decked with gold, whose ceilings were of lazuli and the walls therein. The floors [ ], The doors were of copper, the bolts were of bronze, *made for everlastingness,* at which eternity fears." [49]

By the XVIII Dynasty our information is less conjectural, because, in addition to the large palace built by Amenhotep III at Thebes, we have the remains of Amenhotep IV's palaces at Tell el-Amarna. The palace of Amenhotep III covered a large area on the west bank at Thebes and "consisted of a number of vast, rambling, one-storied structures, built independently from time to time." [50] One section of the palace-city included the quarters for the artisans engaged about the palace, houses for nobles, the royal residence, and most interesting of all, the royal *harim*. The central feature of the *harim* building was the banquet-hall from which opened the private suites of the king and the ladies of his household. These suites, all more or less identical in size and appointments, and providing accommodations for eight ladies and their servants, each consisted of a bathroom, its roof supported by wooden columns; a reception-room with a dais, and from this lounging-room, doors opening into

[48] Page 61.

[49] Breasted, *op. cit.*, III, No. 483; the references to "lazuli" in the decoration of palaces and temples must refer to the color used either as paint or glaze. It must also be kept in mind that Egyptian descriptions of architecture tend to follow a formula and to exaggerate.

[50] H. E. Winlock, "The Work of the Egyptian Expedition," *Bulletin of the Metropolitan Museum*, VII (1912), pp. 184-190; A. Lansing, "The Egyptian Expedition of 1916-17," *Supplement to Bulletin of the Metropolitan Museum,* XIII (1918), pp. 8-14; H. A. Evelyn-White, "The Egyptian Expedition of 1914-15," *op. cit.*, X (1915), p. 255.

a private bedroom and wardrobe. "The king himself had a large bedroom, retiring rooms, a bath, and a special banquet-chamber in which there was a throne placed opposite the large door through which he could be seen seated from the banquet-hall."

Another section (Plate LXX–3) consisted of the special residence of the king's favorite wife, Queen Tyi, in which the arrangement of banqueting room, bedroom, bath, etc., was similar to that in the royal *harim*. A third section of the palace complex was the Festival Hall, the "House of Rejoicing," constructed to celebrate Amenhotep's second jubilee, in the thirty-fourth year of his reign. From its large forecourt ramps led up to the terrace at the west end, where a central doorway with a projecting vestibule gave access to the first hypostyle hall, which, in its turn, opened into a smaller columnar hall, where three flights of steps rose to three sanctuaries.[51] As one of the special attractions of the palace, "His majesty commanded to make a lake for the Great King's Wife, Tyi, in her city of Zerukha. Its length 3700 cubits: its width 700 cubits." It was here on the great artificial lake, surrounded by trees, shrubs and flowers, that Amenhotep and his much loved queen sailed in their magnificent *dahabiyeh,* called in the inscriptions "Aton-gleams." It was here also that their son, Akhenaten, got his idea for the pleasure gardens of Maru-Aten, which he built at Tell el-Amarna.

Amenhotep IV built two palaces at Tell el-Amarna. His great palace was in the center of the city, and, like so many building activities of the king, was planned on a scale which was never carried out in finished form.[52] The Weben-Aten, or "Broad Hall", was a part of the original plan, which after a few years was rebuilt and then razed to the foundations and covered with sand to form a central parade ground. None of the squares marking the position of columns show any signs of having been used. The parade-ground was surrounded by colossi, and in the center of the north side was a pavilion, frequently represented in the Amarna paintings, which formed the entrance to the palace (Plate LXX–4). Immediately back of the pavilion was a long colonnade hall from which a ramp descended into an open court, filled with stelæ, and with ramps leading out of it to the north, east, and west. Back of this court and still on axis was a large hypostyle hall, ending abruptly without any throne-room. At either side of the hypostyle hall were courts, and beyond the part of the palace already excavated are the remains of a large, pillared hall. The *harim* was on the eastern side of the parade ground, set back from the wall to leave a passage for the guards.[53] In the *harim* was discovered a richly painted pavement, representing a garden pool in lovely colors, with fish, ducks, and lotus pads in it, and with various grasses and flowering shrubs around its borders.

The North Palace (Plate LXXI–1) which was built in the later part of Akhenaten's reign, presumably as a more protected winter residence, was much smaller, and for that reason more comprehensible. It was an example of the fully developed palace of the XVIII Dynasty, with the component parts, which in earlier palaces had been separate buildings, organized into a compact unity. It consisted of a rectangular block of exterior walls, nearly square in plan, divided longitudi-

[51] A. Lansing, "Excavations at the Palace of Amenhotep III at Thebes," *Bulletin of the Metropolitan Museum of Art,* suppl., XIII (1918), p. 8.

[52] Petrie, *Tell el Amarna,* 1894; J. D. S. Pendlebury, *Journal of Egyptian Archaeology,* XXI (1935), XXII, (1936).

[53] For plan of *harim* see *Journal of Egyptian Archaeology,* XXI (1935), Pl. x.

PLATE LXX: TOWNS AND PALACES

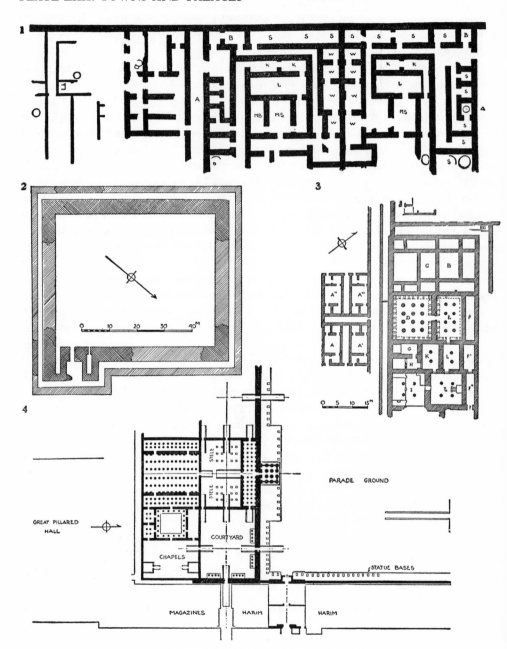

1

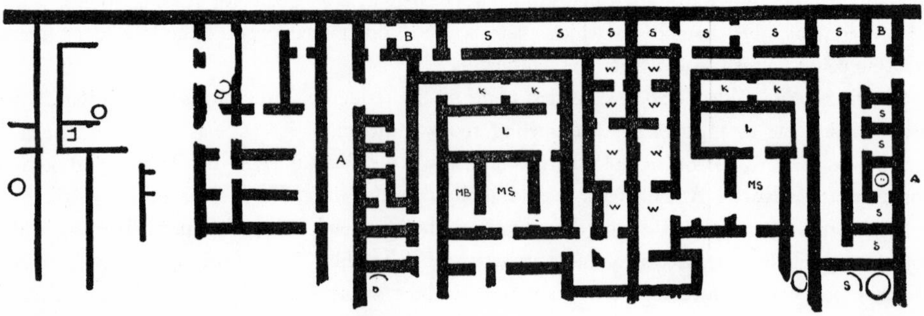

2

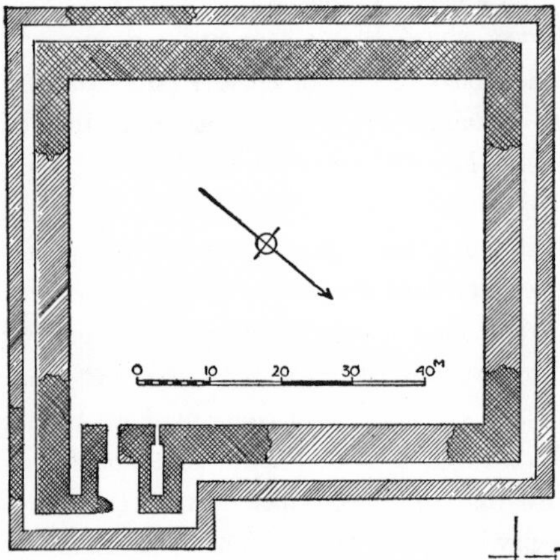

3

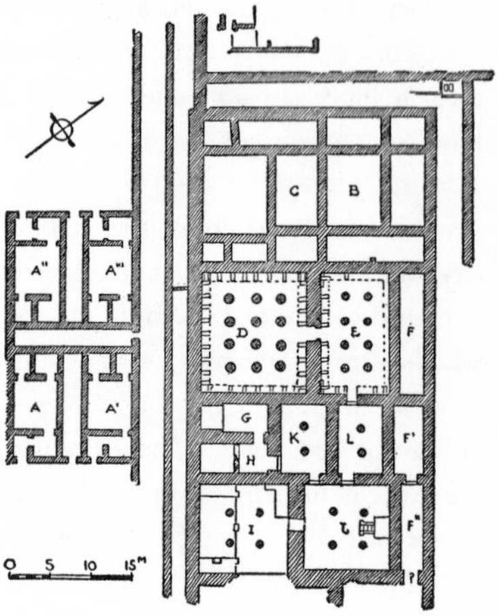

4

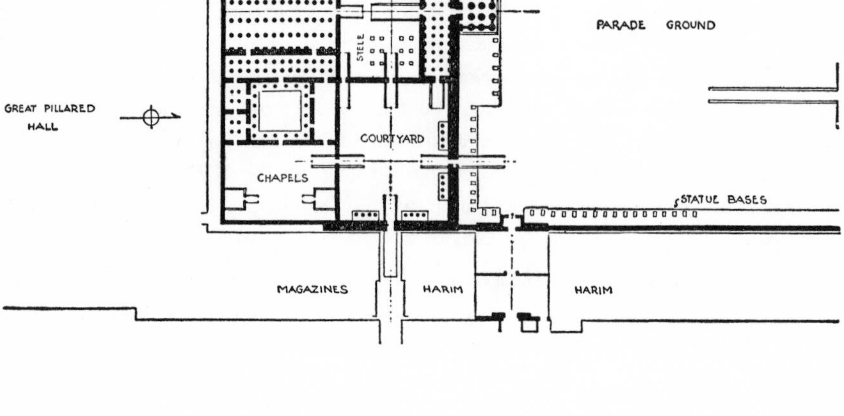

nally and laterally into three parts.[54] The forecourt was flanked on the north by an altar-court, with nine cell-like chambers on both sides of it, and on the south by a service-court in which there were three buildings, one on axis and two peristyled structures, one at either side. By analogy with the mortuary temples of Ramses II and III, where supplies and tribute in kind were received in a small building at the right of the temple forecourt, this space at Amarna was the official section of the steward in charge of the business of the palace. From the first court three gates led into the water-court, which was terraced and shaded by trees. It had a large pool in the center which undoubtedly supplied the whole palace with water. Flanking this open area on the north was an enclosed space for the king's pets, with mangers richly carved for the bulls, the ibex, and the gazelles of the royal zoölogical garden, and on the south side were the residential quarters of the officials of the palace, for there were ministers and special attendants for each part of the king's daily routine of bathing, dressing, eating, painting, and perfuming.

The royal quarters, still preserving the triple division of the palace, extended across the eastern side of the enclosure. In the center was the hypostyle hall, with smaller halls and chambers, including a bathroom and bedroom, perhaps for the king, on either side. The hypostyle hall was entered by a double doorway, preceded by a stone pavilion, in which the king and queen made public appearances, as they do in the scenes on the frescoes from the Tell el-Amarna tombs. The hypostyle hall, which tomb paintings show as a banqueting-room, had twenty-six columns in six rows, the columns of the four inner rows being larger and therefore rising higher to form a clerestory. Around the bottom of the wall was a painted dado of squares decorated with papyrus and lotus flowers, while above the dado were scenes undoubtedly connected with the life and activities of the king. From the large hall a doorway on axis opened into a long vestibule, or private dining-room, with twelve columns, running north and south; and from this room another door led into the throne-room with its dais for the son of Aten. On both sides of the throne-room were narrow halls with rectangular piers, and with pantries at one end, as their glazed decorations of molded grapes and the fragments of wine jars marked "Good Wine of the House of Aten" would indicate.

At both ends of the transverse, columnar vestibule, corridors ran north and south to the wings of the palace, terminating at each end in a flight of stairs which went up to a window. The win-

[54] The walls of the palace had bonding courses of wood probably at intervals of about one meter.

PLATE LXX

1. Town of Aahmes, Abydos:
   A street, *B* porter's lodge, *K* men's apartments, *L* master's private room, *MS* master's sitting room, *MB* master's bedroom, *S* servants and storerooms, *W* women's apartments (E. R. Ayrton, *Abydos,* III, Pl. LIII).
2. Plan of the stronghold at Hierakonpolis (J. E. Quibell, *Hierakonpolis,* II, Pl. LXXIV).
3. Plan of the residence of Queen Tyi in palace of Amenhotep III at Thebes (H. A. Evelyn-White, *Bulletin of the Metropolitan Museum of Art,* X, 1915, p. 255, Fig. 3).
4. One section of Great Palace at Tell el-Amarna (J. D. S. Pendlebury, *Journal of Egyptian Archaeology,* XXII, 1936, Pl. XVIII).

PLATE LXXI: PALACES

1

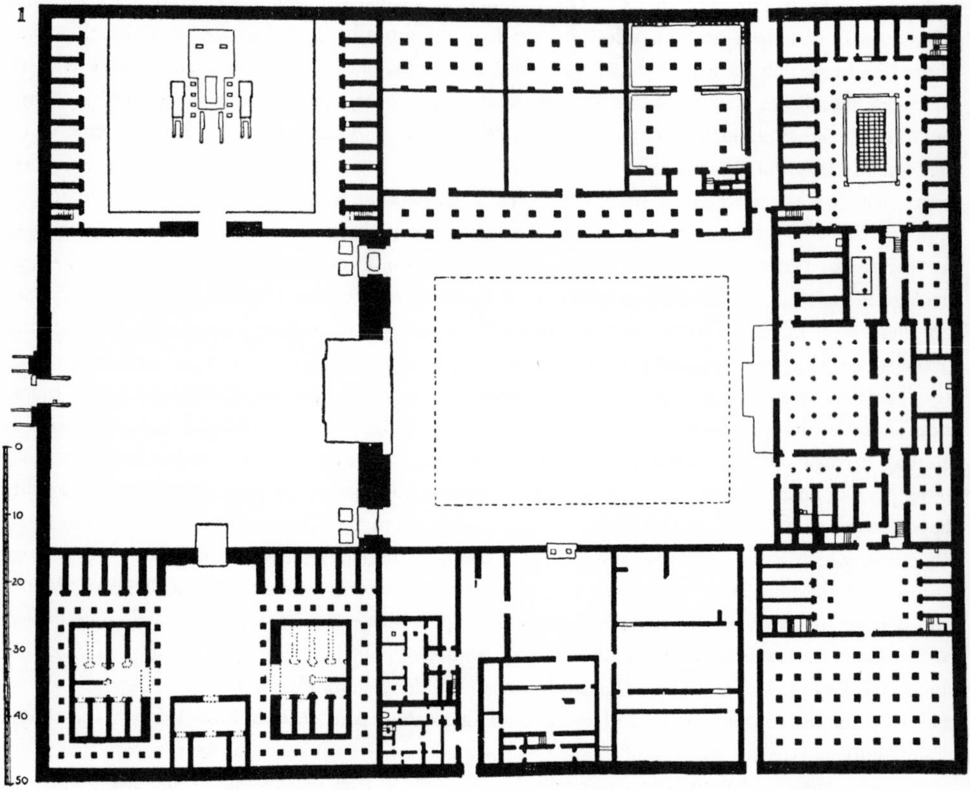

2

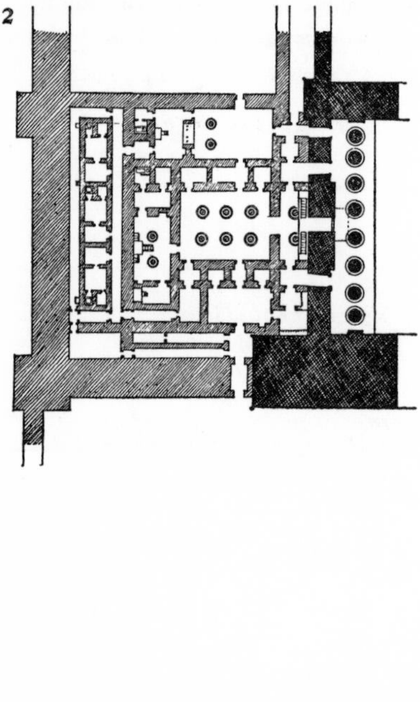

3

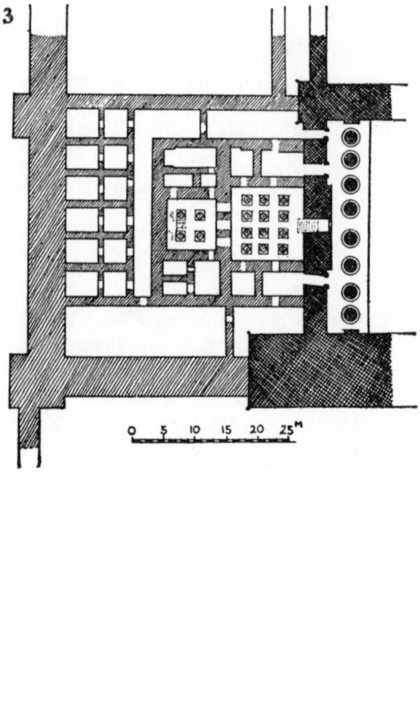

dows probably opened on a balcony where Akhenaten could look down upon the picturesque peristyled courts of his palace. The south court, with chambers opening from it, and beyond it a pillared hall, was for the men. The north court, which was the most charming part of the palace, presented an attractive picture to the Pharaoh standing in his window and looking down at his *harim*. The oblong court of the *harim,* enclosed by colonnaded loggia, had a garden in the center laid out in reticulated flower beds surrounded by a border of running water. Opening off from the covered peristyle were small rectangular chambers, suggestive more of cells for ascetics than for ladies in the king's favor. At the center of the north end was one special room, known as the "Green Room," which had a large window facing the court. Originally this "Green Room" may have been an aviary, as the niches in the wall have suggested, but it was turned into a painted arbor by decorating all its walls with one continuous scene of remarkable richness. Around the bottom was sparkling water in deep blue with floating lotus flowers and pads; then a variety of flowering weeds and grasses growing on the water's edge; and finally a band of flowering shrubbery, as a transition to the wall of papyrus reeds which extended up to the ceiling, with the flowers and birds spotted through the reeds, made a gorgeous tapestry of color.[55] Two stairs from the court led up to the roof and probably to a second story. As in the case of the "Precinct of the Southern Pool" an unfortunate suspicion creeps in to lessen the idyllic charm of the *harim* court. Not only is there no mention of the much loved queen, but the name of Meryt-Aten, the favorite daughter, appears on erased surfaces as it did in the gardens of Maru-Aten. There is no place for speculative gossip in the study of architecture, but the Amarna art is sufficiently exotic, sensuously naturalistic, and partly free of ideographic formality, to suggest a royal recluse whose interests were not entirely religious.

After the XVIII Dynasty the permanent royal residence, certainly under the Ramesside Pharaohs, was in the Delta, probably at Kantir, and only smaller palaces were built in different parts of the kingdom, with always at least one at Thebes, where the Pharaoh had to officiate in so many religious ceremonies.[56] Ramses II had his Theban residence built within the sacred precinct of his mortuary temple (Plate XXXVIII–3). Still later, Ramses III followed his example and so fully copied

[55] N. de G. Davies, "The Paintings of the Northern Palace," *The Mural Painting of El 'Amarneh* (1929).

[56] Nothing remains of the palace buildings at Kantir except some of the glazed tiles from the throne daises (W. C. Hayes, "Glazed Tiles from a Palace of Ramesses II at Kantir," *The Metropolitan Museum of Art Studies,* 1937; M. Hamza, "Excavations at Qantir," *Annales du Service,* XXX, pp. 31-68). Other palaces of no architectural significance are: Palace of Apries (Petrie, 1909) and the palace of Mer-en-Ptah at Memphis (C. S. Fisher, *University of Pennsylvania Museum Journal,* VIII, 1917, p. 211-237).

PLATE LXXI

1. Plan of North Palace at Tell el-Amarna (T. Whittemore, "Excavations at El-Amarnah," *Journal of Egyptian Archaeology,* XII, 1926, Pl. II).
2. Plan of the Second Palace of Ramses III at Medinet Habu (U. Hölscher, "Medinet Habu," *Oriental Institute Communications,* no. 5, Fig. 30).
3. Plan of the First Palace of Ramses III (*op. cit.,* Fig. 29).

PLATE LXXII: PALACES

1

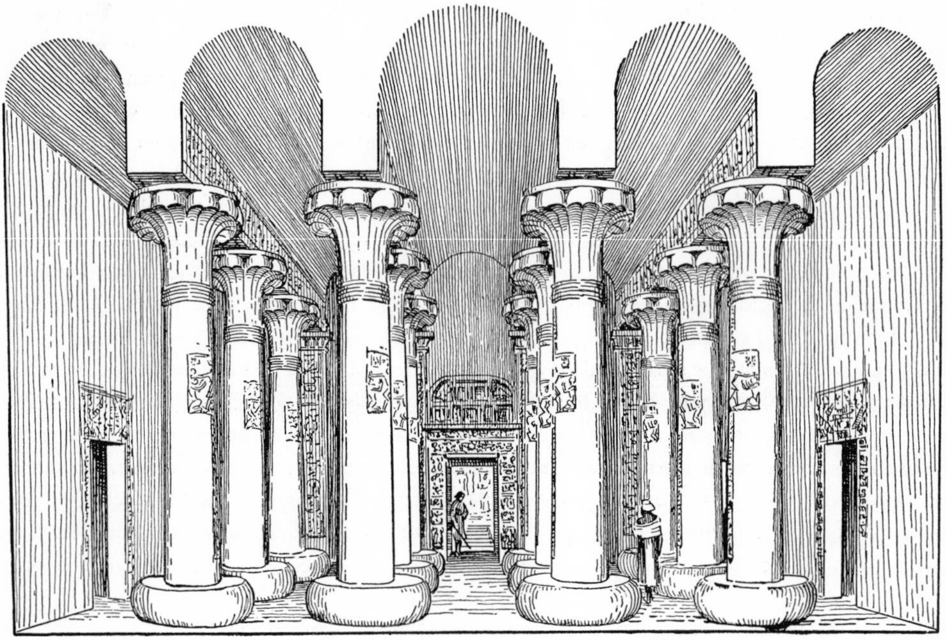

2

the plan of the Ramesseum palace in his own mortuary temple at Medinet Habu that his palace will illustrate a XIX Dynasty royal residence.

The first palace which Ramses III built was planned simultaneously with the temple, and, as the plan shows (Plate LXXI–3), its entrances were through the outer forecourt of the temple, so that the portico of the temple court became the portico of the royal residence. The plan was basically a traditional house plan, consisting of an audience hall of twelve limestone columns with palm leaf capitals (Plate LXXII–1), a private throne room of four columns and a raised dais, and smaller rooms for the accommodation of the king. The audience-hall was roofed with five tunnel-vaults of mud-brick covered with painted decorations, and from it a flight of steps led up to a window opening on the portico of the temple-court (Plate XLI–2). In this window, with its sill supported by the sculptured heads of prisoners, Ramses sat upon a wooden balcony and made his godlike appearances to the public, enjoyed the procession of slaves and plunder dedicated to the god, amused himself with the gladiatorial contests and dancing in the court, and from his elevation rewarded his followers by throwing down chains of gold. Behind his dais in the throne-room was a sculptured "false-door," the derivative of the *serekh* façade, "through which the king might be imagined as emerging from his private apartments," for beside it stands the inscription, "The King appears in the palace of his august temple." This inscription leaves no doubt that the Egyptians thought of their palaces and temples as essentially the same.

Some time after the building of the first palace, Ramses had his residence remade (Plate LXXI–2). He substituted two rows of columns for the four rows in the audience-hall, and raised its roof, still covered by tunnel-vaults (Plate LXXII–2), above the surrounding roofs, so as to get direct, clerestory lighting. At the same time, he isolated the stairs to the Window of Appearances in a vestibule, and built a wooden canopy above the balcony in front of the window. He also improved his private quarters, built three suites of rooms for women in back, and at the west side of the hypostyle hall constructed a *harim* court and a women's salon with an alabaster dais for the Pharaoh. A wide window, probably grated, afforded a view from the dais into the open *harim* court. Obviously the second palace was more a residence than the first. The fact that both palaces were roofed with tunnel-vaults is proved by the outlines formed by the holes on the temple wall (Plate XLI–4) in which the centering timbers were set.

The Fortified Gate of Ramses III's palace-temple at Medinet Habu is an imposing architectural monument. It is interesting not only as the only existing gateway of its kind in Egypt, but also because of its possible origin and use.[57] This towered gateway, built into the defensive walls,

[57] A gateway of similar ground plan was found in the city of "Raamses" (Petrie, *Hyksos and Israelite Cities*, 1906, Pl. XXXV).

PLATE LXXII

1. Audience hall in the First Palace of Ramses III at Medinet Habu (Hölscher, "Medinet Habu Studies," *Oriental Institute Communications*, no. 7, Pl. II).
2. Section through Audience Hall of Second Palace of Ramses III (Hölscher, *Oriental Institute Communications*, no. 5, Fig. 35).

PLATE LXXIII: FORTIFIED GATEWAY, MEDINET HABU

1

2

3

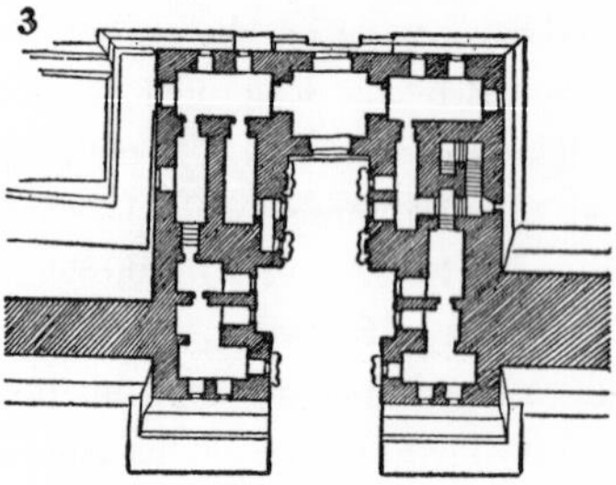

4

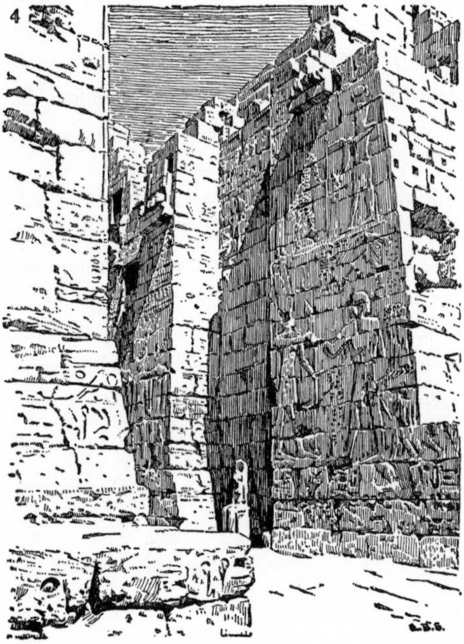

5

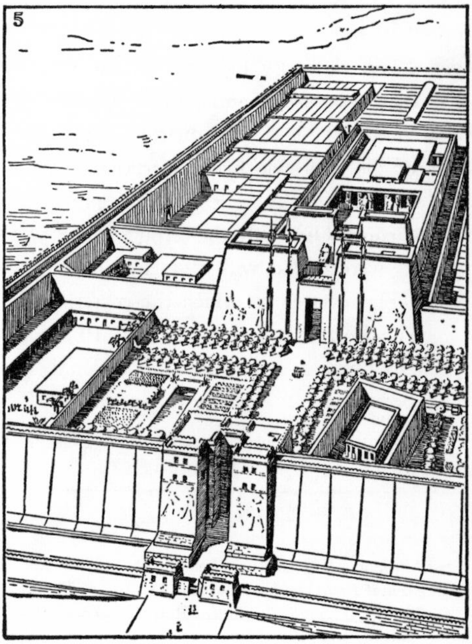

consists of two stone towers with vertical walls which project beyond the defenses (Plate LXXIII–1). The space between the towers is like a narrow court growing narrower at the back where the towers come together to form a gate. Only the two projecting towers, the gateway, and the sides towards the slype are of sandstone, the rest of the gateway having been constructed of mud-brick, faced with mud and finished with whitewash. The ground floors of the towers are of solid masonry without rooms, but the second and third floors (Plate LXXIII-3) had suites of rooms, wooden-roofed in the stone portion and barrel-vaulted in the rest of the structure (Plate LXXIII–2). The stone walls were covered with colored reliefs and on the upper stories can be seen the windows opening from the apartments above. Two of the windows facing on the slype have lintels supported by carved heads of prisoners (Plate LXXIII–4).

Inasmuch as the apartments on the upper floor are decorated with reliefs of the king enjoying his *harim,* the tower is frequently described as the quarters of the royal *harim,* but Hölscher has shown that the women's quarters were back of the palace, and the towers, outside their defensive purpose, were "a royal kiosk," a cool and pleasant retreat for the king and his maidens. In origin this gateway has been at times described as an architectural intrusion borrowed from the brick architecture of the East, because of its resemblance to Assyrian city gateways, its designation by the Syrian name *migdol,* its vaulted chambers, and its vertical instead of battered walls. While its use and even its adoption at Medinet Habu may have been influenced by Ramses' wars in the East, the tradition of a towered gateway goes back to the beginnings of Dynastic architecture. A Predynastic fresco from a tomb at Hierakonpolis shows a towered gateway on a boat, and the *serekh* façade on the stele of King Zet (Plate IV–1) depicts a towered stronghold of the I Dynasty. It is probable that Zoser's defensive walls about his mortuary palace at Saqqara had towered portals, and it is a strong possibility that other fortified palaces, such as the early "fort" at Hierakonpolis, had similar towers. By the New Kingdom, there are too few preserved fortifications to prove this type of gateway was not indigenous. As Hölscher says, "Especially at the frontiers, in the Delta and in Lower Nubia, there must have been similar structures, ruins of which will perhaps later be recognized." [58]

[58] U. Hölscher, "Excavations at Ancient Thebes, 1930-31," *University of Chicago, Oriental Institute Communications,* No. 15, p. 9.

PLATE LXXIII

1. Façade restored (Hölscher, "Excavations at Ancient Thebes," *Oriental Institute Communications,* no. 15, Fig. 9).
2. Section looking west (*op. cit.,* Fig. 8).
3. Plan of third floor (*op. cit.,* Fig. 7).
4. View looking northwest.
5. Reconstruction of gateway, temple and palace (Hölscher, *Das hohe Tor von Medinet Habu,* 1910).

PLATE LXXIV: FORTS AND GARDENS

1

2

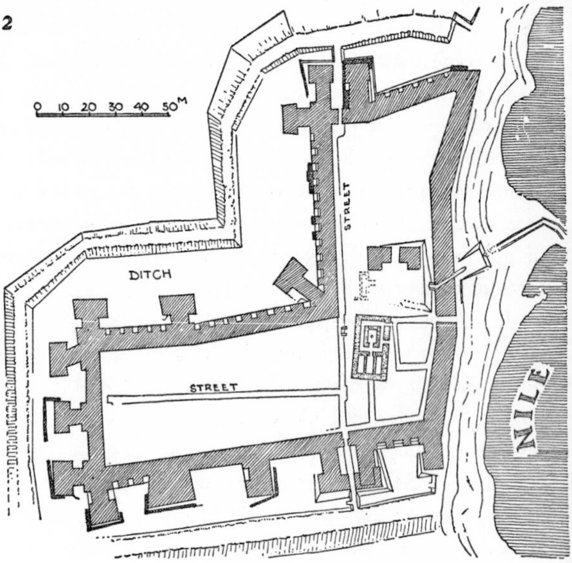

4

3

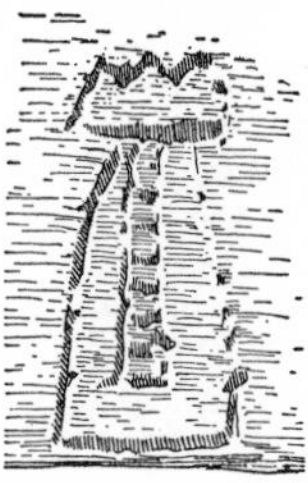

5

GARDENS AND VILLAS

Every Egyptian who could afford it had a garden in his yard (Plate LXVII–6), and if possible a villa outside the city where he could have what was so rare in Egypt, shade trees, flowers, and an artificial pool (Plate LXXIV–5). Although the Egyptians began by valuing the lotus and papyrus flowers as emblems of life-giving fertility in the dry valley, they ended by enjoying them for their own sake. Flowers were hung on their walls, giving rise to painted floral patterns; they were collected from different parts of the world and cultivated, as shown by Queen Hatshepsut's famous expedition to obtain myrrh trees from the land of Punt; and they were heaped upon the tables and presented in many of the ceremonies, for in spite of the sober architecture, the preoccupation with death and the persistence of primitive ideas, the Egyptians were a cheerful, happy and pleasure-loving people. All the New Kingdom palaces had lovely gardens, and the estates of Aten at Tell el-Amarna, as depicted on the wall paintings, had park-like gardens laid out within the precinct walls (Plate LXXIV–4). These gardens, because they were artificial, difficult to keep alive, and such a contrast to the barren desert, were one of the great joys of Egyptian life. Even though they never disentangled their experiences of life from their primitive beliefs, and, therefore, did not consider art as an æsthetic vehicle for transmitting pleasurable experiences of nature, it was in their love of gardens that the Egyptians and their art came nearest to an escape from the tyranny of immemorial ideas.

FORTS

Forts are a grim contrast to gardens, and yet military architecture, which was developed to a remarkable efficiency even before the Middle Kingdom, was a direct outgrowth of the defensive palace architecture at the opening of Dynastic history. The *serekh* building (Plate IV–1), with its towers and parapets, was a wooden stronghold of Delta chieftains;[59] the forts at Abydos (Plate VI–4) were early defensive castles of brick[60]; and the fort at Hierakonpolis (Plate LXX–2), as well as Zoser's stronghold at Memphis, which he reproduced around his tomb at Saqqara (Plate XIII), shows how the domestic architecture of the ruling class had already become military even at the beginning of the Old Kingdom. On a wooden tablet from Abydos (Plate LXXIV–3) is the representation of a defensive tower which probably dates from the time of Menes.

[59] Pages 33-34.
[60] Page 40.

PLATE LXXIV

1. Fort depicted in reliefs of Ramesseum (Perrot et Chipiez, *op. cit.*, I, Fig. 287).
2. Plan of fort at Semna (Reisner, *Boston Museum of Fine Arts Bulletin*, XXIII, 1925, p. 22).
3. Defensive Tower, wooden label, Abydos (Petrie, *The Royal Tombs*, II, Pl. V).
4. Egyptian plan of the estate of Aten (N. de G. Davies, *The Rock Tombs of El Amarna*, I, Pl. XXXII).
5. Restoration of a villa (*after* Perrot et Chipiez, *op. cit.*, I, Fig. 267).

The greatest incentive to the growth of military architecture came when Egypt, especially in the Middle Kingdom, began to fortify her eastern and southern borders, extending her frontier beyond Elephantine, and finally pushing it beyond the Second Cataract in order to protect the profitable trade with Nubia and central Africa. Most of the strongest forts were built in Nubia during the XII Dynasty, some of them being so strong that they give no indication of ever having been captured. Of these fortresses on the southern frontier[61] the most interesting and exceptional is the fort at Semna, on the west side of the Second Cataract. The two forts which guarded both sides of the river were built in the XII Dynasty by Senwosret III and called "Sekhem-Khakauw-R" (Senwosret III-is-Powerful) and "Itenuw-peduwt" (Warding-off-the-bow-peoples). Unlike most Egyptian forts, which were rectangular, Semna West (Plate LXXIV-2) was L-shaped, having been at first rectangular and then extended to one side. It had two gateways through which all north and south traffic along the river was directed; it also had a small postern gate next to the water gate which opened on a covered causeway leading down to the river.

The fort was so constructed as to take full advantage of the terrain, having no unfortified spur on which the enemy could get a foothold. It was built on a platform of granite rubble, and surrounded on the three sides away from the river by a dry ditch, made by an embankment with glacis of stone. At both gateways this moat was crossed by a causeway, penetrated by a drain. The walls of the fortress were built of crude brick, strengthened, as was the custom, by frequent layers of wooden beams, laid both longitudinally and transversely, thereby making a banding effect. It is also to be noted that these brick walls had vertical grooves, recalling the sunken panels of the forts at Abydos, the walls of Zoser's mortuary temenos, and hence the traditional *serekh*-façade sinkings of the old defensive palaces. The walls were from 5 to 8 m. thick and about 10 m. high. Inside the fort at the junction of the two cross-roads was a temple, first built by Senwosret, then rebuilt by Thutmose II and III, by Amenhotep II, and finally by Taharka. The space at either side of the streets was filled by blocks of houses.

Although it is unlikely that the Middle Kingdom fort looked like the New Kingdom fortress pictured on the Ramesseum (Plate LXXIV–1), still the relief gives us a clear idea of an Egyptian stronghold. It shows the banding of wood and brick, the use of towers, and the typical Egyptian battlement, consisting of a scalloped parapet.

[61] Somers Clarke, "Ancient Egyptian Frontier Fortresses," *Journal of Egyptian Archaeology,* III (1916), p. 155-179; Randall-Maciver and L. Woolley, *Buhen* (1911); Reisner, "Excavations in Egypt and Ethiopia, 1922-1925," *Boston Museum of Fine Arts Bulletin,* XXIII (1925), p. 23 *seq.;* "Ancient Egyptian Forts at Semna and Uronarti," *op. cit.,* XXVII (1929), p. 64 *seq.;* N. F. Wheeler, "Harvard-Boston Expedition in the Sudan" (Fortress of Shalfak), *op. cit.,* XXIX (1931), p. 66 *seq.;* A. H. Gardiner, "An Ancient List of the Fortresses in Nubia," *Journal of Egyptian Archaeology,* III (1916), p. 184-192.

10. *EGYPTIAN ARCHITECTS AND THEIR METHODS*

I shall be praised because of my wisdom in years to come, by those who shall imitate that which I have done. I did not fail—I obeyed superior orders.—INENI, "CHIEF OF ALL WORKS."

THE BUILDING of an Egyptian temple involved an elaborate series of ceremonies [1] which were represented on all Egyptian temples down to the end of the Græco-Roman period. Inasmuch as the temple was a house concept,[2] the ceremonies of foundation and consecration were essentially the ritual of a son, the Pharaoh, building a permanent residence, i.e., house, tomb, or temple, for his fathers, who, in the case of temples, were the gods. By Ptolemaic times when the king and his priests decided to build a temple, they consulted the "Book of Foundation of Temples," which was believed to have been written by the god Imhotep, chief official of the cult of his father Ptah. This book was carried up to the sky when the gods withdrew from the earth, but Imhotep "let it fall from heaven north of Memphis." [3] It was by following the prescriptions of this book that the general plan of the temple at Edfu was established. The plan of the temple at Dendera was believed to have been found on a hidden parchment of the time of either Khufu or Pepi. In other words it was the desire of the king to construct the house of his fathers after the plans laid down by the gods themselves when they lived and ruled in the valley. Every important Egyptian temple had its archives in which were preserved the instructions and precedents of those who had gone before.

After his deliberations on the plans the king is depicted leaving his palace, preceded by the standards of the primitive tribes of Upper Egypt, the emblems of his fathers. This ceremony took place at night so that the king, with the assistance of the gods, could orient the temple by the Great Bear, stretch the cord, and establish the corners. After the king has pegged out the limits of the temple area, he turns the first sod, makes the first brick, and throws seed or incense into the foundation ditch. When the temple is finished, he purifies it by magic, knocks at the door for admittance, and finally "gives the house to his master."

These formulas were rigidly observed because the priests, at least, demanded that their buildings should conform with regulations laid down at the earliest times. The temples had to have "their height *good,* their width correct, the whole well reckoned, squared according to the wisdom of Thoth, and therefore set forth in the sacred writings." [4]

[1] A. Moret, *Du Caractère Religieux de la Royauté Pharaonique* (1902), pp. 130-145.
[2] Moret, *op. cit.*, p. 130; G. Steindorff, "Haus und Temple," *Zeitschrift für Aegyptische Sprache,* XXXIV (1896), p. 107.
[3] Moret, *op. cit.*, p. 130.
[4] A. Erman, *A Handbook of Egyptian Religion* (1907), p. 209.

All the dimensions of the temples were measured in the Royal Cubit,[5] divided into seven palms, which, in turn, were subdivided into four digits. All the actual work was done under the supervision and control of a state architect who was responsible to the king.

There can be no doubt that these Egyptian architects had the practical ability to achieve whatever was required of them. At a very early date they had methods of representing buildings by linear conventions of plans and elevations, as a means of controlling the shape and dimensions of the various elements. It is assumed that throughout Egyptian history there were palace and temple archives, in which the traditional plans were conserved.[6] As early as the III Dynasty there were diagrammatic methods of conveying building instructions. An *ostracon* from Saqqara depicts a curve by what appears to be coördinates, or at least by vertical and horizontal measurements taken from an existing model to be copied.[7] Inasmuch as all the important plans were drawn upon papyrus, they have not been preserved, with the single exception of the plan for the tomb of Ramses IV in the Turin papyrus.[8]

For all simple building instructions the working drawings were only rough sketches made upon flat flakes of limestone, called *ostraca*. These flakes of stone, as used by architects, builders, scribes, and artists, furnished a cheap and available surface on which to make studies; but they were by necessity small, and the plans on them were never drawn to scale. There are three such flakes in the Cairo Museum: one with a plan of the tomb of Ramses IX[9] another showing the elevation of a doorway,[10] and a third showing a builder's plan (Plate LXXV–6) intended as a general guide for the foreman in working out various dimensions.[11] This plan has a central axis as a means of controlling the symmetry; the spaces between the columns, between the walls and the columns, and the size of the columns, are indicated by "ticks" on the edge of the plan, each "tick" representing a cubit; and the main dimensions of the building are written at the bottom in hieratic. An *ostracon* in the British Museum, of the XVIII Dynasty from Deir el-Bahari, gives the plan of a shrine within a semi-covered court, which was probably made by the architect, or by the foreman for his gang.[12] The plan on the *ostracon* recalls the sanctuary of Hatshepsut at Medinet Habu, but there is very little resemblance between its proportions and a scaled drawing based upon the given measurements.

There is also an architect's plan of an estate, on a wooden panel,[13] and a sketch of an architect's project for setting out trees in front of Mentuhotep's temple at Deir el-Bahari.[14] This last

[5] The cubit was about 20.6 in., but varied in different periods from 20.1 to 20.77 in.

[6] Clarke and Engelbach, *Ancient Egyptian Masonry,* p. 46.

[7] Gunn, *Annales du Service,* XXV, p. 197; Clarke and Engelbach, *op. cit.,* Fig. 53.

[8] H. Carter and A. Gardiner, *Journal of Egyptian Archaeology,* IV (1917), pp. 130-158, Pl. XXIX; Clarke and Engelbach *op. cit.,* Fig. 49.

[9] Daressy, *Ostraca* (Catalogue général du Musée du Caire), Pl. XXXII, No. 25184; *Revue archéologique,* XXXII (1898), p. 235; Clarke and Engelbach, *op. cit.,* Fig. 50.

[10] Clarke and Engelbach, *op. cit.,* Fig. 52.

[11] R. Engelbach, *Annales du Service,* XXVII, p. 72.

[12] S. R. K. Glanville, "Working Plan for a Shrine," *Journal of Egyptian Archaeology,* XVI (1930), p. 237.

[13] N. de G. Davies, *Journal of Egyptian Archaeology,* IV, p. 194.

[14] H. E. Winlock, *Bulletin of the Metropolitan Museum of Art,* XVI (1922), Part II, p. 26; Clarke and Engelbach, *op cit.,* Fig. 59.

plan, drawn upon two pieces of limestone from the ambulatory of the temple, represents the temple and ramp on a curiously small scale compared with the squares for the planting. Instead the building is a mere symbol. Also the sketch shows the corrections which were made when the designer discovered that his actual façade was not symmetrical, and therefore would not allow of four rows of trees on each side of the causeway. This lack of scale, which is characteristic of all Egyptian plans, is indicative of the Egyptian's attitude towards architecture. Proportions were matters of convention, and not problems of design and æsthetic effect. As in all the trades, the Egyptian builders acquired a practical method of attaining their ends, but seem to have had little interest in making their technical conventions more logical and precise.

The architects undoubtedly had accurate outline elevations for all important details, which were precise copy-book patterns (Plate LXXV–1), carefully squared, and hence capable of being enlarged to any size. The one example which has been preserved is a working drawing of a shrine from Ghorab, presumably of the XVIII Dynasty. It is a papyrus with the outlines in black and the square in red. This quadrated method of copying paintings, sculpture, and architecture shows the meticulous emphasis which was placed upon duplication, and helps to account for the lack of scale in so much Egyptian art. If the mechanical devices of the craftsmen allowed them to make a small object very large without altering either its proportions or its details, then the patrons and architects were not critics of scaled proportions, because the Egyptians looked upon bigness, like everlastingness, as a concept rather than as an æsthetic experience.

In addition to the working drawings already considered, the Egyptian artists depicted buildings in their reliefs and paintings. These graphic representations, while often very detailed and complicated, are nearly always difficult for us to interpret. In the first place, the Egyptians never used perspective, and in the second place, it never occurred to a craftsman to sit down in front of a building with the purpose of showing how the building looked to him. All Egyptian forms of imagery were ideographic and consisted of memory images which were in part representational and in part conventionally symbolic. The picture of one of the pylons of the Temple of Amon-Re at Karnak, in the tomb of the priest Amenhotpesi-se,[15] might be any pylon with two seated colossi in front of it. On the other hand the view of the front pylon of the Aten temple at Tell el-Amarna (Plate XLII-3) shows an open colonnade in front of the gateway. Because this portico had two rows of columns the artist put one row above another, so that they look like superimposed orders.

As a rule the Egyptian draftsman combined the two most descriptively significant aspects of a building, its plan and its elevation. The elevation, however, was not by necessity a single exterior view from one side. More often there was a series of elevations, one for each important section of the plan, flattened out upon the ground plan (Plate LXXIV–4). In making this descriptive combination of several mental aspects of a building, the artist sought to convey the greatest amount of essential information, and it is for this reason that the modern student, bound by habit to photographic and visual experience, and somewhat in doubt as to what the Egyptian considered essen-

[15] N. de G. Davies, *The Tombs of Two Officials* (1923), Pl. XIV; L. Borchardt, *Zur Baugeschichte des Amonstempels von Karnak*, p. 28.

PLATE LXXV: GRAPHIC CONVENTIONS

1

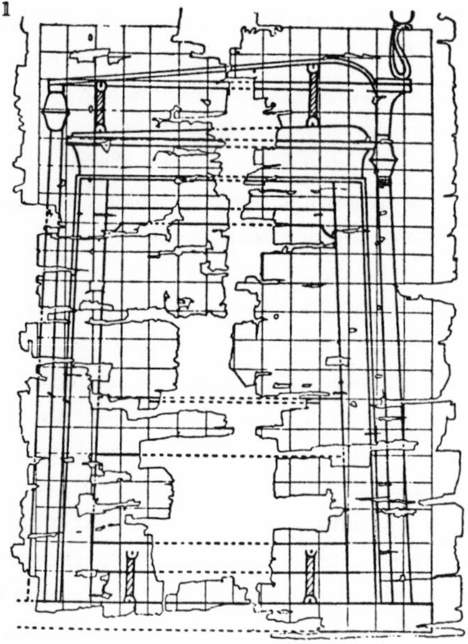

2

3

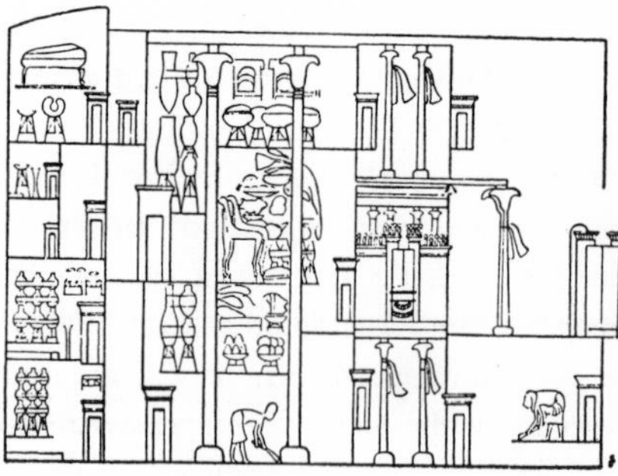

4

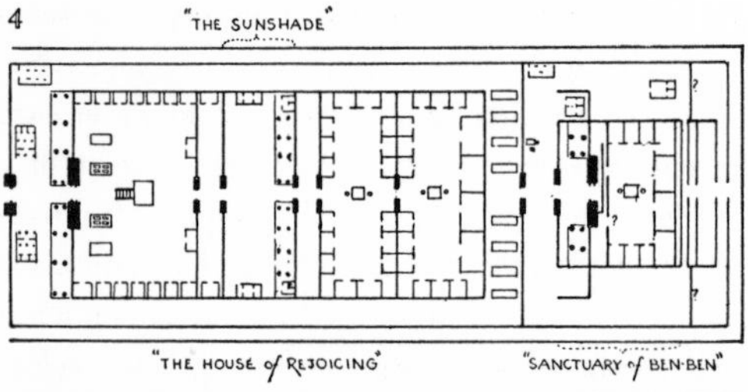

5

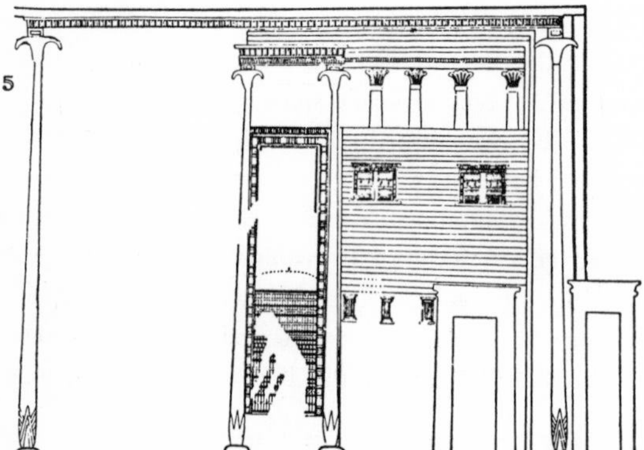

6

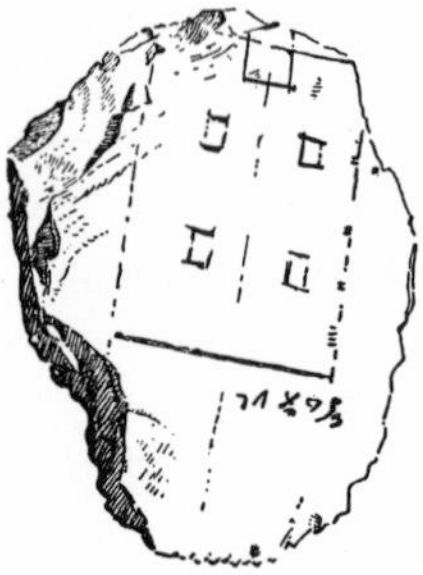

tials, finds it difficult to translate his drawing back into reality. For example, the XVIII Dynasty drawing of the so-called house of Neferhotep (Plate LXXV–5) in his tomb at Thebes is "not much better than a hieroglyphic sign of indeterminate value, only the general meaning of which can at present be surmised by us."[16] We cannot be sure what details represent interior or exterior, what is convention rather than fact, and what is mere expedience in order to compress all essential details into the limited space.

Frequent efforts have been made to restore the destroyed palace of Akhenaten from the representations of it in the tomb paintings of Tell el-Amarna,[17] but all the drawings are no more than very general memory images when compared to what the recent excavations have revealed of the actual plan of the palace.[18] The two most interesting drawings of the palace are the front and side views from the tomb of the high priest Meryra (Plate LXXV–2, 3). The front view consists of a series of elevations of successive sections of the palace superimposed above one another in separate registers. The lowest register shows the three gateways into the outer court, and even here there is the presumption that the artist added the third gateway for symmetry; the second register depicts the actual front of the palace, with the Pavilion of Appearances in the middle and a colonnade on either side; above the façade comes the interior, still preserving the triple division, and with the Hall of Appearances laid out for a royal banquet; then there is a corridor; and finally, in the last register, are the storerooms and bedroom of the king. In this last section the drawing carefully shows that the back rooms, or at least the royal bedroom, had a ventilator on the roof. The other drawing is a quasi-section with pavilion and doorways swung into front view, and the contents of the room now arranged in registers within their architectural units.

The significant point to be kept in mind is that the few people of importance who ever saw these drawings knew the palace intimately, and for them the drawings were only symbols. The pictures conveyed the idea of a palace with the elements of a royal abode clearly specified and distinctly readable; but the actual proportions and the number of small rooms and columns were of no significance.

16 N. de G. Davies, *New York Bulletin of the Metropolitan Museum of Art,* XVI (1921), Part II, p. 26.

17 N. de G. Davies, *The Rock Tombs of El-Amarna* I, p. 23, Pl. XVIII; Erman (*Egypt,* p. 177-180) first interpreted the drawings as representing the house of the priest Meryra; J. Capart, *Egyptian Art* (1923), Chapter X, "Conventions of Egyptian Drawings"; Herbert Ricke, *Der Grundriss des Amarna-Wohnhauses* (1932), p. 58-63.

18 Page 221.

PLATE LXXV

1. Side elevation of a shrine on a papyrus of XVIII Dyn. from Ghorab (Clarke and Engelbach, *op. cit.,* Fig. 48).
2. Front view of Amarna palace from tomb of Meryra (N. de G. Davies, *The Rock Tombs of El-Amarna,* I, Pl. XXVI).
3. Side view of same palace (*op. cit.,* Pl. XVIII).
4. Plan of the Great Temple of Aten at Amarna, made from pictorial descriptions (Davies, *op. cit.,* II, p. 20).
5. The *harim* of King Ay, usually called the house of Neferhotep (Davies, *Metropolitan Museum Studies,* I, Fig. 3).
6. Plan on *ostracon* from Thebes (Clarke and Engelbach, *op. cit.,* Fig. 51).

Obviously there were many more columns than the artist had space to represent. Also the number of columns might be varied in any one of the king's palaces. Hence their exact number was not particularly essential. On the other hand the number and position of the doorways were important. Doors conditioned action and marked the prescribed stages of ritualistic procedure. At one door only servants might enter; at another the visitor to the divine king had to prostrate himself; while at the central door the incarnate god appeared to greet his followers, to present gifts, and to render justice. Therefore in Egyptian art the doorway is ideographically one of the most essential elements of a building, and as such was emphasized in the drawings.

The most detailed architectural drawings are the series of painted reliefs from the Amarna tombs representing the Great Temple of Aten.[19] No one can study these drawings without agreeing with Davies, who says, "The remarkable correspondence in detail, which all the laxity exhibited by the artists does not invalidate, makes it plain that these are studied views of the great building. Though it cannot be claimed for them that they satisfy the requirements of architectural plans, in the main they present us with a clear and complete knowledge of the building." Yet when the plan of the Temple of Aten (Plate LXXV–4), made up from the various Egyptian representations, is compared with the recent excavations of the temple,[20] we are forced to one of three explanations to explain the discrepancies: first, that the Egyptian craftsmen were very careless about what we would consider essential architectural facts; second, that the excavators were overimaginative in restoring the meager data which remained of the temple; or third, that the Egyptian drawings represent a first building of the temple, while the modern restorations show a later rebuilding. In spite of the unsatisfactory results these Amarna drawings give us a detailed insight into Egyptian graphic methods, and offer us our only check on the accuracy of their architectural drawings.

ARCHITECTS

The Egyptians, it has been seen, venerated usage because they valued the useful. Their practical habits of thought, which at first gave them such efficient methods and later became such a deterrent to change, made them the first people in the history of civilization to honor the architect as an efficient man. To them the master-builder was the personification of intelligence. Therefore, from the time when the use of stone made building both a royal privilege and a difficult profession, the king's architect was an executive, at times a friend and counselor of the ruler, and in some instances the most powerful person in the realm after the Pharaoh. The first master-builder to be honored was Kanofer, "architect of Upper and Lower Egypt" under Khasekemui, who was the first king to have his tomb chamber made of cut stone. Following Kanofer came the great Imhotep,[21] who was perhaps his son. In addition to being the first architect to develop a monumental architecture in stone, he was, as his

[19] The whole temple is represented three times, twice in the tomb of Meryra (Davies, *The Rock Tombs of El Amarna,* I, Pls. x[a], xxv) and once in the tomb of Panehesy (*op. cit.,* II, Pls. XVIII, XIX), while part of it is represented five times in other tombs (*op. cit.,* p. 20).

[20] Pages 172-178.

[21] Page 61.

inscription reads, "The Chancellor of the King of Lower Egypt, Chief under the King of [Upper Egypt], Administrator of the Great Mansion, Hereditary Noble, Heliopolitan High Priest, Imhotep." So great was his fame that he became a legendary figure, the mythical father of medicine, a sage whose wisdom schoolboys copied and memorized, and, finally, two thousand years after his death he was worshiped as a divinity. As late as the Fifth Century B.C. architects traced their descent from him through a direct line of builders.[22]

In the V Dynasty Senezemib was "the chief of all works of the King" in addition to his other duties of vizier, chief scribe, and chief judge,[23] while in the VI Dynasty Merire-meriptah-onekh was a master-builder and "sole companion of the king."[24] During the Middle Kingdom there were several architects who were distinguished administrators. In the XI Dynasty Amenemhet[25] was an hereditary Prince, governor of the city, vizier, and favorite of the king. Under Senwosret I in the XII Dynasty, Senwosret-ankh[26] was "Priest of Ptah," "Chief of the Artisans of the Two Houses," "Dean of the College of Scribes," and "Royal Sculptor and Builder"; Meri[27] was the architect entrusted with constructing Senwosret's mortuary temple at Lisht; Simontu[28] was a royal scribe, a register of grain, and "chief of all works in the entire land"; and Mentuhotep[29] was an hereditary prince, vizier, chief judge, prophet of Mat, "supreme head in judgment, putting matters in order," "good at listening" and chief of all works.

There were, however, no architects in Egyptian tradition comparable to Imhotep until the XVIII Dynasty. In the New Kingdom Amenhotep, son of Hapu,[30] was a royal builder of Amenhotep III who acquired such fame for his wisdom that he was probably deified in his own lifetime and considered by subsequent ages as the equal of Imhotep. Amenhotep was a member of a noble family, "born of the lady Yatu," and began his public career as a scribe. Although during his long life of about eighty years he became a friend and counselor of the king, chief of all the king's works, steward of the king's daughter, chief of the prophets of Horus, and festival leader of Amon, he was proud of being the "King's Scribe." During his lifetime he was granted many special privileges, including the right to erect for himself a mortuary temple of almost royal proportions at Thebes,[31] and was given a statue in the temple of Amon (Plate LXXVII–4)

Another distinguished builder of the XVIII Dynasty, although never deified, was the efficient Ineni[32] who in his long life served Amenhotep I, Thutmose I and II, Hatshepsut and Thutmose III. He was an "hereditary prince," "chief of all works in Karnak" and "overseer of the double gran-

22 In 495-491 B.C. the architect Khnum-ib-re gives his family tree, listing twenty-five master-builders back to Imhotep, J. L. Hurry, *Imhotep*, p. 193; H. Brugsch-Bey, *A History of Egypt under the Pharaohs*, II (1879), p. 299.

23 Breasted, *op. cit.*, I, 271-273.

24 Breasted, *op. cit.*, I, 298, 299.

25 Breasted, *op. cit.*, I, 442-445.

26 A. Lansing, "The Egyptian Expedition of 1932-33," *Bulletin of the Metropolitan Museum of Art*, Sect. II (1933), p. 11.

27 Breasted, *op. cit.*, I, 509.

28 Breasted, *op. cit.*, I, 598.

29 Breasted, *op. cit.*, I, 531.

30 Breasted, *op. cit.*, II, 912-927; G. Maspero, *New Light on Ancient Egypt* (1909), pp. 189-195.

31 Page 135.

32 Breasted, *op. cit.*, II, 43-46, 99-108, 115-118 and 340-343.

ary of Amon." As "chief of all works" most of his time was spent supervising the rebuilding of various parts of the "estate of Amon" at Karnak, but he also "inspected the excavation of the rock cut tomb of his majesty (Thutmose I), alone, no one seeing, no one hearing." Ineni was proud of his wisdom in the construction of this royal tomb, and it may have been his suggestion which persuaded the kings of the XVIII Dynasty to conceal their burial places in the Valley of the Kings. Few architects to-day can record, as Ineni did, "I continued powerful in peace, and met with no misfortune, my years were spent in gladness—*I never failed, but always obeyed superior orders.*" Great he was, if in all his dealings with Egyptian labor he could truthfully say, as he did, "I never blasphemed sacred things."

THE ARCHITECT SENMUT, SKETCH IN HIS TOMB, THEBES
H. E. Winlock, *Bulletin of the Metropolitan Museum of Art,* XXIII (1928), p. 36, Fig. 35.

What is perhaps equally curious, from a modern standpoint, is Ineni's failure to praise any of his architectural works as creations of which he was proud. He was proud of his wisdom in excavating the tomb of Thutmose I, he was proud to do that which "the god of the city loved," but in his tomb he merely mentions that he was "the foreman of foremen." The dignities and duties which he most valued are those included in his final mortuary inscription, "the revered dignitary, the overseer of the granary of Amon, the scribe, Ineni, triumphant."

Contemporary with Ineni during the later part of his life, but far excelling him in power, was Senmut,[33] "architect of all the works of the Queen." He rose to power with Hatshepsut, during her regency, became her chief counselor, "secure in favor and given audience alone," and was undoubtedly her adviser when she declared herself king. As "Chief Guardian of the King's Daughter," "Overseer of all the Works of Amon," "Governor of the Royal Palace" Superintendent of the Private Apartments, of the Bathroom, and of the Royal Bedrooms, he was practically a collaborator in the government. There are statues of him holding the queen's daughter in his lap (Plate LXXVII–6). He built the queen's mortuary temple at Deir el-Bahari, was responsible for the quarrying and transportation

[33] H. E. Winlock, "The Egyptian Expedition 1925-1927," *Bulletin of the Metropolitan Museum of Art,* XXIII (1928), Sect. II, pp. 34-58; Breasted, *op. cit.,* II, 345-368.

of her great obelisks from Aswân to Karnak, and supervised her works at Karnak and in the temple of Luxor.

He could truthfully record, as he did in his tomb, "I was the greatest of the great in the whole land—one to whom judges listened and whose very silence was eloquent." But he shows his vanity and ambition, not because he had it recorded, "there was nothing from the beginning of time which I did not know," but because he planned a secret tomb directly under the queen's mortuary temple and had his portrait executed (undoubtedly with the queen's permission) behind every door in the queen's temple. The significant fact is, however, that Senmut, like all the other great architects of Egypt, was above everything else an administrator. Starting as a "Steward of Amon," and always keeping that title, he was Overseer of Amon's Granaries, Storehouses, Fields, Gardens, Cattle, and Slaves. To these duties he added the supervision of the royal household.

The XVIII Dynasty seems to have had an exceptional number of capable builders, for besides the famous ones already mentioned, there was the hereditary noble Rekhmire [34] who was a chief of works under Thutmose III, and with Akhenaten at Tell el-Amarna there was the vizier Ramose,[35] and Bek,[36] who was the son of a master sculptor. In the XIX Dynasty Hui [37] worked for Seti I, and Hatey [38] records how he erected the great columns in the Hypostyle Hall at Karnak for Ramses II. During the XX Dynasty Ramses-nakht [39] was First Prophet of Amon and chief of works, and Amenhotep [40] was a king's scribe and High Priest of Amon. Several hundred years later it is recorded that Haremsaf [41] in the XXII Dynasty built the Great Pylon of Bubastides at Karnak, and was commended by the king for neither sleeping at night nor slumbering by day, "but building the eternal work without ceasing."

The many and varied activities of these Egyptian architects, of which they were supremely proud, show how fully they were men of affairs rather than creative artists. The fact that many of them began as scribes makes it evident that the ability to write and transmit orders was the first and most important requisite of a chief of works. None of the Egyptian architects in their sepulchral eulogies ever mention the appearance of their buildings.[42] Like Senmut they record with great satisfaction all their duties, honors, and actions; they stress their unhesitating obedience to superior orders; but they never praise the beauty and appearance of their creations. They were respected for their wisdom, and not for their originality and taste, because taste, æsthetic discrimination, and creative originality were not criteria of ability in the practice of a profession dedicated by royal command to the perpetuation of tradition.

[34] Breasted, *op. cit.*, II, 757; P. E. Newberry, *The Life of Rakhmara* (1900).
[35] Breasted, *op. cit.*, II, 936.
[36] Breasted, *op. cit.*, II, 975.
[37] Breasted, *op. cit.*, III, 210.
[38] Breasted, *op. cit.*, III, 513.
[39] Breasted, *op. cit.*, IV, 466.
[40] Breasted, *op. cit.*, IV, 491.
[41] Breasted, *op. cit.*, IV, 706, 708.
[42] In the XII Dynasty Meri, in describing the mortuary temple of his master, says, "I myself rejoiced, and my heart was glad at that which I had executed"; but the inscription makes it clear that Meri was really proud of the height of the columns and the great gates "towering heavenward." Also he records, "I was a zealous servant, great in character, amiable in love."

11. *THE ARCHITECTURE AS CULTURAL EXPRESSION*

> *My beloved son, Menkheperre, how beautiful is this beautiful monument, which thou has made for my beloved son, King of Upper and Lower Egypt, Khekure* (Senwosret III). *Thou has perpetuated his name forever, that thou mayest live.*—Breasted, II, 174

WHEN WE UNDERTAKE TO ESTIMATE the art of an extinct culture, we are confronted by barriers of time, customs, and habits of thought. Hence we see the danger of imposing our modern prejudices upon the unsuspecting Egyptians. It is difficult for man to resist the "egotistical enjoyment"[1] of finding what he values in the past, and it is impossible for him to be impersonal when dealing with human activities. In fact, the history of Egyptian architecture developed in the previous chapters must be unconsciously colored by the author's interpretation of Egyptian culture. Nevertheless, since any act of exposition involves interpretation, and interpretation necessitates evaluation, it is desirable to face the interpretation squarely, for at least it makes the issues clear, even if the deductions prove unsatisfactory.

The Greeks, like Herodotus, were impressed by what they considered to be the wisdom of Egypt. Seeing the colossal size and expressionless passivity of the Great Sphinx at Gizeh (Plate LXXVI–1), they assumed that something very wise and mysterious must lie behind such an otherwise irrational effort. Therefore they interpreted the Sphinx as all-knowing, a creature of another world who transcends the actual and impassively looks through the past into the future. Men to-day are still reluctant to admit that the Sphinx-head, expressionless like all Egyptian sculpture, is only the mask of a dead Pharaoh who, like all Egyptians, was interested in preserving the material form of the living, in order to serve a useful purpose in the hereafter. Not unlike the Sphinx, the inanimate head of the mummified Seti I also looks out into the unknown with a mysteriously expressionless fixity (Plate LXXVI–3). It, too, is a material form devoid of life and preserved because the Egyptians believed literally in the idea of holding in death to the material aspect of physical reality. At the outset, therefore, we must entertain the possibility that the Egyptians expected from art something so much more practical than anything we may hope to find in it, and based their expectation upon naïve assumptions which seem to us so incredible and superstitious as to make it impossible for us to understand their conceptions of art and life in exactly the same way that they did.

The most stimulating interpreter of Egyptian art, Wilhelm Worringer,[2] points out what the Egyptians and their creations so obviously lacked in the forced stimulation of a hothouse culture; but because this brilliant critic had no sympathy for their cultural and environmental limitations, he fails to

[1] H. Schäfer, *Von Ægyptische Kunst* (1919).
[2] W. Worringer, *Egyptian Art* (Eng. trans.) (1928).

explain why the poor Egyptians were so sadly lacking in those invigorating, sensuous, and emotional qualities which he, the intensely modern German, values so highly. Egyptian builders, it is true, had little feeling for organic unity, were devoid of any enjoyment of space relations, and were persistently rigidified in all their habits and methods. But was the lack of these qualities so exceptional? The Greeks had many of the same limitations during the archaic period of their art, and they developed no feeling for interior space and little enjoyment of architectural space composition until the Hellenistic Age, when, it must be remembered, they had become self-conscious and critical observers, rather than unconscious and convinced believers. Even though the Romans acquired a remarkable architecture of interior space and decorative effects, they never attained to the Greek sense of plastic form. Hence if we start by using space, proportions, organic unity, and "functionalism" as criteria of what Egyptian architecture should have been, or was meant to be, we will end up hopelessly entangled in questions of taste.

HABITS OF IMAGERY. No analysis can attribute one set of mental habits to architecture and another set to sculpture and painting. The most direct approach to the Egyptians' conception of art is to consider their method of representing the objects of nature. The Egyptians were primarily concerned with the descriptive clarity of artistic forms because of their interest in the magical significance and traditional meaning of those forms. Therefore they tended to treat art like a conventionalized language, in which there was a rigid dependence upon established usage in order to preserve the overwhelming importance of the idea. *Like all primitive arts, Egyptian art was persistently ideographic, dealing always with the fundamental, communal ideas, rather than with transient and personal experience.*

As a result of this conceptual rather than sensuous use of art, Egyptian objects were not copied directly from nature but were made up of the most memorable, significant, and hence traditional aspect of things. A bowl of flowers was never pictured in any foreshortening which would distort the actual and permanent shape of the bowl and perhaps conceal the equally significant presence of the flowers as ritualistic offerings and fertility emblems. Instead, the bowl was drawn in profile and the flowers were diagrammatically placed above it, seen either from above or in side view (Plate LXXVI–2). In the same fashion, human figures were made up from outlined profiles of the most distinctive shapes of the different parts of the body. This so-called "fractional method" of combining memory images of different views of the same object resulted in what seems to us either fascinating abstractions of nature, or unnatural wholes. That the Egyptian was ignorant of perspective was only natural, since he was never thinking of how figures appeared to him personally at any given moment. Had he thought of it, perspective would have been totally unsatisfactory, for it would have distorted the specific and inherent reality of things, reduced the idea of a man to a mere dot in the landscape, concealed the essential by the unessential, made servants larger and more important than their masters merely because they chanced to be in the foreground, and in every way would have confused, and even denied, those ideas of nature upon which the Egyptian felt himself absolutely dependent. Thus the Egyptian had no thought of transcribing in art what he as an individual chanced to see, but was

PLATE LXXVI:

1

2

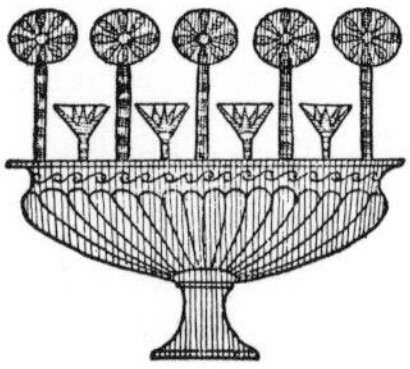

3

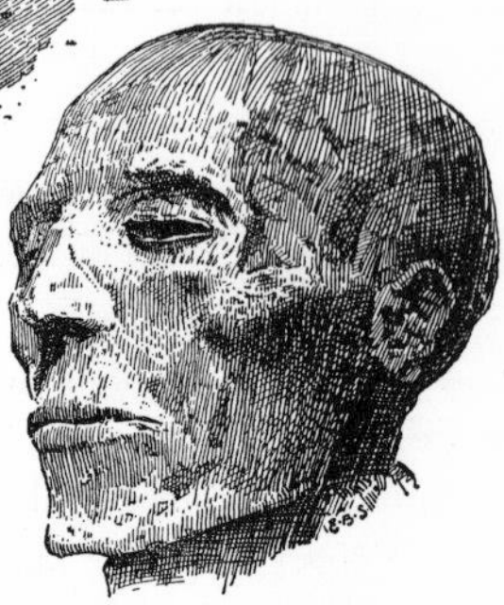

4

5

only interested in what he as a member of a collective group had acquired by communal rule and precept, for "primitive people, like children, retain in their memory what has taken place before their eyes far less than what has been transmitted to their ears." [3]

The Egyptian craftsman put none of his own bodily sympathy into his figurative art because he was not recreating a personal experience. Instead, he was faithfully describing in a prescribed language an idea to which he was so bound by his beliefs that he had no interest in experiencing the forms as organic and living wholes. When an Egyptian craftsman depicted an act of offering (Plate LXXVI–4) it was inconceivable, even sacrilegious, for him to imagine himself as the king making a gift to the god. As a result he did not feel the weight of the basket, its pressure upon the hands, and its pull upon the muscles of the shoulders. To the modern artist such impersonality is unnatural. Picasso relives the act before he makes it (Plate LXXVI–5); he does not add the balancing boy to the ball, and merely juxtapose the man and the box; instead he feels how one element conditions the other, so that the man's hips spread as his weight bears down upon the box, while the boy's body is tense with action as it tries to preserve its unity with the ball.

The curious feature of Egyptian representational art is not that its figures are lifeless and unemotional pictographs,—*a mere adding together of traditional memory images without organic unity.* Primitive art always adheres to strict ideographic conventions. What is revealing, however, is the Nilotic complacency which allowed the craftsmen for three thousand years to go on repeating the same conventions and ideas with magnificent clarity, unsurpassed dexterity and unquestioning assurance.

For such finality the craftsmen had to work in precise linear outlines, bringing all essential elements up to the same frontal plane. The type of line used shows the strength and limitations of this impersonal art, for Egyptian outlines are unmodulated and unaccented. In many instances they surround a whole figure without any variation in the width of the line and apparently without the brush having been lifted from the surface. Technically such lines are astonishingly skilful, but they are emotionally dead.

The same conditions must have prevailed in sculpture as in painting, even though the modern critics differ in their opinions as to the results. Some contemporary writers, themselves hypnotized by abstractions, praise the "cubistic," "plastic" and "abstract" directness of Egyptian sculpture.[4] Yet it may be argued that Egyptian sculpture was neither conceived nor enjoyed plastically. It is true that

[3] Léon Brunschvig, *History and Philosophy*, p. 27.
[4] H. Frankfort, "On Egyptian Art," *Journal of Egyptian Archaeology*, XVIII (1923), pp. 33-49.

PLATE LXXVI

1. Great Sphinx at Gizeh before excavation.
2. Egyptian vase (Prisse d'Avennes).
3. Head of mummified Seti I.
4. Relief from Temple of Seti I, Abydos.
5. Modern painting by Picasso.

PLATE LXXVII: SCULPTURE

1

2

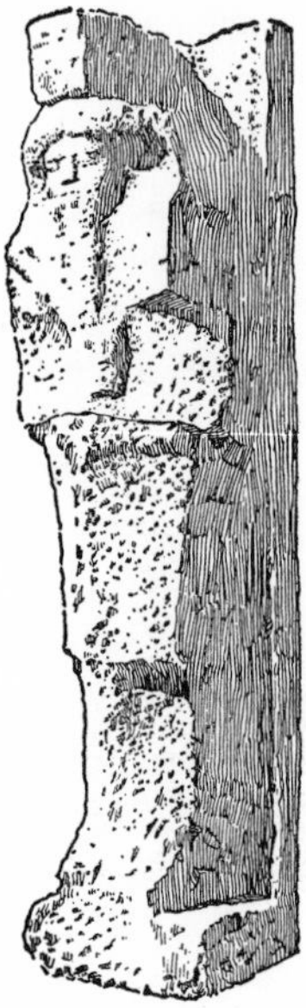

3

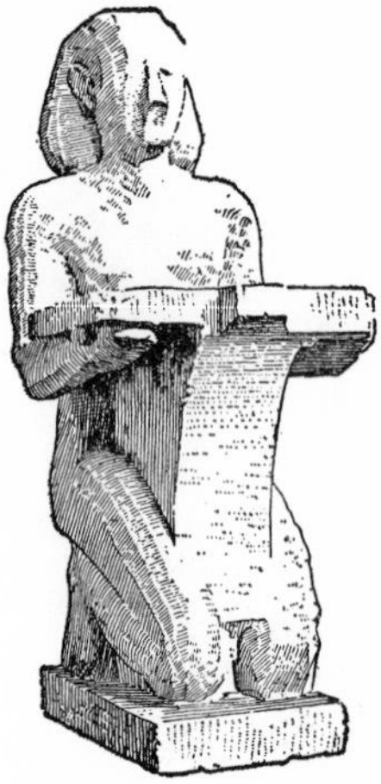

4

5

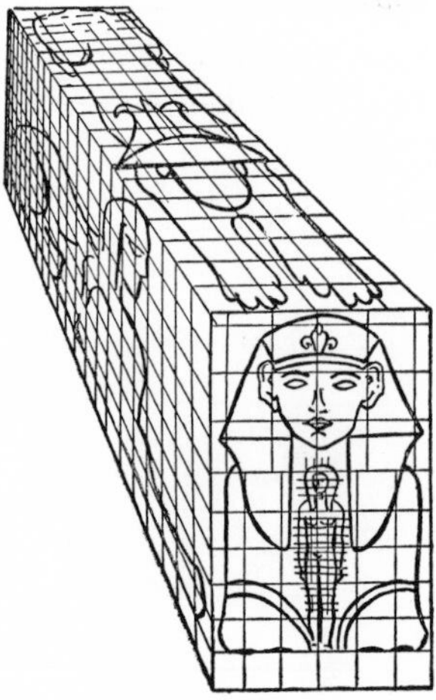

6

nearly all Egyptian sculpture in the round appears solidly three-dimensional, looks rectilinear and seems geometrically organized; but the modern, seeing these figures without any interest in ideological purpose and with little realization of the Egyptian methods of laying out figures in the round, is only aware of his own sensuous and æsthetic experience. He recognizes the apparent solidity of the forms, and assumes that it was the result of a conscious choice, instead of realizing that it was the product of the same linear conventions used in the painting.

Unfinished Egyptian statues or representations of their own methods of carving figures in the round (Plate LXXVII–2, 3,) show how little the apparent abstractions were plastically conceived. Instead, the traditional and linear memory images were drawn upon the four sides of a rectangular block of stone and the profiles were cut through until the planes intersected before any modeling was undertaken. Partly because of this conventional means of making form, and partly because of the hieratic formality of the ideas, Egyptian statues are *always frontal, mechanically axial, and with the parts not organically articulated*—characteristics which are equally true of their architectural composition. Since the statues were conceived ideographically, like the paintings, they are immobile and tensionless as if each figure were a soldier at attention, or a man in the fixed posture of either his social or professional status (Plate LXXVII–1).

While the faces of Egyptian statues are at times remarkable portraits, since individual appearance, like social posture, was a physical distinction by which a man could preserve his identity and his rank in the after life, they are nevertheless masklike in their expressionless immobility. Every statue was a possible embodiment for the spirit after death, and any deviation from essential fact and social convention meant both a loss of permanency and a change in the existing and prescribed status. Therefore there had to be fixed postures for the various social grades, and the purpose of such art was too seriously concerned with material reality to be interested in transient moods and fleeting expressions. As Worringer says, "That there is *not* one kind of naturalism only but several, that above all there is one naturalism of primitive stages and another of the advanced stage of civilization, is, of course, incontestable. Primitive naturalism is not an affair of the eyes but of the whole man and his spiritual attitude towards his experience of nature." [5]

[5] Worringer, *op. cit.*, p. 27.

PLATE LXXVII

1. Statue of Ranofer, IV Dyn., Cairo Museum.
2. Unfinished figure, III Dyn., Saqqara (Lauer, *La Pyramide à Degrés*, Pl. XCIX).
3. Unfinished statue, Saïtic Period, Cairo Museum (C. C. Edgar, "Sculptor's Studies and Unfinished Works," *Catalogue général du Musée du Caire*, 1906, Pl. IV).
4. Amenhotep, Son of Hapu, XVIII Dyn., Cairo Museum.
5. Block drawing for a sphinx after a papyrus (H. Schäfer und W. Andrae, *Die Kunst des alten Orient*, 1925, Fig. 25).
6. Senmut and Princess Nefrure, XVIII Dyn., Berlin Museum.

ARCHITECTURAL LIMITATIONS. How, then, do such limitations of the Egyptian's experience of nature explain his architecture? If the Egyptian in the representational arts was satisfied to add traditional parts together as a descriptive substitute for an organic unity, if he dealt primarily with the non-sensuous aspects of nature, created with memory images, and was unable to stand back so as to see his forms critically either in relation to himself or to the life about him, it would be disconcerting to find him behaving differently in his forms of architectural expression. In what ways, therefore, could his inherently ideographic habits of thought be reflected in the structural considerations of architecture? While his earliest architectural efforts were restrained by tectonic limitations, we have already seen that the Egyptian did develop his trabeated principle of stone construction beyond the mere structural requirements of the post and lintel. Ideas transformed construction into a consistent and persistent style of architecture. The style, however, had its limitations when measured by subsequent styles whose purposes were totally outside the needs and desires of the Egyptian environment.

Even the Egyptian's most ambitious plans are indicative of his creative limitations. In addition to the imitative character of nearly all his types of building, the Egyptian, when erecting his largest temples, was satisfied to enlarge traditional parts, adding them together uncritically and inorganically to make still larger wholes (Plate XLV–2). Unlike modern designers, he did not feel the necessity to think himself into his plan before building it; he did not go around the building in his mind, viewing it critically from all angles; he never imaginatively led crowds of people through it; and he never imposed, as it were, one tentative design upon another until he had a theoretically ideal arrangement of all the parts. He had no need of such methods because he was only the servant of the Pharaoh and because most of his buildings were established and venerated types. Temples, as we have seen, were not places ostensibly where people congregated for communal services, but instead they were the royal dwellings of the gods, where a time-honored ritual was observed. Therefore they were a relatively fixed concept which had to be preserved if the king, who was an incarnation of the gods, was to be assured in the hereafter of such formal protection and service as he believed to be essential to his continued existence. Continuity, and the effort to thwart time, destruction, and death, bound the architect to the service of tradition.

Nevertheless, in his planning, the Egyptian builder advanced beyond the early expedient of a casual agglutination of separate hut units. He evolved architecture, even though his designs always adhered symmetrically to a longitudinal axis along which the traditional temple units of pylon, court, hypostyle hall, and *sekos* were repeated in straight horizontal extension. As in sculpture, the adherence to this axial symmetry was primarily the result of the formal, hieratic conventions of the social and religious ritual which emphasized the procession; but at the same time the axial convention gave the builders a simple and balanced control over the otherwise unassimilated elements, and so made their architecture ordered even if it was not organized. The endless repetition of halls and corridors, as well as the New Kingdom's desire for magnitude, were the instinctive result of the primitive desire for certainty. Like the monotonous reiteration of long and formalized prayers for the dead, like the insistence of Ramses II on having his doubtful victory at Kadesh carved upon every possible surface, and like the countless altars which Akhenaten set up in his Aten temple, the Egyptian iteration of architectural units was all a part of the same, fearful quest for certainty. The Bellman understood the conviction which comes to man from repetition when he assured skeptics about the Snark, "What I tell you three times is true."

Egyptian plans also show how little any feeling for space entered into the creation of the architecture. The isolated interior rooms seem either carved out of massive piles of masonry or compressed around a forest of columns. Is this "space shyness," however, exceptional enough in the history of architecture, especially when conditioned by the limitations of the trabeated principle of construction, to be considered "one of the most characteristic traits of Egyptian architecture"? [6] Worringer forces the issue of space upon the Egyptians and as good as says, let us not excuse the Egyptians for such an unnatural and unspiritual disregard of space, inasmuch as they went out of their way to increase the space-filling size of their columns and walls out of all relation to structural necessity. "The complete indifference of the Egyptian attitude towards the spatial potency of existence," he writes, "was thus converted into a carefully considered renunciation of the space-factor, and the setting of this renunciation against the deepest metaphysical backgrounds was in agreement with the tradition of Egyptian profundity and wisdom."

The issue, however, is not the extent to which "space is always only a form of the relationship of the ego to the surrounding world"; it is the reason why the Egyptians had so little interest in space. No culture still at grips with the phenomena of nature is interested in the intangible. Even the Greeks before the Hellenistic Age looked upon space as something vague, indefinite, and hence undesirable. Moreover, no treatment of the trabeated principle of architecture, dependent as it must be upon multiple points of support and narrow spans, can escape from the inherent limitations of the structural system. Why then should the Egyptians have developed a space architecture? They may have lacked any emotional or spiritual desire to escape from the constrictions of a prescribed existence; it may be granted that they had no subtle, metaphysical ideas about the freedom of space; but in a culture in which all beliefs were bound up with the primitive struggle for existence and were inevitably dependent upon a prescribed and uncontrolled reality, there could be no desire for any overpowering vacancy in which the individual would feel isolated. What Egyptian religion did not require was interior space for emotional transfiguration. Because the stone architecture was a sculptural imitation of venerated and specific house-forms, which had originated in wood and mud-brick, and because the stone itself, as well as its massive shapes, was developed in order to make the buildings more permanent and indestructible, the Egyptians had no need and no conception of tri-dimensional extension in any spiritual or æsthetic sense. Therefore it was impossible for them to make "a considered renunciation of the space-factor." The metaphysical valuations of space are so relatively modern as to be inconceivable in any but a highly individualistic and self-conscious age.

Architectural space must not be confused with mere voids between structural elements. Any room has physical or natural space, but it is not architectural space unless the height, character, and proportions of the enclosing surfaces have been consciously designed to make the space purposeful, scaled, articulate, and hence appreciable. Where there is architectural space, the relation between voids and

[6] Worringer, *op. cit.,* p. 80.

solids governs the design, and voids are the controlling consideration to which the structure is made subordinate. In this sense, Egyptian architecture had no feeling for space. Instead it exhibits an antithesis between solids and voids, so that at one moment we see the long aisles or corridors, and at another feel only the overpowering supports. Moreover, the enclosing walls are long and inarticulate expanses, suitable for the recording of pictographic themes in relief and paint, but never thought of as in any way reflecting the interior (Plate XLI–4). This is because the walls are never imaginatively freed from their primitive and tectonic inception as protective barriers. They bear, enclose, and cut off, but never express, because they are neutral, impersonal, and hence unemotional conventions of construction. The fact that Egyptian stone walls were so frequently plastered and covered like great bill-boards with painted reliefs on a white ground is evidence of how fully the Egyptians disregarded the expressive possibilities of walls, and how they failed to enjoy the texture and physical weight of stone. The only really strange characteristic is their inability to get away from the monotony of such primitive habits. When instinctive conventions are perpetuated for thousands of years in an iron formalism, they grow less wise, refuse to appear mysterious, and finally cease to be wholly natural. Back of this architecture there must have been an environmental despotism stronger and more deeply rooted than mere social tyranny.

In any treatment of trabeated construction the formal character of the upright post and its relation to the horizontal lintel are the two most indicative aspects of stylistic expression. The forms of Egyptian columns were the result of ideas totally different from the ordinary conception of supports in Classic and European architecture. The Greek column started out tectonic and imitative, somewhat like the Egyptian columns, but it gradually became an expression of the Greek's personal enjoyment of three-dimensional form and so took on something of the proportional and controlled vigor which he felt in his own body. Hence the imitative and traditional elements of the Greek column, such as the entasis, diminution, trachylion and echinus, which in the archaic architecture existed for their own sake and made the supports look soft and lifeless, were reduced to imperceptible subtleties or strengthened into plastic emphasis in a conscious effort to make the stone uprights look vigorously and elastically alive. Instead of adhering to time-honored usage, the Greek columns were proportionally related to the entablature in an organic fashion so that they would look strong enough to carry the apparent load with vigorous ease. At the same time, they were so integrated that their parts were subordinated to the whole, and a module of measurement was made to govern both the height and the breadth of all the parts in much the same fashion as the human body is proportioned.

No such bodily energy and personal awareness animated the sculptors of Egyptian columns. The columns followed no fixed rules and canons of proportion. At first under the influence of the slender wood and bundled reed prototypes, the stone columns were tall in proportion to their diameter; then as the weight of stone architraves became an inescapable consideration in the large temples, and mere size was considered both a symbol of power and an assurance of indestructibility, the columns grew shorter and stouter. Such as it was, the development was quite different from that of the Greek column, for in the Old Kingdom the columns vary in height from five and one-half to seven diameters, or even more, then get as heavy as four diameters in the New Kingdom, and finally lengthen out in the Ptolemaic period to five and one-half and six diameters.

From the outset, Egyptian columns were either structural or ideographic forms. In the end it was not the tectonic considerations so much as the symbolic ideas which dominated the architecture. The bracket capital of bundled reeds reproduced at Saqqara on Zoser's sepulchral palaces and chapels did not survive, while the symbolic lotus and papyrus columns were never abandoned. The bulge, or entasis, of Egyptian columns, being an imitation of plant-stalks, makes them look dropsical and flabby (Plate XXXIX–1). In such forms stone seems to lose its rigidity and so looks crushed by the weight upon it. The square abacus block of Egyptian columns, when it is a structural transition from the horizontal lintel to the vertical support, appears logical until the spreading papyrus capital is introduced between it and the column (Plate XLVI–2). Then the effect is, as Worringer says, of a "tensionless juxtaposition of two irreconcilable categories of architectural speech." Here, again, the columns are a combination of traditional elements, customary memory images, such as cavetto cornice, lintel, structural abacus block, symbolic capital, and naturalized shaft, all unreflectively added together into an inorganic whole.

As in the case of their other forms of expression, the reason why the Egyptians took no interest in the columns as an expression of organic unity was the persistence of the ideographic significance of the primitive idea. Columns were fertility emblems, symbols of the land, and of sacred plants which rose out of the fertilized soil to bring protection, permanency, and sustenance to the land and its people. Structurally, the columns began as poles, or bundles of reeds, on which were tied the palm fronds, the lotus and papyrus flowers (Plate LXXVIII). Back in the inner recesses of Egyptian memory, which never seems to have forgotten anything, was always a mental image of the earliest fertility shafts, made for the first shrines by binding together the *growing* stalks of the marshes and before which their ancestors had worshiped as they did before the *dedu* emblem of Osiris.[7] As long as such memories persisted, even in stereotyped forms, the Egyptians could have no interest in the apparent strength and texture of stone, and could never stand back to think critically of the organic relation between support and load, for they saw not the stone but the symbol.

As long as Egyptian columns are considered æsthetically by modern critics, they will continue to present a baffling contradiction between the "loud cubistic tones" of their mighty size and the "whisper" of the delicate bas-reliefs which cover them from base to capital. Viewed critically, most Egyptian columns present an antithesis of overpowering mass versus minutely elaborate surface. If the Egyptian enjoyed his columns in any æsthetic sense, which was it then that pleased him, for obviously he could not see the "pure tectonic abstractions" of his columns when he was close enough to decipher the cobwebs of hieroglyphs? The contradiction and its æsthetic implications disappear if we realized how completely the Egyptians valued mass, solidity, and bigness as an idea of durability, a guarantee of unlimited security and indestructibility, and how, on the other hand, they thought of the elaborately carved pictographs as a permanent record of their possessions, their material attainments, and their divine relations. The reliefs, which were frequently far above the eye

[7] W. Andrae, *Das Gotteshaus und die Urformen des Bauens im Alten Orient* (1930), p. 48.

or inaccessible on the exteriors (Plate L), existed not to be read, but to preserve essential ideas. The monumental mass, which astounds the modern, existed because of its usefulness and not for its optical effect. A temple they called, "Thy House of millions of years", Senwosret had inscribed in praise of the house of his father, Atum, "Eternity is that excellent thing which I have made."

Much has been written about the inherently lithic character of Egyptian architecture and the architectonic purity, amounting to geometric abstraction, of the structural elements. The triangular simplicity of the pyramids, the rectilinear regularity of the plans, the emphatic polygonal solidity of many of the supports, and the rigid horizontality of the roofs, are all evident characteristics of the style, but do they prove that in intent and origin Egyptian buildings were any more cubistic and plastic than the apparent abstractions of the sculpture? The pyramid was an ideographic form, —the *ben-ben* symbol of the Sun-god, which was gradually imposed upon the mastaba because of an association of ideas and for the practical consideration of attaining greater security for the material remains of the incarnate Sun-god who ruled the land. The æsthetic expressiveness of Egyptian architecture, which is and should be fascinating to the modern visitor to Egypt, seems less considered and intentional the more we realize how completely its stone forms were the sculptural imitation of symbolic and structural elements which first took shape in pliable materials.

The technically dexterous, but none the less imitative character of the stone architecture, which is quite different in both cause and effect from the sculpturally plastic character of Greek architecture, is evident not only in the shapes, but also in the methods of cutting the masonry. Stone columns of any size, starting with their inception by Imhotep at Saqqara and rising to monumental dimensions at Karnak, were built like masonry walls by means of small blocks of rough hewn stones laid in courses around a central core and only carved to the final shape after they were erected. As a result of this imitative method, the courses of Egyptian columns have no relation to the parts, for the capital was not thought of as a structural element, and therefore the courses could cut the shaft and capital at any convenient levels. The literal result of this mimetic habit of Egyptian stonemasons is illustrated by the treatment of the base. In the primitive construction of wood and bundled reeds the columns with their attached floral emblems, which later in stone became capitals, were complete units, while the bases were sockets of earth, or hollowed stones, into which the shafts were set. Later, when these columnar prototypes were imitated in stone, it was only structural expediency that set the height and the number of stone courses for the columns, but, with faithful adherence to tradition, the bases were always carved separate from the shafts, as a raised part of the pavement upon which the columns stood.

The history of Egyptian masonry shows an intuitive preoccupation with practical results and a tendency to disregard the inherent principles of true masonry construction as long as the surface and formal aspect of the buildings were meticulously accurate. In the earliest stonework, as seen at Saqqara, the stone-cutters not only took little advantage of rectangular shapes for their joints, but also made themselves extra work by carving the outer surfaces of the walls like a skin of carefully smoothed surface, each stone cut with splayed sides so that the edges would fit smoothly together, while the interior was a loose rubble precariously retained by the ashlar surfaces. Obviously, the intent of the Saqqara masons was imitative rather than structural. While Egyptian builders soon learned some of the advantages of solid, megalithic masonry, they never abandoned the early habit of forming walls by courses of oblique joints, with a loose fill between two carefully carved faces (Plate LI–2). Because their interest was essentially imitative, they never developed a feeling for the inherent possibilities and limitations of solid masonry. Their use of dowels and dovetail cramps, which occurs as early as the IV Dynasty, seems to have been more reflective of methods of wood joinery than structurally useful in masonry, because the cramps, usually of wood, although at times of lead, copper, and even stone, were too weak to strengthen the masonry.[8] They went to infinite pains to patch a chipped surface by marvelous inlays, they economized by recutting pilfered material and irregular fragments into intricate and perfectly fitted pavements, and at the same time went on neglecting foundations and building walls with loose rubble cores which endangered the stability of their structures. This neglect was neither the result of carelessness nor of impatience. The workmen had the time and the skill, but the royal and priestly preoccupation with the conceptual values of architecture kept the craftsmen bound to traditional methods which gave the desired formal appearance of exactness and massiveness. As late as the Ptolemaic period, the stone-cutters continued to carve the whole width of a doorjamb, with all its interior and exterior projecting moldings, out of the stone courses of the enclosing wall. They did it that way because after twenty-five hundred years the forms of stone architecture, such as the moldings around a doorway, were still considered to be imitative rather than structural in stone.

That the Old Kingdom builders practised a magnificent quadrated masonry for their sepulchral monuments and manifested both ingenuity and accuracy in cutting complicated portcullis stones and the earliest known wedge-shaped voussoirs for arches, is no proof that the Egyptians were interested in lithic construction as either an art or science. Subsequent periods did not benefit from the painstaking efforts of the Old Kingdom masons, but considered the solid masonry too time-consuming; and they did not develop the possibilities of the cut-stone voussoir arch initiated by the ingenious experiments of their predecessors until the Saïtic Dynasty. Therefore we may assume that the excellent Old Kingdom masonry was a practical expedient to get permanence, and its lessons were overlooked because it had not evolved any theory and principles of lithic construction. The technique of building, like all the crafts in Egypt, was at an early date raised to the point of practical service so that it could satisfy a specific requirement, but it never was formulated into a conscious art or a theoretical science.

This lack of any speculative interest is most clearly shown by the conventions of mathematical calculations which the builders must have used.[9] The Egyptian's conception of figures never divested itself of its practical origin; he "does not speak or think of 8 as an abstract number; he thinks of 8 loaves or 8 sheep." When he multiplied or divided, the astoundingly complicated methods he used were "little more than a system of trial and error carried out by doubling, halving and multiplying by two-thirds." While he had no provisions, with the exception of $\frac{2}{3}$ and $\frac{3}{4}$, for deal-

[8] Clarke and Engelbach, *Ancient Egyptian Masonry,* p. 113.
[9] Clarke and Engelbach, *op. cit.,* pp. 217-223.

ing with fractions whose numerators were greater than unity, and so had to express $\frac{2}{29}$ as $\frac{1}{24} + \frac{1}{58} + \frac{1}{174} + \frac{1}{232}$, still he extracted square roots, got an approximate area of a circle, computed the volume of a cylinder, and even determined the volume of a truncated cone. Every computation, however, was a laborious and time-consuming series of operations. As one Egyptologist has expressed it, "Despite the reputation for philosophic wisdom attributed to the Egyptians by the Greeks, no people has ever shown itself more adverse to speculation or more whole-heartedly devoted to material interests."[10]

ÆSTHETIC ATTITUDE. If the Egyptians did not enjoy speculative thinking, it is difficult to imagine that they had an æsthetic attitude towards art, for both require some degree of critical detachment and an interest in theoretical comparisons. Æsthetic purpose also involves individual self-consciousness and personal self-confidence which the static and collective uniformity of Egyptian thinking did not cultivate. In spite of our modern awareness of a kind of beauty in Egyptian forms of expression, all the evidence indicates that the Egyptians had very little interest in the æsthetic appeal of their artistic creations. Certainly all the monumental stone architecture, most of the sculpture, and much of the painting were executed and located without regard for the appreciative spectator. Tombs and temples were either hidden away in cities of the dead or concealed behind great walls. Columnar halls and surfaces of wall decoration, which are to-day beautiful in their ruined isolation, were originally inaccessible and completely concealed in dark interiors. Even the processional ways, which were the only open approaches to their buildings, ended abruptly at blank enclosing-walls or concealing pylons.

Furthermore, if we assume that the Egyptians created and valued art in the same way that we do, then we must also assume that they must have expressed their experiences of beauty in somewhat the same fashion that we do. Yet in spite of their great pride which impelled them to cover the walls of their buildings with long accounts of their accomplishments, the royal patrons and master craftsmen are curiously silent regarding the artistic merits of their creations. The architects certainly treated architecture as a practical activity of far less significance in their estimation than the administrative duties connected with the service of Amon and the Pharaoh. Royal patrons of art, like Ramses II, who covered every square foot of their tombs and temples with scenes and inscriptions relating to their greatness, may be relied upon to have extolled what they valued most highly. In architecture they praised above everything else the everlastingness of their buildings and the wealth of burnished metals lavished upon them. But not once, in tens of thousands of inscriptions, do they actually praise the beauty of their works of art.

When they do employ the word *nefer,* or other words such as *'n,* as an adjective, and it is translated "good," "fine" or "beautiful," we have to be sure in what sense the Egyptians meant a thing was beautiful. Even in English we do not always mean that an object is a feast for the senses when we call it beautiful. At times it only means "well made," or of "fine" material; and when we say a "good man is beautiful in the eyes of God," the pleasure implied is not æsthetic. There-

[10] A. Gardiner, *Egyptian Grammar,* p. 4.

fore we cannot assume that the Egyptian word *nefer* connotes æsthetic enjoyment.[11] Frequently it is used for "good" oxen or bread, and in the title "good god" it refers to the virtue, beneficence, and greatness of the king. Usually when applied to architecture, it has the significance of "fine" as applied to the quality of material and the thoroughness of the execution. Therefore when we read, "he buried her in this beautiful tomb,"[12] we cannot infer that *nefer* means more than "fine" or "excellent." In fact when translating the inscription, "Behold, his majesty beautified the temple," Breasted introduces a note[13] to say that *snefer* in this instance means no more "than to supply with inscriptions."

On the other hand there is every indication that the Egyptians enjoyed fine craftsmanship, flowers, gay paintings of Nile scenes in their palaces, and were in no sense oblivious of sensuous delights. They were human beings with the accomplishments to satisfy their desires; and while the masses found pleasure in the excitement of crowded religious festivals, the upper-class loved flowers, gardens, gay villas, and bright colors. But an appreciation of flowers and painted Nile scenes in an arid desert is something different from æsthetic consciousness. In fact, there are ample indications that a keen horticultural interest can even in modern times be distinct from artistic sensibility, just as an appreciation of fine craftsmanship and a love of brilliant colors may be very remote from æsthetic interests.

The differences between the Egyptian and the modern attitude towards art are neither a matter of degree nor a question of human possibilities. They are almost entirely the result of the cultural values which are placed upon art. Within the limits of their conceptual valuation of art, Egyptian artists exhibit a wide range of expressive power. The inferiority of the coarse effectiveness of Ramesside reliefs to the delicacy and feeling of XVIII Dynasty sculpture and to the powerful and direct simplicity of IV Dynasty craftsmanship makes it clear that the art was not a mere matter of rote. Behind the strength and finish of Old Kingdom art there must have been a workman's conviction, pride, and enthusiasm—which meant some kind of pleasure to its creator.

Under the surface of the formal art of Egypt are intimations of individual feeling. A caricature of Akhenaten, a sketch of Senmut, and numerous *ostraca,* on which craftsmen recorded uncensored personal impressions, all show that the artists were very human, and, if not bound by usage, would have been much more personal in their interpretation of nature. For a brief period, when Akhenaten did free his artists from the control of Amon, a fresh and somewhat sensuous naturalism softened the hieratic formulas. Hence when we say that the Egyptians had no æsthetic attitude towards art, we mean that the communal ideas of art were so much more important than the tran-

[11] I am indebted for my familiarity with *nefer* and *snefer* to the Egyptologist Mr. W. C. Hayes of the Metropolitan Museum of Art. Hayes writes: "I should be inclined to read *nfr* as meaning 'goodly,' 'fine,' or just plain 'good,'—'beautiful' if any one wants to insist on it, but only with the implication that the building is well built, its material of good quality, of practical and useful design, and of approved appearance. The verb *snfr,* when applied to a building, means 'to restore,' literally 'to make good (again).' In general the stem *nfr* refers almost always to the virtues of an object or person, rather than to its æsthetic appeal; and I rather think that the virtues of which the ancient Egyptian was thinking were of the most homely, practical, and materialistic sort." (Personal letter to Author.)

[12] Breasted, *Ancient Records of Egypt,* I, 186.

[13] Breasted, *op. cit.,* II, 794.

PLATE LXXVIII: PAINTED COLUMNS

1

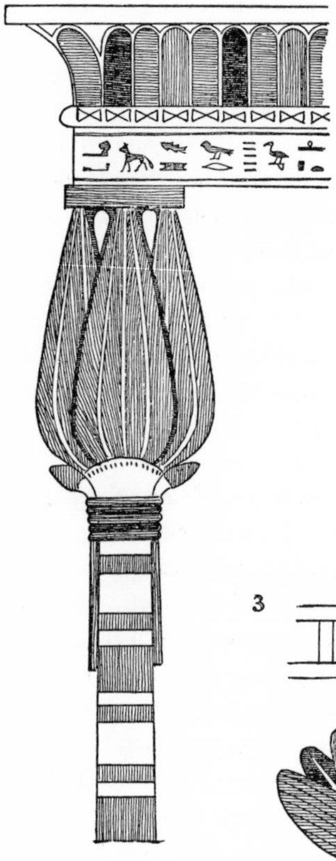

2

3

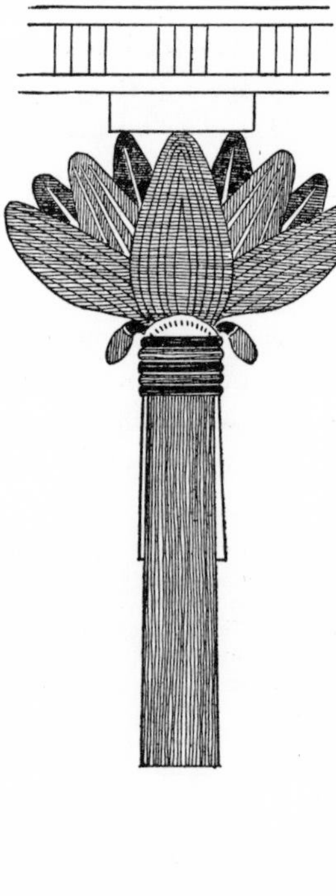

sient effects that the Egyptians did not develop a contemplative and critical approach to formal art. By and large, Egyptian art was the quintessence of elegance and technical refinement petrified at the animistic stage of cultural development where man is too convinced of the potency of his imagery to stand back as a critical observer.

SUMMARY. Whatever we may feel about the artistic merits of Egyptian creations, the outstanding characteristic of the architecture and of the culture itself is its persistent uniformity, which can only be explained by an environmental despotism. The real phenomenon of Egyptian art is its unending iteration and rigid dependence upon formulas—formulas that were frequently highly intelligent and nearly always skilfully executed. This stultifying dependence of a complicated, and in many ways such an accomplished culture upon habit and tradition is only in part explained by the isolation of the country, by the beneficent tyranny of the Nile, which made life easy and so stifled initiative, and by the practical serfdom of the people. It is not even fully explained by the fact that art and religion were finally so centered around the needs of the Pharaoh, and through him of the ruling class, that they both became ritualistic formulas, controlled by a wealthy, despotic, and all-powerful priesthood, whose one interest was the preservation of the established order. Even though this environmental and social despotism may explain much that appears in the culture, still it does not explain itself. It is the position in the society of the individual, having in his capacity as a human being the possibility of personal expression, which perhaps furnishes the key to the art.

In Egypt the continuous coöperative effort and the necessary discipline required in prehistoric times to formulate an order which would make life and civilization possible in the swamps of the Nile "left a mark on the internal articulation of the growing society in addition to the change which it produced in the society's relations with its external environment." As a result, the individual was set in the mold of this collective and primitive routine; in the end, the wills of the rank and file were permanently subordinated to the direction of a few outstanding leaders. Therefore the individual was merged in the communal order, relied upon mimesis, which is the greatest instrument and faculty of primitive man, and in his search for permanence allowed himself to become an unquestioning element in a static culture. Egypt never divested itself of the materiality of nature, never, as Toynbee says, withdrew into its own imagination and then returned to a life of new meaning and incentive; it never found its soul; Akhenaten may have tried, but he failed. Egypt lacked individual self-determination and self-expression, and her art was therefore bound to the formulas of ideographic conventions.

PLATE LXXVIII

1. Lotus column of XII Dynasty (Prisse d'Avennes).
2. Column from XVIII Dynasty tomb, Thebes, *op. cit.*).
3. Lotus column of VI Dynasty (*op. cit.*).

Admitting that the Egyptians were not essentially "beholders of architecture," still they made so many contributions to the history of architecture that we must not overlook their greatness in the process of discovering their cultural limitations. As early as about 3000 B.C., they knew the arch and the tunnel-vault; also in their brick architecture they could construct laminated vaults, knew how to build small cupolas without centering, and had developed an interlocking brick arch. Undoubtedly their masonry construction was the first in the history of man, and before the end of the Old Kingdom they had relieving arches in stone, cut-stone voussoirs, and intricate portcullis-blocks. In wall construction they anticipated, if they did not originate, the architectural convention of a base, or dado, at the bottom of a wall, and a frieze, or cornice, at the top. Their cavetto cornice, which capped all their walls and doorways, was the first crowning stone molding in architecture, and from it, perhaps, developed certain forms of classic cornices. As far as we know they were the first to use columnar porticoes, peristyled courts, and peripteral temples, while their columns probably supplied the Mediterranean world with such elements of the subsequent Classic orders as the abacus block, foliate capitals, entasis, diminution, and channeling.

Without any question they originated the idea of clerestory lighting, were the first to use ventilators for cooling their houses, gave the Greeks the form of the lion-headed water spout, and anticipated the Christian use of crypts under their temples. They had the earliest known vertical city house, and used the rectangular grid arrangement of town-planning two thousand years before any other Mediterranean culture saw the advantages of regular town planning. From their decorative patterns, especially the lotus and papyrus, evolved many of the motives of subsequent European ornament, such as the egg-and-tongue, and the Greek palmette. Egyptian civilization may have suffered a long and progressive petrifaction, but before it was completely entombed, its forms had "gone West" to be reborn, like Osiris, in the new civilizations of the western world.

INDEX

Italics indicate illustrations